*To all who have ever raised a voice, a hand or some hell
to save Oregon's remaining wilderness. And to all those who will.*

Oregon Wild

Endangered Forest Wilderness

Published by
Oregon Natural Resources Council
5825 North Greeley Avenue
Portland, OR 97217 USA
www.onrc.org
503-283-6343 voice
503-283-0756 fax
info@onrc.org

Distributed by
Timber Press
33 SW 2nd Ave., Ste. 450
Portland, Oregon 97204 USA
www.timberpress.com
800-327-5680 toll-free
503-227-2878 voice
503-227-3070 fax
info@timberpress.com

Printed in Oregon, USA. This book is printed on acid-free paper.

Front cover: Old-growth ponderosa pine (*Pinus ponderosa*) in the Lookout Mountain Unit of the proposed Ochoco Mountains Wilderness. Photo by Larry Olson.

Previous page: old-growth Sitka spruce (*Picea sitchensis*) in the Cascade Head Unit of the proposed Coast Range Wilderness. Photo by Gary Braasch.

Back cover: Old-growth Douglas-fir in the Big Bottom Unit of the proposed Clackamas Wilderness. Photo by Bob Holmstrom.

Library of Congress Cataloging-in-Publication Data

Kerr, Andy, 1955-
Oregon wild : endangered forest wilderness / by Andy Kerr ; photography by
Sandy Lonsdale ... [et al.] ; cartography by Erik Fernandez ; foreword by
Kathleen Dean Moore.
256 p ; 24.13 x 30.48 cm.
Includes bibliographical references (p. 210).
ISBN 0-9624877-8-3 (pbk.)
1. Wilderness areas--Oregon. 2. Natural history--Oregon. 3. Forests and
forestry--Oregon. I. Title.
QH76.5.O7K47 2004
333.75'09795--dc22
                         2004000419

Woe to them that join house to house;
that lay field to field,
till there is no room, that you may dwell
alone in the midst of the earth.

Isaiah 5:8

Fancy cutting down all those beautiful trees to make pulp
for those bloody newspapers and calling it civilization.

Winston Churchill

Have you gazed on naked grandeur where there's nothing left to gaze on,
Set pieces and drop-curtain scenes galore,
Big mountains heaved to heaven, where the blinding sunsets blazon,
Black canyons where the rapids rip and roar?
Have you swept the visioned valley with the green stream streaking through it,
Searched the Vastness for a something you have lost?
Have you strung your soul to silence? Then for God's sake go and do it;
Here the challenge, learn the lesson, pay the cost.

Robert Service, in The Call of the Wild

The West of which I speak is but another name for the Wild; and what I have
been preparing to say is, that in Wildness lies the preservation of the World.

Henry David Thoreau

Map 0-1. **Oregon Forest Wilderness and Major Ecoregions**

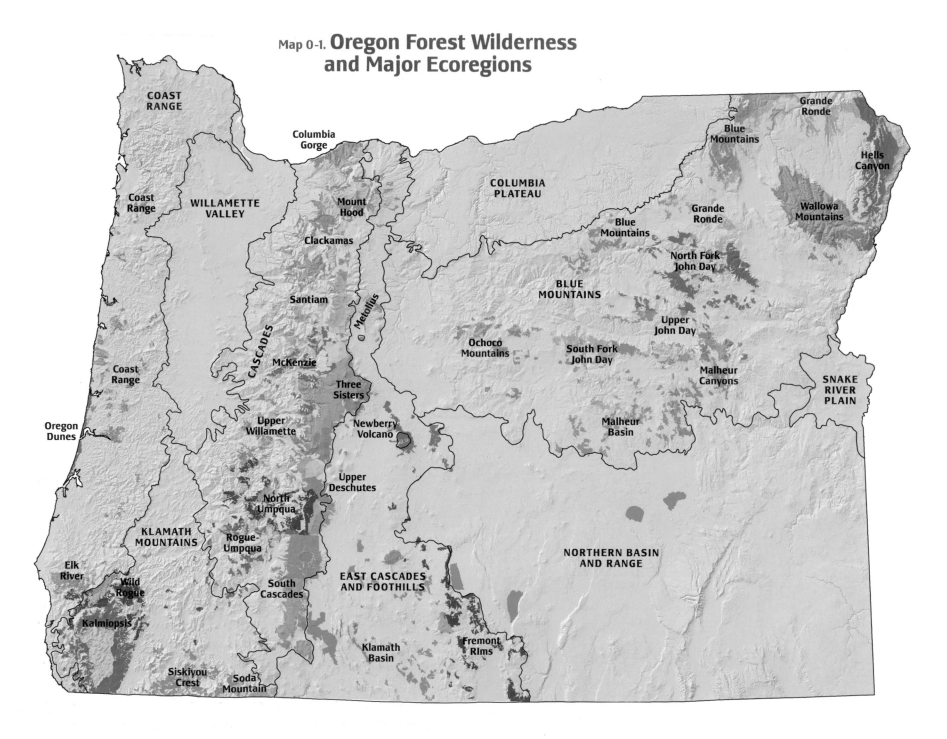

COAST
RANGE

Columbia
Gorge

Coast
Range

WILLAMETTE
VALLEY

Mount
Hood

COLUMBIA
PLATEAU

Grande
Ronde

Blue
Mountains

Hells
Canyon

Clackamas

Blue
Mountains

Grande
Ronde

Wallowa
Mountains

Santiam

Metolius

North Fork
John Day

BLUE
MOUNTAINS

CASCADES

McKenzie

Ochoco
Mountains

Upper
John Day

Coast
Range

Three
Sisters

South Fork
John Day

Malheur
Canyons

SNAKE
RIVER
PLAIN

Newberry
Volcano

Upper
Willamette

Malheur
Basin

Oregon
Dunes

Upper
Deschutes

North
Umpqua

KLAMATH
MOUNTAINS

Rogue-
Umpqua

NORTHERN BASIN
AND RANGE

Elk
River

South
Cascades

Wild
Rogue

EAST CASCADES
AND FOOTHILLS

Kalmiopsis

Klamath
Basin

Fremont
Rims

Siskiyou
Crest

Soda
Mountain

Table of Contents

Chapter 9:
Dry Open Forests: East Cascades
Slopes and Foothills Ecoregion · · · · · · · · · · · · 154

Chapter 10:
Neither Cascades nor Rockies, but with Attributes
of Both: Blue Mountains Ecoregion · · · · · · · · 172

List of Maps, Tables and Charts

MAPS

TABLES AND CHARTS

Foreword

The trail brings us to a creek that carves tight curves through a marshy meadow. The creek is deeper than it is wide, and so clear we can make out every ripple in the sand, every caddis fly larvae and pickerel weed bent to the current. Red-wing blackbirds sway on reeds, raising their beaks in song. We hear the winnowing of a snipe and the Sora rail's descending song, but we can only imagine the hidden rail, padding on spread toes across mud below the reeds. In the creek, the shadow of a rainbow trout darts under a lotus in yellow bloom. Above the creek, swallows swoop after midges. So high we lose it in the sun, a bald eagle soars on broad wings. We raise binoculars to watch a sandhill crane hunt for frogs. Sunlight reflects on the bright new needles of lodgepole pines that circle the valley.

The meadow is whole, intact, singing with light and life. It has the feel of a place where every bird is in its tree, every mouse and snake is in its burrow, each tree and wind-riffled reed is in its place. I had forgotten.

Accustomed to the stripped down and hacked up habitats at the edge of town, I had forgotten this richness and complexity, the wholeness of an intact ecosystem. Like so many others, I live in the silence of places that have been abused for more than a hundred years — forests cut and cut again, rivers emptied of the abundance of life, marshes paved for parking lots. But changes often happen slowly, and losses are often hard to see. People who remember a healthy landscape die or move away, and others move in who have no memory of the forests and marshes. So it's easy to forget what a healthy habitat looks like, easy to assume that degraded, cut-over landscapes are the way things have always been, will always be.

Ecologists call this the problem of the sliding baseline. If we no longer know healthy, beautiful habitats, our standards of natural health and beauty slide down to meet the degraded landscapes that we know.

There are dozens of compelling reasons why we need to preserve forest wilderness — to clean, store and replenish fresh water and fresh air; to find solace and renewal for tired spirits; to preserve species diversity; to honor God's creation; to protect places of safety where wild plants and animals can thrive. The list goes on. But in my mind, one of the most important functions of wilderness is to remind people of what normal is. Wilderness reminds us that the natural state of this world is to be healthy and beautiful, the way it once was and the way it might be again. By showing us a vision of what we have destroyed in our everyday lives, wilderness is a standard by which we can measure our loss, as it is a standard to measure our hopes.

Old-growth forests are not so much an inheritance from our ancestors as a loan from our successors. ▶

There is another sliding baseline — an ethical baseline. Along with the degradation of the land has come the degradation of our standards for human behavior. We think of ourselves as good people, while we destroy the ecosystems that provide the fresh water and air that we all depend on. We congratulate ourselves on supporting our children, while we bulldoze the habitats of species that no person's child will ever see again. We think of ourselves as patriots, as we poison our country's air, deplete its fields, mine out its resources, dam its rivers. We are not ashamed. We see no hypocrisy in loving our children and the land, while we act in ways that sicken both. On the contrary, measuring ourselves against degraded moral standards, we think we're doing the best we can.

But in wilderness — in remnant patches of unspoiled land — there is a high, clear moral standard. The wilderness ethic requires that when we enter a wilderness, we enter a place where we must do no harm. We enter into the peace of a place that must not be plundered. Shouldering our packs, we step onto the land with relief and celebration, but also with restraint, transformed by our responsibility to be care-full, to safeguard the well-being of an unspoiled place. We may not always live up to the wilderness ethic, but we know what it requires of us. The wilderness ethic is a moral standard by which we can measure the hypocrisies of our everyday lives. This is a standard to measure what we can hope for from human beings. It's a vision of the possibility of living in harmony with the land, of walking on earth as a guest, with gratitude and respect.

So I celebrate the advent of a new book about forest wilderness in Oregon. In Oregon, there still are some glistening, bird-graced, bountiful wildlands beyond the end of the road. These must remain intact. Here, in the healthiest places, we can become our best selves. Here, in the wholeness of unfragmented wilderness, in the entirety of ecosystems with all the pieces in place, we can remember what it means to be whole ourselves.

Kathleen Dean Moore
Corvallis, Oregon

Kathleen Dean Moore writes about water and wilderness in her books: Riverwalking; Holdfast; *and* The Pine Island Paradox, *from Milkweed Editions. She is professor of philosophy at Oregon State University, where she directs the Spring Creek Project for Ideas, Nature and the Written Word.*

Industrial foresters considered the Pacific Yew (*Taxus brevifolia*) worthless slash because it didn't make good lumber. Then scientists discovered that the yew's bark contains the cancer-fighting compound paclitaxel (a.k.a. Taxol®). They remarked that the molecule is so complex that only a tree could have thought of it. ▶

Preface

(T)he love of wilderness is more than a hunger for what is always beyond reach; it is also an expression of loyalty to the earth, the earth which bore us and sustains us, the only home we shall ever know, the only paradise we ever need – if we only had eyes to see. Original sin, the true original sin, is the blind destruction for the sake of greed of this natural paradise which lies all around us – if only we were worthy of it.

—Edward Abbey[1]

Common in northeast Oregon are forest "stringers" flanked by grasslands. The cooler, wetter north-facing slopes favor forests.

Once while walking in the Three Sisters Wilderness, I encountered a fellow who lived there most of the year. Usually he stayed away from the main trails and camped where no one was likely to come across him — and therefore likely to cross him. He was walking to town for supplies. He didn't like town. "If I spend too much time in town, all I do is get into fights and end up in jail," he said. "Out here, I'm at peace and the town is peaceful too."

Much later, I met George Atiyeh — nephew of a former Oregon Governor, and, more importantly, the person who would become the leading savior of Opal Creek. He credits the wilderness of Opal Creek with allowing him to deal successfully with the post-traumatic stress caused by his tour of duty in Southeast Asia. Before George was old enough to legally drink, his government sent him off to Cambodia with an M-16 and later denied he was ever there. After returning home, he retreated to a remote old mining camp that his family owned on the Little North Santiam River. There, Atiyeh heeded the words of John Muir:

Camp out among the grass and gentians of glacier meadows, in craggy garden nooks full of Nature's darlings. Climb the mountains and get their good tidings. Nature's peace will flow into you as the sunshine flows into trees. The winds will blow their freshness into you, and the storms their energy, while cares will drop off like autumn leaves.[2]

Several years passed before George was again ready to deal constructively with society (and vice versa), but when he was, he went to battle on behalf of the land that had healed him. Thanks to George and many others, Opal Creek and the historic mining camp are now protected as the Opal Creek Wilderness and Opal Creek Scenic Recreation Area.

The Three Sisters hermit and George Atiyeh are but two of countless Oregonians who have gone — and go — to Oregon's forests for solace, comfort, restoration and yes, even recreation. Oregon's forest wildlands provide that and much, much more. They are home to countless species of plants and animals — some that live, swim, crawl and creep nowhere else in the world. They protect soil from erosion, provide nutrients for the Pacific Northwest's amazing anadromous fish and provide pure drinking water for thousands of Oregonians. Precious little of these wildlands remain. The time to protect them is now.

Andy Kerr
On the right bank of Rock Creek
May 2004

Acknowledgements

This book contains little original research or original thought. It is an assemblage of information and argument for these times. Much of the information contained herein comes from published sources; some does not. The books, publications and other sources I consulted and relied upon are generally noted, but I also wish to generously thank and acknowledge all of the contributing scientists and researchers for their invaluable work. Since this book is written for the lay reader, its popular style cannot do citational justice to those whose published works I used to write the book. Of course, I did cite sources wherever I could, including attribution for direct quotations.

I also wish to thank people who contributed their time and knowledge to help write the book. First, my colleagues at the Oregon Natural Resources Council: Tim Lillebo, Wendell Wood and Regna Merritt, who are tireless warriors in defense of the wild. They (along with James Monteith, ONRC's former executive director) have done more than nearly anyone else in recent times to preserve Oregon's wild. While they did not act alone to protect Oregon's protected Wilderness, without them, it would not have been protected at all. That as much wild roadless forestland is still available for permanent protection is attributable to ONRC's Doug Heiken and his colleagues who are using science, the courts and public opinion to stop an endless assault of timber sales.

The next generation of tireless wilderness warriors is coming on-line. ONRC's GIS (Geographic Information System) jockey and map maestro Eric Fernandez compiled both the research and final maps for the book, as well as cheerfully responded to my endless requests. Leeanne Siart found obscure government records for me. Erin Madden collected critical roadless area files. Nanci Champlin compiled almost thirty years of the organization's image archives. Sumner Robinson aided immeasurably in the digitalization of the images in this book. Susan Ash, Alex Brown, Jeremy Hall and other ONRC staff previously mentioned reviewed text. Several of the ONRC staff contributed photography to the book. Jacki Richey and Candice Guth managed the finances for this project, and David Wilkins helped find the money to pay for it. Joellen Pail meticulously reviewed the final pages. Seeing a need for the book, Regna Merritt recognized its potential and Ken Rait — then with ONRC, now with Campaign for America's Wilderness — helped focus the effort into the campaign book it is. Finally, Jay Ward is leading the effort to make the dream described in this book a reality.

Other wild warriors that helped in large and small, but always important ways include: Ric Bailey, Jim Baker, Sharyn Becker, the late Joy Belsky, Omar Bose, John Brandt, Dan Brummer, Chris Burford, Jim Cahalan, Greg Clark, Romain Cooper,

LEON WERDINGEF

Forests in Oregon co-evolved with fire. Most fires are not stand-replacing, but cool-burning ground fires. Both renew forest ecosystems.

Gerald and Buff Corsi, Ken Crocker, Dominick DellaSala, Paul Dewey, Tom Dimitre, Linda Driskill, Nancy Duhnkrack, Greg Dyson, Francis Eatherington, Erin Fagley, Edwin Florance, Evan Frost, Stu Garrett, Patty Goldman, Kevin Gorman, Gary Guttormsen, Ashley Henry, Bob Holmstrom, Mark Hubbard, Tim Ingalsbee, Kurt Jensen, Jimmy Kagan, Jim Kauppila, Joan Kittrell, William Leonard, Penny Lind, Jay Lininger, Cameron LaFollette, Darilyn LeGore, Christine Masters, Steve Miller, Jason Miner, Jim Myron, Frazier Nichol, Reed Noss, Ken Olsen, Ralph Opp, Randal O'Toole, Mike Piehl, Sally Prender, Jim Rogers, Leslie Salvo, Robert Schofield, Doug Scott, Mary Scurlock, Leslee Sherman, Jenny Young Seidemann, Chant Thomas, Dave Thomas, Pepper Trail, Barbara Ullian, Joseph Vaile, Dick VanderShaff, Sherry Wellborn, Boyd Wilcox, Chuck Willer, Dave Willis, Robin Wisdom and Tonia Wolf.

My debt owed to the many photographers who contributed images to this book is immeasurable. Sandy Lonsdale, George Wuerthner, Elizabeth Feryl and Gary Braasch all cheerfully offered selections from their vast stocks and invited me to choose as many as I wished. Other professional photographers who generously offered their work include Ellen Morris Bishop, Dominic DeFazio, Don Getty, Richard Grost, David Stone and Leon Werdinger. Wildlife researcher Evelyn Bull contributed some hard-to-find shots of increasingly harder-to-find animals. Larry Olson, with his large format camera, provided the front cover image. Others who contributed images are noted in my previous acknowledgements above.

I am deeply appreciative of Kathleen Dean Moore for contributing her wise and eloquent words for the foreword.

Sandy Bryce and Glen Griffith were very helpful in explaining the intricacies of ecoregion classification.

David Marshall, co-editor of the new *Birds of Oregon*, generously shared draft species accounts from that book for this one.

Mark Salvo provided the legal research to help me recall Oregon's wilderness history, prepared the logging history chart, ensured that all the citations were in order, and cheerfully and compulsively proofread and improved the final pages.

Rick Brown was always there to answer questions, suggest sources and review copy.

Elizabeth Grossman shepherded this book through conception, creation, editing and production.

Nancy Peterson correlated the Wilderness proposals with published hikes for www.oregonwild.org/hikes and reviewed the final text. She also provided immeasurable tangible and intangible support.

Bryan Potter, Eldon Potter and Josh Nusbaum of Bryan Potter Design gave the "look" to the book and cheerfully cajoled us all and acceded to most of our fancies.

Allen King of Environmental Paper and Print was invaluable in aiding ONRC to produce a book that is environmentally friendly and affordable.

Thanks to Eve Goodman and Max Gibson of Timber Press for their assistance and suggestions.

Generous support for the book was provided in part by the Brainerd Foundation, Bullitt Foundation, Campaign for America's Wilderness, Evergreen Hill Education Fund of The Oregon Community Foundation, Lazar Foundation, The Pew Charitable Trusts and Wilburforce Foundation.

I am certain I have missed people who deserve thanks, and for that, my apologies. While I'm apologizing, I will do so again for any errors that survived the gauntlet of research, writing, editing and review. Any errors are mine alone.

About the Maps

The maps in this book represent five years of wildlands research and mapping. Initially developed through examination of satellite imagery and high-resolution digital orthophotography, the maps were then subjected to further review and evaluation through extensive field checking involving over four hundred people. A variety of source data was used for analysis including, but not limited to: Land Use /Land Cover from the U.S. Geological Survey, TIGER road data from the U.S. Department of Commerce, detailed road data from the thirteen national forests in Oregon, data from the Bureau of Land Management for Western Oregon and past logging data from five western Oregon national forests. The maps were based on the Oregon Roadless Areas Mapping Project — a cooperative effort between the Oregon Natural Resources Council and Pacific Biodiversity Project.

Introduction

Whatever you do will be insignificant, but it is very important that you do it.

—Mahatma Gandhi[3]

I did not want to write this book. I would prefer not to share any secrets about Oregon's remaining wild forests, but there was no other choice.

Despite the fact that the wildlands described in this book would be even better protected if they remained as unknown and unvisited as many currently are, I share them with the hope that if more people know and care about them, they will not be lost to exploitation but instead become protected for future generations of Oregonians to cherish and conserve.

Oregon has 2.3 million acres of designated Wilderness, which amounts to about 3.7 percent of the state. However, Oregon has an additional five million acres of publicly owned forests (an additional 8 percent of the state's land area) that are both wild and unprotected.

Most of Oregon's protected land is classified as "forest." But with a few notable and glorious exceptions, the land that has been designated Wilderness is of little economic or biological productivity. Most is either rock and ice above timberline, or is above the commercial timberline — where the trees are smaller and slower growing. Oregon's unprotected wilderness is just as wild, just as natural and just as important as its protected Wilderness — and these unprotected forested wildlands provide irreplaceable and inimitable ecological, economic, social goods and services. However, the benefits of these wildlands will be lost if Congress does not protect them from roading, logging, mining, off-road vehicles and other threats.

The Oregon Wild Campaign of the Oregon Wild Forest Coalition advocates for the protection of Oregon's remaining forest wildlands. To help identify these areas and secure legislative protection for them, we have organized the five million roadless acres into 32 Wilderness proposals that incorporate and expand upon Oregon's 37 existing forested Wilderness areas. Each of the more than 1,200 individual units identified within these 32 proposals qualify for inclusion in the National Wilderness Preservation System; some are large, some are small; however, all are important to protect for future generations.

These Wilderness proposals are designed for landscape conservation, and are centered on major watersheds or mountain ranges. A wild swath of forest is not an island, but part of a larger, ecologically connected whole. Our goal is to protect Oregon's entire remaining wilderness, not in isolation, but as part of a conservation and restoration framework that extends throughout the state beyond the borders of the individual Wilderness areas. This will ensure that our children — and theirs for generations to come — will benefit from functioning forests across the landscape and over time.

In addition to these forested wildlands, there are also at least 6.2 million acres of de facto wilderness within Oregon's Sagebrush Sea (another 10 percent of the state's land area) in need of protection. That brings the total of the state's remaining wilderness to 13.5 million acres, or 21.7 percent of Oregon. Does that sound like a lot? It does not to a wolf, or a salmon or a grizzly bear. Or to anybody who understands how wildlands contribute to Oregon's quality of life.

Unless enough wilderness-loving Oregonians know about these endangered places, they will be lost to timber beasts, cattle barons, mining conglomerates, land developers, unenlightened (and sometimes venal) bureaucrats and motorheads who have forgotten how to walk. Whether attributed to greed, stupidity, convenience or ignorance, the result would be the same: wilderness lost.

We have a challenge ahead of us. As Vice President Al Gore noted,

The maximum that is politically feasible, even the maximum that is politically imaginable right now, still falls short of the minimum that is scientifically and ecologically necessary.[4]

Political realities can be changed; ecological realities cannot.

So dear reader, in exchange for learning some secrets about these wonderful and wild places, I make this request: do something for Oregon's threatened forest wilderness.

Pick up the phone or a pen, or reach for a keyboard and contact the elected and appointed officials in whose hands the fate of these last wildlands rests.

Give money and/or time to organizations working to save these places. If one does not have the time, one may well have the money.

Encourage your friends, family and colleagues to do the same. No one person acting alone can save these wild places. Working together, we can.

UNLESS someone like you cares a whole awful lot, nothing is going to get better. It's not.

—The Lorax (Dr. Seuss)[5]

KEN CROCKER

Notes

[1] Abbey, Edward. 1968. DESERT SOLITAIRE: A SEASON IN THE WILDERNESS. Ballantine Books. New York, NY: 190.

[2] Muir, John. 1901. OUR NATIONAL PARKS. Houghton, Mifflin & Company. New York, NY: 56.

[3] This quote is widely attributed to Gandhi.

[4] McKibben, Bill. *Not so fast.* New York Times Magazine (July 23, 1995).

[5] Geisel, Theodore Seuss. 1971. THE LORAX. Random House. New York, NY (unpaginated).

◄ Madrones (*Arbutus menziesii*) in the Kalmiopsis country resprouting just after the Biscuit Fire of 2002 was extinguished by rains.

A Brief Natural History of Oregon's Forests

The Forests of Oregon

The curious world which we inhabit is more wonderful than it is convenient; more beautiful than it is useful; it is more to be admired than to be used.

—Henry David Thoreau[1]

Oregon is known for its wonderful, beautiful, admirable forests. And, while all forests are unique, here's why some of Oregon's forests are especially so. As naturalist Daniel Mathews notes:

The area made rainy by the Cascades, Olympics and other Pacific coastal ranges is the Conifer Capital of the World. This is the only large temperate-zone area where conifers utterly overwhelm their broadleaf competitors. It grows conifers bigger than anywhere else, and the resulting tonnage of biomass and square-footage of leaf area, per acre, are the world's highest, even greater than tropical rain forests.[2]

Oregon's inland conifer forests are much drier than those near the coast and the trees are less supremely massive than in westside forests, yet eastside forests are still unique and their trees majestic.

Approximately half of Oregon is — or was — forested. Ecologists usually classify forests by the type of tree(s) that currently dominate the forest, or by the tree(s) that would be most prevalent given enough time and if spared human and natural disturbance. To classify broader ecoregions, ecologists also study the geology, soils and climate. Forest vegetation types do not fall precisely into generally accepted ecoregions, but then few things in nature are easily ordered.

Major Oregon Forest Ecoregions

Natural scientists categorize terrestrial Earth on a scale that ranges from the very broad to the increasingly detailed. The broadest scale or so-called "Level I" category divides the continents in the Western Hemisphere into twenty-four huge ecoregions.

Oregon contains portions of three, of which this book focuses on two: the "Northwestern Forested Mountains" and "Maritime West Coast Forest." (The third Level I ecoregion in Oregon is the "North American Deserts.") The "Northwestern Forested Mountains" includes most of Oregon's forests, with the exception of the Coast Range. Because it is more maritime than mountainous, the Willamette Valley is included in the "Maritime West Coast Forest" along with the Coast Range.

The "Level II" category further divides our hemisphere into 82 very large ecoregions. Oregon forests occupy part of just two Level II ecoregions that are subparts of Oregon's Level I ecoregions. The "Marine West Coast Forest" includes the Oregon Coast Range and the Willamette Valley, while the "Western Cordillera" includes the remainder of Oregon's primarily forested landscapes. (To complete the description, the rest of Oregon, which is generally tree-free, occupies the "Western Interior Basins and Ranges" Level II ecoregion.)

Oregon is then further divided into nine separate "Level III" ecoregions. (The entire Western Hemisphere has approximately 311 Level III ecoregions.) These are "large areas with similar physical conditions and biological features,"[3] and are based on the interplay of geology, landforms, soils, land use, vegetation, climate, wildlife and hydrology. Five of Oregon's Level III ecoregions are primarily forested and the subject of this book. The vast majority of Oregon's forests (moving west to east) lie within the "Coast Range," "Klamath Mountains," "Cascades," "East Cascades Slopes and Foothills" and "Blue Mountains" Level III ecoregions. The Wilderness proposals described in this book are organized by Level III ecoregion.

Oregon also has four generally non-forested Level III ecoregions. Three — the "Columbia Plateau," "Snake River Plain" and "Northern Basin and Range" ecoregions — are primarily sagebrush steppe and related ecosystems (also known as the Sagebrush Sea), although they do contain significant amounts of aspen forest, juniper woodland, and relic pine groves and fir forests.[4] These small bits of forested wildlands that are surrounded by hundreds of thousands of acres of Sagebrush Sea are not addressed in this book. Similarly, while both forested and non-forested wildlands occur in the Blue Mountains Ecoregion, only the predominantly forested areas are considered in this book.[5]

The fourth generally non-forested Oregon Level III ecoregion is the Willamette Valley. The Oregon Biodiversity Project notes that the valley is:

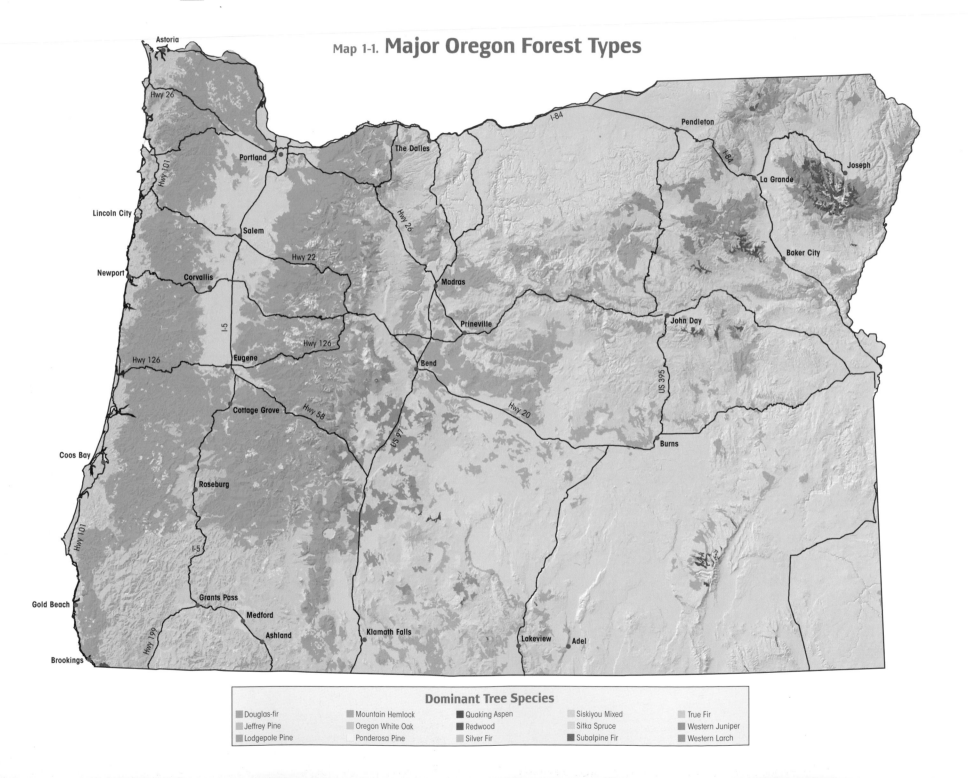

Map 1-1. Major Oregon Forest Types

Astoria

Hwy 26

Hwy 101

Portland

The Dalles

Hwy 26

Lincoln City

Salem

Hwy 22

Newport

Corvallis

Madras

I-5

Prineville

John Day

Hwy 126

Eugene

Bend

US 395

Cottage Grove

Hwy 58

Hwy 20

US 97

Coos Bay

Burns

Roseburg

I-5

Grants Pass

Medford

Hwy 199

Ashland

Klamath Falls

Lakeview   Adel

Gold Beach

Hwy 101

Brookings

Pendleton

I-84

La Grande

Joseph

Baker City

I-84

Dominant Tree Species

Douglas-fir	Mountain Hemlock	Quaking Aspen	Siskiyou Mixed	True Fir
Jeffrey Pine	Oregon White Oak	Redwood	Sitka Spruce	Western Juniper
Lodgepole Pine	Ponderosa Pine	Silver Fir	Subalpine Fir	Western Larch

Table 1-1. **Major Oregon Forest Types**[8]

Dominant Tree Species on Map 1-1	Forest Types	Dominant Tree Species on Map 1-1	Forest Types
Douglas-fir	Douglas-fir/Broadleaf Deciduous	**Quaking Aspen**	Quaking Aspen
	Douglas-fir/Oregon White Oak		
	Douglas-fir/Ponderosa/ Incense Cedar	**Redwood**	Redwood
	Douglas-fir/Ponderosa/True Fir	**Silver Fir**	Silver Fir/Western Hemlock/Noble Fir
	Douglas-fir/Western Hemlock		
	Douglas-fir/True Fir/Ponderosa Pine/Western Larch	**Siskiyou Mixed**	Siskiyou Mixed Conifer (High Elevation)
Jeffrey Pine	Siskiyou Jeffrey Pine		Siskiyou Mixed Conifer
			Siskiyou Mixed Evergreen
Lodgepole Pine	Lodgepole		
	Lodgepole/True Fir	**Sitka Spruce**	Sitka Spruce
	Lodgepole/Western Larch		
	Subalpine Lodgepole	**Subalpine Fir**	Subalpine Fir/ Engelmann Spruce Parklands
Mountain Hemlock	Mountain Hemlock		
	Mountain Hemlock/Parklands	**True Firs**	True Fir/Douglas-fir
	Mountain Hemlock/Red Fir		True Fir/Lodgepole
	Mountain Hemlock/ Red Fir/Lodgepole		True Fir/Lodgepole/ Western Larch/ Douglas-fir
Oregon White Oak	Oregon White Oak/Douglas-fir	**Western Juniper**	Juniper/Big Sage
	Oregon White Oak/ Pacific Madrone		Juniper/Bitterbrush
			Juniper/Grasslands
	Oregon White Oak/Ponderosa		Juniper/Low Sage
			Juniper/Mountain Big Sage
Ponderosa Pine	Ponderosa		Juniper/Ponderosa
	Ponderosa/Douglas-fir/True Fir		
	Ponderosa/Douglas-fir/ Western Larch/Lodgepole	**Western Larch**	Western Larch/Douglas-fir/ True Fir
	Ponderosa/Grasslands		Western Larch/Douglas-fir/ Ponderosa/Lodgepole
	Ponderosa/Lodgepole		
	Ponderosa/White Oak		
	Ponderosa on Pumice		
	Ponderosa/Scrub		

Old-growth incense-cedar (*Libocedrus decurrens*) on the Umpqua National Forest. ▶

SANDY LONSDALE.

...among the state's most altered ecoregions. Development for agriculture, urbanization, fire suppression, construction of dams and impoundments, drainage of marshes and wetlands, commercial forestry, livestock grazing, and the introduction of exotic plants and animals have all dramatically reshaped the valley's ecosystem.[6]

The Willamette Valley also has an expanding population of 2.3 million people and no forested — nor probably any other kind of — wilderness of large size remains in the Willamette Valley Ecoregion.[7]

The introduction to each (Level III) ecoregion presented here includes a description of the area's Level IV ecoregions.

There are Level V ecoregions, but we won't be going there, particularly since such delineations are still being developed. Suffice to say that every piece of nature has biologically and ecologically unique characteristics. The same cannot be said of strip malls.

Major Oregon Forest Types

Scientists have defined forty-four forest and woodland types in Oregon between the Pacific Ocean and the Snake River. "Woodlands" have fewer trees than forestlands, but more trees than "grasslands." Precipitation, soil type, elevation and other factors determine an area's vegetation, which further determines the forest type. While each forest type is named after its dominant tree species, one will often find that the range of that species is much broader and occurs in several other forest types. The introduction to each ecoregion chapter in this book describes the region's major forest types (see Table 1-1). However, for readability, the forty-four types have also been simplified to seventeen types as depicted on Map 1-1 on page 2.

In addition to the forty-four forest types, scientists have identified twenty-six other non-forest vegetation types. Many, but not all, are interspersed with the forest types and are described in the introductions to the ecoregion chapters as follows: Agriculture, Alpine Barren Fell Fields, Barren Playa, Big Sage/Scrub, Big Sagebrush, Bitterbrush Scrub, Built-Up Area, Cleared Grasslands, Cottonwood/Willow Riparian, Cutover/Burned, Grasslands/Bunchgrass, Inland Dunes, Low Sagebrush, Manzanita/Buckbrush Chaparral, Marsh/Wet Meadow, Montane Shrublands, Mountain Big Sage, Open Lava, Sage on Lava, Other Sagebrush, Pasture/Riparian Bottomlands, Rimrock Shrublands, Saltmarsh, Scrub and Shorelands.

Bald eagles in Lodgepole pine (*Pinus contorta*) forest on the Deschutes National Forest. ▶

FEATURED SPECIES
Whitebark Pine

"I love all trees, but I am in love with pines."

—Aldo Leopold[9]

The whitebark pine (*Pinus albicaulis*)[10] is often the last tree to give way to the harshly cold conditions above timberline. Most whitebark pine are now protected in designated Wilderness, national parks, or in areas so high in elevation that they have mostly been spared from human disturbance.

From the interior coastal ranges of British Columbia, across the Canadian Rockies to the Wyoming Basin, down the Cascade Crest and the Sierra Nevada, whitebarks often consort with subalpine fir, mountain hemlock, lodgepole pine and Engelmann spruce. Individual trees have been found to live over 1,000 years. Ecologists call the whitebark pine a "keystone species" as it determines the ability of a large number of other species to exist in whatever biological community it occurs.

The very large (for a pine) and nutritious pea-sized seed is coveted by the Clark's nutcracker, which plays a critical role in the dispersal of the wingless seed. At least 110 species of wildlife, including bears, eat the seed, as can humans.

Although it is protected throughout much of its range, whitebark pine faces a bleak future in Oregon and throughout the rest of its range unless critical steps are taken soon. The species suffers from three major deadly threats: lack of fire, an excess of mountain pine beetles and an exotic fungal disease.

Due to active fire suppression, the fire frequency in whitebark pine stands is perhaps one-tenth of what it was naturally. Unless frequent fire is rapidly restored, whitebarks will continue to be replaced by shade-tolerant conifers that also serve as reservoirs of mountain pine beetles, a native killer of whitebarks. Periodic fire is essential to the propagation of whitebark pines because it creates optimal conditions for seedlings.

An exotic blister rust (*Cronartium ribicola*) was introduced to North America in the early twentieth century and has since ravaged whitebark and other five-needle pines species. The blister rust causes cankers on the bark that kills the tree by girdling it. Thus far, rust-induced mortality in Oregon has been light to moderate. Ghost-like snags can be seen on Mount Hood. Up to 20 percent of the whitebark pines in Crater Lake National Park are infected, and a 46 percent decline in the park's mature whitebark pine is predicted by 2050. In some places outside of Oregon, whitebark pine stands have suffered 90 percent mortality.

Some scientists expect the blister rust will eventually spread to the entire range of the species within one to several decades. The telltale signs of the fungus are red-brown foliage on the dying upper branches and cankers on branches and boles. Some specimens are naturally resistant or, by sheer luck, avoid infection. To complicate matters, the rust also affects all other native five-needle pines and finds an alternative host on *Ribes* species (currants and gooseberries), often found in association with whitebark pine.

GEORGE WUERTHNER

Whitebark pine (*Pinus albicaulis*) on the Fremont National Forest.

In a few cases, killing competing tree species may encourage whitebark pine growth, but this is not economically feasible. In some places rust-resistant seedlings grown from local stock are being planted. However, planting is best done indirectly by letting Clark's nutcrackers distribute the seed. The birds instinctively know better (even if they don't know so) than humans (even if they think so) as to where the trees should be planted.

After a fire, five to seven decades must pass before a whitebark pine starts producing cones. The more whitebark pines there are, the more rust-resistant specimens there will be to carry on.

Some forest managers favor chainsaws over fire, usually more for social than scientific reasons. They anticipate objections from tourists who don't like to see charred and smoky Wilderness areas and parks, and who have an overriding aversion to and fear of fire that has been instilled in them by Smokey Bear for the past fifty years. Fire, however, is a vital and necessary component of the alpine ecosystem. The end of fire suppression and concurrent reintroduction of fire in these areas must begin immediately to save whitebark pines.

To aid conservation and restoration of whitebarks, the Whitebark Pine Ecosystem Foundation has been established and could use your support. [11]

Major Oregon Forest Owners

Contrary to myth and common perception, less than one-half of Oregon is forest-land. The federal government — more importantly, *the public* — owns more than half of that land (state, county and other public ownership brings the total to nearly 60 percent). From the standpoint of timber-production, private lands are inherently more productive than public lands. They generally are lower elevation (with a longer growing season), have more productive soils and are dedicated solely to producing timber.

Old, Mature and Young Forests

It is impossible to state precisely what is at stake biologically and ecologically, because as (former Forest Service Chief and scientist) Jack Thomas succinctly pointed out, these forests are not only more complex than we think, they are more complex than we can think. But there is little question that "(m)uch of the biological diversity of the Pacific Northwest is associated with late-successional and old-growth forests."

–Seven noted Pacific Northwest forest scientists[13]

Before determining the current and historic extent of old-growth forests in Oregon, agreement must be reached on exactly what constitutes an "old-growth" forest. The problem is that the ecological, social and political complexities of old-growth forests defy simple definition.

The definition of old growth can vary with the perspective (or axe) one has (to grind). As a Supreme Court justice once said, "I shall not today attempt further to define (pornography), but I know it when I see it."[14] In the same sense, one knows an old-growth forest when one sees it.

It's easy to see the difference between a real forest and a timber plantation. A real forest has multiple species of trees, usually of different ages, heights and diameters, a biologically diverse understory and a full complement of fish and wildlife species. A timber plantation is usually a monoculture of a single species, all the same size, all planted the same distance apart and all to be clearcut again within a half to a full human lifetime.

An industrialist seeking to maximize financial profit may consider old growth anything older than economic "rotation" age — the age at which it is first profitable to cut a tree down and send it to a mill. But the tree is not "old" by any biological definition and would continue to grow for centuries if left uncut.

A forester seeking to maximize wood volume considers old growth anything older than the silvicultural "rotation" age (also called the "culmination of mean annual increment"), or that point at which the tree's annual growth rate reaches its maximum

Table 1-2. Forestland Ownership in Oregon[12]

Land Owner	Acreage	Total Acreage
Federal		**18,157,000**
Forest Service	15,135,000	
Bureau of Land Management	2,368,000	
National Park Service	166,000	
Fish and Wildlife Service	13,000	
State		**1,022,000**
Department of Forestry	645,000	
Common School Fund (forested)	133,000	
Parks and Recreation Department	60,000	
Department of Fish and Wildlife	39,000	
Department of Transportation (rights-of-way)	7,000	
Board of Higher Education	15,000	
County and Municipal (various)	123,000	
Non-Public		**10,872,000**
Indian Land	480,000	
Non-Industrial (generally small woodlots)	4,438,000	
Industrial (generally large corporations)	5,954,000	
Total Oregon Forest Land		**30,051,000**
Total Oregon Land		**61,441,280**

and begins to decline. (For Douglas-fir, this is traditionally thought to be approximately 80 years, but may actually be 150 to 200 years of age.) The tree continues to grow — in fact, it will grow until it dies — but not as quickly as the forester's theoretical replacement tree.

Scientists, for the most part, have agreed on other quantitative definitions of old growth, which are usually determined by forest type. An old-growth forest must have a certain minimum of large trees of a certain size, per given area. Besides standing live trees, the forest will also have standing dead trees (snags) and downed trees in various states of decomposition. Age and the growing site determine the size of a tree. A good growing site will produce a forest that develops older forest characteristics sooner than a

FEATURED SPECIES
Quaking Aspen

SANDY LONSDALE

The quaking aspen (*Populus tremuloides*) is the most widely distributed tree in North America. It is found at sea level in the north end of its range and at 11,500 feet elevation at the southern end. The species ranges from Alaska to Newfoundland and from Virginia to Northern Mexico. In Oregon, the brilliant spring green and magnificent gold fall foliage of quaking aspen can be seen in the Cascades, East Cascades Slopes and Foothills and Blue Mountains ecoregions. Only a few aspen stands occur in the Coast Range and Klamath Mountains. More can be found in the high ranges of the Oregon Desert such as Steens Mountain and Hart Mountain.

The slightest breeze will make quaking aspen leaves dance. The leaves' bright green tops contrast sharply with their dull green undersides against the backdrop of their white bark and the blue sky. Viewing quaking aspen turning gold on a crisp and clear autumn day is a powerful reminder that all is not wrong in the world.

Aspen forests are biologically rich and provide cover, nesting and feeding habitat for a wide range of birds. Deer and elk heavily graze aspen twigs and foliage, as they do the associated understory. A quaking aspen grove may have 3,000 pounds of understory growth per acre, compared to 200 pounds per acre in a conifer forest. Aspen grow in wet areas and are a favorite of beavers. Rabbits eat the bark and grouse feed on aspen's winter buds. Humans like to carve their initials and ideograms in the bark. Those carved by lonely late nineteenth and early twentieth century sheepherders can still be found and are often sexual in nature.

While individual trees (which are actually stems of a much larger, underground organism) are relatively short-lived, a stand of aspens is not. Aspens typically grow twenty to seventy feet high and live 70 to 90 years. However, an aspen grove can survive indefinitely even if it burns occasionally. Within six weeks of a burn, aspen shoots will rise through the forest floor from the clonal rootstock below and have a distinct advantage over any conifer seeds from cones.

If you see several clumps of aspen trees, each with a distinctive color, know that each cluster consists of clones (genetically identical) from the same original tree that sprouted from a seed 8,000 to 10,000 years ago. In one case, some 47,000 trees have been found to come from one original ancestor.

Any amount of grazing by domestic livestock is harmful to aspen, as the bovines trash the understory and nip off all the replacement shoots from the root system.

Quaking aspen (*Populus tremuloides*) (foreground) and ponderosa pine (*Pinus ponderosa*) (background) on the Ochoco National Forest.

In the American West, the original 9.6 million acres of quaking aspen is down to just 3.9 million acres. In Oregon's Malheur National Forest, aspen have been reduced by 80 percent from historic levels from livestock grazing. While domestic livestock are unquestionably a large part of the problem, another culprit is Smokey Bear.

Aspen sprout profusely after a fire. The first year after a burn may result in 150,000 sprouts per acre. A few years later, the aspen will be a few feet tall with a density of 40,000 to 50,000 sprouts per acre.

The absence of fire — as is now the case throughout most of the West due to federal fire-fighting policies — allows shade-tolerant conifers to slowly invade aspen stands. The conifers then out-compete new aspen shoots by using the aspen's biology against them. Live and healthy adult aspens send a growth-inhibiting hormone down their trunks and into their roots to discourage excessive shoot production, thereby inhibiting the growth of young aspens. When adult aspens die, this hormonal impediment to new shoots ceases. If conifers have overtaken the forest floor by the time the adult aspens die out, the new aspen shoots cannot get established and the aspen stand may eventually be replaced by conifers.

poor growing site. The quality of a growing site is determined by rainfall, soil depth, elevation, aspect, latitude and other factors.

Generally, in western Oregon the onset of old-growth characteristics begins at 150 years of age. Historically, old-growth stands were typically between 250 to 650 years old, though some were over 1000 years old. Individual trees can live longer. If undisturbed by humans for long enough, they are often killed by stand-replacing events: fire, wind, insect, disease or other natural events.

There is a general scientific consensus that — historically, across the landscape and over time — as much as 80 percent of western Oregon forests were over 80 years old, and about two thirds were older than 200 years, or "old growth." The age of trees and percentage of old growth varied, but that was the average. Researchers estimate that today, only 13 to 18 percent of the forested area of western Oregon is old growth, a reduction of over 75 percent. In eastern Oregon, the amount of old growth that existed before European-American invasion averaged about 90 percent for the low elevation ponderosa pine forests, while today it is approximately 20 percent. The rate of old growth loss in Oregon slowed somewhat at the end of the twentieth century, but it still continues.

While the public debate in the Northwest has centered on old-growth forests, "mature forests" (natural forests that are between 80 and 150 years of age) are just as important in the larger and longer scheme of things. Mature (also called "late successional") forests are not old growth, but they are approaching that stage. These forests are home to many of the same species as old growth, though in different proportions.

Therefore it is important to save not only old-growth forests, but mature forests as well, including those that are fragmented by roads and logging. By saving more habitat we can increase the probability of the continued existence of species and ecosystems. As a group of eminent scientists noted, "The more saved now, the greater the buffering against such losses…. Protecting all that remains buys some insurance."[15]

Mature forests have great ecological and watershed values and are the forest stands that will eventually augment and replace current standing old-growth forests. The cycle repeats as the old growth stands are replaced by natural young forests, which will then become mature forests on their way to becoming old-growth forests again. The National Research Council has noted that:

Forest Management in the Pacific Northwest should include the conservation and protection of most or all of the remaining late-successional and old-growth forests…. The remaining late-successional and old-growth forests could form the cores of regional forests managed for truly and indefinitely sustainable production of timber, fish, clean water, recreation, and numerous other amenities of forested ecosystems.[16]

Young Sitka spruce (*Picea stichensis*) growing out of a very old and long dead Stika spruce on the Siuslaw National Forest. ▶

ELIZABETH FERYL, ENVIRONMENTAL IMAGES

FEATURED SPECIES
Western Larch

Not all conifers are evergreens. The ten species of larch (*Larix* spp.), located mostly in the colder climates in the Northern Hemisphere, are conifers (they have cones), but also lose their needles each fall. Three larch species are found in North America: the alpine larch found primarily at high elevations in western Canada; the eastern larch found in boggy areas of the northern forests of eastern North America; and the western larch found in the American West. Commonly called tamarack in the east, this name is sometimes used out west, too. The only other North American "deciduous conifer" is the bald cypress (*Taxodium distichum*), found in the American southeast.

Oregon's larch is the western larch (*Larix occidentalis*). This tallest larch species can reach 150 feet in height, four feet in diameter at the base and 500 years of age. Some specimens reach 200 feet, six feet at the base and live up to 1,000 years. Their great height often makes them an easy target for lightning.

The western larch is easily identified at a distance. During the spring and summer, the bright, almost iridescent, green color of the needles sets it apart from the duller green of the forest's other conifers. Starting in October, the needles turn yellow; by the end of the month they are a brilliant yellow-gold. During the winter, the trees remain distinctive, standing tall and straight without needles.

From a distance, the branches often look feathery, in that the branches are covered with a uniform row of light-green needle clumps. In hand, the needles are very soft and are one to two inches long. There are 14 or more needles per bud. The western larch's small cones are woody and brown.

The bark at the tree's base is quite thick, up to six inches in an old growth specimen. The bark is a furled reddish orange and jigsaw-shaped somewhat like that of ponderosa pine. The thickness of the bark, and the fact that the first limbs often begin up to 50 feet from the ground on large tree, make the western larch the most fire resistant tree in the Pacific Northwest.

Occasionally fire does win the battle with the larch. The dying larch responds by producing huge numbers of seeds that can be dispersed – by the wind – up to 400 feet away. The large-winged seeds are very small; it takes about 143,000 seeds to make a pound. After a fire, western larch often re-establishes itself at the same rate as lodgepole pine, another fast growing species. As the canopy closes, western larch is eventually replaced by other, more shade-tolerant, species in the stand until fire again gives the fire-tolerant larch the advantage.

In Oregon, larch can be found between 3,000 and 7,000 feet in elevation along the east side of the Cascade Range south to the Metolius watershed, but are most abundant in the mountain ranges of the Blue Mountains Ecoregion (Ochoco, Strawberry, Aldrich, Greenhorn, Elkhorn, Wallowa and Blues). Outside Oregon, the western larch ranges through southeastern British Columbia, southwestern Alberta, central and eastern Washington, northwestern Oregon, northern Idaho and western Montana. It prefers the generally moist locations of north slopes and valley bottoms.

Western larch (*Larix occidentalis*) on the Wallowa-Whitman National Forest. The larch has a contrary nature as a deciduous conifer. After turning color in the fall, the needles fall off.

The utility of the western larch is not limited to its beauty. Rotting cavities within larch trunks provide homes to several songbird species, woodpeckers, owls and flying squirrels. Occasionally osprey, bald eagle and even Canada geese make their large platform nests in western larch trees. Both blue and spruce grouse eat the buds and leaves. Black bears favor larch trees for escape because the textured bark and large size make for easy climbing (if one is a bear).

Glactan, the natural sugar gum in the wood, resembles a slightly bitter honey and can be made into baking powder (in case you're running low and can't get to a store).

The native quinine conk (*Fomes officinalis*) that grows perpendicular on tree trunks can be deadly to western larch, but has medicinal value to humans. In earlier times, conk growing high above the forest floor was harvested by rifle shot and sold to European pharmaceutical firms.

The larch casebearer (*Coleophora laricella*), a native of Europe, was introduced to the range of the western larch and is now a serious pest that defoliates the victim trees. In Europe, the casebearer is naturally controlled by parasites, as it is in eastern North America. But importing the parasites to the West has not been effective as a control measure. Fortunately, the western larch is accustomed to losing its needles and will grow a second crop if defoliated in the spring. However, repeated defoliation stresses the trees and does not bode well for the larch's ability to compete in the forest environment in the future.

For much of the last half-century, government and industry has routinely "salvage" logged forests after major natural disturbances such as wild fire, windthrow, insect infestations or disease outbreaks. This has caused scientists to note the importance and rarity of natural young (0-80 years old) forests, as well as older forests.

Indeed, naturally developed early-successional forest habitats, with their rich array of snags and logs and nonarborescent vegetation, are probably the scarcest habitat in the current regional [Pacific Northwest] landscape.[17]

The continued siege by federal forest managers and timber companies against young, mature and old-growth forests in Oregon, and the increasing rarity of all three forest types, certainly strengthens the case for more forest wilderness.

Selected Fish and Wildlife in Oregon's Forests

Idaho is full of elk. Ohio isn't. The reason is obvious.

–Howie Wolke (Wyoming guide, wilderness defender and co-founder of Earth First!)

Northern flying squirrels (*Glaucomys sabrinus*) do not actually fly, but do glide between trees using a flap of skin that extends between their front and rear legs. They mostly eat underground fungi and are mostly eaten by northern spotted owls.

Approximately 579 wildlife species are regularly found in Oregon, including 31 amphibians, 31 reptiles, 370 birds and 137 mammals. Many of these species are in trouble. In Oregon, 139 vertebrate species (most species are *invertebrates*) are categorized as "endangered," "threatened" or "sensitive." This means that their populations are neither stable nor increasing — as a matter of scientific, if not legal, determination. As of 1996, this list included 36 fish, 19 amphibian, 8 reptile, 54 bird and 22 mammal species. Not included are the grizzly bear and other species that have been extirpated from Oregon.

Excessive exploitation (hunting, fishing and trapping), disease and other factors contributed to the decline of several species. However, in almost every case, the overwhelmingly critical factor contributing to species' decline is the loss of habitat caused by development, agriculture, logging, grazing and mining. If the full complement of Oregon's native fish and wildlife are to have a future, we must leave room for nature.

Conservation biologists have developed the concept of "focal species" to help gauge and manage ecosystem health. Focal species are "organisms used in planning and managing nature reserves because their requirements for survival represent factors important to maintaining ecologically healthy conditions."[18] Several types of focal species exist.

▶ **Keystone Species** "enrich ecosystem function in a unique and significant manner through their activities," with an "effect… disproportionate to their numerical abundance."[19] For example, when beaver disappear from an area, the ecosystem structure changes, resulting in a loss of diversity.

▶ **Umbrella Species** "generally cover large areas in their daily or seasonable movements."[20] Large mammalian carnivores, because they are wide-ranging and ecological generalists, often serve as umbrella species, although large herbivores and raptors can also serve this role. Protecting enough habitat for these species often provides habitat sufficient for numerous other species. Grizzly bear, wolf and elk are good examples of umbrella species in Oregon.

▶ **Flagship Species** "are charismatic creatures."[21] Globally, giant pandas, harp seals, whales and sea turtles fill this role. These species attract public attention for the conservation objective they are associated with. Fortunately, the northern spotted owl is warm-blooded, has feathers and is telegenic, making it an ideal flagship species for old-growth forests. (Though Pacific salmon are cold-blooded, slimy and difficult to photograph, they too have charisma.) In Oregon, grizzly bear and wolf can be additional flagship species if ever they are returned to their former habitat in the state. Flagship species are also sometimes called "lightning rod species" because they can attract intense opposition to conservation goals.

▶ **Indicator Species** "are tightly linked to specific biological elements, processes or qualities; are sensitive to ecological changes; and are useful in monitoring habitat quality."[22] In Oregon, there is no better indicator of westside forest ecosystem health than the northern spotted owl. An indicator species can indicate something as narrow as stream temperature or as broad as wilderness quality.

Each of the four types of focal species has a different, but critical function.

A keystone species is defined by ecological value. An umbrella species is a basis for management decisions, particularly about size, shape, and spatial distribution of protected areas. A flagship species is charismatic and used in public relations and fundraising. Finally, an indicator species is useful in assessing and monitoring quality of habitat.[23]

One species can represent more than one type of focal species. The spotted owl, as noted above, is both a flagship and an indicator species. The grizzly bear — temporarily absent from Oregon — can be all four.

Below are a selection of brief accounts of wildlife species that do, could again or may still inhabit Oregon's wild forests. Additional natural history of certain species can be found in the individual descriptions of proposed Wilderness areas.

Carnivorous Mammals

Carnivora. These are flesh eaters.

Oregon's forests are short on carnivores due to habitat destruction, trapping for sport and profit, as well as simple human meanness and fear. Regardless of size or species, most Oregon carnivores are not prospering, save for the wily coyote, which is in no trouble at all, and the cougar, whose numbers have been growing steadily.

The gray wolf and the grizzly bear are presently missing from Oregon, although the wolf is beginning to make a comeback.

There are four medium-sized flesh eaters in serious decline throughout Oregon's forests and elsewhere: lynx, marten, fisher and wolverine.

Carnivores, at or near the top of the food chain, serve important regulatory functions in ecosystems and as indicators of an ecosystem's overall health.

To date, species that fly or swim have received more conservation, legal and political attention than those that roam the land. The Pacific Northwest Forest Plan, for example, was designed primarily to protect marbled murrelets, northern spotted owls and Pacific salmon. While the habitat requirements of birds and fish often overlap those for carnivores, taking specific steps to provide habitat needs for mid- and top-level carnivores will likely also protect the needs of small carnivores and their prey species.

If lynx, wolverine, fisher and marten are to survive in Oregon (and if the wolf and the grizzly bear are to return) we need to protect our remaining wilderness — including that which is already designated Wilderness, and especially that which is not.

Lynx *Lynx canadensis* was thought to have been extirpated from Oregon, but it turns out that the species is just very rare and, until now, hard to detect. Over the last several decades there has been a string of credible lynx sightings from south of Crater Lake all the way to the Wallowa Mountains. Adding to the sightings, the lynx's

GEORGE WUERTHNER

The large paws of the lynx *(Lynx Canadensis)* allow them to hunt atop heavy snow. The blood is not lynx blood.

presence in Oregon was recently proved by analysis of hair samples.

Listed as a threatened species under the Endangered Species Act, lynx are almost perfectly calibrated to snowshoe hare populations, especially in the boreal regions of its range. As hare numbers rise and fall, so do lynx populations. In the southern portion of its range, lynx eat a variety of other prey species, including small mammals and birds. Red squirrels are an alternative food source for lynx throughout much of its range. In Oregon, red squirrels are found only in the Blue Mountains. Douglas squirrels, first cousins to the red, are found in the rest of Oregon's forested ecoregions. Times are particularly difficult for lynx both when squirrel numbers decline (due to a scarcity of conifer cones) and the hares are also at the bottom of their natural cycle (due to reduced food supply).

In Oregon, lynx prefer forest habitats that are similar to northern boreal forests. They live in high elevation areas where the snow is deep in winter. Their oversized paws are natural snowshoes, giving them a competitive advantage over other predators like the bobcat when pursuing prey atop the snow. Lynx paws are comparable in size and shape to those of a cougar, though the latter weighs three to five times more. Bobcats and coyotes may compete with lynx in some (lower elevation) areas, limiting lynx populations. This may be especially so in places where snowmobiles provide perfectly groomed pathways through deep snow, aiding bobcats and coyotes to pursue prey where they would not otherwise go. If wolves are returned to Oregon, research indicates that coyote numbers would probably decrease, affording some respite to lynx.

Lynx need large areas of contiguous habitat. They won't persist in small isolated refuges, which might otherwise be suitable habitat.

Recently disturbed forest stands (preferably by wildfire rather than logging) are highly productive for snowshoe hares, but these open habitats are transient, as they develop quickly into early succession forests. Late-seral (old) forests, on the other hand, are moderately productive for hares and support stable populations for long periods. Lynx find refuge in these older forests.

Controversy is now brewing over how lynx habitat should be defined in the southern extent of its range. Wildlife and forest management agencies — preferring not to consider lynx needs when developing timber sales, roads and winter recreation — have arbitrarily categorized millions of acres of Oregon's national forests so that they are no longer considered lynx habitat.

The American marten (*Martes americana*) needs mature closed-canopy forests.

Marten

We know little firsthand of the marten in Oregon, but we suspect that populations here likely will not increase greatly if short-rotation timber harvest and single-species replanting continue as recommended forest-management practices. Other practices, more of the past than of the present — such as burning or otherwise removing slash, snags and downed logs, and large clearcuttings — likely are detrimental to marten populations.

—B. J. Verts and Leslie N. Carraway, in *Land Mammals of Oregon*[24]

We do know that from 1834 to 1837 the Hudson's Bay Company, through its headquarters near present day Vancouver, Washington, bought 334,362 American marten (*Martes americana*) pelts. For comparison with a better-known fur, during the same three years the company bought 307,186 beaver pelts.

Research shows that martens live longer, more productive lives and suffer less natural and trapping mortality in undisturbed old forests, compared to logged forests.

They can live in a variety of older forest types. In Oregon, martens are most abundant in the southern Cascade Range but also live in the Blue and Wallowa mountains. A few are also found in the Coast Range. Once believed extinct, the

Humboldt subspecies (*M. a. humboldtensis*) may have been recently rediscovered just south of the Oregon border and may range into the Kalmiopsis country.

Martens are opportunistic feeders, eating not only small birds and mammals, but also carrion.

Fisher In Oregon, the fisher (*Martes pennanti*) once ranged through all forested ecoregions of the state. It now appears to be limited to a portion of the Klamath Mountains and the Cascades Ecoregion.

Classified in the same family of carnivores as river otter and mink, the fisher is larger than both of these and the marten. It is renowned for its unique ability to kill porcupines. Contrary to lore, the fisher does not flip the porcupine over and then attack its quill-free underbelly. (In 1979, I saw Senator Mark Hatfield get down on his hands and knees in his capitol office to demonstrate the technique.) Rather it bites the porcupine's quill-free face until it dies, which can last a half-hour before the real eating begins.

The fisher in its west coast range has been found to be warranted for protection under the Endangered Species Act. Only three small populations of fishers remain in the Sierra Nevada, northern California and the Oregon Cascades. The species is extirpated from the rest of Oregon, including the Blue Mountains.

The only native fisher population in Oregon is in the Klamath Mountains. The current Oregon Cascades population is the result of a successful reintroduction of individuals from British Columbia and Minnesota. To please the timber industry, the Oregon Department of Fish and Wildlife reintroduced fishers, hoping to control the porcupine populations that were decimating tree seedlings in timber plantations.

Very rare in Oregon, the fisher (*Martes pennanti*) has been the victim of trapping and habitat loss. It needs dense, mature forests with a deciduous component.

While porcupines can adapt to such severely simplified ecosystems, fishers require a variety of densely forested habitats at low and middle elevations. Fishers require large blocks of intact old forests with snags and continuous closed canopies, especially along riparian areas. Fishers need the cavities of large trees for dens. Swamps and other forest wetlands are important fisher habitat. Timber plantations have none of these. An estimated 60 to 85 percent of the fisher's original habitat has been destroyed across its range.

Despite the name, fishers don't eat fish, but they do eat small mammals and birds, carrion, fruit and truffles.

Wolverine

The wolverine occurs in a broad range of wilderness habitats. Coastal forest, inland forest of coastal composition, boreal forest, and even tundra areas are occupied depending on elevation and latitude. Within these types, ecotonal areas, especially those near marshes, seem to be significant components of habitats used by wolverines. Open areas seem to be avoided, skirted or crossed rapidly. Nevertheless, the critical component seems to be the absence of human activity or development.

—B. J. Verts and Leslie N. Carraway, in *Land Mammals of Oregon*[25]

Wolverines (*Gulo gulo*) are legendary for their savage disposition, although this reputation is probably derived from observing the behavior of individuals caught in cages or traps where they display unparalleled defensive aggression compared to other trapped species. (Wouldn't you?)

Wolverines are large, powerful animals, and sometimes weigh over 50 pounds. They often escape from traps, break into structures or food stores and can even kill large deer and elk. An adept climber and swimmer, the wolverine is about the size of a bear cub. While primarily a meat eater, it will also take berries in season. Wolverines kill some of their own meat and also eat carrion. The extirpation of wolves in Oregon has meant less carrion lying around for wolverines (and other carrion eaters) and that has probably affected the species.

Wolverines can be found in boreal (northern) forests that receive deep winter snow. Recent wolverine sightings in the southern Oregon Cascades and southern Blue Mountains — and mostly in designated Wilderness and de facto wilderness — are exciting news. Wolverines were thought to have been extirpated from Oregon until 1965 when a large male was killed on Three Fingered Jack (Mount Jefferson Wilderness). Since then, tracks, sightings and trappings have been reported on Steens Mountain (Wilderness), Broken Top (Three Sisters Wilderness), Mount Thielsen (Wilderness), Mount McLoughlin (Sky Lakes Wilderness) and Mount Bailey (proposed North Umpqua Wilderness).

GERALD AND BUFF CORSI

Wolverines (*Gulo gulo*) do not get along well with people or development.

Cougar In Oregon, cougar or mountain lion are the most common names for *Puma concolor*. Since the species originally had the widest range of any mammal in the Western Hemisphere, it also picked up some other names, including puma, catamount, panther and painter.

Oregon's largest cat is doing well. Before hunting cougars with hounds was eliminated in 1994 by a vote of the people, the population was growing 4 to 5 percent annually. After the hounds were held at bay, the annual cougar population growth spurted to 8 to 12 percent, but has since returned to about 5 percent.

Cougars average 120 pounds with extremely large males having been reported at as much as 264 pounds.

Three of the 15 recognized cougar subspecies occur in Oregon. The smaller *P. c. californica* is found in the Siskiyou Mountains and southern interior valleys of southwestern Oregon. The lighter colored *P. c. missoulensis* makes its home in the Wallowa Mountains and Hells Canyon, while the darker *P. c. oregonensis* is found throughout the rest of Oregon.

The cougar has a wide distribution and a wild spirit that symbolizes wilderness. In Oregon, cougars range widely in a variety of habitats, but are most often found in forested areas, especially in winter. The most productive cougar habitat in western Oregon is of the Douglas-fir/trailing blackberry type with an old growth component. In northeastern Oregon, the best habitat appears to be open mixed-conifer, including pine-bunchgrass canyons. Home ranges can be from 60 to100 square miles.

Cougars don't like clearcuts, roads and humans and generally try to avoid all three. Cougars don't prefer other cougars much either, as they spend most of their lives

alone, save for mating and when mothers are rearing their young.

Deer and elk are primary prey for the cougar, but the big cat also eats porcupine, snowshoe hare, small mammals and grass. A cougar will kill a deer or elk every seven to ten days. Domestic livestock can also cure a cougar's hunger, but such predation is relatively rare, even though livestock are pervasive in cougar country.

While hungry cougars have been seen on the edge of urban areas, your chances of seeing one are only a little better than being struck by lightning. Your chance of being killed and eaten by a cougar is not much greater than your chance of winning the lottery without buying a ticket.

Wolf The gray wolf was officially extirpated from Oregon in 1946 when the last state bounty was paid on a dead wolf. However, since then there has been tantalizing evidence of *Canis lupus'* return to the state. Carcasses confirmed to be wolves were found in Baker County in 1974 and Douglas County in 1978. Were these remnants of the native Oregon population, or renegades that crossed the border from elsewhere?

Some speculate that wolves have persisted all along at unnoticeably low levels in the southern Cascades.

Three wolves have been confirmed in the state during the last few years. The first was captured near the Middle Fork John Day River and returned to Idaho. A vehicle on Interstate 84 hit and killed a second wolf in Baker County. Both of these wolves came from an experimental population in Idaho and had collars to prove it. A third, found dead without any collar, was shot near Ukiah. (Though some yahoo likely had a beef with this wolf for threatening domestic livestock, an analysis of the wolf's stomach contents found no beef.) There have been 40 additional gray wolf sightings since 2001, including a reliable one as far west as Klamath County, although some of the animals reported were probably not wolves.

"Official" Oregon has never been charitable to wolves. A reason for organizing the first state government in 1843 was to institute a $3 bounty ($52.95 in 2001 dollars) on wolves and other predators.[26] Before that, from 1834 to 1837, the Hudson's Bay Company bought 19,544 wolf pelts from trappers. Fortunately, times have changed. Killing an endangered wolf in Oregon today is a federal offense punishable by a maximum of a $100,000 fine and one year in jail.

Until recently, the position of the Oregon Department of Fish and "Wildlife" policy on wolves (the department used to be called "Fish and Game," which reflected the agency's bias against non-game species, including predators) was that the federal government should give any wolf found in Oregon a free ride (back) to Idaho. ODFW was not only kowtowing to a minority of hunters who detest sharing their prey with wolves, but worse, the agency was pandering to the concerns of private livestock interests who oppose the wolf's return. It is no wonder this agency has little public support.

◄ Few are lucky enough to encounter a cougar (*Puma concolor*) in the wild.

GEORGE WUERTHNER

The gray wolf (*Canus lupis*) was once common in Oregon, then was extirpated and now is moving back into the state from Idaho.

The largest canid in the world, the gray wolf once ranged across the continent from the central plateau of Mexico to the lower Arctic and from coast to coast. Usually gray, the wolf can also be yellowish or light brownish with black. Two subspecies historically ranged in Oregon. The smaller, darker *C. l. fuscus* was found in the western three-fifths of the state while the lighter, larger *C. l. irremotus* was found elsewhere.

Over the last 150 years the wolf population in the continental United States has been reduced from hundreds of thousands of individuals to about 1,000 (mostly in Minnesota). Wolves have since been reintroduced in Idaho and Yellowstone National Park in 1994. An individual wolf can disperse nearly 500 miles in search of a new home and mate. So their return to the Pacific Northwest and elsewhere is almost inevitable. Wolves are beginning to reappear in Washington's Cascade and Selkirk ranges. It is only a matter of time until the wolf becomes a full-time resident of Oregon again.

The Oregon Cattlemen's Association (OCA) opposes the return of wolves to Oregon. Their predecessors worked hard to kill off Oregon's wolves last century, and they worry about the potential threat of wolf predation on their livestock that range on the public lands.

These cowboys are acting more like Little Red Riding Hood than John Wayne. It doesn't matter to the OCA that Defenders of Wildlife will pay 100 percent of the value of livestock confirmed to be killed by wolves and 50 percent for probable wolf kills. Under this program, Defenders has paid out more than $206,000 to 180 ranchers since 1987. However, more important to the larger debate on wolf restoration is a comparison of wolf predation to other causes of livestock loss. In Montana, for every eight to ten livestock taken by wolves, approximately 1,000 livestock are killed by domestic dogs (*Canis familiaris*). In 1996, more than 97 percent of livestock deaths nationwide were attributed to digestive problems, respiratory difficulties, calving complications, weather and other causes. Less than three percent were attributed to predation by all classes of predators.

Oregon's Klamath, Siskiyou, Cascade and Blue mountains all have good wolf habitat because they have good prey populations of deer and elk. Where there is prey there should be predators. One of the reasons for the exploding coyote (*Canis latrans*) population in Oregon and across the West, despite the cattle industry's best efforts to wipe them out, is that nature's coyote control, the gray wolf, has been missing from the top of the food chain. Oregon has more wolf habitat than Montana and it is mostly on public lands. It's time to fill it up with these beautiful animals again. Defenders of Wildlife reports:

> *Predators and predation play a dynamic and essential role in maintaining the health of ecosystems. By preying mostly on the young and elderly, the sick and injured and the weak and unfit, wolves help keep prey population healthy and vigorous.... In fact, ... a classic study... showed that the reproductive rate of deer herds remains stable and may even rise in the presence of wolves. More fawns survive as wolves remove older animals, thus reducing competition for food and other resources.*[27]

Polls indicate that 70 percent of Oregonians would welcome the wolf back for both ecological and cultural reasons. If the Oregon Department of Fish and Wildlife is worried about decreased deer and elk tag revenue from wolf restoration (unlikely), it should consider offering people who purchase deer and elk hunting tags the opportunity to waive their tags in favor of these new fanged Oregonians. They might be pleasantly surprised by the support for such a program.

Black Bear Currently, Oregon's only native bear is the black bear (*Ursus americanus*). Take note: black bears can be black or brown and are occasionally white or bluish. Much smaller than grizzly bears, female adult black bears average 175 pounds and males about 275 pounds. On all four feet, they are about three feet high. Standing upright, black bears measure five feet. With short powerful legs, they can reach bursts of speeds of 35 mph. Black bears can live up to 20 years in the wild. Their natural enemies include other bears, cougars and humans.

Black bears are forest-dwellers. Oregon has two recognized subspecies. *U. a. altifrontalis* is larger, occurs west of the Cascade Range and has a four to one chance of actually being black. The smaller *U. a. cinnamomum* is common east of the Cascades and has 55 percent chance of being brown. It is possible that a third subspecies, *U. a. californiensis*, occurred in the southern portion of the Cascade Range, but historical data is inconclusive. Black bear numbers are increasing in Oregon with an estimated population of 25,000.

Largely herbivorous, black bears eat the new growth of grasses and forbs (wildflowers) in spring. In summer, they eat mostly berries and fruits. In fall, their diet

Black bears (*Ursus americanus*) prefer dense conifer-deciduous forests, but will munch on the cambium layer of little trees in timber plantations (since there is little else around). Consequently, the timber industry advocates severely reducing their numbers.

consists primarily of acorns, nuts and berries, as well as insects and fish. Black bears will never pass up carrion (dead animals), but only about 10 percent of their diet is animal protein. In winter, the only thing they eat during dormancy is the soles of their own footpads. (Really!) The hairless pads shed and have been found in bear scat near dens. Until the new pads harden with use, emerging bears with tender feet are limited in their movements.

While black bears eat well in young forests, wet meadows and even clearcuts, they do require dens in winter, often provided at the base or within the trunks of large hollow trees. A large hollow tree must first have been a large, living tree. And the large, living tree must first have been allowed to grow into an old tree, at least 150 to 200 years. In northeast Oregon, top-entry bear den trees average 57 feet in height (the tree was once taller) and over 43 inches in diameter at the base. Grand fir, western larch and western redcedar provide the best dens. While subject to heart rot, western white and lodgepole pines, Douglas- and subalpine fir and Engelmann spruce seldom form hollow chambers needed by bears.

Grizzly Bear

There seems to be a tacit assumption that if grizzlies survive in Canada and Alaska, that it's good enough. It is not good enough for me.... Relegating grizzlies to Alaska is about like relegating happiness to heaven; one may never get there.

—Aldo Leopold[28]

At the time of Lewis and Clark, as many as 100,000 grizzly bears (*Ursus arctos*) could be found in what are now the lower 48 United States. Today, about one percent of their original population remains in the lower 48 states in about two percent of their historical range.

Grizzlies once ranged from Alaska and the Canadian north to the Great Plains to the Pacific Ocean and central Mexico. Today, the species' range is limited to the far northlands: northeastern Washington, the northern most part of Idaho, western Montana and northwestern Wyoming.

The last grizzly bear was killed in Oregon on September 14, 1931, on Chesnimnus Creek in Wallowa County. Oregon has plenty of black bears (*U. americanus*), but no grizzly bears, also known as "brown bears," even though they are sometimes black. The best ways to distinguish the species are by size (the grizzly is usually much larger) and shape (the grizzly has characteristic humped shoulders and a dished [concave] face). Verts and Carraway in *Land Mammals of Oregon* note that:

(G)rizzly bears seemingly were widespread in Oregon before European settlement; they occurred in the Cascade Range; the Siskiyou, Blue, Steens and Wallowa mountains; the Klamath, Rogue, Umpqua and Willamette valleys; and some of the high desert country south and east of Bend. [29]

The United States Geological Survey lists 29 natural features in Oregon named "Grizzly." They include ten summits (peaks and mountains), three ridges, three valleys, nine streams and four flats in thirteen Oregon counties from Wallowa to Lake and from Curry to Clatsop. Verts and Carraway describe the habitat needs of the grizzly bear.

The grizzly bear is a species of the rugged, largely inaccessible spacious wilderness areas where either by law or by remoteness its populations are protected from overexploitation by humans. Within such areas, the requirements for food, dens, and cover may be met by a variety of vegetative and physiographic types. A variety of forest types, alpine and subalpine communities, early seral communities in riparian or burned-over areas, grasslands, and shrublands appropriately intermixed and interconnected with travel lanes serve as habitat for these wide-ranging mammals. Succulent, high-protein, and high-energy foods; dry dens not subject to being disturbed by humans; and sufficient vegetation to serve as a shield from human view seem to be habitat requisites for grizzly bears. Thus, precisely how communities provide these elements (which plant and animal species are involved) does not seem as critical as the elements themselves.[30]

Grizzly bears are opportunistic feeders and eat varied plant and animal matter. Because they hibernate, they must put on lots of fat, which means eating lots of flesh. New evidence suggests that the grizzly bear cannot successfully return to Oregon until

GEORGE WUERTHNER

The last grizzly bear (*Ursus arctos*) in Oregon was shot in 1931. It is possible that they are returning to the state from Idaho.

Table 1-3. Causes of Death in National Parks in Grizzly Country[32]

Yellowstone National Park Deaths (1839-1994)	
Drowning	101
Falls	24
Climbing	21
Airplane Crashes	20
Burns from Hot Springs	19
Suicides	15
Hypothermia	9
Horse Drawn Wagons	9
Indian Battles	7
Horses	7
Accidental Shootings	7
Carbon Monoxide Poisoning	7
Missing/Presumed Dead	5
Murder	5
Avalanches	5
Falling Trees	5
Lightning	5
Bear Attacks	**4**

Glacier National Park Deaths (1913-1998)	
Drowning	48
Heart Attack	31
Vehicle Accidents	26
Falls	24
Bear Attacks	**10**
Natural Death	9
Avalanches	8
Falling Object	7
Missing/Presumed Dead	7
Airplane Accident	6

salmon runs are adequately restored. Scientists have analyzed museum specimens and determined that most of what Northwest grizzly bears ate was salmon.[31]

Thus, as part of an astounding biological cycle, the grizzly bear and salmon link the Pacific Ocean and the magnificent old-growth forests of the Pacific Northwest. Washington State University researchers say that as a result of bears eating salmon, 400 pounds of phosphorus and nitrogen are deposited in adjacent forests each year. As bear scat, these elements are in a more usable form as nutrients for trees than even manufactured fertilizers. The nutrients-to-salmon-to-bear (and other species)-to-forest connection can account for up to 20 percent of tree growth. These old-growth forests depend not just on climate, genetics, soils and time, but also on nutrients transported and deposited by healthy fish and wildlife populations.

So the answer to the age-old question of "does an ursine defecate in the forest?" has been answered unequivocally. (The infamous companion question about the religion of the Pope is not addressed by these studies.)

Like most natural processes, this one is entirely circular. When trees that have benefited from wildlife-deposited nutrients fall into streams they return nutrients to riparian and oceanic systems downstream that support an aquatic food chain that features salmon at the top. Interestingly, Hawaiian natives made dugout canoes from old-growth trees that originated in North American Pacific Coast forests and washed up on the islands' shores, after floating down rivers and out to sea.

This natural ecosystem can again accommodate grizzlies, but can human society accommodate the bears? Grizzlies do kill people. Although more people die from mosquito-borne disease, it is somehow not the same. In grizzly country, humans are species *numero dos* and that makes many people uncomfortable. Perhaps it is because a grizzly bear can weigh up to 800 pounds, stand eight feet tall and run 35 to 40 miles per hour. Still, while an individual grizzly can easily overwhelm a human, humankind is utterly overwhelming bearkind.

Humans and grizzly bears can co-exist. Whether we choose that future depends on whether society believes that humans are all-important or that humans are only the most important part of an all-important biosphere. To put the grizzly-human balance in perspective, consider the causes of human death in both Yellowstone and Glacier National Parks, the two locales in the continental United States where grizzlies and humans most often meet (Table 1-3).

In 1979, a grizzly bear was sighted in Oregon. It was heading east up Steep Creek into the proposed Homestead Addition to the Hells Canyon Wilderness. The bear was apparently coming from the proposed Lake Fork unit of the proposed Wallowa Mountains Wilderness across the road. Oregon is not complete without the grizzly bear. The wildest wilderness exists where our largest ursine colleague can find a home.

DON GETTY

Herbivorous Mammals

Not all mammals eat mammals. Oregon's forests contain majestic and interesting herbivorous mammals as well. But even these, on their worst days — but as nature intended — can end up as dinner for carnivorous mammals.

Beaver [33]

The destruction of salmon habitat in the rivers of the Pacific Northwest started with this near annihilation of beaver in the last half of the nineteenth century.

—Jim Lichatowich, in *Salmon Without Rivers*[34]

Yes, Oregon's official state mammal is a rodent. But this largest rodent on the continent, which can weigh 55 pounds, is by no means a riparian rat. The beaver (*Castor canadensis*) enriches its ecosystem far in disproportion to its numbers. Because the beaver modifies its environment to make a living and creates habitat for numerous other species, it is what biologists call a keystone species.

Perhaps 200 million beavers once inhabited North America. Beavers were everywhere there was water. However, after centuries of severe over-trapping and the resulting decline in the fur market, the beaver is only now beginning to recover and make a partial comeback.

Beavers live to dam moving water and don't care if the water moves through irrigation ditches or highway culverts. Beavers can be a nuisance to human notions about order and territory but, on the whole, any annoyance or damage beavers cause to human development is far outweighed by the great ecological benefits they provide. According to *Oregon's Living Landscape*, beaver benefits include:

- *Raised water tables and related sediment settling, which contributes to the creation of meadows behind beaver dams and to the enhancement of fisheries downstream*

- *Control of streambank and channel erosion by trapping silt eroding from adjacent lands*

- *Creation of large carbon-absorbing reservoirs that greatly boost the amount of nitrogen available to plants*

- *Regeneration of riparian vegetation, which increases food and shelter for numerous invertebrates, other mammals, waterfowl and songbirds*

- *Enhancement of fish habitat behind dams by increasing water depth*

- *Reduction of stream velocity and overall improvement of water quality as riparian vegetation intercepts contamination from agricultural runoff*

Beaver (*Castor americana*) are a "keystone" species that creates habitat upon which many other species depend. ▶

• *Recharging of groundwater reservoirs and stabilization of stream flows throughout the summer and during droughts*

• *The protection of downstream croplands and urban areas from floods by the beaver's enhancement of upstream water storage (through the creation of meadows and wetlands)*[35]

Four subspecies of beaver can be found in Oregon: the small, dark *C. c. idoneus* in northwestern Oregon; the large chestnut brown *C. c. leucodontus* in the northern two-thirds of Oregon east of the Cascades; the small, dull and pale *C. c. baileyi* in the Harney Basin; and the bright, chestnut brown *C. c. shastensis* in south central and southwestern Oregon.

Elk There are two subspecies of elk (*Cervus elaphus*) in Oregon. The typically larger and darker Roosevelt elk (*C. e. roosevelti*) is found west of the Cascade crest. Males have larger antlers with a narrower spread than do the Rocky Mountain elk (*C. e. nelsoni*) that are found east of the Cascade crest. Individual variation within the two subspecies makes identification difficult, so geography is the best way to differentiate the two.

Best known as forest-dwelling animals, the Rocky Mountain subspecies, for reasons not clear, are also reinhabiting the Oregon Desert portion of the Sagebrush Sea. Across Oregon, elk are most abundant in the Blue and Wallowa mountains (Rocky Mountain) and in the north Oregon Coast Range (Roosevelt).

Also called wapiti, the elk is Oregon's largest native ungulate, save for the very occasional stray moose, and can weigh in at over 1,100 pounds. Bull antler size is related to nutrition, as is female reproductive success. Rocky Mountain cows (females) are likely to bear a calf every year, while Roosevelt cows usually give birth every other year. From late August through mid-November, mature bulls gather harems for autumn mating. It's good work if you can get it, but dominant bulls are so busy servicing the harem and fending off challengers that they often suffer from a lack of sleep and nutrition. Calves are born the following spring.

During the summer, elk try to build up fat reserves for winter by eating lots of grasses and wildflowers. They can often be found in moist meadows and streambanks, which provide food and cool places to escape the heat. If you come across a dug-out mud hole in a meadow, it's probably an elk wallow used to both cool the occupant and create a urine- and feces-soaked mud defense against insects. It makes one appreciate modern bug spray.

In the winter, elk browse on woody vegetation such as oak, aspen, alder, yew and willow. During very cold times — especially in eastern Oregon, but also in the Coast Range — elk require the thermal cover provided by older forests.

In Oregon, elk hunting was banned from 1908-32 in an attempt to rebuild herds

GARY BRAASCH

Roosevelt elk (*Cervus elaphus roosevelti*) are found west of the Cascade Crest.

that had been decimated by commercial hunting (some for the meat, mostly for the hides, antlers and upper canine teeth) and competition from livestock grazing.

In the publicly owned mountains of eastern Oregon, domestic livestock compete with elk for summer forage. Obviously, any forage that is appropriated by domestic livestock is not available for native wildlife. Livestock typically spend their winters back at privately owned ranches in the mountain valleys where the elk also wander to avoid deep snow.

Hearing elk is as exciting as seeing them. Bulls bugle a deep bellowing whistle for obvious reasons in the fall, but cows also vocalize in spring while calving.

Rocky Mountain Bighorn Sheep.

Rocky Mountain bighorn sheep (*Ovis canadensis canadensis*) are now at 5 percent of their pre-European invasion numbers. Over 90 percent of all remaining Rocky Mountain bighorns spend part of their life on the national forest system. In Oregon, Rocky Mountain bighorns are found primarily in the Wallowa-Whitman and Umatilla National Forests. The original native population was extirpated from Oregon by 1945. Unrestricted hunting, diseases transmitted from domestic sheep and other conflicts with domestic livestock contributed to the demise of wild sheep in Oregon.

Rocky Mountain bighorns have since been reintroduced in limited areas in Oregon. Ten herds of bighorns are now found in the proposed Hells Canyon, Wallowa Mountains and Grande Ronde Wilderness areas in the Grande Ronde, Burnt and Imnaha Basins, which also include the existing Hells Canyon, Eagle Cap and Wenaha-Tucannon Wilderness areas.

Rocky Mountain bighorn sheep (*Ovis americana americana*) are often fatally susceptible to diseases from domestic sheep.

In 1971, twenty Rocky Mountain bighorns were transplanted from Jasper Park, Alberta to Hells Canyon, but they eventually disappeared. Another twenty were released the same year on the Lostine River in the Eagle Cap Wilderness. Fortunately, that population thrived and became the source of successful transplants elsewhere in Northeastern Oregon (including Hells Canyon) and other states. Today, Oregon has an estimated 700 Rocky Mountain bighorn sheep.

The Rocky Mountain subspecies usually has heavier horns and is a little larger, stockier and darker in color than the California subspecies (*O. c. californiana*). The general geographic boundary between the two subspecies ranges is the John Day-Burnt River Divide.

The California subspecies, while found mostly in the Oregon Desert, also occurs on Strawberry Mountain and in some other forested areas. Conversely, Rocky Mountain bighorns are found at Sheep Mountain at the south end of Hells Canyon in the Oregon Desert.

The Oregon Department of Fish and Wildlife has identified numerous additional potential transplant sites for both subspecies, mostly in designated Wilderness or proposed Wilderness areas. These sites provide both winter and summer range, generally contain the sheep's preferred precipitous terrain and have few trees or other vegetation that obstructs long-distance vision. In some places, unless the trees burn periodically, conifer encroachment will degrade bighorn habitat.

In Oregon, the single most effective limitation on increased populations of Rocky Mountain bighorn sheep is the U.S. Forest Service, particularly in the Wallowa-Whitman National Forest. There — and elsewhere — the Forest Service insists on continuing domestic sheep grazing that, although at best a marginal enterprise on these public lands, is deadly to wild sheep. Where domestic and wild sheep interact, wild sheep often die in large numbers. Domestic sheep are carriers of, but are not affected by, a strain of pneumonia (*Pasteurella* spp.) that is lethal to bighorn sheep. All ages of wild sheep are affected and lamb mortality rates are adversely affected for three to five years after each outbreak of the disease.

Responding to litigation and public concern, the Forest Service has reluctantly ended domestic sheep grazing in most parts of the Oregon side of the Hells Canyon National Recreation Area (NRA). Nonetheless, the Hells Canyon wild sheep recently suffered a large die-off, which was directly linked to a domestic sheep allotment on the edge of the NRA in the Seven Devils Mountains on the Payette National Forest in Idaho.

The Wallowa-Whitman National Forest still hosts 33,885 sheep-months of grazing on various parts of the forest, which prohibits the re-introduction of wild bighorn sheep in these areas. The government takes in less than $10,000 a year in grazing revenue, while spending several-fold more than that to facilitate such grazing. Meanwhile, in 2001, one hunter bid and paid $67,500 for the opportunity to hunt for an Oregon bighorn sheep (either subspecies). The proceeds from hunting license auctions fund bighorn sheep research and management.

A Maybe Mammal

Bigfoot

"I hope there's an animal somewhere that nobody has ever seen. And I hope nobody ever sees it."

—Wendell Berry (quoting his daughter in his poem, "To the Unseeable Animal")[36]

Although it has been given a scientific name (*Gigantopithecus americana*) Bigfoot or Sasquatch probably doesn't exist. However, it might.

Is Bigfoot legend or reality, or both a legend and reality? No one really knows if Bigfoot exists or not. It is always more difficult to prove a negative. If Bigfoot does exist, is it more ape-like or human? Also called Sasquatch, is *Gigantopithecus canadensis* a carnivore, herbivore or an omnivore?

The U.S. Army Corps of Engineers has speculated that Bigfoot exists.[37] A Washington State University anthropology professor has studied enough evidence to convince himself that Bigfoot is a living descendant of *Gigantopithecus*, known from Pliocene and Pleistocene fossil records in Southeast Asia.[38]

Thus, tantalizing evidence of this creature exists.

However, because Bigfoot has always been more than a matter of science, but also of myth, legend and dreams, the question of its existence has tended to attract as many dreamers, schemers, crackpots and pranksters (including some who have recently admitted to hoaxes long cited as evidence by believers) than serious scientists. If Bigfoot does indeed exist and has thus far escaped our detection, then there is no doubt that Bigfoot is the ultimate wilderness species.

In *Where Bigfoot Walks*, Pacific Northwest naturalist and author Robert Michael Pyle opens his excellent exploration of the science, myth and hope behind Bigfoot by saying:

> *Something definitely is afoot in the forests of the Pacific Northwest. Either an officially undescribed species of hominoid primate dwells there, or an act of self- and group-deception of astonishing proportions is taking place. In any case the phenomenon of Bigfoot exists. Whether the animals themselves are becoming scarcer or whether they even walk as corporeal creatures at all, their reputation and cult are only growing. More and more people, including credible and skeptical citizens and scientists, as well as the gullible, the wishful and the whacko, believe that giant hairy monsters are present in our midst. What does it mean? Who is this beast described by the great ecologist G. Evelyn Hutchinson as "our shadowy, perplexing and perhaps non-existent cousin"?* [39]

Birds

Many birds have co-evolved with particular forest habitats so individual species often become the proverbial "canary in a coal mine," each warning of the decline of their individual forest types.

Brown Creeper Behold the brown creeper (*Certhia americana*). It is the only bird on the continent that relies on both the trunk and bark of a tree for foraging and nesting. It is a small bird, with a down-curving bill to reach insects hiding deep in the bark. Streaked with white on its otherwise brown back, the species is one of the most camouflaged forest birds.

Brown creepers are found in most forested regions of the continent. Nine subspecies are recognized, three or four of which are found in Oregon. Generally, wherever there are large, old forests, there are brown creepers.

Brown creepers usually nest under the loose bark of large standing dead trees. The life of a dead standing tree (snag) can be quite long, but the bark usually loosens and sloughs off relatively quickly. Thus, a forest must contain many large, old live trees to produce a sufficient number of large, old dead trees in varying stages of decay to yield

GREG CLARK

The brown creeper (*Certhia americana*) specializes in exploiting the short period in the life of a snag where the bark is beginning to fall off, but hasn't quite.

enough bark-sloughing snags for brown creepers.

Brown creepers eat animals with at least six-legs and these are abundant in old forests.

Want to see a brown creeper creeping up the side of a tree? The next time you are in an old forest during the spring or summer, listen for the call that sounds like "trees, trees, beau-ti-ful trees!"

Goshawk When thinking of hawks, one usually conjures images of majestic birds soaring high above open coastlines, estuaries, lakes, meadows, mountaintops and tundra. There are, however, three "forest" hawks that specialize in more confined surroundings: goshawk, Cooper's hawk and sharp-shinned hawk. Because of its size and aggressiveness, the goshawk is the most magnificent of the three.

Goshawks (*Accipiter gentilis*) evolved with short, very powerful wings and protective eye tufts that allow them, amazingly, to fly unscathed (mostly) and rapidly through the forest in search of small mammals, songbirds and grouse.

Approximately the size of a common raven, individual goshawks increase in size as their range goes north. The color of the adult plumage is generally silver-gray on the bird's upper parts and barred pale grayish-white on their under parts. Look for the distinctive eye-stripes that flare behind their eyes.

Scientists generally recognize three subspecies of goshawks: the Queen Charlotte (*A. g. laingi*), the northern (*A. g. atricapillus*) and the Apache (*A. g. apache*). The Apache lives far south of Oregon while the Queen Charlotte now lives north of our state. In Oregon, northern goshawks (*A. g. atricapillus*) need mature and old-growth forests between 1,900-6,100 feet in elevation like those found in portions of the Cascades, Blue and Klamath mountains. The highest concentrations of northern goshawks are found in the drier forests east of the Cascade crest. Northern goshawks may also be on Steens Mountain, a sky island in the Sagebrush Sea.

Goshawks do not occur in the Oregon Coast Range. However, some scientists suspect that the goshawk subspecies that did (and can again) inhabit the Coast Range is the Queen Charlotte goshawk that is adapted to wetter marine forests.

Northern goshawk (*Accipter gentilus*) nestlings. This species prefers big trees and open understory.

Seeing a goshawk is a rare treat because of its reclusiveness and specialized habitat requirements. A pair of goshawks builds and maintains three to nine nests each year, but only defends one nest each year. The others are free for use by northern spotted owls, great gray owls, great-horned owls, short-eared owls, Cooper's hawks, red-tailed hawks, squirrels and many other species.

A goshawk's reproductive home range has three critical components: a foraging area, a nesting area and a post-fledging family area. Foraging areas are 4,900 to 5,900 acres, comprised of a forest mosaic that includes large trees, snags and downed logs with interspersed openings. Under natural fire conditions, the forest floor is generally open, allowing goshawks to see their prey with relative ease. Fire exclusion allows the understory to fill with shrubs to the detriment of goshawks.

One of the reasons goshawk forage areas are so large is that the birds remove so much prey from localized areas that prey from adjacent areas must recolonize them. This is also a reason for the goshawks' multiple nests.

Goshawks usually nest in very large Douglas-fir, true fir, lodgepole pine, ponderosa pine, western larch or quaking aspen, in mature forest stands that have a high canopy closure. The loss of both big nesting trees and of closed canopy, open-floored forests for foraging have greatly reduced goshawk numbers. Halting and reversing the loss of these forest types halt and reverse the declines in goshawk populations.

Marbled Murrelet

In 1985, an Oregon State University wildlife graduate student was hiking on the east side of Marys Peak in the Coast Range when she heard what sounded like a seabird. Being 30 miles inland, S. Kim Nelson was perplexed, but eventually identified the bird as a marbled murrelet (*Brachyramphus marmoratus*), a sea bird that is primarily found within a few miles of shore during the breeding season and up to six miles out to sea in winter.

At that time, however, no marbled murrelet nest had ever been found in Oregon and only one had been identified in northern California. That the species nested so far inland in interior forests had never been confirmed. Nelson went on to do her master's degree research on cavity nesting birds in the Oregon Coast Range, finding many more marbled murrelet nests in Oregon's marine forests and has since become one of the leading experts on marbled murrelets.

The marbled murrelet is an amazing little dove-sized bird. It can speed through the air at up to 98 miles per hour. It can dive for small fish 160-feet under ocean swells and nest in old-growth trees 150-feet above the ground, as far as 36 (and possibly 80) miles inland from the ocean. Marbled murrelets do not actually build a nest but use a large moss-covered limb — usually of an old-growth tree — as a nesting platform, where one egg is laid in the moss. Eggs and chicks are vulnerable to edge-dwelling generalists such as crows and ravens. Mom and Dad murrelet each take dawn-to-dawn shifts on the nest while their mate makes up to eight round trips to the nest per day delivering fresh fish from the ocean to the chick. When the young fledge, they fly to the sea unescorted.

A seabird, the marbled murrelet (*Brachyramphus marmoratus*) can nest up to 50 miles inland from the ocean, but only in big old trees.

Marbled murrelets exhibit strong site fidelity to a particular stand of trees. Nest success is higher in larger intact old-growth stands than smaller and/or fragmented forests.

The first marbled murrelet nest was discovered in 1974, in California's Big Basin Redwoods State Park. None were found in Oregon until 1990, the first near Five Rivers in Benton County. The species is uncommon to rare along the entire Oregon coast, but has the greatest concentration between Cascade Head (north of Lincoln City) and the California border. This concentration coincides with the relative abundance (compared to clearcut private lands) of nearby onshore publicly-owned mature and old-growth forests in the Siuslaw and Siskiyou National Forests.

GARY BRAASCH

Between 6,600 to 20,000 marbled murrelets call Oregon home. Population declines are currently estimated at four to seven percent annually (do the math). Murrelets are typically counted at sea, so these numbers do not represent the nesting population. While only 10 percent of their original nesting habitat remains, life on the ocean is often no picnic these days for marbled murrelets either. At sea they are vulnerable to oil spills, often to gillnet fisheries, and to the vagaries of El Niño messing with their food supply. Because it's a long-lived species and it is displaced by logging, there may be many "homeless" (non-nesting) marbled murrelets.

The species was listed as threatened under the Endangered Species Act in 1991. While the Northwest Forest Plan's late successional reserves will eventually provide adequate habitat once the clearcuts in the reserves grow back to something approximating real forests, the marbled murrelet's status will remain tenuous for the next half to full century. To fully return the species to its former range, private lands must be restored to provide suitable habitat.

Northern Spotted Owl

I rejoice that there are owls. Let them do the idiotic and maniacal hooting for men. It is a sound admirably suited to swamps and twilight woods which no day illustrates, suggesting a vast and undeveloped nature which men have not recognized. They represent the stark twilight and unsatisfied thoughts which we all have.

—Henry D. Thoreau[40]

It has been said that if the northern spotted owl didn't exist, conservationists would have had to invent it. Far from an invention, *Strix occidentalis* is a real bird that has had an incredible impact on old growth logging in the Pacific Northwest. Three subspecies are generally recognized: the Northern (*S. o. caurina*), California (*S. o. occidentalis*) and the Mexican (*S. o. lucida*).

For the last three decades, this inconspicuous species has conspicuously dominated the debate over the Pacific Northwest's last old-growth forests. Fortunately, the northern spotted owl is a charismatic (a.k.a. "telegenic") species. It is also a guileless bird with no innate fear of humans that can be enticed to pose for the cameras with either a human or recorded rendition of the male territorial call. (It also helps to dangle a small mammal, screaming loudly, on a string.) Spotted owls will even follow humans through the woods.

Northern spotted owls are very strongly associated with wet (but not too wet; they don't like Sitka spruce) old-growth forests from southwestern British Columbia through northwestern California. In Oregon, low- and mid-elevation coniferous forests of Douglas-fir, grand fir, ponderosa pine and incense cedar are preferred habitat, but the species also ranges into Shasta red fir and Pacific silver fir zones. The subspecies is

◄ The northern spotted owl (*Strix occidentalis caurina*) is the most famous resident of old-growth Douglas-fir forests.

not found in high-elevation forests. It is most abundant in mature and old-growth forests on either side of the Cascade crest and in the Klamath Mountains and Coast Range ecoregions. Where northern spotted owls are found in young forests, they are undoubtedly associated with residual old trees that survived disturbance, be it logging or natural events. The owls nest in cavities, on broken tops or natural platforms in big trees or snags.

Median home ranges are typically 3,000 to 4,500 acres per breeding pair. Ninety percent of their diet is small forest mammals such as flying squirrels in northwest Oregon and voles and woodrats in southwest Oregon, with the occasional insect, frog or snake.

The northern spotted owl was protected under the Endangered Species Act in 1991 (making the cover of *Time*) and was the driving factor in the creation and implementation of President Clinton's Northwest Forest Plan. The plan is equal parts political and biological (actually an improvement over past plans). But its formula for saving the species is predicated on the debatable premise that continued current logging of mature and old-growth forest habitat is permissible because of the anticipated existence of more old-growth habitat a century from now. Yet while less logging of mature and old-growth forests has occurred than originally envisioned by the plan since its implementation, owl numbers are still declining precipitously.

The northern spotted owl, with its dark eyes and creamy white mottling on the breast, is distinctive, but can be confused visually with a barred owl (although its bars aren't "spots"). The barred owl (*Strix varia*) was historically limited to the east coast of North America where it was similarly dependent upon old-growth forests. In the twentieth century, due to increased forest openings caused by logging and development, the species rapidly expanded west across Canada, then south, reaching northeast Oregon by 1974. The barred owl is now a permanent resident of every forest region in Oregon and appears to be more tolerant of logging activity than the spotted owl.

Barred and spotted owls have interbred (the offspring are not fertile). Despite the havoc barred owls are causing, the primary factor in the decline of spotted owls continues to be the destruction of old-growth and mature forests.

Pileated Woodpecker

Pileated Woodpecker The pileated woodpecker (*Dryocopus pileatus*) is in all likelihood the largest woodpecker left on the continent, since the similarly colored ivory-billed woodpecker (*Campephilus principalis*) is probably extinct. Some birders continue to search desperately for ivory-bills in a swamp near the lower Mississippi River. There have been sporadic reports of sightings in Cuba, but essentially all the old forest upon which the ivory-billed woodpecker depended has now been eliminated.

The continued existence of the pileated woodpecker (the subspecies found in Oregon is *D. p. picinus*) depends upon the willingness of humans to allow sufficiently

EVELYN BULL

The pileated woodpecker (*Dryocopus pileatus*) requires trees at least 70 years of age for nesting.

large snags (standing dead trees) and downed trees to remain in forests. We must also allow very large old trees to die naturally and become large snags and/or downed trees.

The large dull black and white woodpecker with a red crest is usually heard before it is seen. You're likely to hear it pecking on a snag seeking its insect food or hear its distinctive and lengthy (up-to-eight-note) "wok" sounds. Alternatively, you may hear the bird drumming on a hard snag in 11-30 beat bursts, usually to mark territory. Even if you don't spot one, you are likely to notice their excavation of rectangular holes in large snags. Over four-fifths of a pileated woodpecker's diet is ants and termites — both insects that live in downed and standing dead trees. (Dead trees almost always support more life than live ones.)

A keystone species, the pileated woodpecker excavates a new nest every spring. Their old nests are used by a variety of other species, as are the dozens of roosts each pair of woodpeckers excavates each year.

Pileated woodpeckers inhabit mature and old-growth conifer forests of the Blue Mountains, Cascades, East Cascade Slopes and Foothills, Klamath and Coast Range ecoregions. They are rarely found in pure ponderosa pine forests. They sometimes occur in deciduous forests at the bottom of the Willamette, Rogue and Umpqua valleys. Logging and forest fragmentation lead to a less dense canopy overall, leaving pileated woodpeckers more vulnerable to predation.

White-headed Woodpecker

White-headed Woodpecker The white-headed woodpecker (*Picoides albolarvatus*) is to old growth ponderosa pine what the northern spotted owl is to old-growth Douglas-fir. The habitat of these medium-sized woodpeckers consists of pure stands of big old yellow-bellied ponderosa pines, or where ponderosas otherwise dominates a mixed conifer forest. Although heavily dependent on ponderosa pine seeds in winter, white-headed woodpeckers will also eat sugar pine seeds and small insects. The species usually excavates nest cavities in snags, but also uses stumps, leaning logs and the dead tops of live trees.

White-headed with a glossy black body, the males of the species have a red patch on the nape and juveniles are a dull black with the nape patch tending toward orange.

In Oregon, the white-headed woodpecker is a permanent, although uncommon, resident of the Ochoco, Blue, Wallowa and the eastside Cascade mountains where suitable habitat can be found. White-headed woodpeckers occasionally occur in the upper reaches of the Umpqua River and Siskiyou Mountains. Stronger populations are centered in the Winema and Deschutes National Forests.

In Oregon, the white-headed woodpecker (*Picoides albolarvatus*) has a strong affinity for ponderosa pine.

The more old-growth ponderosa pine there is, the more white-headed woodpeckers there are. Unfortunately, ponderosa forests have become one of the most endangered forest types in the West. Ponderosa pine forests have been dramatically reduced by logging, and fire suppression has curtailed the low-intensity ground fires that burn out the young trees under the big old pines. The result of fire suppression is that fir forests grow up underneath and eventually replace the pine forests. Competition from this understory also reduces pine seed production. Livestock grazing also removes grass that carries these beneficial fires. As an increasing shrub and tree layer replaces the open forest floor, predation by small mammals of white-headed woodpecker nests increases.

Coho salmon (*Oncorhynchus kisutch*) eggs and alevins (more than just an egg, but not quite a fry) need clean and gravelly stream bottoms.

Fish

The very best habitat for native fish exists in undisturbed roadless areas. Habitat destruction has led to a long and dramatic decline of native fish species in Oregon. In addition, fish managers have a long history of introducing exotic species valued for sport fishing, introductions which have proven harmful to native species.

Bull Trout Before the European-American invasion, abundant populations of bull trout (*Savelinus confluentus*) existed in the Klamath, Willamette, Deschutes, John Day, Umatilla, Walla Walla, Grande Ronde, Imnaha, Pine Creek, Powder and Malheur River basins of Oregon. The species presently ranges from northern British Columbia to northern California and east to western Montana. In the clear, unpolluted refuges in Upper Klamath Lake (where clean water from creeks and underwater springs enter the lake), bull trout can weigh over 20 pounds.

Today, healthy bull trout populations occupy only 3.8 percent of their historical range. Fully 76 percent of the remaining habitat occurs in large — greater than 5,000 acres — roadless areas, Wilderness, Wilderness Study Areas and national parks. If one factors in small roadless areas (1,000 to 5000 acres), the number of bull trout in roadless areas is undoubtedly higher.

Bull trout are the aquatic canary in the (forest) coal mine. The species has exacting standards for habitat and water quality. As watersheds are degraded, bull trout decline.

Biologists recognize three distinct population segments of bull trout in Oregon.

1. Upper Columbia Basin (John Day River and Columbia tributaries upstream to the mouth of and including the Snake River);

2. Lower Columbia Basin (Willamette, Deschutes and Hood River basins); and

3. Klamath Basin.

SANDY LONSDALE

Bull Trout (*Savelinus confluentus*) require cold, clear water and are an excellent indicator of watershed health.

Bull trout have three major life histories. *Resident* bull trout permanently reside in their natal streams. *Fluvial* runs migrate from the smaller tributaries where they spawn and rear as juveniles to larger streams where adults forage and live for the majority of their lives. *Adfluvial* runs are similar to fluvial runs except that adult rearing occurs in lakes or reservoirs.

Bull trout require shaded and stable streams with overhanging banks and large amounts of woody debris; plenty of gravel and riffles with little sediment; and corridors of clean, cold and free-flowing water through which the fish can migrate.

The limiting factors identified for bull trout populations are:

(1) genetics (too few fish in a population leads to inbreeding);

(2) overfishing (catching more than can be sustained by the population);

(3) passage barriers (dams, etc.);

(4) exotic species (of trout and other aquatic organisms);

(5) habitat loss and degradation (channelization, dewatering, removal of streamside vegetation and debris, etc.);

(6) global climate change (especially at the edge of the species range); and

(7) ecosystem change (wholesale decimation of watersheds).

Bull trout evolved to co-exist with a suite of native salmonid and aquatic species, but did not co-evolve with introduced non-native salmonids such as lake trout, brown trout and brook trout that often out-compete bull trout in degraded stream conditions.

Adult bull trout prey upon chinook salmon fry. Since both species are at risk of extinction, it is essential to restore chinook runs for their own benefit, as well as for bull trout.

Roads, logging, grazing, mining, dams and cropland agriculture are all major contributors to the decline of bull trout. Additional factors are residential and urban pollution, as well as past management practices such as intentional chemical poisoning of bull trout by fish agencies to make room for more popular non-native game species.

Fishing regulations have been modified to conserve bull trout over non-natives to help improve the species' prospects in the short-term. For the long-term, habitat conservation and restoration is the key. The conservation of roadless areas is critical to the survival of bull trout.

Pacific Salmon Each of the seven Pacific salmon species that inhabits, once inhabited or could again inhabit Oregon's rivers and streams has a unique life history. Of course, their central common and fascinating trait is that of anadromy. All salmon are born in fresh water, migrate to saltwater to feed and live much of their lives, and return to fresh water to spawn the next generation. Their common life cycle aside, each salmon species is distinct in appearance, size, distribution, abundance, age of maturity, juvenile rearing and migration and spawning habitat.

There are seven salmonid species native to the Pacific Northwest. Two additional salmonid species are found in the northwestern Pacific (commonly called amago and masu) and one species is native to the Atlantic. The seven northeastern Pacific salmon species are:

Pink Salmon - *Oncorhynchus gorbuscha*
Coho Salmon - *Oncorhynchus kisutch*
Chinook Salmon - *Oncorhynchus tshawytscha*
Chum Salmon - *Oncorhynchus keta*
Sockeye Salmon - *Oncorhynchus nerka*
Steelhead Trout - *Oncorhynchus mykiss*
Cutthroat Trout - *Oncorhynchus clarkii*

All but pink salmon spawn in Oregon waters.

Several species can inhabit the same watershed, using different areas at different times. Sockeye spawn only in association with a lake. Fall chinook favor a river's lower main channel for spawning, as do chum and pink salmon. Summer chinook spawn further up the watershed, with spring chinook spawning the farthest upstream.

Salmon are the ultimate keystone species. From bears to killer whales, forty-one

Coho salmon (*Oncorhynchus kisutch*) preparing to spawn. ▶

mammal species feed on salmon during some part of the species' life cycle. So do 89 species of birds, including bald eagles. Even five reptile and two amphibian species feed on salmon, for a total of 137 species. This does not include insects, like caddis fly larvae that feed on salmon carcasses and later become food for both trout and salmon. (And we certainly cannot forget the importance of salmon to the survival of the Northwest's native people!)

Pacific salmon co-evolved with Pacific Northwest forests. As fisheries biologist Jim Lichatowich writes:

Between 5,000 and 4,000 years ago, the climate began to shift toward the cool, moist maritime conditions that persist today. This change in the environment enabled forests to grow. Early in the cooling period, Douglas-fir, which favors drier conditions, dominated; then western hemlock and western red cedar took hold, especially in the wetter areas. Eventually, what we now call old-growth forests emerged, creating stable, well-shaded streams and high-quality salmon habitat. The extensive root systems of the large trees held the streams to defined channels and prevented erosion, while the thick foliage filtered out the sun's heat, helping to maintain cool water temperatures. When the large trees died and fell across stream channels, they created pools and added structure and diversity to riverine habitats. The logs accumulated and eventually backed up water, creating productive side channels and sloughs. The thousands of trees falling across streams also functioned as small check dams, holding back sediment and stabilizing streambeds, thus enabling streams to run clear. As a result, these rivers carried far less sediment than the unshaded rivers had. Old-growth forests created complex and stable stream habitats and it's possible that salmon populations first reached levels of eighteenth- and nineteenth-century abundance around 5,000 years ago.[41]

Most salmon stocks in the Pacific Northwest are now in danger of extinction. Many are listed under the Endangered Species Act. Those that are not listed should be.

Currently, twenty-six distinct salmon populations are listed under the Endangered Species Act. At the time of this writing, a legal dispute about wild and hatchery fish and the role of hatchery fish under the Endangered Species Act has become a distraction to conservation efforts that further jeopardizes the continued existence of wild salmon. Detractors would have you believe that, since hatcheries produce salmon, wild fish are unnecessary. However, while similar genetically, hatchery and wild fish are quite different. To avoid going into extreme technical detail, consider this analogy: dogs and wolves are very similar genetically and can even interbreed. However, domestic dogs are not comparable to wild wolves.

Hatchery fish are more susceptible to predators and are less healthy, having been raised on processed, pelletized junk food rather than natural food. Hatchery managers tend to use the first returning fish as brood stock for the following year's production, resulting in successive runs returning before river conditions are really ready for natural spawning migration.

Salmon face many trials and tribulations downstream from the forested areas where they emerge as fry and later return to spawn before dying. Lichatowich notes:

While native people made good use of the region's watersheds, their impact on salmon habitat was probably negligible. In contrast, the newly arrived pioneers and entrepreneurs fully exploited all the watersheds' economic resources through trapping, mining, logging, grazing and irrigation. As a result, the salmon's habitat came into direct contact with the industrial economy throughout the entire length of the chain of habitats that make up its ecosystem — logging and mining in the headwaters, agriculture in the rivers' lower elevations, cities and industry in the broad alluvial plains and estuaries and finally pollution and large-scale fishing in the ocean. A major part of the salmon's problem, then and now, is that there is not just one threat to their existence but a continuous series of threats at nearly every point in their range, throughout their entire lifecycle. At every point of contact with the industrial economy, from the headwaters to the sea, the salmon have long engaged in a losing struggle for habitat.[42]

Salmon will be lost unless all of the so-called "four 'H's" are addressed: habitat, hatcheries, harvest and hydropower. This includes Wilderness designation of salmon sanctuaries as a vital part of what must be done to restore healthy salmon runs with sustainable harvestable surpluses.

Enigmatic Microfauna

Not all species can be charismatic megafauna. Wilderness is also home to infamous and little known species in Oregon. Many of these creatures play an important part in the web of forest life. Without them, forest ecosystems are incomplete.

Mollusks In 1994, Senator Bob Packwood — no fan of President Clinton's Northwest Forest Plan — faced a tough election challenge. In an attempt to woo undecided voters, his campaign manager tested a variety of messages. Among these was the fact that the Northwest Forest Plan protected the Malone jumping slug. The mollusk doesn't really "jump" but falls, however, if you don't know your malacology, you may believe it jumped on you. The media never bit, so the public never swallowed.

Well over 150 species of terrestrial snails and slugs are found in the Pacific Northwest's moist forests. Undoubtedly, many new species — perhaps half again as many — will be discovered as soon as someone takes the time to look.

WILLIAM LEONARD

The Malone jumping slug (*Hemphilla malonei*) is only found in older forests.

Mollusks in Pacific Northwest forests can number 4.5 million per acre and, merely by eating, are responsible for recycling up to 90 percent of the biomass in a forest. Because they tend to have very exacting ecological needs and because they are rather small and very slow, Northwest forest mollusks don't disperse well. Imagine being an inch long with one foot and trying to cross a 40-acre clearcut to get to "greener pastures."

As a group, mollusks are some of the Northwest's most endangered species. They are very sensitive to forest fragmentation, grazing, fire, fertilizers, herbicides, pesticides, turbidity and water impoundments. In water bodies, mollusks are indicators of stream health. Many species have adapted specifically to oligitrophic (nutrient-poor, oxygen-rich) mountain streams and springs. These mollusk species are the primary herbivores in freshwater aquatic systems. They also serve as food for fish, crayfish, raccoons, herons and other wildlife. In pristine freshwater streams there are usually more species of insects than mollusks. However, mollusks often comprise up to 90 percent of a stream's invertebrates by weight.

There are over 100,000 different taxa (kinds) of mollusks — from barely moving slugs to fast-moving squids. Gastropods (slugs and snails) and bi-valves (clams and mussels) are all members of the Phylum Mollusca.

For the record, the annoying slugs that decimate Pacific Northwest gardens and flowerbeds are introduced exotic species. However, while this garden pest has not wreaked havoc on Northwest forests, the recent discovery of the New Zealand mud snail in three Oregon locations is a serious development for native ecosystems, especially for salmon and trout streams.

Despite their lack of charisma, mollusks received a disproportionately large amount of attention in the Northwest Forest Plan. That is because the Forest Service requested one of the world's foremost malacologists, Dr. Terry Frest, provide information on mollusks for the plan. Although the agency had carefully avoided asking the question, Frest nonetheless provided a long list of the region's mollusks and noted which species — in his professional opinion — qualified as threatened or endangered under the Endangered Species Act.

Oregon Natural Resources Council thereafter used the Frest report to petition for protection of several hundred species of mollusks under the ESA. The government rejected the petition but covered its official posterior by promising to survey for mollusks before offering timber sales.

An inch-long snail, the rare blue-grey tail-dropper (*Prophysaon coeruleus*) "cannot cross your fingernail in five minutes, but could stop a timber sale," says Jim Rogers of Friends of Elk River. It has been affectionately renamed the "blue-grey sale-stopper."

Alas, the federal forest agencies and the timber industry, exploiting their chances under the more mollusk malevolent Bush Administration, have skipped the surveys and decimated species that depend on old-growth forest. Wilderness designation affords permanent protection for both enigmatic microfauna and charismatic megafauna, as well as not subject to the whims of changing administrations.

STU GARRETT

A stronghold for the pumice grape fern (*Botrychium pumicola*) is the proposed Newberry Volcano Wilderness.

Baker City gets its drinking water from the Elkhorn Mountains in the proposed North Fork John Day-Elkhorns Wilderness.

It's the Water [43]

Do you know where your tap water comes from? Two thirds of Oregonians get their water from surface sources and most Oregon tap water originates on federal lands, primarily national forests. Rain and snowmelt from forests are collected, treated (sometimes only minimally because the initial quality is excellent) and delivered to businesses, schools and household taps.

Intact forests are natural reservoirs that absorb, store, filter and gradually release water to forest streams. Logging and road building in forest watersheds degrades their natural hydrology. Water that once percolated slowly through stable soils runs off more quickly, carrying with it soil and other sediments. Logged watersheds have both earlier peak flows and greater storm volumes than do pristine watersheds that maintain more consistent flows through the hot summer months.

Logging reduces water quantity in other ways as well. An intact old-growth conifer forest "harvests" water from fog, as droplets condense from the moist air onto the needles, then drop to the ground. The surface area of the needles of a single old-growth Douglas-fir tree, if spread flat, would cover a football field. This "fog drip" contributes up to one third of all precipitation in Portland's Bull Run municipal watershed and, in many Northwest watersheds, may be the only source of summer precipitation.

Of course, when the trees are logged, fog drip no longer occurs. Moreover, without shade from the standing forest, the sun evaporates even more water from the soil. This decreases the amount of water "migrating" into the streams and rivers during the dry summer months when the demand for municipal and irrigation water is greatest. The combination of high summer demand (related to increased population and per capita consumption) and reduced supply (related to roading and logging) may ultimately force us to drink from dirty rivers full of agricultural chemicals, dioxin and sewage. Clackamas area water planners, for example, could be driven to tap the polluted lower Willamette River (home to toxic three-eyed fish), while timber interests continue to deforest and dewater the Clackamas River watershed.

Roads can affect the hydrology of watersheds as much or more than logging. Municipal watersheds have already been damaged by past roading and logging. Further logging operations (with or without more roads) bring more flood and water quality risks. Yet the continuing controversy over the mismanagement of Oregon's forests has rarely centered on drinking water. Federal forest management plans are focused more on addressing fish and wildlife issues than on protecting people's water supplies. However, securing safe and plentiful drinking water should not be a coincidental after-thought of other forest management priorities. Occasionally, water quality and quantity for domestic, commercial and industrial use does become a political issue.

In Oregon, the greater Portland area relies primarily on water from the Bull Run River, a tributary of the Sandy River, which is a tributary of the Columbia River that empties into the Pacific Ocean. At the turn of the last century, Portland was growing and had polluted its water supply in its West Hills. Faced with the prospect of having to drink out of the polluted Willamette River, Portland instead chose to make the pristine Bull Run Watershed its water source because it was far away, federally owned and not subject to human development. In 1904, Congress passed the Bull Run Trespass Act to keep the public out and prevent most activities that could be harmful to the watershed.

After World War II, the Forest Service went on a timber binge (it hasn't quite ended yet), ignoring the law and seriously roading and logging a good portion of the Bull Run Reserve. In the 1970s, the agency was successfully sued to stop the logging. In 1978 Congress responded with a law that legalized logging in the Bull Run watershed. An increasingly outraged (and, more importantly, an organized) citizenry finally prevailed upon Congress in 1996 to essentially prohibit logging in the Bull Run water-shed Management Unit. In an attempt to further protect Portland's water supply, the unit was expanded in 2001 to include the Little Sandy Watershed, upstream of Aschoff Creek.

The Forest Service has officially recognized several other municipal watersheds on national forest lands in Oregon, including Dallas, Corvallis, Medford, Ashland, Cottage Grove, Bend, The Dalles, Baker City, La Grande and Walla Walla (a Washington city, but most of its watershed is in Oregon). While most of these watersheds are clearly marked on forest recreation maps, that recognition does not necessarily mean protection from logging, roading, grazing, mining, excessive human recreation and other abuses. Other municipalities, like Eugene, Salem, Idanha, Mill City, Stayton, Jefferson, Sweet Home, Lebanon, Oregon City, West Linn, Lake Oswego, Albany, Beaverton, Gresham, Estacada, Long Creek and Sandy also take their water from streams that rise on federal forests. In fact, more than half of the inventoried (large) roadless areas discussed in this book are located in municipal drinking watersheds.

The better the water's initial quality, the less treatment is needed to make it potable. Two Oregon watersheds — greater Portland's Bull Run and Baker City's Elkhorns Front — are so pure that they don't require filtration before use and need only minimal treatment.

Many current federal forest plans carelessly target municipal watersheds for logging, which has numerous detrimental effects. Logging in the "rain-on-snow" zone (that elevation band where it does often snow, but it also usually rains which rapidly melts the snow) results in flooding and sedimentation of the water. It can also result in lower summer and autumn flows, when water is most needed.

Turbid (sediment-laden) waters create multiple problems for many municipal water supplies. Water treatment becomes more difficult and more chlorine is usually added. For some systems, frequent backwashing of filters is required, which increases expense and the risk of operator error with subsequent contamination by waterborne

Heavy logging has soiled Fish Creek, a tributary to the Clackamas River on the Mount Hood National Forest.

disease. Muddy water forces some municipal water systems to shut down completely.

Other communities are now looking to Portland's Bull Run protections as an example of how to safeguard a water supply. The cities of Salem and Sandy have recognized that their watersheds, damaged by an ugly legacy of clearcuts that produce muddy water, are further threatened by new logging. Both city councils have passed resolutions and requested the withdrawal of federal timber sale proposals. Citizen support for permanent legislative protections — such as Wilderness designations — is building dramatically around the state to protect water supplies.

Some of Oregon's municipal watersheds do not lie within public forestlands or have private or municipal inholdings within the boundaries of the public lands. Where undeveloped, these watersheds could be better managed under federal ownership. Municipal ownership is generally a bad idea, because many water departments have chosen to log the forests in their watershed for short-term revenues to help keep water rates low while spoiling the water supplies they were supposed to protect. The best way to protect a municipal watershed is through federal ownership with an informed and active municipality which can watchdog the watershed's management.

The primary reason that roadless forestlands lack roads is that it has been too expensive to build any. Slopes in these areas are steeper and more unstable than those in surrounding forests. Consequently, roading and logging these last wildlands would have a disproportionately greater impact on municipal watersheds than all comparable

The vast majority of Oregonians get most of their drinking water not from groundwater, but from surface sources.

GARY BRAASCH

development that has occurred to date.

Oregon's 1.7 million acres of domestic watersheds include many areas of both protected Wilderness and unprotected wilderness. If these wildlands receive permanent protection, they will continue to serve their essential role in providing some of the best and most plentiful water on earth. It's time for Oregonians to stand up for the forests that produce our clean drinking water — a move that will also benefit the fish and wildlife that call these watersheds home.

The Carbon Connection

Perhaps the greatest threat facing the planet is that of global climate change, accelerated by human activities that are loading the atmosphere with excessive amounts of greenhouse gases (most commonly carbon dioxide).

We now understand the impacts of increased temperatures due to elevated greenhouse gases in the atmosphere to be enormous and these will worsen if we don't phase out our use of fossil fuel. These impacts include: a rise in global sea level great enough to wipe out numerous island nations (and flood much of our own coastal areas where most Americans live); melting polar ice caps from underneath polar bears and penguins; the loss of coral reefs in tropical waters; increased frequency and intensity of inclement weather (including hurricanes); increased spread of what were once "tropical" diseases; and large-scale disruption of ecosystem function and agricultural production.

In the Pacific Northwest, temperatures increased 1 to 3° F over most of the region during the twentieth century. Unless we significantly change our behaviors, summer and winter temperatures are anticipated to rise 7 to 8° F and 8 to 11°F, respectively, by the end of the twenty-first century.

The annual Columbia River Basin snowpack, for example, is projected to decrease and melt earlier, possibly resulting in increased winter flooding and reduced summer and fall river flows. By the 2090s, projected snowpack on March 1 will be only slightly greater than what we presently have on June 1. Increasing temperatures will mean added stresses on salmon runs, increased coastal erosion due to rising sea-level, increased forest fires and resulting changes to forest composition, including notable migrations of forest species both elevationally and latitudinally (assuming the trees can adjust their range faster than the climate changes).

Today, while most atmospheric carbon increase results from humans burning carbon-heavy fuels (oil, gas and coal) that had long been ensconced under our feet in the lithosphere, nine percent of annual U.S. emissions are attributable to logging. Logging transfers biospheric carbon (stored as living or newly dead organic matter) to

Old-growth forests store massive amounts of carbon taken from the air. Excess carbon dioxide and other greenhouse gases cause global warming. To end human-induced climate change, we must phase out our use of fossil fuels, preserve all remaining native forests and re-establish real forests (not timber plantations). ▶

the atmosphere. After traveling through the atmosphere, large amounts of previously lithospheric carbon (fossil fuel) are sequestered in the hydrosphere (i.e., the ocean). Increased oceanic carbon levels are a contributing factor of coral reef decline.

Until the exponential proliferation of fossil fuel use in recent decades, human-caused excess atmospheric carbon was due about equally to fossil fuel burning and the destruction of forests — especially of old-growth forests that contain massive amounts of stored carbon. "Reforestation" does not balance the carbon equation. A better term than reforestation would be "weeforestation" because with replanting, massive old-growth forests are replaced with diminutive young plantations, which can sequester far less carbon. Well before reaching old growth conditions, these young trees are cut again, releasing any carbon stored over their short lives.

The Kyoto Protocol — which the second Bush Administration renounced as too radical — would only slow (not stabilize, let alone reverse) increasing atmospheric carbon levels. To return to safe levels of atmospheric CO_2, we need to end our use of fossil fuels, truly reforest our wildlands and protect remaining virgin forest from further logging. We also need to reduce human population to sustainable levels.

Protection of roadless areas and old-growth forests in the Pacific Northwest is particularly important because of these forests' relatively high carbon loads (as compared to other forests). Logging of old-growth forests has resulted in 117 times the release of carbon into the atmosphere than from average land use conversions:

> A mere 0.017% of the earth's land surface, old-growth forest conversion [in western Oregon and western Washington] appears to account for a noteworthy 2% of the total [Carbon] released [into the atmosphere] because of land use changes in the last 100 years.[44]

Biomass equals carbon, so large tracts of large old trees provide more carbon sequestration. Leaving forests intact and not logging them prevents the conversion of biospheric carbon to atmospheric carbon. Letting forestlands grow to be real forests again can increase biospheric carbon and thus reduce harmful levels of atmospheric carbon. Let's not forget the coincidental benefits of watershed protection, biodiversity conservation and human recreation (pronounced "re-creation") that intact forests provide. Intact forests are both more resilient and more resistant to the effects of global climate change. ◆

Notes

[1] Porter, Eliot. 1967. In Wildness is the Preservation of the World. Sierra Club and Ballantine Books. San Francisco: 11.

[2] Mathews, Daniel. 1999. Cascade-Olympic Natural History Guide: A Trailside Reference. 2nd ed. Raven Editions. Portland, OR: 11.

[3] Oregon Biodiversity Project. 1998. Oregon's Living Landscape: Strategies and Opportunities to Conserve Biodiversity. Defenders of Wildlife. Portland, OR: 1.

[4] This region was previously classified as Basin and Range, Columbia Basin, Owyhee Uplands and Lava Plains ecoregions.

[5] For more information on the (generally) "tree-free" wildlands of Oregon, see Andy Kerr. 2000. Oregon Desert Guide: 70 Hikes. The Mountaineers. Seattle, WA.

[6] Oregon Biodiversity Project. 1998. Oregon's Living Landscape: Strategies and Opportunities to Conserve Biodiversity. Defenders of Wildlife. Portland, OR: 190.

[7] A few thousand acres of the Cowlitz/Chehalis Foothills Level IV Ecoregion (Puget Lowland Level III Ecoregion) exist along the left bank of the Columbia River downstream from Portland. It is not further considered in this book.

[8] Adapted from William Loy, Stuart Allan, Aileen R. Buckley, James E. Meacham. 2001. Atlas of Oregon. 2nd ed. University of Oregon Press. Eugene, OR: 176-77 (data from Jimmi Kagan and Steve Caicco. 1992. Manual of Actual Oregon Vegetation. Oregon Natural Heritage Program; Idaho Cooperative Fish and Wildlife Research Unit; Oregon Geospatial Data Clearinghouse. Salem, OR (GAP vegetation, 1:250,000)).

[9] Leopold, Aldo. 1970. A Sand County Almanac: With Essays on Conservation from Round River. Ballantine Books. New York, NY: 74.

[10] The Forest Service, Rocky Mountain Research Station, Intermountain Fire Sciences Laboratory publishes an informative newsletter, "Nutcrackernotes" on whitebark pine research and management, available at http://nrmsc.usgs.gov/nut-notes/.

[11] Whitebark Pine Ecosystem Foundation, P.O. Box 16503, Missoula, MT 59808 (www.whitebarkfound.org).

[12] Oregon Department of Forestry (www.odf.state.or.us); Torgerson, Tim (ed.). 1999. Oregon Blue Book 1999-2000. Office of the Secretary of State. Salem, OR.

[13] Perry, David A., Reed F. Noss, Timothy D. Schowalter, Terrence J. Frest, Bruce McCune, David R. Montgomery, James R. Karr. 2001. Letter to Regional Interagency Executive Committee to implement Northwest Forest Plan (Sept. 4, 2001) (citing in part National Research Council. 2000. Environmental Issues in Pacific Northwest Forest Management. National Academy Press. Washington, DC: 5).

[14] Jacobellis v. Ohio 378 U.S. 184 (1964) (Justice Potter Stewart concurring opinion).

[15] Perry, David A., Reed F. Noss, Timothy D. Schowalter, Terrence J. Frest, Bruce McCune, David R. Montgomery, James R. Karr. 2001. Letter to Regional Interagency Executive Committee to implement Northwest Forest Plan (Sept. 4, 2001).

[16] National Research Council. 2000. Environmental Issues in Pacific Northwest Forest Management. National Academy Press. Washington, DC: 5-6.

[17] Lindenmayer, David B. and Jerry F. Franklin. 2002. Conserving Forest Biodiveristy: A Comprehensive Multiscale Approach. Island Press. Washington, DC: 69.

[18] Miller, Brian, Richard Reading, James Strittholt, et al. 1998. Using focal species in the design of nature reserve networks. Wild Earth 8 (4): 82

[19] Ibid.

[20] Ibid.

[21] Ibid.

[22] Ibid.

[23] Ibid at 82-83.

[24] Verts, B. J. and Leslie N. Carraway. 1998. Land Mammals of Oregon. University of California Press. Berkeley, CA: 411.

[25] Verts, B. J. and Leslie N. Carraway. 1998. Land Mammals of Oregon. University of California Press. Berkeley, CA: 427.

[26] The first "state" government in Oregon also paid bounties of $0.50 for a small wolf; $1.50 for lynx; $2.00 bear; $5.00 for "panther." Terry, John. Missteps turned into strides toward statehood. The Oregonian (Apr. 6, 2003): D12.

[27] Ferris, Robert. M., Mark Shaffer, Nina Fascione, et al. 1999. Places for Wolves: A Blueprint for Restoration and Long-Term Recovery in the Lower 48 States. Defenders of Wildlife. Washington, DC: 8.

[28] Leopold, Aldo. 1966. A SAND COUNTY ALMANAC. Sierra Club; Ballantine Books. Ballantine Books. New York, NY: 277.

[29] Verts, B. J. and Leslie N. Carraway. 1998. LAND MAMMALS OF OREGON. University of California Press. Berkeley, CA: 379.

[30] Ibid.

[31] Olsen, Ken. *Unbearable conditions: could grizzlies be fat and happy without salmon runs?* Spokesman-Review (Nov. 29, 1998).

[32] Ibid.

[33] The section on Beaver is adapted with permission from Andy Kerr. 2000. OREGON DESERT GUIDE: 70 HIKES. The Mountaineers. Seattle, WA: 56-57.

[34] Lichatowich, Jim. 1999. SALMON WITHOUT RIVERS: A HISTORY OF THE PACIFIC SALMON CRISIS. Island Press. Washington, DC: 55

[35] Oregon Biodiversity Project. 1998. OREGON'S LIVING LANDSCAPE: STRATEGIES AND OPPORTUNITIES TO CONSERVE BIODIVERSITY. Defenders of Wildlife. Portland, OR: 157.

[36] Impastato, David (ed.). 1997. UPHOLDING MYSTERY: AN ANTHOLOGY OF CONTEMPORARY CHRISTIAN POETRY. Oxford University Press. Oxford, England: 135.

[37] U.S. Army Corps of Engineers. 1975. WASHINGTON ENVIRONMENTAL ATLAS OF WASHINGTON STATE. Seattle, WA: 53.

[38] Pyle, Robert M. 1995. WHERE BIGFOOT WALKS: CROSSING THE DARK DIVIDE. Houghton Mifflin Company. New York, NY.

[39] Young, Bob. Big Hoax: *The abominable truth can finally be told.* The Oregonian (Dec. 6, 2002): A1.

[40] Thoreau, Henry. 1942. WALDEN: OR LIVE IN THE WOODS. Signet Classics/New American Library of World Literature. New York, NY: 88-89.

[41] Lichatowich, Jim. 1999. SALMON WITHOUT RIVERS: A HISTORY OF THE PACIFIC SALMON CRISIS. Island Press. Washington, DC: 20.

[42] Ibid at 46.

[43] This section coauthored with Regna Merritt, Executive Director, Oregon Natural Resources Council, and long-time water quality advocate.

[44] Harmon, Mark E., William K. Ferrell, Jerry F. Franklin. 1990. *Effects on carbon storage of old-growth forests to young forests.* Science 247 (4943): 701.

A Brief Unnatural History of Oregon's Forests

Deforestation in Oregon

If a man walks in the woods for the love of them half of each day, he is in danger of being regarded as a loafer; but if he spends his whole day as a speculator, shearing off the woods and making earth bald before her time, he is esteemed an industrious and enterprising citizen.

–Henry David Thoreau[1]

D eforestation in Oregon began well before statehood in 1859. John McLoughlin, the last Chief Factor of the Hudson's Bay Company in what is now Oregon, built a sawmill during the winter of 1842-43 at Oregon City that employed thirty Hawaiians to produce 3,000 board feet per day — about half of a modern flat bed trailer — for export. He was later deemed to be the "Father of Oregon."

Is "deforestation" an overstatement? No. In earlier times, deforestation clearly occurred as forests were eliminated to make way for farms and cities. Deforestation also occurred as forests were logged and left behind because loggers always believed there were more trees over the next hill. Deforestation is still occurring today. Although the law requires "reforestation" after logging, there are legal loopholes that are regularly invoked to avoid it. Even when clearcuts are replanted, the natural forests that were logged are replaced with very unnatural timber plantations.

A more accurate term to describe the conversion of large old forests to plantations of small young trees would be "*wee*forestation." While tiny trees may qualify as "forest cover" under the law, tree plantations are not real, diverse forests. Equating a timber plantation with a forest is like saying a sewer lagoon is a mountain lake, a cornfield is a native grassland or a blue-velvet Elvis is art.

As Oregon's timber industry grew, Oregon's forests were steadily deforested, first for local needs, then for the California Gold Rush, and later to rebuild San Francisco after the 1906 earthquake. After a brief decline during the Great Depression, logging levels ramped up to an all-time high in 1955. Another noticeable peak came in 1988, when the cut rose to extremely unsustainable levels. This continued until the cut was finally curtailed by a combination of over-cutting (on both private and public lands),

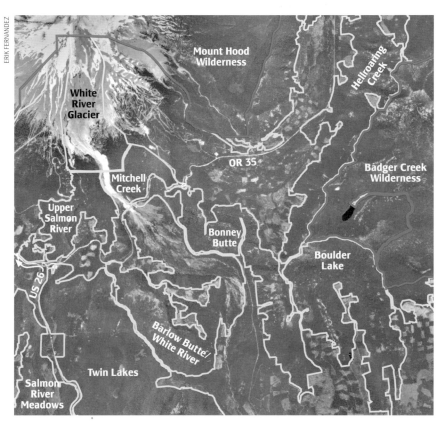

Mount Hood and vicinity. Green Wilderness boundaries and yellow roadless area boundaries in this photograph and elsewhere indicate simply what hasn't yet been roaded and logged. The tragedy of forest fragmentation is apparent to anyone who flies over or drives off of US 26 or OR 35.

court-ordered reductions imposed in the early 1990s to protect spotted owls, marbled murrelets and Pacific salmon and public lands agency actions to avoid more court orders.

Current controversies over endangered species and decimated watersheds are simply hastening the inevitable day of reckoning when Oregon must face the fact that it has severely over-cut its forests.

Only until recently (the last three decades) have a substantial number of

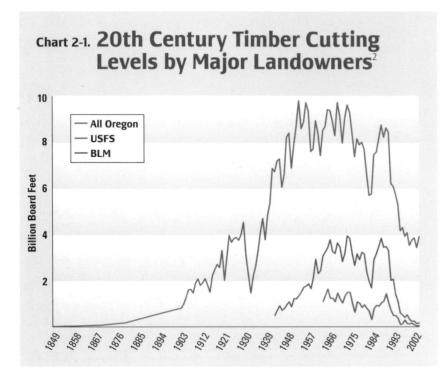

Chart 2-1. 20th Century Timber Cutting Levels by Major Landowners[2]

Billion Board Feet

- All Oregon
- USFS
- BLM

(x-axis: 1849, 1858, 1867, 1876, 1885, 1894, 1903, 1912, 1921, 1930, 1939, 1948, 1957, 1966, 1975, 1984, 1993, 2002)

ERIK FERNANDEZ

Warm Springs Creek

Dread and Terror Ridge

Forest fragmentation in the North Umpqua River Watershed on the Umpqua National Forest. The smallest visible clearcuts are approximately 40 acres in size. The Warms Springs Creek (4,019 acres) and Dread and Terror Ridge (2,504 acres) roadless areas are highlighted. A new timber sale has been awarded in these units. Litigation to block the sale was not successful. Now, it can only be stopped by an Act of Congress.

Oregonians questioned cutting levels. For more than one hundred years increasing timber cutting was generally viewed as a good thing. A few visionaries could see where these trends were headed (see *The Worst of All Microbes*, page 37), but the liquidation of old-growth forests in the Pacific Northwest was mostly seen as our "peculiar institution." Old-growth forest logging was questioned no more in mid-twentieth century Oregon than was slavery in mid-nineteenth century Mississippi. It is very difficult to get someone to understand something when their profits, wages, election or lifestyle depends upon them not understanding it.

Of course, much logging was necessary to make way for farms and to develop the state. However, logging has gone way too far. We have now reached the point where the state's landscape is literally being torn down. This is precipitating the extinction of species and entire ecosystems, the decimation of watersheds and the loss of clean drinking water. Logging has gone too far in Oregon when we have:

- *83-90% loss of old-growth forests in Douglas-fir region of Oregon and Washington;*

- *96% of original coastal temperate rainforests in Oregon logged; (and) …*

- *92-98% loss of old-growth ponderosa pine forests in three sample national forests (Deschutes, Fremont, and Winema) in Oregon.*[3]

Logging in Oregon must be balanced with forest and other ecosystem values — something that society is still trying to achieve. This balance is easier to define by what it is not than what it is. Logging is not in balance when it causes species extinction, decimates salmon runs or pollutes our streams. Wood consumption is not in balance when the two items most prevalent in our landfills are wood and paper.

Although the timber industry in Oregon has downsized, it is still not in proportion with the state's forests' ability to provide sustainable levels of various forest products such as wildlife, fish, water and wood. Because it took several generations to log off Oregon's wildlands, many were under the impression that such logging was infinitely sustainable. The forests of the Pacific Northwest were so big and so vast that it took three generations of loggers to cut through them, unlike the forests of Maine, Mississippi or Michigan, which took only one generation. Many Oregonians assumed — their thinking often fogged by greed and selfishness (what did posterity ever do for us anyway?) — that if their granddaddies logged, their grandchildren would too.

Too few Oregonians ever considered forests as principal and the timber that could be had in perpetuity as the interest. Oregon not only allowed most of its forest capital to be consumed, but also ran up quite a debt on the ecological credit card. The boom is over now. We've just about cut it all. The timber industry isn't up against the spotted owl, it's up against the Pacific Ocean.

Charles Erskine Scott Wood

Charles Erskine Scott Wood is the most interesting Oregonian ever (so far). Familiar to many modern day Oregonians as "C. E. S. Wood," he was a poet, author, anarchist, lawyer (who defended Margaret Sanger on obscenity charges for selling the booklet "Family Planning" in Portland and also collected a $1 million fee for brokering and litigating one of history's largest land transfers from public to private ownership), artist, divorcee, bohemian, co-founder of the Arlington Club, co-founder of the Oregon National Guard, soldier, translator of Chief Joseph's most famous speech, founding trustee of the Portland Art Museum, director of the Portland Library Association and originator of the idea of what became the Rose Festival. In 1908, Wood lamented the loss of Oregon's old forests in the Pacific Monthly.

The Worst of All Microbes[4]

by Charles Erskine Scott Wood

Charles Erskine Scott Wood.

L ike our great counterparts the Romans, we are, as I have said, a commercial and a utilitarian, not a poetic or artistic people. Our genius, too, is for construction; construction in institutions, as well as in stone and mortar. Our art finds its place in skyscrapers and bridges.

The dream has no place with us, though all which truly lives forever has begun as a dream. Three hundred billion board feet of timber in Oregon are impossible figures to count on the fingers, but they are easily grasped by arithmetic. It is no trouble to divide them by Portland's own cut of lumber (which is only part of the total cut), five hundred and fifty million feet a year, and guess at the day when Oregon forests shall not be.

The City of Roses carved from that forest will have to take its visitors even now far to show them so much as a few acres of an unbroken forest, and it is so everywhere. The dollar rules, and except for the Government reservations there has been no thought of preserving a specimen of what mysterious Nature was a thousand years in building into infinite beauty with infinite patience.

When I see a dead giant rising from the river and placed dripping and naked before the saw, stripped of its armor of rugged bark to which the lichens and mosses clung lovingly till the last, I am foolish enough to think of the past ages and the future, and to believe that it is not necessary all should be wiped off clean, and when I hear the shriek of the log at the first bite of the saw I am Greek enough to think of Daphne and the dryads* and the hamadryads,** and I like to think of the shadowy aisles of an untouched Oregon forest, where the sky is blotted out by the dark and over-arching roof of green and into the sky, smooth and clear and round, for one hundred, two hundred feet rise the great solemn columns of this cathedral, I smell the balsam and feel the soft carpet of needles and of moss and look into those bluish depths where the giant trunks become almost ghostly and, behind that veil, it sees to me still lingers the Great Spirit of Creation. The brooding Silence shuts out the world and in these temples there is perfect rest.

It seems to me that this great beauty and solemnity is perhaps as valuable as the shriek and clamor of the mill. It is a pity to have all this majesty of antiquity wholly destroyed. Man cannot restore it. It cannot be rebuilt by Nature herself in less than a thousand years, nor indeed ever, for it never is renewed the same. Nor do Government reservations preserve this to us; they, too, are wholly utilitarian and their plan contemplates the gradual sale and destruction of these Titans. There is no spot where the primeval forest is assured from the attack of the worst of all microbes, the dollar.

* In Greek Mythology, a divinity presiding over forests and trees; a wood nymph.[5]

** In Greek and Roman Mythology, a wood nymph who lives only as long as the tree of which she serves as the spirit.[6]

ELIZABETH FERYL, ENVIRONMENTAL IMAGES

Logging on both public and private lands.

Roading Oregon's Forests

(S)tudies in a variety of terrestrial and aquatic ecosystems have demonstrated that many of the most pervasive threats to biological diversity — habitat destruction and fragmentation, edge effects, exotic species invasions, pollution, and overhunting — are aggravated by roads.

Roads have been implicated as mortality sinks for animals ranging from snakes to wolves; as displacement factors affecting animal distribution and movement patterns; as population fragmenting factors; as sources of sediments that clog streams and destroy fisheries; as sources of deleterious edge effects; and as access corridors that encourage development, logging and poaching of rare plants and animals.

Road-building in National Forests and other public lands threatens the existence of de facto wilderness and the species that depend on wilderness.

—Reed Noss[7]

So, what is a sustainable level of logging in Oregon? It all depends on what you want to sustain. From the standpoint of timber production, one must first decide if you want to sustain profits, jobs or timber volume. You can only choose one. Profits, jobs and logging levels do not correlate. If you choose profits, remember shareholders demand that profits must always be increasing (forcing companies to eradicate forests at far above sustainable levels). If you want to sustain jobs, you must factor in automation and modernization — both in the woods and the mills — which mean fewer timber workers are required to produce the same and higher volumes of timber. Corporations consider jobs a cost, rather than a benefit, of doing business, so they cut their workforce with automation whenever possible. If you want to sustain a constant output of timber, decide if you want that volume to be in the form of big trees for dimension lumber, or small trees for pulp and chips.

If you want to sustain clean water, salmon runs, grizzly bears, beautiful forests and other "non-timber" forest values, logging levels must be much lower.

The question now facing Oregonians is: What do we want forests — especially public forestlands (as opposed to private timberlands) — for?

For example, Siuslaw National Forest contains some of the best coniferous timber-growing land in the world. It is also a coastal rainforest that produces an infinite number of other environmental products and services, including tremendous quantities of salmon. Should the Siuslaw be primarily a producer of timber where we can only hope the salmon runs will not go extinct, or is this forest more valuable as a producer of salmon (among many other things)? Would not fishing jobs, derived by protecting and restoring the forest salmon habitat, have a greater probability of being sustainable than logging jobs that destroy forests?

Whether a four-lane freeway blocking migration of large ungulates and predators, or a one-track forest road depositing sediment into a mountain stream, roads are one of the world's greatest ecological threats.

The National Forest System contains at least 370,000 miles of roads. There are more, but the Forest Service has lost count of them all. That's at least eight times more miles of roads than the U.S. Interstate Highway System, or enough to reach all the way to the moon and halfway back. Most of the Forest Service road system is in disrepair. To repair and maintain all Forest Service roads to minimum environmental and safety standards would cost taxpayers $8.2 billion — funding the agency is not likely to receive from any administration. The Forest Service would be wise to stop building new roads, repair and maintain only those roads that are necessary, as well as close and naturally rehabilitate the rest of its deteriorating road system.

Ecologist Reed Noss has summarized both the direct and indirect effects of roads. The direct effects include:

Road Kills. The Humane Society of the United States and the Urban Wildlife Research Center estimate that one million animals are killed each day on the nation's highways. Mammals are attracted to de-icing salts, birds to roadside gravel that aids their digestion and cold-blooded species to the warmth of dark asphalt on sunny winter days and cool mornings. Scavengers seek out roadkill, often becoming new roadkill themselves. Opportunistic omnivores such as crows and magpies tend to forage along road corridors, increasing the vulnerability of small animals trying to cross exposed roadways and of birds that nest in the roadside forest fringe. Noss believes the reported kill figure is conservative and that roadkill figures are biased toward mammals, and against reptiles, amphibians and probably birds. Of course, the figures don't include insects at all because counting smashed bugs on grills and windshields is such a thankless task.

Road Aversion and Other Behavioral Modifications. Studies show some animals — especially game species — avoid roads because they associate them with humans (who carry weapons). When disturbed by and forced to flee from vehicles, animals use up important energy that may later increase their vulnerability to predators, weather and disease.

Fragmentation and Isolation of Populations. Roads are barriers to migration. Networks of roads isolate species into smaller and smaller populations. It's not just freeways and charismatic four-legged megafauna that we need to worry about, but also beetles, salamanders, mollusks and other enigmatic microfauna that can be impeded by a simple closed dirt track.

Pollution. Noise bothers animals. Air pollution from motor vehicles releases heavy metals that accumulate in roadside vegetation and can build to harmful levels as they climb the food chain.

Impacts on Terrestrial Habitats. Roadways directly destroy wildlife habitat and lead to further destruction of surrounding habitat from logging and other uses. Regardless of their surface and use, all roads severely compact soil, reducing its capacity to absorb water and make slopes more vulnerable to erosion and landslides. Finally, and perhaps most importantly, roads facilitate the invasion of exotic species and allow opportunistic species to take advantage of edge effects to the detriment of interior dwelling species.

Impacts on Hydrology and Aquatic Habitats. Groundwater levels, stream channel morphology, water quality and water quantity are all affected by alterations in hydrology caused by road construction. Next to every road is a ditch that collects run-off from the crowned, unnaturally hardened road surface. Rather than percolating into the soil, the surface water is directed into forest streams at much greater volumes and at much faster rates than in an unroaded forest. The resulting "peak flows" erode stream banks, scour out fish eggs and kill aquatic insect larvae.

The indirect effects of roads include:

Access. Roads create easy access for insensitive (and often unlawful) humans with off-road vehicles, chainsaws, weapons, unleashed pets, boom-boxes, careless smoking habits, tendencies to litter and misguided development plans — all to the detriment of wildlife.

Cumulative Effects. Combined, the sum of a road's effects on a forest is greater than the aforementioned individual harms.

For example, consider the impact of roads on native trout.

Stream sediment from roads can be greater than that from all other land activities combined. Excess sediment can give introduced non-native species a competitive advantage over native species. Native fish are an excellent indicator of ecological

Dead Port Orford-cedar (*Chamaecyparis lawsoniana*) caused by root rot disease spread by roads. ▶

JEREMY HALL

Road failures cause massive erosion.

integrity. If we want to conserve and restore our native trout, we need to conserve, protect and restore roadless areas. According to the Western Native Trout Campaign:

Trout require four habitat types during their life history: spawning habitat, rearing habitat, adult habitat and over-wintering habitat. Road construction negatively affects all of these habitats.... Though road construction effects can be many and complex, some of the more serious impacts are increased sediment loads, damaged riparian areas, increased water temperatures, and changes in peak flow timing and magnitude. When fish spawn, they lay eggs in the gravel in the stream bottom. Fine sediment from roads can completely cover the stream bottom, smothering eggs. Sediment also reduces available habitat by filling in pools, reducing their number or frequency. Pools are vital to trout survival and production.[8]

Roads have additional direct impacts on native trout as they create increased access for overfishing, livestock grazing, stocking of non-native fish, pathogens (such as whirling disease) and an increased risk of toxic spills.

Scientists have found that roadless watersheds (1) recover from fire better than roaded watersheds, (2) that their pool-riffle ratios are stable or increasing (thereby slowing the stream's velocity), (3) that their downstream water quality and habitat quality are better and (4) that they are havens for native trout.

Why are roadless areas still roadless? Because there is most likely a combination of lower exploitation opportunities (for example, relatively small, few or no trees) and

higher extraction costs (steeper slopes and unstable soils require more expensive road building and logging). Building roads in the last roadless areas, given their relatively steeper and unstable slopes, will have a disproportionately high impact on watersheds.

(T)he scientific literature, and pertinent government assessments indicates that in the face of the severe declines of these native trout and their dependence on high quality habitat frequently associated with roadless areas, the full protection of all roadless land, including uninventoried areas greater than 1000 acres, is essential for the restoration and protection of native trout in the West. While such protection is essential, it is not enough. Ensuring even the long term persistence of sensitive trout species will require widespread protection of depressed and scattered populations, and the recovery and restoration of much habitat. Full recovery of western trout will require proportionately more action yet.[9]

Forests and Fire

We must restore fire to fire-adapted ecosystems on a large scale. We need to face up to this – that fire is with us.

— Jack Ward Thomas (scientist and former U.S. Forest Service Chief, formerly of La Grande, August 1996)[10]

It is not a question of whether a forest will burn, but when.

Both ecology and economics require us to rethink our attitudes toward wildfire. Smokey Bear needs to go to school and then get a new job.

Thanks to fifty years of indoctrination, 98 percent of Americans can finish this sentence: "Only you...." While humans can and should be careful with campfires and devices that can cause fire, humans cannot prevent lightning from starting thousands of fires in the West each year, nor should we want to.

In the arid West, fire is an ecologically vital component of ecosystem health and function. The same is true in the moister parts of the Pacific Northwest where periodic stand-replacing fires are part of a fully functioning natural ecosystem.

Much of the public, but few conservationists and no scientists, view a stand of trees as a picture of how it will be forever. We must look at forests broadly both across the landscape and over time. A stand of burned trees is but the beginning of the next forest; a stand of trees that has grown up nearby will help seed and replace the burned area (assuming it was not completely logged).

In Oregon's eastside forests, periodic fire is especially important for rejuvenating ecosystems. Fires maintain ecological integrity, control forest pests and release a steady supply of nutrients into the soil. Some trees need fire to open their cones and release

KEN CROCKER

seeds. In low- and mid-elevation ponderosa pine and mixed conifer forests, the natural fire-return interval is as short as seven years.

More than a century of logging, livestock grazing, fire suppression, road building and development have resulted in the degradation of these magnificent forests. Without periodic fires, fire-tolerant, sun-loving species such as ponderosa pine and western larch give way to fire-sensitive, shade-tolerant species such as Douglas-fir and true firs. (Logging has further decimated sun-loving tree species, which are more economically valuable than other eastside forest species.)

Natural fire frequency is much lower in moist, north-slope and streamside forests and in high elevation lodgepole pine and Engelmann spruce/subalpine fir forests. Consequently, these forests remain relatively unchanged by fire suppression. Unlogged roadless areas are also in relatively good shape. Fire suppression has caused the greatest ecological imbalance in low-elevation, south-slope ponderosa pine stands that evolved with a naturally high fire frequency and have been affected by logging and grazing. To restore these fire-dependent forests to complete health and function, fire must be reintroduced and logging and livestock grazing eliminated. During the transition period to this new management, sometimes the careful cutting of certain small-diameter understory trees can be ecologically beneficial in restoring natural conditions.

Logging not only diminishes the quantity and quality of a forest, it makes fires more intense. "In general, rate of spread and flame length were positively correlated with the proportion of area logged," states a report by Forest Service scientists.[11]

Where it is permitted, domestic livestock grazing has eliminated the fine fuels needed to carry low-intensity surface fires. This in turn allows ever-greater numbers of tree seedlings to survive to maturity, creating fuel build-ups.

Economically, fire suppression is foolish.

The government spends billions of dollars each summer on fire suppression and accomplishes almost nothing but environmental harm and fiscal waste. The science is clear. While most fires go out almost immediately, little can be done to stop those that persist due to high temperatures, low humidity and/or high winds. Notice that almost every news story about almost any fire will report that the fire was "contained" or "controlled" when the weather changed or there was nothing left to burn — not because thousands of firefighters were set to digging fire lines. It might be less expensive and more effective for the government to pour dollar bills out of C-5A cargo planes directly onto backcountry fires in an attempt to smother them.

Often, more ecological damage occurs "fighting" a fire than is caused by the fire itself. Bulldozed fire lines cause erosion and scar the land. However, fire lines can only work where there is a low-intensity burn — the most common (and the most environmentally beneficial) type of forest fire. In the summer of 2002, embers from a fire on the Oregon side of the Columbia Gorge ignited spot fires on the Washington

◄ Much of the 2002 Biscuit Fire in the proposed Kalmiopsis Wilderness Additions was a low-intensity ground fire.

The Warner Creek Fire

On October 10, 1991, an arson-caused fire burned in the mostly roadless Warner Creek area in the western Cascades, east of Oakridge, Oregon. The fire burned over Bunchgrass Ridge, covered 8,900 acres and was the object of a massive fire-fighting effort until it was extinguished by snow on October 23. The traditional response of the Forest Service is to fight fire, and on the Warner Creek fire it wasted one million dollars and deployed 2,500 firefighters on a fire far removed from any human habitation. (One third of the burned acreage was scorched by "backfires" designed to deny the encroaching wildfire any fuel. Do not waste your time trying to determine the logic.)

After the fire was out, the Forest Service began planning to "salvage" the burned timber. According to existing management plans designed to protect the northern spotted owl, the Warner Creek area was off-limits to logging, but there was a loophole big enough to drive a convoy of log trucks through. If the area burned, it would no longer qualify as spotted owl habitat and could be clearcut. "Light it, then log it" was becoming the latest way to perpetuate unsustainable logging levels.

In its zeal to log, local Forest Service officials were caught in numerous lies during their long disinformation campaign. They argued that to protect and restore the forest around Warner Creek, it had to be logged.

Local conservationists proposed that the area be preserved for research purposes to study the ecology of fire. Because the Forest Service has for so long routinely logged after wildfire, relatively little is known about natural recovery after a fire.

The Warner Creek timber sale was challenged in court. In 1995, the magistrate recommended to the judge that he rule in the plaintiffs' favor. However, that same year, Senator Mark Hatfield rammed through his "logging without laws" legislative rider that insulated all timber sales from federal environmental standards. So before the judge could finalize the magistrate's recommendation, the case was dismissed. No legal action could stop the sale.

With judicial review denied, a motley but heroic group of primarily young conservationists blockaded the sale area. The Forest Service had banned all entry here, except to loggers. These activists literally dug in for the winter and hand dug big pits (think "tank traps") across Forest Service Road 2408 to prevent the passage of logging equipment. They spent the winter in the woods, resupplied by other activists who trudged eight miles through the snow to reach them. To protest the sale, one activist went on a 75-day hunger strike in front of the federal courthouse and Willamette National Forest office in Eugene.

The protests received lots of publicity, including a story on the front page of the *New York Times*. Then, astoundingly, in August 1996, senior officials in the Forest Service (prodded by the Clinton White House) reconsidered the timber sale and ordered that it be bought back from the purchasers. Victory was at hand. However, a few weeks later local Forest Service officials, emulating Keystone cops, invaded the protest site and arrested several people, including two newspaper reporters. The concurrent

Natural recovery is rapid in the Warner Creek Burn on the Willamette National Forest (the fire scars at the base of the tree trunks are barely noticeable).

confiscation of the reporters' First Amendment-protected notes did not endear the agency to the media.

The "logging without laws" law expired in late 1996 and the sale was canceled. However, the Forest Service persisted and, under the cover of the so-called "lawless logging salvage rider," proposed a new and much larger timber sale in the Warner Fire Area. This sale was ultimately withdrawn (after much hard work by ONRC and many others) after the Clinton-appointed Secretary of Agriculture issued a directive prohibiting the Forest Service from using the authority of the salvage rider to log in inventoried roadless areas such as Warner Creek.

On October 30, 1996, the Oakridge Ranger Station was torched. The Oregon Natural Resources Council immediately offered a $1,000 reward for information leading to the arrest and conviction of the arsonist(s). The reward has yet to be claimed. The ranger station was rebuilt in 2002 in the Cascadian architectural style.

If you walk the Bunchgrass Ridge Trail in the proposed Upper Willamette Wilderness today, you'll see a healthy recovering forest, where the spotted owls remained even after the fire.

SANDY LONSDALE

side several miles away. If the unnatural firebreaks of I-84, U.S. 30, Washington 14, two railroad tracks and a dammed Columbia River couldn't prevent a fire from spreading, what chance does a single bulldozer-width ditch hastily bladed across the forest landscape have as soon as a breeze comes up?

An insidious fire-industrial complex, consisting of a severely bloated fire bureaucracy and a corps of fire contractors (fire-fighting crews, food service, transportation service, helicopters, tankers, lodging, et al.) has been created to "fight" fires. Every summer federal and state agencies are given what amounts to a blank check for fire fighting and have essentially no accountability. Some of those who stand to gain financially from "fighting" fires actually start fires.

Consider also that August, when many wildfires burn, is a slow news month. Congress isn't in session and much of the East Coast is on vacation. To escape the eastern humidity many reporters come West in search of "news." Though most forest fires are generally slow-burning ground fires, they make for lousy video. Footage of the relatively atypical "crown fires" is what makes the news as editors have to justify the expense of the mobile satellite feed trucks. Many reporters are lazy and are fed their news by government public relations flacks who are part of the fire bureaucracy. For example, in 1988 headlines screamed that Yellowstone Park was "destroyed" by fire. It wasn't.

Increasingly, resources are spent in an attempt to defend not forests from fire, but individual buildings located in the backcountry. "We should recognize that people who construct homes in fire-prone environments are just as imprudent as someone who parks their car on a railroad track," says ecologist and author George Wuerthner. Like a flood or a hurricane, a wildfire may not come often, but when it does the results are predictable. People who choose to live in the path of nature should accept the risks themselves and take appropriate steps to mitigate and insure against them.

While front-line fire fighters most always exhibit great valor and determination, their lives are often needlessly put in jeopardy in futile attempts to oppose natural and beneficial phenomena or to defend an isolated building from fire. The number of fire fighters that die in action is increasing.

Is it reasonable to expect taxpayers to repeatedly spend unlimited amounts of money and firefighters to repeatedly risk their lives to save a poorly maintained vacation retreat from natural fires?

The government should spend less money "fighting" fire and more money on fire management, including firebreaks around towns and property that can and should be defended. The most effective actions that can be taken, in terms of cost and fire prevention, involve making buildings less susceptible to inevitable wildfires. The single most important thing to do is to make roofs inflammable (metal roofs). The second is to remove vegetation and other flammable fuels directly adjacent to the building.

◄ A controlled burn in ponderosa pine on the Deschutes National Forest. Most forest fires naturally burn low and "cool" along the ground.

ELIZABETH FERYL, ENVIRONMENTAL IMAGES

Modern logging in the Oregon Coast Range.

Top Dozen Threats to Oregon's Forest Wilderness

Depending on a particular site (or one's mood), the threats at the bottom of this list may shuffle positions a bit, but those at the top are there to stay.

1. Logging. If logged, and especially if clearcut, a forest is no longer a forest. If logging looks bad, it is bad. Yet even if logging looks good, it is still bad. Even selective logging of virgin forest, while less displeasing to the eye than a clearcut, still impoverishes wildlife habitat, degrades water quality and quantity, compacts soil and fragments the landscape. (A small exception can sometimes be made for the logging of small-diameter trees in plantations or fire-suppressed and/or livestock-grazed stands where the ultimate goal is the restoration of naturalness and/or wildness.)

2. Road Building. Besides allowing the conveyance of cut trees away from and of alien species into a forest, roads degrade watersheds by altering hydrology, boosting peak flows and increasing erosion. Roads are also a barrier to both local wildlife movement and longer migrations.

3. Livestock Grazing. Bovine bulldozers have done more environmental damage in some forests than chainsaws. Livestock grazing severely degrades both streamside and upland areas by compacting soil and removing vegetation that is mostly converted to disgustingly large amounts of fecal material, much of which ends up in forest streams.

4. Excessive Consumption. Americans consume wood products at levels far greater than the rest of the world, greater even than comparably developed countries such as Japan and those in Western Europe. Gluttonous consumption has long ceased to have any correlation to individual happiness. While many other countries are more densely populated than the United States, excessive and unsustainable demands on the earth's resources make America the world's most overpopulated nation. In the short-run, unless we curtail both our population growth and rates of consumption, there will be no room for nature. And in the long run, nature won't have room for us. Nature bats last.

5. Exotic Species. Exotic species, including weeds, insects and diseases, are an increasing problem for forest ecosystems. The threat is worth mentioning even though most of the problem would abate if the other threats listed here were brought under control.

6. Mining. Even if a site where minerals, oil, gas or geothermal heat were extracted is "reclaimed," such does not yield a native forest ecosystem. Mining processes have both direct and long-term indirect impacts on forest ecosystems. Hard rock mineral claims on public lands can be bought for no more than $5.00 per acre. That price, set in the Mining Law of 1872, if indexed to inflation would be still be a bargain at $71.04 in today's dollars.

7. Climate Change. Deforestation has released significant amounts of carbon into the atmosphere, as has the burning of fossil fuels. Humans can adapt somewhat to climate change. As the climate warms, to stay in historic climatic conditions, forest species (trees and wildlife) will likely try to move both northward and upslope. These attempts will probably prove futile, as the climate will likely change faster than these species can move away from the heat.

8. Developed Recreation. Ski areas, off-road vehicle staging areas and destination resorts degrade wilderness values.

9. Off-Road Vehicles. ORVs are loud, noxious and obnoxious to both people and wildlife, and are a primary vector for the introduction of alien species to forest eco-systems. They also compact soils, leave ugly scars on the landscape, pollute excessively and inevitably crush many living things. To be fair, it's the 90 percent of off-road vehicle users that do not follow the rules that make the other 10 percent look bad.

10. Primitive Recreation Overuse. The loss of wilderness means the loss of elbow-room. Too many hikers and backpackers can overrun protected Wilderness. In the short-term, increasing the supply to meet demand and diluting these recreational impacts can be achieved by designating more Wilderness areas. In the long-term, population must be stabilized.

11. Utility Corridors. Pipelines and powerlines have enormously detrimental impacts on public lands. For example, they create barriers to wildlife migration, they are subject to regular chemical spraying to control vegetation, become vectors for weeds and are aesthetically appalling. They are also some of the longest, linear clearcuts in the world.

12. Privatization. Any transfer of public lands out of public custody inevitably results in lost public values for those lands. Besides the usual closure to public access, private lands must produce income, usually at the expense of nature. Forest ecosystems quickly pay the price.

If only the list of threats stopped at an even dozen. Globalization of trade and the concurrent reduction in enforcement of national environmental laws, could result in successful corporate lawsuits against the United States for profits lost due to Wilderness protection. Genetically modified organisms, including the transfer of genes from one species into another, can pollute the wild gene pool that wilderness preserves and fosters. Greed is another, if not the overarching, threat to forest wilderness.

MINERAL POLICY CENTER

A very small cyanide heap leach mining operation.

Salvage logging after a wildfire is akin to mugging a burn victim.

Wood decks and woodpiles next to a house can act as carefully laid kindling and facilitate forest fire flames or radiant heat to ignite the structure.

We should never forget that the only thing truly predictable about wildfire is that it is usually unpredictable. As land managers reintroduce controlled burns to these fire-dependent ecosystems, sometimes plans will go awry. Fires can burn out of control and cause damage to property and even to people. However, prescribed fires will cause nowhere near as much damage as continuing the futile policy of trying to prevent or suppress every wildfire. Summer firefighters should become year-round fire-technicians. Much work is needed to restore the natural fire balance that is beneficial to nature and can safely coexist with human communities.

The timber industry has its own axe to wield in this matter. Because the American people have rejected industry's arguments that national forests serve merely as timber mines, or that wildlife needs clearcuts, the timber industry is falling back on its last remaining argument: that logging mimics the ecological benefits of fire without the ecological costs. The only problem with this argument is that it is not true. Fire is natural and nature needs fire. Chainsaws and bulldozers are not part of the natural cycle. Post-fire salvage logging after a fire is not a solution to forest health problems either. Salvage logging after a wildfire is akin to mugging a burn victim.

However, in some cases, as part of a careful program to reintroduce natural fire into dry forest ecosystems, some logging of small-diameter trees that have grown in response to the lack of regular ground fires resulting from fire suppression and livestock

grazing is appropriate. But additional logging of the large-diameter, fire-resistant trees in the same forests is not.

The ecological debt created by decades of fire suppression must be paid off by investing federal dollars in truly ecologically balanced forest restoration, not merely by continuing to subsidize timber sales of big old trees.

Livestock Grazing: A Major Factor in Unhealthy Forests

Livestock have actively participated in the destabilization of ponderosa pine and mixed coniferous forests. The hot fires that swept through central and eastern Washington and Oregon during the summer of 1994 may have, in fact, been partially a result of a century of livestock grazing.

—Dr. Joy Belsky and Dana Blumenthal[12]

The classic "park-like" stands of ponderosa pine and mixed conifer forests that once blanketed the interior West from British Columbia to New Mexico have changed dramatically for the worse since the European-American invasion. Only 2 to 8 percent of Oregon's original old-growth ponderosa pine stands still exist. The numbers are similar throughout the rest of the West.

What were once widely spaced, fire-tolerant stands of trees with a dense grass sward underneath have been converted over the last century into thick forest stands that are more susceptible to both fire and disease. Scientists, government foresters, the timber industry and conservationists point to two major causes of this transition: (1) suppression of low-intensity fires that prevented the establishment of fire-sensitive and shade-tolerant tree species such as Douglas-, grand and white firs and (2) logging of the economically valuable and fire-resistant ponderosa pine and western larch.

Today, there is much talk about the "forest health crisis." Of course, forest ecologists, mill owners or government bureaucrats will differ on what constitutes a healthy forest. They also differ vehemently on the relative importance of logging, fire suppression, disease and road building to forest sustainability. However, while these are very important factors in forest health, another factor that has been utterly overlooked in the debate is the effects of a century and a half of livestock grazing.

Livestock currently range over 284 million acres or 91 percent of all federal land in the eleven western states, including forested landscapes. Although livestock do not wield chainsaws or use fire-fighting equipment, they have a their own dramatic impact on forest composition and density.

Livestock grazing has modified forest dynamics by annually removing the understory grasses that serve two critical roles in a natural forest. First, healthy, thick

GEORGE WUERTHNER

Cow-bombed landscape along the Sprague River in the Fremont National Forest.

infestation. Fuel loads have thus increased ten-fold in the last 25 years.

In their review of the scientific literature, Dr. Joy Belsky and her associate Dana Blumenthal found numerous studies comparing grazed and ungrazed forest stands (where domestic livestock was excluded, but not native wildlife). They found that ungrazed stands retained their park-like character, in spite of active fire prevention efforts.

To restore the stability and sustainability of our interior public forests, we must not only end logging of big trees and carefully reintroduce fire into the ecosystem, but also eliminate domestic livestock grazing from these forests so that native grasses can return.

The cow may be mightier than the chainsaw — not only in myth, but also in fact. ◆

Notes

[1]Bode, Carl. 1964. THE PORTABLE THOREAU. Viking Press. New York, NY: 633 (originally published in Henry David Thoreau, LIFE WITHOUT PRINCIPLE, in 1863).

[2]Bourhill, Bob. 1994. HISTORY OF OREGON'S TIMBER HARVESTS AND LUMBER PRODUCTION. Oregon Dept. of Forestry. Salem, OR; Oregon Dept. of Forestry. "25-Year Harvest History" (chart), available at www.odf.state.or.us/DIVISIONS/resource_policy/resource_planning/Annual_Reports/rpt25YearHistory.asp; Oregon Dept. of Forestry. "Oregon's 2002 Timber Harvest Highest since 1997" (press release). ODF. Salem, OR (July 17 2003) (available at www.odf.state.or.us/divisions/resource_policy/public_affairs/news_releases/nr02180.htm).

[3]Noss, Reed F., Edward T. LaRoe, J. Michael Scott. 1995. Endangered Ecosystems of the United States: A Preliminary Assessment of Loss and Degradation. Biological Report 28. USDI-National Biological Service. Washington, DC: (unpaginated) (*citations omitted*) (available at biology.usgs.gov/pubs/ecosys.htm).

[4]Originally published in Wood, Charles Erskine Scott. 1908. *Portland's feast of roses*. Pacific Monthly (Portland, OR) 19(6): 623-633.

[5]American Heritage Dictionaries. 1996. THE AMERICAN HERITAGE DICTIONARY OF THE ENGLISH LANGUAGE. 3rd ed. Houghton Mifflin Company. Boston , MA. (electronic ver.).

[6]Ibid.

[7]Noss, Reed F. 1990. The ecological effects of roads, or the road to destruction. Available at www.wildlandscpr.org/resourcelibrary/reports/ecoleffectsroads.html (originally published as Diamondback. 1990. *The ecological effects of roads, or the road to destruction*. Special Paper. Earth First! Tucson, AZ.).

[8]Western Native Trout Campaign. 2001. Imperiled Western Trout and the Importance of Roadless Areas. Center for Biological Diversity, Tucson, AZ; Pacific Rivers Council, Eugene, OR; Biodiversity Associates, Laramie WY: 12.

[9]Ibid, Executive Summary, unpaginated.

[10]Kerr, Andy. *Re-educating Smokey Bear on Merits of Fire*. Wallowa County Chieftain (Aug. 29, 1996).

[11]Huff, Mark H., Roger D. Ottmar, Ernesto Alvarado, et al. 1995. HISTORICAL AND CURRENT LANDSCAPES IN EASTERN OREGON AND WASHINGTON. PART II: LINKING VEGETATION CHARACTERISTICS TO POTENTIAL FIRE BEHAVIOR AND RELATED SMOKE PRODUCTION. Gen. Tech. Rep. 355. USDA-Forest Service, Pacific Northwest Forest and Range Experiment Station. Portland, OR: (unpaginated abstract) (available at www.fs.fed.us/pnw/pubs/gtr355/gtr355a.pdf).

[12]Belsky, A. Joy and Dana M. Blumenthal. 1997. *Effects of livestock grazing on stand dynamics and soils in upland forests of the Interior West*. Conservation Biology 11(2): 324

stands of grass out-compete conifer seedlings for space and water, preventing the establishment of dense stands of small trees.

Before the intrusion of domestic livestock, the typical eastside forest floor was carpeted with Idaho fescue, bluebunch wheatgrass, pine-grass and elk sedge. The old-growth grasses with their extensive roots could out-compete small seedlings for moisture and nutrients. A source of nutrients and organic matter, the grass cover was also critical for slowing surface water flow, enhancing water infiltration, insulating the soil from freezing and mitigating the erosive force of raindrops.

The second role of grasses in dry eastern forests is to carry forest-cleansing low- intensity ground fires that kill large percentages of seedlings and maintain open park-like stands of old growth. On dry, low-elevation south-facing slopes, the dominant tree is ponderosa pine. In wetter mid-level north-facing stands, the dominant trees are western larch, Douglas-fir, grand fir and white fir. Trees that survive to maturity evolve with fire by having self-pruning lower branches and thick fire-resistant bark. Ground fires that occur approximately every five to twelve years throughout the West usually pose no problem for the big old trees.

Gone with the grass are these beneficial fires. Dense stands of sapling- and pole-sized fire-sensitive species are now all too common. These species are more susceptible to stress during drought, which makes them more vulnerable to disease and insect

A Brief Political History of Oregon's Wilderness Protections

Government protection should be thrown around every wild grove and forest on the mountains, as it is around every private orchard, and trees in public parks. To say nothing of their values as fountains of timber, they are worth infinitely more than all the gardens and parks of town.

–John Muir[1]

Inadequacies of Administrative Protections

There is "government protection," and then there is *government protection*. Mere public ownership — especially if managed by the Bureau of Land Management — affords land little real or permanent protection. National forests enjoy somewhat more protection than BLM lands, but to fully protect, conserve and restore federal forests often requires a combination of Wilderness designation and additional appropriate congressional protections.

The best and most permanent protection available for federal wildlands is their inclusion in the National Wilderness Preservation System. Once an Act of Congress designates wildlands as "Wilderness", they are very rarely undesignated (a few acres have been lost to nefarious boundary shifting and some have been willfully removed for ski area expansion). Congressional Wilderness designation is very difficult to achieve politically, but an order of magnitude more difficult to undo.

The standards of protection under the Wilderness Act of 1964 — apart from the gaping loophole for domestic livestock grazing — are quite strong. The relatively few problems with management of designated Wilderness are usually caused by the managing agency's abuse of their limited discretion under the Act.

A far more serious problem is the abuse of agency discretion in managing wildlands *not* formally protected as Wilderness. In fact, a driving force behind the passage of the Wilderness Act four decades ago was the need to end the Forest Service's practice of declassifying "wilderness" areas the agency had previously administratively established on the national forests (i.e., on its own, without congressional prompting or direction).

Although the Forest Service pioneered the concept of wilderness protection in the 1920s and 1930s, by the late 1940s and 1950s, it was methodically undoing whatever good it had done earlier by declassifying administrative wilderness areas that contained any commercial timber.

Just prior to the end of its second term, and after receiving over a million public comments in support of protecting national forest roadless areas, the Clinton Administration promulgated a regulation (a.k.a. "the Roadless Rule") to protect the remaining unprotected wildlands (greater than 5,000 acres in size) in the National Forest System from road building and logging. At the time, Clinton's Forest Service chief Mike Dombeck asked rhetorically:

Is it worth one-quarter of 1 percent of our nation's timber supply or a fraction of a fraction of our oil and gas to protect 58.5 million acres of wild and unfragmented land in perpetuity?[2]

Dombeck's remarks echoed those of a Forest Service scientist from an earlier era. In 1922, Aldo Leopold persuaded the Forest Service to designate the nation's first administrative wilderness area in the Gila Mountains of New Mexico. In the following decades, under Leopold's prodding and that of others, the Forest Service designated millions of acres of additional administrative wilderness. Leopold noted:

Such a policy would not subtract even a fraction of 1 percent from our economic wealth but would preserve a fraction of what has, since first the flight of years began, been wealth to the human spirit.[3]

Unlike Dombeck and Leopold, many Forest Service personnel oppose congressional Wilderness designation. Formal Wilderness designation intentionally limits agency discretion to manage the protected areas. Control and discretion are very important to agency bureaucrats. Most land managers believe that they can do a better job managing the landscape than nature can — a belief not limited to the Forest Service and Bureau of Land Management, two agencies that are institutionally biased toward natural resource extraction. The U.S. Fish and Wildlife Service and National Park Service, two agencies

RALPH OPP

The forests on Pelican Butte in the proposed South Cascades Wilderness have some administrative protection, but not enough to prevent the Forest Service from seeking to allow a ski development, which would harass bald eagles, spotted owls and other imperiled species.

for disaster. Administrative land management plans, which can provide protection to an area, can be later undone. They can also be amended or ignored to accommodate pet development schemes.

Consider the case of Pelican Butte in Oregon's Southern Cascades. At 8,036 feet, Pelican Butte is one of the two highest Oregon Cascades peaks not included in the National Wilderness System. The Winema National Forest Land and Resource Management Plan designated the area as a "semi-primitive area" and a "bald eagle management area" due to the large number of eagles that winter there. President Clinton's Northwest Forest Plan also designated the area a "late successional reserve," the strongest administrative protection possible. Under provisions of the Endangered Species Act, the U.S. Fish and Wildlife Service designated the area as "critical habitat" for the northern spotted owl. However, despite all these administrative designations and recognitions, local Forest Service officials supported building a ski area on the butte.

The proposed Pelican Butte Ski Resort is presently dead. But it has died a dozen times before. Yet another new plan to haul downhill skiers up hill by snow machines is currently being proposed, and the Forest Service is considering the proposal, despite a longstanding seasonal closure on motorized vehicle use to protect bald eagles. The Forest Service's constant flirtation with proposals for a ski area on Pelican Butte is enabled by the fact that all protections for the area are administrative designations, allowing the Forest Service some discretion to bypass them. Congressionally designating the butte as Wilderness would finally resolve the issue in favor of protection by severely restricting the agency's discretion to manage it.

While Chief Dombeck was in office, he told Forest Service employees that:

Values such as wilderness and roadless areas, clean water, protection of rare species, old growth forests, naturalness — these are the reasons most Americans cherish their public lands. (T)wenty percent of the National Forest System is wilderness, and in the minds of man, more should be. Our wilderness portfolio must embody a broader array of lands — from prairie to old growth. As world leaders in wilderness management, we should be looking to the future to better manage existing, and identify new wilderness and other wild lands.[4]

Chief Dombeck is now retired and the new Bush Administration's Forest Service Chief Dale Bosworth is working to undo essentially every good thing Dombeck did. This is the problem with administrative rulemaking to protect wildlands — they are subject to change by every succeeding administration that comes into office. Only congressionally designated Wilderness areas can survive changing administrations and completely and permanently protect the nation's Pelican Buttes from the vagaries of land management agencies and other development interests.

more traditionally inclined toward conservation, also share this belief.

While some active management of Wilderness is necessary to prevent damage caused by excess visitation, to restore natural fire regimes or to eliminate exotic species, generally the best way to manage Wilderness is to leave it alone. Some land managers even consider Wilderness a potential threat to their jobs. For example, a wildlife refuge manager charged with manipulating habitat to maximize duck production or a park superintendent attempting to accommodate ever more visitors may view their jobs as unnecessary under Wilderness management, since little active management is necessary or allowed.

Opposition to permanent protection — including administrative actions that could lead to later Wilderness designation — often begins at the top. Consider the nation's new national forest roadless policy, designed by the Clinton Administration and desecrated by the second Bush Administration. The Bush II White House judged that the roadless areas policy was too popular to undo directly, so they left the administrative rule on the books, but created new loopholes in the rule large enough to drive log trucks through. Like the old Forest Service administrative wilderness designations, because the new roadless rule was created administratively, rather than enacted by legislation, it is subject to change by later administrations. This is a recipe

Judge John B. Waldo: Oregon's John Muir

An urgent need of the hour would seem to be, not more land to cultivate, but some change for the better in our ideas. There are educational uses in the mountains and the wilderness which might well justify a wise people in preserving and reserving them for such uses.

—Judge John B. Waldo[5]

OREGON HISTORICAL SOCIETY

Lawyer, legislator, granger, Republican, sportsman, chief justice, conservationist, explorer and scholar, John B. Waldo read and quoted Thoreau, Shakespeare, Emerson, Aurelius, Goethe and Wordsworth on his twenty-seven summer sojourns in Oregon's Cascades. From July through September and from Mount Hood to Mount Shasta, Waldo explored, was nourished by and educated by Oregon's mountain wildlands.

Born in 1844, Waldo graduated from Willamette University in 1866 and was admitted to the state bar in 1870. In the 1889 Oregon Legislative Assembly, Representative Waldo introduced a measure requesting that Congress:

... set aside and forever preserve, for the uses herein specified, all that portion of the Cascade Range throughout the State extending twelve miles on each side, substantially, of the summit of the range.[6]

The resolution further stated:

That the altitude of said strip of land, its wildness, game, fish, water and other fowl, its scenery, the beauty of its flora, and the purity of its atmosphere, and healthfulness, and other attractions, render it most desirable that it be set aside and kept free and open forever as a public reserve, park, and resort for the people of Oregon and of the United States.[7]

The resolution urged the proscription of many commercial uses, including grazing, hunting and logging, except for railroads. Resorts would be limited to being no closer than five miles apart.

The Oregon House approved the measure, though it omitted the southernmost Cascades to appease local livestock interests. (Some things have yet to change.)

Unfortunately, the Oregon Senate, at the behest of sheepmen, killed the measure by bottling it up in committee.

Waldo fought on. From Odell Lake on September 4, 1890, he wrote:

The policy of the government in establishing reserves cannot be too highly commended. How splendid for this age to leave to posterity a resort and pleasure ground for the people forever.

Why the need of a resort and pleasure ground? Because the happiness, comfort and development are thereby subserved. Provision for the recreation of the people is now one of the established principles of municipal and civil government.[8]

In 1893, President Grover Cleveland established the Cascade Forest Reserve, which today would be most or all of the Mount Hood, Willamette, Deschutes, Umpqua, Rogue River and Winema National Forests. Waldo later wrote the President thanking him and defending his bold action:

A wise government will know that to raise men is much more important than to raise sheep, or men the nature of sheep; and that this is a question which, ultimately, immeasurably concerns even the purely material interest of men ... .[9]

Why should not all Americans, with a continent in their hands to fashion as they would, have provided broadly for all the needs of men which can be supplied? ... Not only fields to toil in, but mountains and wilderness to camp in, to hunt and fish in, and where, in communion with untrammeled nature and the free air, the narrowing tendencies of an artificial and petty existence might be perceived and corrected, and the spirit enlarged and strengthened.[10]

Waldo never stopped advocating for Oregon's forest wildlands. At Pamelia Lake on August 15 and 17, 1905, a few years before his death, he wrote:

The still woods; surely they are not all made merely to cut down. Let wide stretches still grow for the spiritual welfare of men. How good they seem here today — the untrammeled ... wilderness, untouched by men, and that never has been touched. Cannot wide expanses still be preserved?

The commercial view of the forest is not the whole view, nor the correct view, any more than it is of most things. We do not live by bread alone. A wise compromise is probably the end to be attained. The most useful things are those which have no utility.[11]

His front-page obituary in the Salem *Capital Journal* Sept. 5, 1907, concluded:

To him the mountains ... were a book to which there was no end. The beauty of the hills was a sermon ... . The forest was his temple, and there he worshipped.[12]

The Wilderness Act

The Wilderness Act is somewhat flawed and sometimes at odds with itself.
—Dave Foreman (former Wilderness Society lobbyist, co-founder
of Earth First! and co-founder of The Wildlands Project) [13]

The nation's first administratively protected "wilderness" area was established on the Gila National Forest in New Mexico in 1924 at the instigation of visionary Forest Service ecologist Aldo Leopold. The Boundary Water Canoe Area in the Superior National Forest in Minnesota was established in 1926. It also later became a "wilderness." As noted above, these were not Congressional designations, but administrative forbearers to Wilderness Act "Wilderness."

In 1929, the Department of Agriculture issued "L-20" regulations to establish "primitive areas." No activities were specifically banned, leaving management to the discretion of local Forest Service managers. The L-20 regulations were superceded in 1939 by the U-1 and U-2 regulations for establishing "wilderness" areas (larger than 100,000 acres, designated by the Secretary of Agriculture) and "wild" areas (less than 100,000 acres, established by the Chief of the Forest Service).

Following World War II, a new Forest Service leadership drove the agency toward decidedly more industrial timber production than ever before, for which administrative wilderness classification posed an impediment. Consequently the agency did not classify any additional wilderness or wilderness-like areas, but instead declassified previously protected wildlands with high timber value. It was then conservationists began looking to Congress for statutory protection of public lands. In 1949 at a Sierra Club conference, Howard Zahniser, executive director of The Wilderness Society, proposed the idea of congressionally legislated Wilderness.

Senator Hubert Humphrey (D-MN) and Representative John Saylor (R-PA) introduced the first Wilderness bill in 1956. Sixty-six rewrites and eight years later, the Wilderness Act was signed into law by President Lyndon Johnson.

Fifty-four areas totaling 9.1 million acres were initially included in the National Wilderness Preservation System. As of this writing, the system now includes 662 areas and over 106 million acres.

The passage of the Wilderness Act on September 3, 1964, is an extraordinary landmark in the history of American conservation and law. It culminated an epic struggle begun in the 1950s, the groundwork for which was laid in the 1930s, if not the 1870s. With the President's signature, Congress went on record with a remarkable articulation of the Wilderness ideal. Anyone who has ever been bored or confused reading federal statutory language will be struck by the poetry Congress used in the preamble to the Wilderness Act of 1964:

Cross-country skiers in the Maiden Peak Unit of the proposed Three Sisters Wilderness Additions. ▶

Kalmiopsis leachiana, endemic to Oregon, for which the Kalmiopsis Wilderness was named.

 In order to assure that an increasing population, accompanied by expanding
settlement and growing mechanization, does not occupy and modify all areas within
the United States and its possessions, leaving no lands designated for preservation and
protection in their natural condition, it is hereby declared to be the policy of the
Congress to secure for the American people of present and future generations the
benefits of an enduring resource of wilderness.[14]

Congress then went on to specify exactly what would constitute federally
designated Wilderness:

*For this purpose there is hereby established a National Wilderness Preservation
System to be composed of federally owned areas designated by the Congress as*

*"wilderness areas," and these shall be administered for the use and enjoyment of the
American people in such a manner as will leave them unimpaired for future use and
enjoyment as wilderness, and so as to provide for the protection of these areas, the
preservation of their wilderness character, and for the gathering and dissemination of
information regarding their use and enjoyment as wilderness; and no Federal lands
shall be designated as "wilderness areas" expect as provided for in this Act or by a
subsequent Act.[15]*

Consider just how remarkable the passage of the Wilderness Act was. Our nation's
history has almost entirely been one of ever-expanding settlement and the conquest of
nature. Destruction of wilderness was simply a byproduct of "progress." In the waning
days of the 88th Congress, our elected officials not only waxed poetic, but stated
unequivocally that "progress" can go too far and that, unless specific actions are taken to
preserve wilderness, an "increasing population," "expanding settlement" and "growing
mechanization" would eventually "modify *all* areas" of the country (emphasis added).

For an institution that rarely can see beyond the next election, the passage of the
Wilderness Act was unusually prescient. Most of the Wilderness initially preserved by
Congress in the Act remains protected to this day. Even those who profit or receive
psychic benefit from the inexorable march of "progress" recognize the political folly of
trying to undermine the value of protected Wilderness. Since enactment of the
Wilderness Act, the debate has evolved to how much, what kind and where, but no
longer whether we need wilderness.

But the status quo is not static. In their relentless assault on the wild in pursuit of
financial gain, wilderness destroyers have the advantage over wilderness protectors. In
response to those seeking a new water supply for the increasing population of San
Francisco by constructing a dam in Yosemite National Park, John Muir railed:

*These temple destroyers, devotees of ravishing commercialism seem to have a perfect
contempt for Nature, and instead of lifting their eyes to the God of the Mountains, lift
them to the Almighty Dollar. Dam Hetch Hetchy! As well dam for water tanks the
people's cathedrals and churches, for no holier temple has ever been consecrated by the
hearts of man.[16]*

Once an area is protected as Wilderness, it is relatively safe from most threats (logging, road building, mining and water developments, but *not* grazing). This legislative
protection is as permanent as things get in a democracy. Wilderness, however, is only
safe as long as Americans continue to want it and people stay on guard to protect it.

There have been some reversals — temporary and permanent — in Wilderness
protection. Areas protected in the Wilderness System have had their boundaries

subsequently rearranged by federal politicians seeking to accommodate local interests. For example, Oregon U.S. Senator Mark Hatfield moved the Hells Canyon and the Kalmiopsis Wilderness boundaries in 1978 to accommodate logging roads. In the 1970s, the Forest Service, in the name of "protecting" wilderness values, brought DDT out of retirement to spray for native insects that were defoliating (but rarely killing) trees in the Eagle Cap Wilderness. (The natural infestation was exacerbated by the agency's overzealous fire suppression policies).

Congress was very careful to distinguish *what kind of land qualifies* for inclusion in the Wilderness System and *how such lands are to be managed* once part of the Wilderness System. Congress described wilderness in Section 2(c) of the Wilderness Act:

A wilderness in contrast with those areas where man and his own works dominate the landscape, is hereby recognized as an area where the earth and community of life are untrammeled by man, where man himself is a visitor who does not remain.[17]

Congress then defined Wilderness in practical terms:

An area of wilderness is further defined to mean in this Act an area of undeveloped Federal land retaining its primeval character and influence, without permanent improvements or human habitation, which is protected and managed so as to preserve its natural conditions and which (1) generally appears to have been affected primarily by the forces of nature, with the imprint of man's work substantially unnoticeable; (2) has outstanding opportunities of solitude or a primitive and unconfined type of recreation; (3) has at least five thousand acres of land or is of sufficient size as to make practicable its preservation and use in an unimpaired condition; and (4) may also contain ecological, geological, or other features of scientific, educational, scenic or historical value[18] (emphasis added).

In providing for the management of Wilderness, Congress was restrictive:

Except as otherwise provided in this Act, each agency administering any area designated as wilderness shall be responsible for preserving the wilderness character of the area and shall so administer such area for such other purposes for which it may have been established as also to preserve its wilderness character. Except as otherwise provided in this Act, wilderness areas shall be devoted to the public purposes of recreational, scenic, scientific, education, conservation and historical use.[19]

Except as specifically provided for in this Act, and subject to existing private rights, there shall be no commercial enterprise and no permanent road within any wilderness area designated by this Act and except as necessary to meet minimum

ELLEN MORRIS BISHOP

Congress has a long history of extending federal protection to natural wonders. Crater Lake National Park was established in 1902.

FEATURED

Other Congressional Protections

W ilderness designation is but one way to protect federal public land. It is clearly the best protection for roadless areas, but there are circumstances when other federal classifications are more appropriate (often in combination with Wilderness designation).

In Oregon, as of 2002, Congress had established 49 wild and scenic rivers, three national monuments (one congressionally legislated and two proclaimed by the President under authority of the Antiquities Act of 1906), two national recreation areas and one of each of the following: national park, scenic-research area, scenic recreation area, national scenic area, national volcanic monument, recreation area, cooperative management and protection area and a watershed management unit. (See Appendices C and D.) Congress has also designated national wildlife refuges, but they are more often wetlands, rather than forested or other major terrestrial habitats.

Unfortunately, nearly all of these alternate designations have some loopholes in them that, under certain conditions, allow mining, grazing, logging or other development. Several of these areas have (or should have) legislatively protected Wilderness within their boundaries to enhance their protection.

requirements for the administration of the area for the purpose of this Act, (including measures required in emergencies involving the health and safety of persons within the area), there shall be no temporary road, no use of motor vehicles, motorized equipment or motorboats, no landing of aircraft, no other form of mechanical transport, and no structure or installation within any such area.[20]

Congress has been flexible about allowing past developments in several Wilderness Areas, including an old clearcut that was one square-mile in size (in the Grassy Knob Wilderness), a major logging road with old clearcuts at its terminus (in the Cummins Creek Wilderness and several others) and numerous "jeep trails." Congress knew that, over time, these unnatural features would be reclaimed by nature. But opponents of Wilderness designation often use the argument that only lands that have been managed as Wilderness without *any* human impacts qualify as Wilderness.

The Wilderness Act is not perfect. It is a political compromise that has loopholes that can be and have been used to the detriment of Wilderness.

Perhaps the most glaring loophole: domestic livestock grazing was grandfathered into the Wilderness Act to continue wherever it occurred before an area is designated as Wilderness. This compromise was necessary in 1964 to overcome the objections of public lands cattlemen against the Act. At the time livestock grazing was considered a minor issue. Conservationists feared more the devastating and immediate threats of road building and logging in areas the Forest Service was busily removing from the administrative wilderness system. In exchange for compromising on grazing in Wilderness areas, proponents were able to pass the Wilderness Act more quickly and begin campaigning for congressional protection for wilderness areas. Today we know more about the ecological destruction caused by seemingly innocuous livestock grazing.

Mining — where claims are both valid and filed before an area is designated as Wilderness — is also grandfathered into the Wilderness Act.

In both cases, the most efficient, just and pragmatic way to address these non-conforming prior uses would simply be for the federal government to acquire the interests in these activities and end them.

There is also a provision in the Wilderness Act, though it has never been exercised, which allows water developments in designated Wilderness Areas at the express order of the President.

Despite its imperfections, the Wilderness Act is a wonderful law, worth defending against all attacks and attackers. Over time, its loopholes and compromises can be addressed through the political process and the goal of "an enduring resource of wilderness" unsullied by any exploitation will finally be attained.

Oregon Wilderness Protection 1930-2002

If we save all the roadless areas that are left as Wilderness, in fifty years it won't be half enough.

—Sen. Bob Packwood (uttered first in 1975 on the edge of Hells Canyon and repeated there again in 1986)

Over the years, the Oregon congressional delegation has included both wilderness saints and scoundrels; and it has been heavily influenced by the politics of Big Timber. Oregon has a smaller proportion (3.6%) of its land protected as Wilderness than do California (13%), Washington (10%) or Idaho (8%). What protected Wilderness Oregon does possess has a smaller percentage of large trees and more "rock and ice" than that of its neighbors to the north and south.

Before the Wilderness Act of 1964

In 1930, the Forest Service designated the Eagle Cap, Mount Jefferson and Mountain Lakes Primitive Areas. The agency also established the Three Sisters Primitive Area in 1937.

In 1940, the agency upgraded the Eagle Cap Primitive Area as an administrative "wilderness area" and the Mountain Lakes Primitive Area as a "wild area." The Mount Hood Wild Area was also established.

World War II did not halt wildland protection in Oregon. The Strawberry Mountain and Gearhart Mountain Wild Areas were established in 1942 and 1943, respectively, and in 1946, the Kalmiopsis Wild Area was designated.

The Forest Service's enthusiasm for wildlands protection waned in the early 1950s. The newly industrialized agency was eager to road and clearcut Oregon's low-elevation old-growth forests, including the west side of the Three Sisters Primitive Area. On February 6, 1957, the agency re-classified the Three Sisters Primitive Area to the Three Sisters Wilderness Area, but removed over 57,000 acres from the protected zone to allow road building and logging. The day before, the agency established the Mount Washington and Diamond Peak Wild Areas to the north and south to mitigate the pending loss of acreage in the Three Sisters area, but neither of the new areas had significant old-growth forests. The lost acreage from the Three Sisters Wilderness Area later became known as "French Pete" (named after a creek in the region) and was an important catalyst and rallying cry for a subsequent congressional Wilderness System.

U.S. Senator
Richard L. Neuberger

Given our state's close marriage (and later separation) with the timber industry, it is hard to imagine that a United States Senator from Oregon could be a co-sponsor of the original legislation that became the Wilderness Act of 1964. Yet Senator Richard Lewis Neuberger was no ordinary United States Senator. According to Michael Frome in *Battle for Wilderness*:

At the first committee hearings in 1957, Neuberger spoke eloquently, tolling the bell at "the eleventh hour" for saving the nation's wilderness heritage. He told of the great forests of the Northwest. "If only such magnificent trees might endure forever," he said. "But are we letting commercialism and exploitation rob us of our chance for unfettered enjoyment under the blue heavens and the stars?" Then he added:

Public life often can be a sort of prison, so my visits to these beautiful places are rare. Yet it reassures me to know that they continue to exist — that, somewhere, the sparking Lochsa foams toward the sea with the same lilting resonance over the same mossy rocks as when Captain Meriwether Lewis called it KoosKooskee, the river which flows fast and clear.

I know that millions of Americans feel likewise. They gain both security and comfort from the fact that a segment of the original wilderness has been saved. The whole continent has not yet been tilled, paved, or settled. Some of these people may never see the real wilderness; their sentiments are purely vicarious. But they are aware of it nevertheless — just as Mount Everest and K-2 inspire pride among people in remote parts of India.[21]

Born in 1912 in Multnomah County, Neuberger attended public schools in Portland and the University of Oregon. He was a correspondent for the *New York Times* from 1939 until he was elected to the U.S. Senate in 1954. He also served in the Oregon House of Representatives in 1941-1942 and was commissioned as an Army lieutenant (later promoted to captain) during World War II. He was elected to the Oregon Senate in 1949. He served in the United States Senate as a Democrat from 1954 until his untimely death from cancer on March 9, 1960.

In a 1959 article in the *Progressive*, Neuberger noted:

Once wilderness is mined or grazed or logged, it never can be true wilderness again. This should induce Americans to proceed slowly when they alter the character of their few remaining primitive realms because such a process

OREGON HISTORICAL SOCIETY

Senator Richard L. Neuberger was the greatest Wilderness advocate (so far) to represent Oregon in the U.S. Senate.

inevitably becomes irreversible. Nature has done well by our United States. It is man's part that needs constant attention and improvement.[22]

Senator Neuberger's wife and fellow Democratic politician Maurine Neuberger succeeded him by winning the next term. However, she didn't run again in 1966 and was replaced by Senator Mark O. Hatfield.

Much of the original acreage protected as "Wilderness," first by the Forest Service and later by Congress, was "rock and ice" with no commercial value.

Mount Jefferson, Oregon Island and Three Arch Rocks

With passage of the Wilderness Act of 1964, all areas then classified by the Forest Service as "wilderness" and "wild" areas became part of the new National Wilderness Preservation System.

The Wilderness Act also required the Forest Service to review all Forest Service-designated "primitive areas," including the Mount Jefferson Primitive Area, and make a recommendation to Congress about possible Wilderness designation. While the agency recommended that most of the Mount Jefferson Primitive Area be upgraded to Wilderness, it also recommended that a portion including Marion Lake be left out. Chafing under the loss of administrative discretion wherever congressional Wilderness was designated, the Forest Service had adopted a "purity" threshold for new additions to the Wilderness System. Because some minor development had occurred at Marion Lake, the agency claimed the area was disqualified for Wilderness protection.

To his credit, Oregon's junior Senator Mark Hatfield, who served on the Senate Interior and Insular Affairs Committee, took the lead on a successful Mount Jefferson

Wilderness bill that included Marion Lake. Some water pumps, a boathouse, picnic tables, fire pits and more than 100 boats stored along the shore were ordered removed. Enraged that its recommendation had been overruled, the Forest Service obeyed with a vengeance, to the point of towing the boats that hadn't been removed from the lake shore to the middle of the lake, burning them to the waterline and sinking them, thereby turning some recreationists against Wilderness protection. The Marion Lake controversy seemingly haunted all of Hatfield's Wilderness dealings thereafter.

In 1970, two small, non-controversial coastal island Wildernesses were established that included the entire Oregon Island and Three Arch Rocks National Wildlife Refuges.

Minam River and Hells Canyon

Controversy returned in 1972 when Congress expanded the Eagle Cap Wilderness by including the Little Minam River and other lands around the boundary perimeter. While a net acreage gain, Congress also declassified certain lands that had been protected in the Eagle Cap, placing them back into the general pool of exploitable lands. Congress also ordered the Forest Service to study the Lower Minam River for possible Wilderness protection.

In early 1975, Congress established the Hells Canyon Wilderness as part of a larger national recreation area and adjacent Wild and Scenic Snake River. The legislation was the culmination of an epic battle to prevent hydroelectric dams from being built on the last free-flowing stretch of the Snake River. The congressional hero in this struggle was Senator Bob Packwood, who had fought tenaciously against the dams and for Wilderness since being elected in 1968. Packwood had defeated Senator Wayne Morse who had served in the Senate since 1944 and never showed great interest in protecting wilderness.

The Endangered American Wilderness Act and More Oregon Islands

In 1978, Congress passed the Endangered American Wilderness Act that included additions to the Kalmiopsis, Mount Hood and Three Sisters Wilderness areas, and established the Wild Rogue and Wenaha-Tucannon Wilderness areas. Hatfield brokered this effort and played both hero and villain. The now senior senator successfully resisted last-minute efforts to reduce the proposed Mount Hood Wilderness additions (33,000 acres) in order to allow natural gas development. He also resisted, with some success, efforts by Representatives Al Ullman (D-OR) and Tom Foley (D-WA) to exclude all the big timber (25,000 acres) from the proposed Wenaha-Tucannon Wilderness. (In the end, 15,000 acres were lost in the Washington portion of the Wilderness).

Two years prior to the passage of the Endangered American Wilderness Act, Hatfield had introduced an "Oregon Omnibus Wilderness Act" that was eventually merged into the final Endangered American Wilderness Act. Hatfield's bill included Boulder Creek (which was dropped from the final bill because of intense opposition from Douglas County timber interests) and Wilderness Study Area status for the "Hidden" Wilderness proposal. (Boulder Creek was eventually added to the Wilderness System in 1984. The "Hidden" Wilderness was protected in pieces, first in the Bull-of-the-Woods Wilderness in 1984 and later in the Opal Creek Wilderness in 1996.)

In 1978, Hatfield's "Oregon Omnibus Wilderness Act" passed the Senate and would have added 82,400 acres to the Kalmiopsis Wilderness Area. However, as originally introduced, Hatfield's bill would have added 134,000 acres to the Kalmiopsis Wilderness. Representative Jim Weaver's (D-OR) own proposal was for a 134,000-acre Kalmiopsis Wilderness addition and an adjacent 136,000-acre Wilderness Study Area. Weaver then persuaded the House to include all 280,000 acres as an addition to the already protected Wilderness. A heated conference committee ensued and, to resolve the differences between the two bills, the final addition was set at 92,000 acres.

The House staff knew the area better than the Senate staff, so the northern boundary of this new Wilderness addition was drawn to prevent the planned Bald Mountain Road. When Hatfield later learned this, he introduced a "rider" to move the boundary so as to allow the logging road to be built. The actual construction of the road was a catalyzing event in the Pacific Northwest Forest War.

By 1978, the long-raging controversy over the exclusion of French Pete from the Three Sisters Wilderness Area had been decisively won by wilderness proponents. Hatfield had long opposed granting Wilderness status to French Pete, claiming concerns about overuse. In fact, the Senator was still smarting from the wounds of his earlier effort on behalf of Marion Lake. After assurances were given that the area would be managed to accommodate or limit non-conforming uses, Hatfield acquiesced.

Even though none of the wilderness lands included in the House version of the Endangered American Wilderness Act were in his district, Representative Les AuCoin (D-OR) voted against the bill, a decision that enraged the conservation community. Even his counterpart, Representative Robert ("Sawdust Bob") Duncan (D-OR) voted for the bill. In a lame attempt at political mitigation later that year, AuCoin pushed through a 496-acre addition (consisting of a few score of small coastal islands) to the renamed Oregon Islands Wilderness.

Additional Wilderness boundary tinkering occurred in 1978 when the Hells Canyon Wilderness boundary was moved inward to accommodate the Hells Canyon Rim Road. Senator Bob Packwood initially opposed the effort, but he eventually caved into the wishes of local Representative Al Ullman. Hatfield also supported the move.

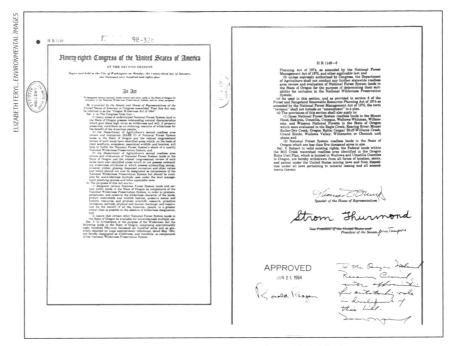

It's not just a piece of paper, but the strongest protection any society has provided wildlands.

The Oregon (Forest) Wilderness Act

A driving force behind the introduction and passage of the Endangered American Wilderness Act was the political fallout from the U.S. Forest Service's Roadless Area Review and Evaluation (RARE) process, initiated by the Forest Service in 1972 to identify roadless areas on Forest Service land that qualify for Wilderness protection. Although the Forest Service had invented "wilderness" protection in the 1930s, by 1972 the agency strongly opposed it, preferring total discretion to build roads and log wherever it wanted. Consequently the RARE process was sloppy and intentionally overlooked millions of acres of qualifying roadless lands.

In 1977, the Carter Administration, responding to concerns about RARE raised during congressional consideration of the Endangered American Wilderness Act, ordered the Forest Service to again review de facto wilderness lands (all roadless areas larger than 5,000 acres and roadless areas of any size bordering a designated Wilderness area) and make recommendations to Congress. "RARE II" began with good intentions, but in the end was co-opted by the timber-dominated agency again. Out of the 2.9 million acres reviewed in Oregon, the Forest Service recommended only 415,000 acres for Wilderness protection. Another 300,000 acres were designated for "further study" to determine whether they should be recommended for Wilderness protection.

The remaining 2.3 million acres were designated "non-Wilderness," to be left open to roading and logging.

In 1978, Democratic Governor Bob Straub went on record favoring 750,000 acres of new Wilderness in Oregon. No Oregon governor — before or since — has recommended so much land for Wilderness protection. Unfortunately, Straub lost his re-election bid to Republican Vic Atiyeh in 1978. When Atiyeh took office, the state's recommendation for new Wilderness designations dropped to 60,000 acres. Atiyeh later thought that was too much.

In 1979, Senator Hatfield promptly responded to the Forest Service's RARE II recommendations by introducing and passing a bill (S. 2031) in the Senate that would have granted Wilderness status to 451,000 acres. While most of the acreage to be protected overlapped with the Forest Service's recommendations for Wilderness, some areas that were recommended by the agency and/or later by the Carter administration never made it into the Wilderness System. The areas omitted include:

- National forest roadless lands (totaling 30,530 acres in six units) adjacent to Crater Lake National Park in the proposed South Cascades and North Umpqua Wildernesses. (Hatfield later expanded the park boundary to include most of these areas.)

- Umpqua Spit (2,370 acres) in the proposed Oregon Dunes Wilderness; and

- Limpy Rock (6,700 acres) in the proposed North Umpqua Wilderness.

The Senate bill died in the House in 1980.

No further congressional action was taken on Oregon Wilderness protection until late 1982. Though Senator Hatfield and Representative Weaver agreed on numerous areas to be designated as Wilderness, they vehemently disagreed about the remaining areas. The open hostility increased dramatically as their individual bills progressed through the dual chambers of Congress.

While half (and the most publicly visible part) of the debate over the Oregon Wilderness Act centered on which areas to designate as protected Wilderness, the other half concerned the fate of the roadless areas not to be protected. The timber industry favored "release" language for areas not slated for Wilderness protection, which would have precluded the areas from ever being considered by the Forest Service for Wilderness again, as was then required by the law. Of course, conservationists opposed releasing any areas from the legal requirements that compel the Forest Service to periodically consider roadless areas for Wilderness and make such recommendations to Congress.

Although Representative Weaver represented the top ranked congressional district for timber production in the nation, he was a strong and tireless proponent of Wilderness. To help frame the wilderness versus timber debate, Weaver stated he

ELIZABETH FERYL, ENVIRONMENTAL IMAGES

Representative Jim Weaver (1975-1986, D-4th District) was the greatest Wilderness advocate (so far) to represent Oregon in the U.S. House of Representatives.

would not support a Wilderness bill that affected more than 2 percent of Oregon's timber supply. Even Weaver was surprised when Oregon conservationists complied by proposing legislation that would have established 1.9 million acres of Wilderness. While only two percent of Oregon's timber supply, the proposal still contained too many acres and board feet for those political times.

To force Congress into action, in late 1982, Oregon Natural Resources Council, National Audubon Society and other conservation organizations threatened to file a lawsuit to prevent the further development of Oregon's national forest roadless areas without preparation of an adequate environmental impact statement for RARE II. The state of California had recently won a similar lawsuit, so it was a slam-dunk case. Like the California case, the (threat of) Oregon litigation was opposed by the Sierra Club and Wilderness Society, who feared a political backlash resulting in the wholesale "release" of roadless areas to development. ONRC was more concerned about nature's backlash, as the areas in question were already being roaded and logged as if they had already been formally "released."

By this time, a new guard of wilderness activists had begun to focus their attention on the importance of Wilderness to protect old-growth forests. The previous generation of activists had generally not advocated for Wilderness areas that included big trees. French Pete was an exception, where big trees had once been protected as part of administratively designated "wilderness," only to be later removed from "wilderness" protection. Logging of heavily timbered roadless areas bothered the new guard. The old guard was more concerned with designating the generally larger, less-timbered, higher-elevation areas. The old guard didn't want to litigate over RARE II; the new guard did.

Also by this time, the timber industry was becoming annoyed that Wilderness legislation was beginning to include significant areas of old-growth forest, rather than the predominantly non-commercial forests or high elevation areas of "rock and ice" that had been periodically doled out to mollify earlier generations of conservationists. Timber country politics were starting to change.

Meanwhile, conservationists were beginning to reframe how Wilderness was perceived, changing the emphasis from a vision of pristine backcountry recreation areas to a consideration of important watersheds containing critical fish and wildlife habitat. The Cummins Creek and Rock Creek Wilderness areas — for example — were probably the first national forest lands designated as Wilderness that at the time did not contain one foot of official Forest Service hiking trail.

During the post-election "lame duck" Congressional session in December 1982, Representative Weaver used the threat of the RARE II litigation to push another Wilderness bill in the House (H.R. 7340). It would have designated 1,118,875 acres of Wilderness and Wilderness Study Areas in Oregon. Though it received a clear majority during House consideration, it had to be brought to the floor under a "suspension of the rules." This meant the bill as presented could not be amended and a two-thirds majority was required for passage. The bill lost with 247 yays and 141 nays.

The bitter division among the Oregon congressional delegation continued throughout 1983. The conservation community remained split over whether or not to file the highly meritorious, but politically problematic RARE II lawsuit. Weaver's failed Wilderness bill, H.R. 7340 of the 97th Congress, was resurrected as H.R. 1149 in the 98th Congress. It passed the House easily in March 1983 and included about 10,000 more acres than H.R. 7340. Had the Senate passed by the House bill, it would have resulted in an additional 1,128,375 acres of Oregon Wilderness.

Weaver led the House effort for Oregon Wilderness in the early 1980s, but Representatives Les AuCoin and Ron Wyden (Oregon Democrats) also played important roles. Weaver can be credited with the 1983 House bill having as much acreage as it did, and it passed the House thanks to AuCoin's leadership. That the North Fork John Day, Salmon-Huckleberry and Badger Creek areas were as large as they were, and that Table Rock was included in the bill at all, are due to Wyden's leadership.

After passing the House, H.R. 1149 went to the Senate where it languished for the rest of 1983. In December of that year, the long-threatened RARE II lawsuit against the Forest Service was filed. The suit successfully prevented the Reagan administration from building roads and logging in the 2.2 million acres of Oregon national forest lands recommended for "non-Wilderness." It also forced Hatfield to finally act on Wilderness legislation. Hatfield passed a modified and diminished version of H.R. 1149 totaling 780,500 acres through the Senate Committee on Energy and Natural

Resources. His bill also included "soft release" of lands categorized as "non-Wilderness." "Soft release" differed from the timber industry's hoped for "hard release," by theoretically requiring future agency consideration of these lands for Wilderness in ten to fifteen years.

The Oregon congressional delegation soon reached a compromise and amended H.R. 1149 (later known as the Oregon Wilderness Act of 1984) so that the final version added 861,500 acres of Wilderness in Oregon. This broke the "logjam" and culminated in the enactment of numerous other state Wilderness bills in 1984.

Table 3-1 depicts the evolution of the Oregon Wilderness Act of 1984. The size of some areas was never controversial. (Minor changes in acreage depicted in the table were either recalculations or mapping refinements.) Some areas became smaller during the legislative negotiation process in response to new roads and clearcuts. Other areas didn't make it into the final bill at all, while still others were added late in the process. Congressman Les AuCoin supported H.R. 1149 in the House but insisted that no Wilderness be designated in his congressional district. Despite AuCoin's objections, the final version of the bill included the old-growth rich Drift Creek Wilderness.

The Oregon Wilderness Act of 1984 added the first extensive stands of Oregon old-growth forest to the Wilderness System. In addition to Drift Creek, these included the Middle Santiam, Waldo Lake, Rock Creek, Salmon-Huckleberry, Cummins Creek, Bridge Creek, Black Canyon, Badger Creek, Bull-of-the-Woods, Boulder Creek, Mill Creek, Grassy Knob, Monument Rock, North Fork John Day, North Fork Umatilla and Rogue-Umpqua Divide Wildernesses. The bill also designated Oregon's first forest Wilderness of less than 5,000 acres in size, the Menagerie Wilderness. The bill included Oregon's first BLM-administered Wilderness, the Table Rock Wilderness. (The Wild Rogue Wilderness also includes BLM lands, but is administered by the Forest Service.)

In addition, previously unprotected lengths of the Cascade crest were finally protected in the Columbia, Mount Thielsen and Sky Lakes Wildernesses. The Diamond Peak, Mt. Jefferson, Mount Washington and Three Sisters Wildernesses along the Cascade crest were also "widened" to include lower elevation and more diverse forestlands, as was the Strawberry Mountain Wilderness.

Finally, some more "classic" Wilderness (small in size, high elevation and/or few trees) was protected in the Red Buttes Wilderness and the Gearhart Mountain and Hells Canyon Wilderness additions.

By 1984 a pattern had become evident in Oregon wilderness politics. Each year that Senator Mark Hatfield was up for re-election, he found time to push through Wilderness bills. When the dust finally settled in 1984, Congress had created 21 new Wilderness areas in Oregon, increased the size of eight others and restored some of the wildlands removed from the Eagle Cap Wilderness in 1972.

Table 3-1. Evolution of the Oregon Wilderness Act of 1984

Wilderness Proposal	Notes	S. 2031 Nov. 79 (Passed Senate)	H.R. 7340 Dec. 82 (Failed House*)	H.R. 1149 Mar. 83 (Passed House)	H.R.1149 May 84 (Passed Senate)	P.L. 98-328 Jun. 84 (Enacted Into Law)
Salmon-Huckleberry	1	8,300	55,000	55,000	44,600	44,600
Bull-of-the-Woods	2	26,700	47,000	47,000	34,900	34,900
Columbia (now Mark O. Hatfield)	3	40,900	40,900	40,900	39,000	39,000
Badger Creek		14,000	27,000	25,000	23,500	24,000
Black Canyon	4	13,400	13,400	13,400	13,400	13,400
Bridge Creek		6,325	7,100	7,100	5,400	5,400
Coleman Rim		7,825	7,825	7,825	-	-
Rock Creek	5	6,500	6,500	6,500	7,400	7,400
Boulder Creek		19,820	19,820	19,820	19,100	19,100
North Fork John Day		65,000	205,000	218,000	121,300	121,400
Sky Lakes		113,000	113,000	113,000	116,300	116,300
Mill Creek		14,400	14,400	17,400	17,400	17,400
Mount Washington Additions		6,000	6,000	6,000	6,400	6,400
Diamond Peak Additions	6	8,200	-	-	-	15,700
Diamond-Thielsen	6	-	155,000	154,000	-	-
Mt. Thielsen	6	-	-	-	-	55,100
Three Sisters Additions		27,300	36,000	36,000	38,100	38,100
Gearhart Mountain Additions		3,730	3,730	3,730	4,100	4,100
Strawberry Mountain Additions		35,100	35,100	35,100	35,300	35,300
Eagle Cap Additions		34,300	34,300	67,000	67,500	66,500
Middle Santiam		-	20,000	19,800	7,500	7,500
Cummins Creek		-	8,800	8,800	9,300	9,300
Rogue-Umpqua Divide		-	55,000	54,000	33,200	33,200
Grassy Knob	7	-	22,000	21,500	7,700	17,200
Red Buttes	7	-	26,000	25,000	3,800	3,400
Joseph Canyon	7	-	31,000	31,000	-	-
Mt. Jefferson Additions		-	13,500	13,000	6,800	6,800
Mountain Lakes Additions		-	3,000	3,000	-	-
Waldo Lake	8	-	65,000	-	39,200	39,200
Hardesty Mountain	7,8	-	7,500	7,000	-	-
North Fork Umatilla		-	-	18,000	22,200	22,200
Glacier-Monument	9	-	-	49,000	-	-
Glacier Mountain	9	-	-	-	18,300	-
Monument Rock	9	-	-	-	-	19,800
Table Rock	10	-	-	5,500	5,500	5,500
Drift Creek		-	-	-	5,800	5,800
Old Cascades	11	-	40,000	-	-	-
Menagerie	11	-	-	-	4800	4800
Hells Canyon Additions		-	-	-	22700	22700
TOTAL (Wilderness & Wilderness Study Area)	**12**	**450,800**	**1,118,875**	**1,128,375**	**780,500**	**861,500**

* This bill was considered under "suspension of the rules," meaning that no amendments could be offered and that it had to pass by a two-thirds majority. The vote was 247-141.

1. Named "Salmon Butte" Wilderness in S. 2031.

2. Named "Hidden Wilderness" in H.R. 7340 and H.R. 1149 (House version). The final Bull-of-the-Woods Wilderness did not include the Opal Creek area, which later became the Opal Creek Wilderness in 1996.

3. Named "Columbia Gorge" Wilderness in H.R. 7340 and H.R. 1149 (House version).

4. Named "Ochoco Canyon" Wilderness in H.R. 7340 and H.R. 1149 (House version).

5. Named "Oregon Coast" Wilderness in S. 2031.

6. S. 2031 designated this area part of a 133,950-acre "Oregon Cascades Conservation Area," a Hatfield alternative to Wilderness (neither Wilderness, nor clearcut, but "wilderness lite"). H.R. 7340 and H.R. 1149 included 155,000-acre and 154,000-acre, respectively, "Diamond-Thielsen" Wilderness which would have incorporated existing Diamond-Peak Wilderness (acreage does not include existing Wilderness).

7. Also included Bureau of Land Management holdings.

8. Included as a Wilderness Study Area in H.R. 7340

9. H.R. 1149 (House version) included a two-unit "Glacier-Monument" Wilderness; H.R. 1149 (Senate version) included Glacier Mountain Wilderness of 18,300 acres.

10. Bureau of Land Management holdings.

11. H.R. 7340 included a Wilderness Study Area of 40,000 acres, containing the Echo Mountain, Gordon Meadows and Menagerie (a.k.a. Rooster Rock) units.

12. Included an additional "Oregon Cascades Recreation Area" ("wilderness lite") of 51,488 acres (not totaled).

S. 2031, 96th Congress, 1st Session (1979), sponsored by Sen. Hatfield

H.R. 7340, 97th Congress, 2nd Session (1982), sponsored by Reps. Weaver, AuCoin and Wyden

H.R. 1149, 98th Congress, 1st Session (1983), sponsored by Reps. Weaver, AuCoin and Wyden

H.R. 1149, 98th Congress, 2nd Session (1984), modified by Sen. Hatfield

P.L. 98-328, 98th Congress, 2nd Session (1984), signed by President Reagan

Wilderness Designations on Hold

After passage of the Oregon Wilderness Act, Hatfield was so politically exhausted that he said he never wanted to confront the issue again. In June of 1984, I found myself on a red-eye flight to Washington, D.C., with the Senator. While changing planes in Chicago at 5:00 a.m., the sleep-deprived Senator asked the sleep-deprived ONRC staffer why he was going to Washington, D.C.

"To work on your timber bailout bill, sir," I cheerfully replied.

"You mean the Federal Timber Purchaser Contract Payment Modification Act," the Senator replied somewhat sternly.

Timber purchasers, in what would later be known as "irrational exuberance" had bid up timber sale prices to levels well beyond their market value. So they were subsequently seeking regulatory relief from Congress to let them off the hook. "Your bill would void some very damaging timber sales in roadless areas, which means conservationists have another shot at designating them as Wilderness someday," I commented with less cheerfulness.

"There are no more roadless areas," said Hatfield in a slightly more patronizing tone.

"Yes, Senator, I know that as a matter of *law* Forest Service roadless areas won't have to be considered again for Wilderness for a long time, but…"

"Andy, there are *no* more roadless areas," he interrupted, even more patronizingly.

"… but as a matter of *fact* there are still areas without roads, so…"

"Andy, I will never ever do another Wilderness bill. This is the last one," Hatfield said with nary a tone of patronization, but with a heavy note of finality.

The godfather of Oregon politics was saying that he would never grant another wish to wilderness advocates. Each year Hatfield had run for re-election (in 1972, 1978 and 1984) he had helped enact exponentially larger Wilderness bills into law. However, Hatfield was now saying in 1984, "no-way" to more Wilderness in 1990. This represented potentially a huge loss for Oregon forest conservation.

With the door to future Wilderness legislation closed by Hatfield, the conservation community was forced to consider other means to slow the destruction of de facto wilderness and other stands of old-growth forest. Thus Hatfield was instrumental in prompting conservationists to seek alternate strategies to save forestland, including safeguarding habitat for spotted owls, marbled murrelets, Pacific salmon and other residents of the old-growth forest. Ironically — and most fortunately — the resultant habitat protection for sensitive fish and wildlife led to far fewer trees being cut than would have likely occurred under conservationists' most optimistic Wilderness scenarios. (That, however, is another book.)

Almost a Thaw

When Senator Bob Packwood sought re-election in 1986, he faced a challenge by Congressman Jim Weaver, the staunch Wilderness supporter. However, running statewide, Weaver had no chance of winning the office. Nonetheless, Packwood wanted to leave nothing to chance and conceived of a victory strategy that sought to win or at least split the environmental vote.

To gain at least some conservationists' support for his re-election bid, Packwood introduced legislation for a 300,000-acre addition to the Hells Canyon Wilderness. Hatfield supported the legislation, despite his recent vow not to become involved in another Wilderness bill. When Weaver dropped out of the race in August and was replaced by a state legislator whose idea of a campaign was to walk from Ashland to Mount Hood, Hatfield correctly perceived no risk to his fellow Republican's re-election and reneged on the 300,000-acre Wilderness deal.

Unfinished Legacy and Even More Oregon Islands

The political polarization and controversy that erupted in the late 1980s around the spotted owl and ancient forests barred any consideration of Oregon Wilderness legislation in 1990, despite the fact that Hatfield was running for re-election. But as Hatfield's last term wound down in 1996, he decided to complete some unfinished business: Opal Creek. Hatfield had tried without success to protect the area in previous legislative efforts. For years conservationists had agitated to save Opal Creek, including making it a state park. By 1990 Opal Creek was a household word in Oregon politics. In late 1994, Oregon Democratic Representative Mike Kopetski pushed Opal Creek Wilderness legislation through the House of Representatives. Although time was rapidly running out on the congressional session, Hatfield had enough time to act, if he wanted to. On November 20, over 4,000 Oregonians rallied at Pioneer Square in Portland to pressure Hatfield into supporting the bill. ONRC also rented the most visible billboard in Oregon (I-5 at OR 217) to post a simple message: "Save Opal Creek. Call Senator Hatfield. 221-3326." Cell phones had become widespread, so motorists stuck in Portland area traffic, keyed in the number and registered their opinion. Hatfield's office telephone lines were jammed for weeks. Still, the Senator claimed there wasn't enough time to introduce a bill and that he'd take up the matter the next Congress (after Kopetski had retired).

In 1996, as he was preparing to leave after thirty years in office, Hatfield did finally save Opal Creek. It still came down to the last minute, with Hatfield tacking the Opal Creek Wilderness legislation onto a must-pass defense appropriations bill. In

Former U.S. Senator Bob Packwood in 2001 at Buckhorn Springs in the Hells Canyon National Recreation Area.

U.S. Senators Mark Hatfield and Bob Packwood

No two people have had more effect on Oregon's wilderness than Mark Hatfield and Bob Packwood, if only because of the timing and duration of their careers in the U.S. Senate (1967-1996 and 1968-1999, respectively).

Packwood believed that roadless areas were de facto wilderness; just as wild, just as natural and just as important as congressionally designated Wilderness. Hatfield believed in the "creationist" theory of wilderness: it wasn't wilderness until Congress designated it so.

Packwood started his Senate career as very pro-environment. He spoke at the first Earth Day in 1970. However, the longer he was in the Senate, the less of a wilderness supporter Packwood became. He felt — somewhat understandably — that he'd never get the political support of the conservation community. When Packwood first ran for the Senate in 1968, the then-small conservation community backed Senator Wayne Morse, more because he was a Democrat and an incumbent than for any environmental record of accomplishment. In 1974, 1980 and 1986, Packwood's Democratic challengers were state legislators with excellent environmental voting records. In 1974 Packwood was so offended by a co-endorsement from the Oregon League of Environmental Voters (now the Oregon League of Conservation Voters) that the League made sure not to repeat the mistake again. In 1980, the League gave its sole endorsement to then state Senator Ted

Kulongoski, who lost his challenge to Packwood. In 1986, Rep. Jim Weaver, who had far better environmental credentials than Packwood, challenged him for his seat, but then failed to finish the race. Packwood felt that environmentalists were always biased toward Democrats, no matter what a Republican's voting record. That contention was reinforced in the 1986 governor's race when most environmentalists backed the Democratic — but markedly un-green — Neil Goldschmidt over the markedly green — but Republican — Norma Paulus.

Packwood was a consummate political opportunist. His national League of Conservation Voters scorecard rating (for "green" votes) oscillated between percentages in the mid-20s and mid-80s. His ratings consistently peaked in re-election years and then plummeted the next, before creeping upward as the next election approached.

In a farewell address to the Senate (after being forced out when some indescretions became known), Packwood said the legislation he was most proud of passing was that which saved Hells Canyon. Too often, it is only after politicians leave the stage that they can see clearly and speak freely.

Senator Mark O. Hatfield proudly claimed that more Oregon acreage was protected as Wilderness during his three decades in Congress than any other time. However, far more wildlands were destroyed by his successful funding of roads and timber sales during his tenure on the Senate Appropriations Committee.

Hatfield's view of wilderness prevented him from understanding why conservationists so adamantly objected to the obscenely high funding of federal road and logging budgets passed during his tenure on the Senate Appropriations Committee. Hatfield later said, with apparent pride, that it was during his time in the Senate that the most Wildernesses in Oregon had been "created." (The correct word is "established.") Considering that Hatfield arrived in the Senate two years after the Wilderness Act passed and was re-elected for 30 years thereafter, this isn't that remarkable of an accomplishment. And he has never been heard to brag that far more de facto wilderness and old-growth forest was also roaded and clearcut during his tenure than that of any other Oregon senator.

Hatfield, like most Republicans who run for statewide office in Oregon, was "liberal" on at least one major issue. He usually opposed war on Earth. But his relentless funding of roads and clearcuts meant that he was usually at war with the Earth. As Hatfield was leaving office in 1996, his colleagues renamed the Columbia Wilderness the Mark O. Hatfield Wilderness. (The Senate also named the new federal courthouse in Portland after Hatfield, a man who several times sought to bar the courthouse door to citizens in order to allow logging of Oregon's forested wildlands and old-growth forests.) Hatfield never had any real love for wilderness. It was politically expedient for him only to support Wilderness when seeking re-election or to polish his tarnished environmental legacy.

addition, he added more islands to the Oregon Islands Wilderness. In the haste and confusion of the concluding Congress, the body actually passed the bill twice, enacting identical language in a separate piece of legislation.

Never had an area taken so long or required such dogged advocacy to save as Wilderness. Opal Creek first became an issue in the early 1970s. The proposed "Hidden Wilderness," which included Opal Creek, was approved by the Senate as a Wilderness Study Area in 1977 and was designated a Wilderness by the House in 1983, but was not included in the Oregon Wilderness Act of 1984. Over the years the Forest Service attempted numerous timber sales in the area, but was always beaten back. Partly to fulfill his commitment to unfinished business, and partly as an attempt to mitigate his legacy of forest clearcuts, Hatfield did at last succeed in pushing Opal Creek protection through Congress in 1996.

Oregon's First Desert Wilderness

Oregon's first mostly non-forested desert Wilderness is the Steens Mountain Wilderness, designated in 2000. With not one but two political "guns to the head," local cattle barons willingly supported establishing Steens Mountain Wilderness. One gun, loaded with ammunition in the form of the Wild and Scenic Rivers Act of 1968, was wielded by a U.S. District Court judge in Portland. A pending lawsuit was likely to rule that livestock grazing was illegal within the Donner und Blitzen Wild and Scenic River corridor. The second political gun, loaded with the Antiquities Act of 1906, was being waved menacingly by Secretary of the Interior Bruce Babbitt, who threatened the cattle barons with the prospect that President Clinton might proclaim the area a national monument. Fortunately, the cattle barons' worst fears of a Clintonian national monument were far greater than the conservationists' best hopes.

Senator Wyden and Representatives Earl Blumenauer (D-OR), Peter DeFazio (D-OR) and Greg Walden (R-OR) deserve the most credit among members of the Oregon congressional delegation who unanimously supported the final legislation. In politics, one never questions — but always should understand — the motives of someone who is voting your way. The personal wishes of the cattle barons and the political circumstances of the times resulted in a very reluctant Republican, Rep. Greg Walden, being responsible for creating the nation's first legislatively mandated livestock-free Wilderness Area. ◆

Notes

[1] Browning, Peter (compiler, ed.). 1988. JOHN MUIR IN HIS OWN WORDS: A BOOK OF QUOTATIONS. Great West Books. Lafayette, CA: 52 (originally published in John Muir, JOHN OF THE MOUNTAINS, IN 1895).

[2] Dombeck, Mike. Forest Service Chief letter to all Forest Service employees re. conservation leadership (July 1, 1999).

[3] Dombeck, Mike. 2001. Roadless Area Conservation: an Investment in Future Generation (statement). (Jan. 5, 2001) (unpaginated). Available at roadless.fs.us/documents/rule/dombeck_stmt.htm.

[4] Ibid.

[5] Meehan, Brian T. An Oregon century: the promise of Eden. The Oregonian (Dec. 19, 1999): A14 (Judge Waldo was quoted in 1896).

[6] LaLande, Jeff. 1989. A wilderness journey with Judge John B. Waldo, Oregon's first preservationist. Oregon Historical Quarterly 90(2): 155.

[7] LaLande, Jeff. 1989. A wilderness journey with Judge John B. Waldo, Oregon's first preservationist. Oregon Historical Quarterly 90(2): 155

[8] Mortenson, Eric. Writings of Judge Waldo. Eugene Register-Guard (Aug. 9, 1987): B1.

[9] LaLande, Jeff. 1989. A wilderness journey with Judge John B. Waldo, Oregon's first preservationist. Oregon Historical Quarterly 90(2): 157.

[10] LaLande, Jeff. 1989. A wilderness journey with Judge John B. Waldo, Oregon's first preservationist. Oregon Historical Quarterly 90(2): 159.

[11] Mortenson, Eric. Writings of Judge Waldo. Eugene Register-Guard (Aug. 9, 1987): B1.

[12] LaLande, Jeff. 1989. A wilderness journey with Judge John B. Waldo, Oregon's first preservationist. Oregon Historical Quarterly 90(2): 165 (note 60).

[13] Foreman, Dave. 1999. Around the Campfire: "Will-of-the-land." Wild Earth 9(2): 4.

[14] The Wilderness Act, 16 U.S.C. 1131(a).

[15] The Wilderness Act, 16 U.S.C. 1131(a).

[16] Browning, Peter (compiler, ed.). 1988. JOHN MUIR IN HIS OWN WORDS: A BOOK OF QUOTATIONS. Great West Books. Lafayette, CA: 65-66 (Originally published in John Muir, Cathedral Peak and the Tuolumne Meadows, Sierra Club Bulletin, Jan. 2, 1911).

[17] The Wilderness Act, 16 U.S.C. 1131(c).

[18] The Wilderness Act, 16 U.S.C. 1131(c).

[19] The Wilderness Act, 16 U.S.C. 1133(b).

[20] The Wilderness Act, 16 U.S.C. 1133(c).

[21] Frome, Michael. 1997. BATTLE FOR THE WILDERNESS. Rev. ed. University of Utah Press. Salt Lake City, Utah: l-li.

[22] Neuberger, Richard. 1988. THEY NEVER GO BACK TO POCATELLO: SELECTED ESSAYS OF RICHARD NEUBERGER. Steve Neal (ed.). Oregon Historical Society Press. Portland, OR: 66-67 (appearing in "Guarding our Outdoor Heritage," first published in The Progressive, January 1959).

A Brief Political Future for Oregon's Forest Wilderness

Why Wilderness?

Without enough wilderness America will change. Democracy…must be fibred and vitalized by regular contact with outdoor growths – animals, trees, sun warmth and free skies – or it will dwindle and pale.

–Walt Whitman[1]

Our village life would stagnate if it were not for the unexplored forests and meadows which surround it. We need the tonic of wildness – to wade sometimes in marshes where the bittern and the meadow-hen lurk, and hear the booming of the snipe; to smell the whispering sedge where only some wilder and more solitary fowl builds her nest, and the mink crawls with its belly close to the ground. At the same time that we are earnest to explore and learn all things, we require that all things be mysterious and unexplorable, that land and sea be infinitely wild, unsurveyed and unfathomable. We can never have enough of nature. We must be refreshed by the sight of inexhaustible vigor, vast and titanic ventures, the sea-coast with its wrecks, the wilderness with its living and its decaying trees, the thunder-clouds, and the rain which lasts three weeks and produces freshets. We need to witness our limits transgressed, and some life pasturing where we never wander. We are cheered when we observe the vulture feeding on the carrion which disgust and disheartens us, and deriving health and strength from the repast.

–Henry David Thoreau[2]

Why wilderness? Why the hell not wilderness!? As Edward Abbey proclaimed, "The idea of wilderness needs no defense. It only needs more defenders."[3] Unfortunately, the default setting of our Western society is that nature does not have intrinsic or practical value unless we can dig it up, cut it down, graze it off, plow it under, drain it dry, make it wet or haul it away. Even wilderness defenders need information and arguments with which to persuade an increasingly on-line – but out of touch – public about the importance of and threats to wilderness. As social philosopher Lewis Mumford wrote:

When we rally to preserve the remaining redwood forests or to protect the whooping crane, we are rallying to preserve ourselves, we are trying to keep in existence the organic variety, the whole span of natural resources upon which our own future development will be based. If we surrender this variety too easily in one place, we shall lose it everywhere; and we shall find ourselves enclosed in a technological vision without even the hope that sustains a prisoner in jail – that someday we may get out. Should organic variety disappear, there will be no "out."[4]

Abbey argued in *Desert Solitaire* that:

No, wilderness is not a luxury but a necessity, and as vital to our lives as water and good bread. A civilization which destroys what little remains of the wild, the sparse, the original, is cutting itself off from its origins and betraying the principle of civilization itself.[5]

What is wilderness? A standard dictionary definition is rather complex:

1a(1): a tract or region uncultivated and uninhabited by human beings.
1a(2): an area essentially undisturbed by human activity together with its naturally developed life community.
1b: an empty or pathless area or region
1c: a part of a garden devoted to wild growth.
2: wild or uncultivated state.
3a: a confusing multitude or mass
3b: a bewildering situation.[6]

When many Americans think about wilderness, the first thing that comes to mind is recreation. Visitors to designated Wilderness can hike, ride a horse, raft, canoe, hunt, fish, appreciate wildlife and wildflowers, take pictures, perform non-disturbing scientific research, make love, swim and camp. However, while recreation (consider the composition of this word: "re-creation") is reason enough to save wilderness, there are many, even more compelling arguments for protecting wildlands.

Some commentators consider wilderness in terms of either anthropocentric or biocentric values. America's first wilderness advocates may have had an intrinsic appreciation of the biological values of wilderness, but often tailored their appeals to the American public and political establishment on the aesthetics of wilderness.

Wilderness areas are reservoirs of natural biodiversity, home to plants and animals that may be of great scientific and medical use to humans. Wilderness areas leave room for the fires, floods and other natural disturbances and processes that fuel evolution and support the whole web of life. Wilderness provides goods and services to our economy without cost.

Wilderness areas are refuges for fish and wildlife. Yellowstone National Park (most of which is still de facto wilderness) was originally preserved as a "pleasuring ground" for people because the geothermal features amused tourists. No one knew in 1872 that creating the park would later become the only reason that the United States still has wild bison and grizzly bears.

Some commercial uses occur (but shouldn't) in designated Wilderness areas. The Wilderness Act prohibits the use of all-terrain vehicles, mountain bikes or jet skis, road building, logging and development of oil, gas and geothermal energy. However, one can (but shouldn't be able to) graze livestock, maintain fences and irrigation ditches, exploit a valid mining claim, or patent (transfer to private ownership) a mining claim for $2.50 to $5.00 an acre in Wilderness. One might even be able to build a new water project, but only with Presidential approval. (However, no approval has ever been granted under this exception.)

Designating Wilderness areas actually saves taxpayers money, because wilderness-destroying activities have only ever been and can only ever be profitably exploited by those who are subsidized by the government to do so. Since these activities are prohibited in Wilderness, taxpayer subsidies to log and road these areas are not available.

The preservation of wilderness is also a rational hedge against ignorance. Nancy Newhall, who wrote *This is the American Earth* with Ansel Adams, said, "The wilderness holds answers to more questions than we yet know how to ask."[7] Until humans know everything, it makes no sense to discard any answers that wilderness may hold.

The World Wildlife Fund (WWF) and Conservation Biology Institute (CBI) recognized the ecological importance of large roadless areas (those 5,000 acres and greater) because they contain:

- *Relatively high levels of intact late-seral/old-growth forests;*

- *Essential habitat for many species of conservation concern (including threatened ones);*

- *Broad array of habitat types and elevation bands;*

- *"Buffer areas" from exotic species invasions and edge effects;*

Long sections of the Pacific Crest National Scenic Trail pass through wildlands that have no protection from logging and other development. ▶

• *Critical winter range for ungulates;*

• *Landscape and regional connectivity; and*

• *Aquatic strongholds for salmon.*[8]

WWF and CBI also note that small roadless areas (those 1,000 to 4,999 acres) are important for many of the same reasons as large roadless areas. They state that small roadless areas are:

• *Essential habitat for species key to the recovery of forests following disturbance such as herbaceous plants, lichens, and microrhizal fungi;*

• *Habitat refugia for threatened species and those with restricted distributions (endemics);*

• *Undisturbed habitats for mollusks and amphibians;*

• *Remaining pockets of old-growth forests;*

• *Over-wintering habitat for resident birds and ungulates;*

• *"Stepping stones" for wildlife movements across fragmented landscapes.*[9]

Small Wilderness

In short all available wild areas, large or small, are likely to have value as norms for land science. Recreation is not their only, or even their principal, utility.
— Aldo Leopold[10]

It is vitally important to protect the values of roadless areas 1,000 acres and larger from all activities that will harm their wild character.
—U.S. Representatives Earl Blumenauer,
Peter DeFazio, Darlene Hooley and David Wu[11]

Much of Oregon's remaining unprotected forest wilderness is between 1,000 and 4,999 acres in size. In eastern Oregon and Washington, 85 percent of all roadless federal forestlands occur in patches less than 5,000 acres.

In defining Wilderness for legislative purposes, Congress said that — in general — an area must be at least 5,000 acres, or "is of sufficient size as to make practicable its preservation and use in an unimpaired condition.")[12] However, since enacting the Wilderness Act in 1964, Congress has designated numerous small Wilderness areas. In Oregon, these include not only anomalies like the 17-acre Three Arch Rocks Wilderness just offshore of Oceanside, but also free-standing (not islands) areas like the 4,800-acre Menagerie Wilderness east of Sweet Home.

◄ Walking is not the only way to enjoy wilderness. Brice Creek Unit, proposed Upper Willamette Wilderness.

The anthropocentric (aesthetic and recreational) — biocentric (nature at her best) distinction should be taken into account when considering an area's size and suitability for Wilderness designation. Aldo Leopold, the great American ecologist and co-founder of The Wilderness Society, once defined a wilderness area as one sufficiently large enough for a two-week animal pack trip. In today's America, where there is more common understanding of horsepower than horses, there are very few such large wilderness areas left.

Bob Marshall, a great American forester and another co-founder of The Wilderness Society, also recognized the scientific values of small roadless areas:

The minimum area necessary for the maintenance of primeval conditions varies with forest type, climate and topography. In general the Forest Service believes that for scientific purposes 1,000 acres is about the smallest area desirable, in special cases where so much as 1,000 acres of virgin forest cannot be found the largest available area will have to be sufficient.[13]

As Michael Frome writes in his book *Battle for Wilderness*, another wilderness prophet also acknowledged the importance of small wildlands:

(Henry David) Thoreau foresaw man's need to reach out from the clatter of the mechanical age for a touch of the natural. He proposed that each community sustain a primitive forest of 500 or 1,000 acres. "Let us keep the New World new," he proposed, "and preserve the advantages of living in the country."[14] [Emphasis in original]

Marshall noted the limits of small areas for human recreation.

A tract of 1,000 acres, while well adapted for research is too small for satisfactory recreation. The person with a yearning for the beauties of the primeval wants to do more than just stroll into a virgin stand of timber and squat. He desires to be able to walk around in it for a considerable period, losing himself for a while in its timeless beauty, forgetting that there is such a thing as a machine-aged world. This is extremely difficult to do in 1,000 or even 5,000 acres.[15]

There is no doubt that the recreational utility of wilderness generally decreases in areas less than 5,000 acres (about eight square miles). If one hikes through a 1,000-acre roadless area, one may miss having an epic "wilderness" experience altogether, as one may look outward and see roads, clearcuts and other signs of human exploitation. There are, of course, exceptions — areas where the topography and grandeur of nature conspire to create a sense of solitude in spite of being small.

The Crabtree Valley Unit of the proposed Santiam Wilderness contains old-growth Douglas-fir and western redcedar perhaps 1,000 years old. The unit is 1,726 acres in size, or approximately equivalent to the area of Portland bounded by the Willamette River, East Burnside Street, SE 33rd Avenue and SE Powell Boulevard.

Small Wilderness areas also help perpetuate larger natural systems essential for fish and wildlife habitat, stream flow and clean drinking water. These are but some of the many modern scientific reasons to protect small roadless and wild areas. In a letter to President Clinton urging the protection of roadless areas, 136 scientists noted:

There is a growing consensus among academic and agency scientists that existing roadless areas — irrespective of size — contribute substantially to maintaining biodiversity and ecological integrity on the national forests. The Eastside Forests Scientific Societies Panel, including representatives from the American Fisheries Society, American Ornithologists' Union, Ecological Society of America, Society for Conservation Biology, and The Wildlife Society, recommended a prohibition on the construction of new roads and logging within existing (1) roadless regions larger than 1,000 acres, and (2) roadless regions smaller than 1,000 acres that are biologically significant.... Other scientists have also recommended protection of all roadless areas greater than 1,000 acres, at least until landscapes degraded by past management have recovered....

As you have acknowledged, a national policy prohibiting road building and other forms of development in roadless areas represents a major step towards balancing sustainable forest management with conserving environmental values on federal lands. In our view, a scientifically based policy for roadless areas on public lands should, at a minimum, protect from development all roadless areas larger than 1,000 acres and those smaller areas that have special ecological significance because of their contributions to regional landscapes.[16]

Wilderness Economics 101

It seems to be a law in American life that whatever enriches us anywhere except in the wallet inevitably becomes uneconomic.

—Russell Baker[17]

For unnumbered centuries of human history the wilderness has given way. The priority of industry has become dogma. Are we as yet sufficiently enlightened to realize that we must now challenge that dogma, or do without our wilderness? Do we realize that industry, which has been our good servant, might make a poor master?... Our remnants of wilderness will yield bigger values to the nation's character and health than they will to its pocketbook, and to destroy them will be to admit that the latter are the only values that interest us.

—Aldo Leopold[18]

We are rapidly building a world in which the questions of health and peace and prosperity sooner or later will be moot because we will have crippled the very engine of life that makes it all possible... The economy is a wholly owned subsidiary of the environment. All economic activity is dependent upon the environment with its underlying resource base. When the environment is finally forced to file under Chapter 11 because its resource base has been polluted, drained, cut down, dissipated, and irretrievably compromised, the economy goes down to bankruptcy with it. The economy, in reality, is just a subset of the ecological system.

—Senator Gaylord Nelson[19]

We could have saved the Earth but we were too damned cheap.

—Kurt Vonnegut[20]

"If you don't cut it, dig it, pick it or pump it, it is not real wealth," an old logger once growled. His thesis that all wealth comes from exploiting the earth conveniently ignores the vast wealth of goods and services provided both from human knowledge and by nature left unmolested. There is real, measurable economic value in fish and wildlife, clean water, clean air, new compounds for medicine and other goods and services that nature provides.

Expert scientists and economists have studied the value of "ecosystem services" —

Construction products need not all come from wood. Bagasse (sugar cane), wheat stalk, industrial hemp, corn stover, ryegrass straw and other agricultural fibers can be manufactured into boards and panels using non-toxic, bio-based binders.

nature's goods and services. One study, in the journal *Nature*, considered selected goods and services as the oceans' constant recycling of nutrients, pollination of domestic and wild crops by birds and insects, as well as the "air conditioning" and oxygen provided by wild plants. The economists estimated what it would cost humans to replace these essential goods and services. They calculated that ecosystem services provided by the earth's soil, forests, marshes, oceans and fish and wildlife species was worth $33 trillion ($33,000,000,000,000). For comparison, the "gross world product" was approximately $18 trillion (both 1996 dollars). Very conservatively, nature's good's and services to humankind are 1.8 times the value of humankind's economic output.

Among these services are medicinal plants. The value of such yet-to-be-discovered extracts from tropical forests is estimated at $147 billion. Over-the-counter medicines with plant extracts are estimated to be worth $84 billion annually.

Paclitaxel (a.k.a. Taxol®), an effective cancer-fighting compound, was originally discovered in the Pacific yew, a tree previously considered by most foresters to be a worthless "weed," of use only to cushion old-growth Douglas-firs as they were felled. The scientist who identified paclitaxel in the laboratory noted that the molecule is so complex that only a tree could have thought of it. Once scientists isolated paclitaxel, modern technology allowed the efficient synthesis of the molecule from other more common yew species. Once perceived to be a worthless tree, the Pacific yew became priceless.

While nature provides us with critically important ecosystem services, a market economy — for all its strengths — is poorly equipped to recognize them. For example, people value both cool and clean air. Cool air may be obtained by purchasing an air conditioner, but clean air cannot be bought in the marketplace (unless one considers the oxygen sold in vending machines on the polluted streets of Tokyo).

If an intact forest is privately owned, it is also difficult for the owner to capture, in traditional economic terms, the economic benefits of not logging it. The market does not usually credit forest owners for providing clean air and pure, cool water to the public. The private owner can only realize an economic return by cutting down the trees. Ironically, it usually costs society more to replace or mitigate the ecosystem services lost by logging a private forest than if the public had simply purchased the forest, or the timber rights, from the private interest.

However, even publicly owned forests have their problems. The perverse incentives of our federal forest system often cause public managers to log at the expense of the public trust to maximize their own budgets and bureaucratic fiefdoms. From both private and public forests, nature provides goods and services without charge, but she charges heavily when we abuse her.

Those who would deny Wilderness protection to Oregon's last wild forests often couch their arguments in economic terms. Their economic arguments, however, are selective, in that usually they only consider the economic value of logging, mining, grazing and other such activities. They conveniently forget that natural forests provide tangible economic values in the form of drinking water, tourism, recreation and commercial fishing.

Wilderness opponents also tend to consider only selected local — rather than regional or national — economic values. In some aspects, federally subsidized mining, logging, road-building and grazing may be considered economically beneficial on a local scale, as they create local jobs and income. However, these jobs come at the expense of other jobs and local and regional economic benefits from conserving nature. In any case, such subsidies are deadweight on the greater economy.

Economic arguments against forest Wilderness center on three topics: timber supply, jobs and profits.

Let's first consider the issue of *timber supply*.

- Roadless areas have proportionally less merchantable timber than do (or did) other public and private lands. That's often why they are still roadless — timber companies could not afford to exploit them.

- If domestic timber supplies are short, then ban the export of raw logs overseas.

- The timber industry's dependence on federal timber is minimal. Of the seventy-one sawmills remaining in western Oregon, only one receives more

ELIZABETH FERYL, ENVIRONMENTAL IMAGES

If Americans need the wood from federal forests as the timber industry says, why are they exporting overseas unprocessed logs from their own tree farms?

than two-thirds of its timber supply from federal lands. Only three are supplied with one-third to two-thirds of their logs from federal lands. Forty Oregon mills buy no federal logs.

- Most logging is to satisfy domestic needs for fiber, not "wood" per se. Fiber, which can be available from many other sources, is used to make construction materials, paper and a thousand other products. Our national policy ought to include obtaining most fiber from other, more ample and sustainable supplies, such as from farms (especially crop wastes now burned).

Now let's consider the *jobs* issue.

- Studies show proximity to Wilderness is economically beneficial to local communities.

- According to the Forest Service, if Oregon's 1.9 million acres of inventoried roadless areas were protected from logging, only 58 logging-related jobs would be lost. By this calculus, if the additional approximately 3.1 million acres of Oregon's uninventoried roadless areas were also protected as Wilderness, only 153 timber jobs would be lost.

- Wilderness, protected or unprotected, provides jobs in commercial, sport and

Top Dozen Reasons for Wilderness

12. Recreation. Wilderness is much more than a place for fun in the outdoors. Recreation is a fine, but far from the only, reason for Wilderness protection.

11. Ecosystem Goods and Services. More jobs, more wealth and more economic activity are generated by leaving forests standing than by cutting them down.

10. Medical Benefits. Every species has a complex and unique circuit of chemical reactions. Most medicines are based on compounds found in plants and animals. Humans haven't even classified all plant species on earth, let alone tested their potential for medical benefits. Wilderness is like a library — most people would choose not to burn down a library, especially if most of the books in it haven't been read yet. Preserving wilderness preserves species that preserve options that can preserve people.

9. Arrogance Insurance. Humans are engaged in a grand experiment of manipulating our environment. However, any valid science experiment must have a control with which to compare the experiment's results. Wilderness is a control for the massive and pervasive environmental changes we are imposing on ourselves.

8. Clean Air. Forests, especially older forests, absorb pollutants, including climate-altering carbon dioxide, and produce oxygen.

7. Drinking Water. According to the Forest Service, four-fifths of Oregonians get their drinking water from federal forest watersheds. It's some of the best water in the world.

6. Biodiversity Conservation. Many species cannot adapt to the highly manipulated and simplified landscapes that humans create. Wilderness itself is a landscape niche to which many species are uniquely adapted. Wilderness protection allows the continuation of ecological processes that support all life on earth.

5. Legacy for Future Generations. Preserving wilderness for future generations is natural estate planning.

4. Freedom. Wilderness offers an escape from daily assaults on our senses and psyches.

3. Humility. Wilderness reminds us that while humans are a very powerful species, we are certainly not the only species on earth and not omnipotent.

2. Re-creation. More than mere "recreation," wilderness is a source of spiritual renewal.

GEORGE WUERTHNER

Many hunters support Wilderness designation to protect both habitat and their recreational experience.

1. Hope. If you've read this far, no explanation is needed.

Wilderness is an anchor to windward. Knowing it is there, we can also know we are still a rich nation, tending to our resources as we should — not a people in despair searching every last nook and cranny of our land for a board of lumber, a barrel of oil, a blade of grass, or a tank of water.

—Senator Clinton Anderson (D-NM)
(principal sponsor of the first Wilderness bill)[22]

tribal fishing, guiding, hunting, birding and related industries. These jobs are sustainable, while logging old growth cannot be.

- Oregon's economy has diversified over the past decades, and the wood products industry is becoming increasingly inconsequential to the state's future. Only 1.9 percent of jobs in Oregon and Washington are in wood products.

- Automation in the woods and the mills has resulted in fewer workers needed to produce the same amount of wood products than a decade ago. Even fewer will be required a decade from now.

- Oregon counties with the most protected natural areas experience the most job and income growth.

- Ecological restoration can create new jobs in the woods, especially in replanted clearcuts:

> Done correctly, thinning younger [managed] stands can produce logs while at the same time enhancing ecological and conservation values by reducing susceptibility to fire and other disturbances, improving habitat for lichens, and structurally diversifying stands. In dry forest types we understand some judicious under-thinning of older forests, removing only trees that have established since fire exclusion, may be warranted to reduce fire hazard.[21]

Finally, let's consider the *profits* issue.

- Who earns the profits from logging federally owned forests? Absentee corporations or local communities? Are such profits limited to the current generation, or are they carried over to future generations? (Sustainable industries, such as fishing or guiding, could provide employment and income to local communities forever.)

- Often only a few make a fortune exploiting nature (such as timber company CEOs and stockholders), while the rest involved (local loggers) miss out. After a multi-national timber company has logged an area, it moves on (local timber companies just go out of business), while the local communities left behind suffer from the damage done to their landscape.

- Corporations maximize profit at the expense of jobs (employees always appear on the *cost* side of a corporate balance sheet). As timber supplies are depleted, jobs are quickly eliminated.

Most neoclassical economists believe that if the value of ecological protection and restoration cannot be assessed exactly in monetary terms, then it should not be counted at all. Although these economists will often admit that ecological protection and restoration are worth *something*, because the value is not easy to quantify, they usually set it at zero. By refusing to estimate an economic value for nature and instead pretending it to be zero, these economists choose to be precisely wrong on nature's worth, instead of estimating its value and being approximately correct.

Those who value nature above profit should attempt to assign a market value to nature — if only to defend it against devastating exploitation. If we don't, the default value of nature will be zero, rather than infinity (think *long*-term, beyond the time value of money), as it should be. The things that we value most — self, health, family and community — could be characterized as irrational economic investments in the capitalist system because the return on investment is too low or "incalcuable." Wouldn't it be better to improve the way society calculates and measures what it truly values? Wouldn't it be a shame to fail to save the Earth — and therefore ourselves — because too many economists consider nature inefficient (or difficult to price) and too many accountants regard investing in nature a poor return on capital?

Across the Landscape and Over Time[23]

> If we are going to whittle away at (significant landscapes), we should recognize, at the very beginning, that the whittlings are cumulative and the end result will be mediocrity.
> —Newton Drury, Director, National Park Service (1940-1951)[24]

This chapter could not be complete without a discussion of the necessity of conserving and restoring the web of life in general, and specifically in Oregon's forests. Scientists call it "biodiversity," shorthand for the term "biological diversity."

> Biodiversity is the variety of life and its processes. It includes the variety of living organisms, the genetic difference among them, the communities and ecosystems in which they occur, and the ecological and evolutionary processes that keep them functioning, yet ever changing and adapting.[25]

Conservation biology is a new branch of science created to address the critical need to end the human-caused mass extinction of species that is now underway and accelerating. Conservation biologists are developing guidelines that must be followed if humans are to leave room for nature. Briefly stated (and not surprisingly), these guidelines require that we stop destroying natural habitat and that critical habitat that has been destroyed be restored. By integrating scientific knowledge about habitat requirements with population dynamics, the effect of pollutants and other factors, conservation biologists have come to the conclusion that wilderness landscapes are the anchors of biodiversity. So much wilderness has already been lost that we must work to conserve every acre that remains and to restore a fair amount that has been degraded or destroyed. We must do so not only because we love wilderness emotionally and spiritually, but also because doing so is ecologically and economically imperative.

If the public wants the grizzly bear and the wolf to return, then we need Wilderness and lots of it. If we want wild salmon — not as museum pieces, but in abundance — we need Wilderness and lots of it. The spaces between Wilderness areas should also be better managed to maintain their role as corridors and links in the greater ecological and economic systems.

Dr. Reed Noss, a renowned ecologist who helped define the discipline of conservation biology, has described the ecological requirements of biodiversity conservation:

1. *Represent, in a system of protected areas, all native ecosystem types and seral (successional) stages across their natural range of variation.*

2. *Maintain viable populations of all native species in natural patterns of abundance and distribution.*

3. *Maintain ecological and evolutionary processes, such as disturbance regimes, hydrological processes, nutrient cycles, and biotic interactions, including predation.*

4. *Design and manage the system to be responsive to short-term and long-term environmental change and to maintain the evolutionary potential of lineages.*[26]

Representation of all ecosystem types means including both common and unique habitats, the lowest to the highest elevations, the wettest to the driest climates, all soil and geologic types, all vegetation types of all age classes and all possible combinations of the above.

Because an ecosystem is more than a collection of species — it is an *interconnection* of species — the health of each and every species is critical. Many species thrive without any special attention, but given our extensive alteration of virtually every ecosystem, some require our special attention. Wide-ranging carnivores, such as wolves, bears and wolverines, are excellent indicators of ecosystem health. Protect and restore an ecosystem or landscape to ensure the continued existence of these wide-ranging carnivores and many other species under the ecological umbrella will benefit as well.

Noss has prescribed additional guidelines for designating and protecting habitat:

1. *Species well distributed across their native range are less susceptible to extinction than species confined to small portions of their range.*

2. *Large blocks of habitat, containing large populations of a target species, are superior to small blocks of habitat containing small populations.*

DAVID STONE, WILDLAND PHOTOGRAPHY

A trail in the North Fork Smith River Unit of the proposed Coast Range Wilderness. ▶

3. Blocks of habitat closer together are better than blocks far apart.

4. Habitat in contiguous blocks is better than fragmented habitat.

5. Interconnected blocks of habitat are better than isolated blocks; corridors or linkages function better when habitat within them resembles that preferred by target species.

6. Blocks of habitat that are roadless or otherwise inaccessible to humans are better than roaded and accessible habitat blocks.[27]

We must preserve and restore large enough tracts of wild nature to allow ecological and evolutionary processes to function unfettered.

The practical application of the principles of conservation biology and landscape ecology requires consideration of three essential components, the three C's of conservation science and policy: cores, corridors and carnivores.

Cores are the heart of a conservation management system — the larger and more numerous, the better. They are of the highest quality habitat. Protecting core habitat is best achieved by designating large areas of Wilderness. This is why Congress needs to designate the larger roadless areas described in this book as part of the National Wilderness Preservation System.

To ensure the proper flow and dispersal of species individuals and populations between core areas, the system must be connected by *corridors*, ideally containing areas of high-quality habitat. This is best achieved by designating smaller Wilderness units (as identified in this book), wild and scenic rivers, as well as other similar protective classifications to connect larger wildlands or serve as stepping-stone habitats.

These cores and connectors must be buffered with restrictions on human activities that degrade natural values — with the most stringent restrictions applying to the actual cores and corridors, and with restraints becoming fewer the further away one is from the protected areas.

The third essential component is protection of umbrella species such as *carnivores*. As top predators, carnivores regulate ecosystems and are essential components of ecosystem health. Large carnivores have generally been extirpated from most ecosystems. Noss and his colleague Michael Soulé admonish us:

(M)any people are uncomfortable in proposing the reintroduction of large and politically troublesome carnivores. But this is no excuse. Timidity in conservation planning and implementation is a betrayal of the land. Even in the relatively populated regions like most of the eastern United States, the land cannot fully recover from past and present insults and mismanagement unless its bears, cougars, and wolves return. The greatest impediment to rewilding is an unwillingness to imagine it.[28]

The cornerstone of any landscape conservation strategy is identifying and conserving what is still wild. To this end, the Oregon Wild Forest Coalition has inventoried the remaining forest wildlands in Oregon and recommends them all for Wilderness designation.

Wilderness: Expanding Concept, Shrinking Supply

Friends at home! I charge you to spare, preserve and cherish some portion of your primitive forests; for when these are cut away I apprehend they will not be easily replaced.

—Horace Greeley, editor, *New York Tribune* (1851)[29]

We dare not let the last wilderness on earth go by our own hand, and hope that technology will somehow get us a new wilderness or some remote planet, or that somehow we can save little samples of genes in bottles or on ice, isolated and manageable, or reduce the great vistas to long-lasting video-tape, destroying the originals to sustain the balance of trade and egos.

—David Brower[30]

Limitations on party size, pack animals, camping sites and campfires have long been in effect to minimize human impacts on delicate environments in Wilderness areas. However, the Forest Service increasingly realizes that protecting the natural character of vegetation and soil alone will not adequately protect wilderness values. The agency is now considering limiting the actual number of visitors to protect another legally mandated wilderness value: solitude. If too many people are in the woods at once, even no-trace camping will not provide adequate protection for Wilderness.

Limits have been considered on visitors to Oregon's Mount Hood Wilderness and Washington's Alpine Lakes Wilderness, which are within easy reach of the Portland and Puget Sound metropolitan areas. In some cases, the Forest Service has contemplated visitor reductions as large as 60 and 90 percent. Such limits are already common on popular floating rivers including the Rogue and Colorado.

Choosing to shoot the messenger rather than solve the problem, former Senator Slade Gorton (R-WA) promoted legislation that would have prevented the Forest Service from imposing limitations on Wilderness visitation. A better solution is for Congress to simply add more areas to the National Wilderness Preservation System. There has been no major expansion of Wilderness in Oregon or Washington since 1984, though both states' populations and the demand for Wilderness recreation have skyrocketed. The National Forest System and Bureau of Land Management's forested

Top Ten Arguments Against Wilderness (and Refutations)

We are not so poor that we have to spend our wilderness, or so rich that we can afford to.

— Newton Drury, Director, National Park Service (1940-1951)[31]

1. Forest fires cannot be fought in Wilderness.

False. Forest fires can and are fought in Wilderness areas. Both the Wilderness Act itself and implementing regulations allow federal forest managers wide latitude to pursue aggressive fire fighting in Wilderness. Temporary roads can be built using motorized equipment. (Note that permanent roads actually increase fire risk from human-caused ignition.) However, the question that first needs to be answered is why do we want to fight forest fires in areas designated as Wilderness. Forests have co-evolved with wildfire and are renewed by them.

2. Designating Wilderness costs jobs.

A plethora of studies has debunked this myth. Less than 2 percent of jobs in Oregon and Washington are in the lumber and wood products industries. In an expanding economy, more jobs are typically added to the regional economy in a single year than the total number of existing jobs in lumber and wood products. Forest Service data indicates that only 153 logging-related jobs would be lost in Oregon if nearly five million acres of the state's remaining roadless forestlands were designated Wilderness as recommended by this book. The logging and milling jobs provided by clearcutting forests are unsustainable. A standing forest provides sustainable jobs for commercial, sport and tribal fishing, hunting, guiding, ecotourism, wildlife watching and nature appreciation businesses. The potential timber that could be extracted from remaining roadless areas would be but a tiny portion of the nation's annual timber supply. Most roadless areas are still roadless because their timber isn't worth exploiting given the low volumes, steep slopes and unstable soils.

3. Designating Wilderness harms the economy.

Industry can only profitably exploit roadless areas with the aid of substantial government subsidies. Subsidies in turn drag on the economy. Such government subsidies can be better invested in programs that achieve greater social and economic benefits. The local data is also clear: counties in the American West with the most Wilderness acreage are doing better economically than those without designated Wilderness.

4. Society needs wood; Wilderness designation cuts our supply.

A slight increase in recycling can offset any decrease in timber supply that occurs due to Wilderness designation. The two types of "garbage" most prevalent in landfills are paper and wood, respectively. Technological improvements in production efficiency and increased recycling, along with the use of sustainable alternative fibers, can meet our needs while allowing for broadscale Wilderness designation. Less than 10 percent of all the logging in Oregon and Washington is on federal land and only a very small fraction of that occurs in roadless areas. We can have Wilderness and toilet paper too.

5. Wilderness is just a playground for urban elitists.

Wilderness is an egalitarian playground. One does not need special equipment to enjoy Wilderness. If one does want to invest in a state-of-the-art and top-of-the-line back-packing ensemble, it would still be impossible to pay more than one-quarter the price of a very low-end all-terrain vehicle (not to mention the cost of motor boats, travel trailers and land yachts). Wilderness, like all public lands, is available to everyone.

6. People with disabilities cannot enjoy Wilderness.

Actually, people with disabilities routinely visit wilderness on foot, by horseback, with the assistance of llamas or other pack animals and by boat. One can also enjoy the wilderness by simply sitting at its edge and relishing the unspoiled vistas and enjoying the grace and power that emanates from it.

7. Wilderness designation locks up valuable minerals.

The best deposits of minerals in this country were located long ago. The few, small deposits that exist in Oregon's roadless areas are generally of very low value. Only if mineral prices skyrocket could these deposits begin to appear economically viable. However, should prices rise, increased recycling and the mining of landfills — where most of our exploitable minerals now exist — would still be more profitable than mining virgin ore.

8. Wilderness is off-limits to mountain bikes.

One could ride a bicycle into a cathedral, but one shouldn't. Adequate mountain biking habitat will continue to exist in areas unsuitable for Wilderness designation. And there are potentially tens of thousands of miles of more trails in the form of poorly maintained logging roads that could be converted into mountain biking trails in the future.

GEORGE WUERTHNER

Forestland recovering from the Tillamook Burn (which burned so intensively and extensively because it was being logged) in the Tillamook State Forest.

9. Wilderness designation makes livestock grazing difficult.

If only it were so. The original Wilderness Act grandfathered in livestock grazing. Since then, Congress has enacted guidelines that further entrench livestock grazing interests in the Wilderness System. Conservationists recommend that the federal government offer generous compensation to any and all ranchers who voluntarily retire their federal grazing permits in Wilderness. Not only is it very good for Wilderness and windfall for ranchers, it's a great deal for taxpayers, who subsidize the federal grazing program.

10. Dams cannot be constructed in Wilderness.

Actually, they can, if their purpose is for water supply. Dam construction in Wilderness requires an express order of the President, but the Wilderness Act allows it. To date, no presidential exemption has ever been granted, as none has ever been justified.

holdings contain many de facto wilderness areas that are worthy of congressional Wilderness protection. These lands already provide significant backcountry recreation opportunities and could absorb additional visitors in the future, if they are not roaded and clearcut. However, if these roadless forestlands are degraded, recreationists will be displaced. This will funnel even more visitors onto existing protected Wilderness areas, threatening their natural character.

In Oregon, the majority of the lands protected as Wilderness are either high-elevation forests or "rock and ice" above timberline. Though small areas of low-elevation old-growth forests have also been protected as Wilderness, much more could be if Congress would act soon.

While the National Park System and National Wildlife Refuge System also have lands that qualify for Wilderness designation, the biggest potential source of new Wilderness areas in the Pacific Northwest lies within federal forests (managed by Forest Service and BLM) and the Bureau of Land Management's desert holdings.

Other Threatened Forest Wildlands

Nearly all of Oregon's remaining forest wilderness is managed by the Forest Service or the Bureau of Land Management. However, the National Park Service, U.S. Fish and Wildlife Service, the state of Oregon and Indian tribes also manage some of Oregon's remaining wild forests.

State Forests. Of the sizeable land grant Oregon received from the United States at statehood, only the Elliot State Forest in the southern Oregon Coast Range still contains any unlogged virgin forest. Oregon's other state forests, the Tillamook and Clatsop, Santiam and Sun Pass State Forests were cutover private timberlands that were received by the state when forfeited to county governments many decades ago for non-payment of taxes. As they grow back, the opportunity to create additional small — but important — protected areas increases. This would require action by the Oregon Legislature or initiative vote of the people. The ecological values of these forestlands make this a goal worth pursuing.

Indian Reservations. Most forested lands owned by Native Americans in Oregon are small and scattered, save for the Warm Springs Indian Reservation which contains some important wilderness values, including, most notably, several miles of the Pacific Crest National Scenic Trail, Olallie Butte and one bank of the lower Metolius River. Although tribal lands are not public lands, the Pacific Crest Trail and Olallie Butte are open to public recreation (as part of a deal that transferred a portion of the Mount Hood National Forest to the Warm Springs Indian Reservation). In Oregon, the Native American tribes are important leaders in regional natural resource management, including salmon conservation and restoration that involve protecting spawning

◀ How many trees must be left standing in a clearcut so that it's no longer called a "clearcut?" An example of "new" forestry, developed by foresters in response to criticisms about clearcutting.

OMAR F. BOSE

Olallie Butte is a roadless Cascade peak on the Warm Springs Indian Reservation.

and rearing habitat in intact forests. But like many Oregon communities, the tribes' economic activities often include logging and sawmills. In Montana, the Confederated Salish and Kootenai Tribes have found a balance by designating certain lands on their reservation as the Mission Mountains Tribal Wilderness. Perhaps the Confederated Tribes of the Warm Springs Indian Reservation could consider doing the same.

Private Lands. There are no statistically significant tracts of virgin forest left on private lands in Oregon. In some cases, small private inholdings exist within designated and proposed Wilderness. While minor in size, their key locations requires their eventual conversion to public ownership through purchase from willing sellers.

Get Involved

Nothing in the world can take the place of persistence. Talent will not; nothing is more common than unsuccessful men with talent. Genius will not; unrewarded genius is almost a proverb. Education will not; the world is full of educated derelicts. Persistence and determination alone are omnipotent. The slogan: "Press on" has solved and always will solve the problems of the human race.

–Calvin Coolidge[32]

Wilderness advocates often debate what the most important reasons for protecting wilderness might be. However, when making the case for Wilderness, you should choose an argument that appeals to your audience. If you're talking to a hunter who likes to hunt big game, you should not dwell on the importance of wilderness as inspiration for literature. If you're talking to a birder, speak of wildlife habitat. If you're talking to an angler, speak of refugia for wild fish. If you're talking to someone who is concerned about health and well being and whose watershed is contained in forest wildlands, stress the importance of wilderness as a source of both high quality and copious quantities of fresh, cold water.

Aldo Leopold noted, "There are some who can live without wild things, and some who cannot."[33] Actually, some people can live without knowing the importance of wild things, but no one can actually live without wildness.

There is a story behind every one of Oregon's permanently protected Wilderness areas. In each case, special people — sometimes just one person — rose to the occasion and worked to protect places that they cared passionately about. They often worked long and hard, and against great odds, but they were eventually rewarded with the permanence of congressionally protected Wilderness.

Today, many wild areas in Oregon are seriously threatened. However, they can be saved — for this and future generations — if at least *one* person decides to answer the call for each special area. Advocating for Wilderness requires no professional skills or particular talent. Mostly it takes time and a willingness to do what needs to be done. If one is persistent, one can help save one of Oregon's next protected Wilderness areas. It may involve writing letters, making phone calls, attending public meetings, contacting elected officials, learning and sharing information with friends, family and colleagues, visiting proposed Wilderness areas and maybe even lobbying in Washington, DC. But imagine what you, your progeny, your community and our nation can gain.

The Oregon Natural Resources Council and other organizations will continue to work hard to save wilderness, but success also depends on committed volunteers who are willing to engage in the political process (see Appendix F). Eighty-percent of democracy is just showing up. ◆

Notes

[1] The Wilderness Society. "On Wilderness." Available at www.wilderness.org/library/documents/wilderness_quotes.cfm.

[2] Thoreau, Henry. 1942. WALDEN: OR LIVE IN THE WOODS. Signet Classics/New American Library of World Literature. New York, NY: 211.

[3] Abbey, Edward. 1977. THE JOURNEY HOME: SOME WORDS IN DEFENSE OF THE AMERICAN WEST. E. P. Dutton. New York, NY: 223.

[4] AndyKerr.net. "Wilderness." Available at www.andykerr.net/Wilderness/WildernessPT.htm.

[5] Abbey, Edward. 1971. DESERT SOLITAIRE: A SEASON IN THE WILDERNESS. Ballantine Books. New York, NY: 192.

[6] MERRIAM WEBSTER'S COLLEGIATE DICTIONARY. 11th ed. 1996. Merriam-Webster, Inc. Springfield, MA: 1433.

[7] Adams, Ansel and Nancy Newhall. 1960. THIS AMERICAN EARTH. Sierra Club. San Francisco, CA; Ballantine Books. New York, NY: 84.

[8] DellaSalla, Dominick and James Strittholt. 1999. Importance of Roadless Areas in Biodiversity Conservation: A Scientific Perspective. World Wildlife Fund. Ashland, OR; Conservation Biology Institute. Corvallis, OR: iv.

[9] Ibid.

[10] Leopold, Aldo. 1970. A SAND COUNTY ALMANAC: WITH ESSAYS ON CONSERVATION FROM ROUND RIVER. Ballantine Books. New York, NY: 276.

[11] Wu, David, et al., letter to President Clinton (October 2000).

[12] The Wilderness Act, 16 U.S.C. 1131(c).

[13] Marshall, Robert. 1933. THE PEOPLE'S FORESTS. Harrison Smith and Robert Haas. New York, NY: 176-177.

[14] Frome, Michael. 1974. BATTLE FOR WILDERNESS. Praeger Publishers. New York, NY: 18 (emphasis original).

[15] Ibid.

[16] Letter to President Clinton from 136 scientists (Nov. 14, 1997).

[17] THE COLUMBIA WORLD OF QUOTATIONS. 1996. Columbia University Press. New York, NY (quote no. 5227, originally published in The New York Times (March 24, 1968)).

[18] Brown, David E. and Neil B. Carmony. 1990. ALDO LEOPOLD'S SOUTHWEST. University of New Mexico Press. Albuquerque, NM: 160-161 (originally published in Aldo Leopold, *A plea for wilderness hunting grounds*, Outdoor Life (Nov. 1925)).

[19] Nelson, Gaylord. 1994 *The bankruptcy files*. Wilderness 57(205): 11.

[20] BrainyQuote.com, www.brainyquote.com/quotes/quotes/k/kurtvonneg108238.html.

[21] Perry, David A., Reed F. Noss, Timothy D. Schowalter, Terrence J. Frest, Bruce McCune, David R. Montgomery, James R. Karr. 2001. Letter to Regional Interagency Executive Committee to implement Northwest Forest Plan (Sept. 4, 2001).

[22] Wilderness.net. "Wilderness Quotes." Available at www.wilderness.net/quotes.cfm.

[23] This section is adapted with permission from Andy Kerr. 2000. OREGON DESERT GUIDE: 70 HIKES. The Mountaineers, Seattle, WA: 74-77.

[24] _____. *The state of the park*. Greater Yellowstone Report. Greater Yellowstone Coalition, Bozeman, MT (Summer 2000). Available at www.greateryellowstone.org/water/rivers/yellowstone/yellowstone_park_sum00nl.html.

[25] Noss, Reed F. and Allen Cooperrider. SAVING NATURE'S LEGACY: PROTECTING AND RESTORING BIODIVERSITY. Defenders of Wildlife and Island Press. Washington, DC: 5, *quoting* The Keystone Center. 1991. Final Consensus Report of the Keystone Policy Dialogue on Biological Diversity on Federal Lands. The Keystone Center. Keystone, CO.

[26] Noss, Reed F. 1992. *The Wildlands Project: land conservation strategy*. Wild Earth (Special Issue): 11.

[27] Ibid at 12.

[28] Soulé, Michael and Reed F. Noss. 1998. *Rewilding and biodiversity: complementary goals for continental conservation*. Wild Earth 8(3): 25.

[29] Arthur Carhart National Wilderness Training Center. undated. Wilderness Awareness Training Module. Missoula, MT (appendix C, "Wilderness Quotes").

[30] AndyKerr.net. "Wilderness." Available at www.andykerr.net/Wilderness/WildernessPT.htm.

[31] AndyKerr.net. "Wilderness." Available at www.andykerr.net/Wilderness/WildernessPT.htm.

[32] Calvin Coolidge: 30th President of the United States. "Quotations." Available at www.calvin-coolidge.org/pages/history/research/quotations/quotesp.html.

[33] Leopold, Aldo. 1966. A SAND COUNTY ALMANAC: WITH ESSAYS ON CONSERVATION FROM ROUND RIVER. Sierra Club/Ballantine Books. New York, NY: xvii (originally published in 1949).

ELIZABETH FERYL, ENVIRONMENTAL IMAGES

The most important decisions about the fate of federal forests in Oregon are made in Washington, DC.

A Long-Term Vision for a Wild Oregon

Comprehensive and detailed ecological assessments suggest that, if society wants to protect all ecosystem functions and umbrella species like large predators, at least one half of Oregon's forestlands must be protected or restored to wild and natural conditions. Table 5-1 depicts the current protected forest Wilderness in Oregon and those roadless and undeveloped lands that are de facto wilderness worthy of formal protection.

Approximately three-fifths of Oregon is publicly owned. But not all of those public lands are dedicated to conservation (yet) and, in some cases, large blocks of uninhabited, poorly managed private lands impede the migration of species within and between publicly owned ecoregions.

Both our ecological needs and the politics of natural resources are inescapable factors in wildlands protection. However, while ecological realities will never change — people, fish and wildlife need clean air, water and wilderness — political realities can change. We can transform our current leaders and elect new ones that support designating large tracts of wilderness. Ecologists Reed Noss and Michael Soulé note:

A cynic might describe rewilding as an atavistic obsession with the resurrection of Eden. A more sympathetic critic might label it romantic. We contend, however, that rewilding is simply scientific realism, assuming that our goal is to ensure the long-term integrity of the land community.[1]

Inviting Nature Back

One of the penalties of an ecological education is that one lives alone in a world of wounds.... An ecologist must either harden his shell and make believe that the consequences of science are none of his business, or he must be the doctor who sees the marks of death in a community that believes itself well and does not want to be told otherwise.

—Aldo Leopold[2]

Most of the timber industry and many federal forest managers argue that — due to fragmentation from clearcuts, roads and other human assaults — the remaining road-less lands in Oregon and across the West are no longer of wilderness quality. Even when forced to concede that such lands are of wilderness quality, industry and the federal forest agencies often still argue that cutting these forests is the best course of

Table 5-1. Protected and Protectable Oregon Forest Wilderness

Level III Ecoregion	Currently Protected Forest Wilderness	Currently Unprotected Forest Wilderness	Total Forest Wilderness
Coast Range	0.69%	4.32%	5.01%
Cascades	5.66%	18.22%	23.88%
Klamath Mountains	13.70%	20.35%	38.05%
East Cascades Slopes and Foothills	0.70%	8.77%	9.47%
Blue Mountains	5.32%	12.50%	17.82%

action. They cite the benefits of logging to local communities in the form of jobs and government revenue. They even claim — most hypocritically — that the very health of the forest depends upon logging (while omitting how logging will improve the bottom lines for industry, as well as bureaucratic budgets).

Just because the Venus de Milo lost her arms, it does not follow that the rest of the statue should be discarded. Unlike human art, nature's art can grow whole again, if humans allow it.

Some of Oregon's forests, especially those in the drier southwest and on the eastside of the Cascades, are out of balance. While neither heavily roaded or logged, many of these forest roadless areas have been grazed by livestock and/or had their natural fire regime disrupted by overzealous disciples of Smokey Bear. To restore ecological health and balance to these federal forests, livestock must be removed and fire returned to these ecosystems. Nature's healing begins when livestock are removed and recovery is rapid. The reintroduction of fire is a bit more complex, but not as complicated as many foresters would have us believe.

In most cases, fire can be safely reintroduced to an ecosystem by simply dropping a match at the right time. There is, however, an art — and a science — to prescribed fire that considers topography, the quantity and moisture content of fuel, as well as current and probable future wind, temperature and humidity. Occasionally, despite the best efforts of all involved, prescribed management fires will burn out of control. The public must be willing to tolerate these occasions, forest managers must be willing to accept the risk of failure — and both must learn from successes and failures. A few out-of-control prescribed management fires in the off-season will result in less out-of-control wildfires during the fire season.

Many industrial and agency foresters contend that logging, or at least the serious use of a chainsaw, is necessary before fire can safely be restored to a forest ecosystem. They argue that the exclusion of fire has caused the forest to grow too thick and that if it burns without prior "treatment" the entire forest stand — not just the small understory trees — will be lost. While there is some legitimacy to this claim, it is often exaggerated to promote commercial logging — not to improve forest health, but to increase timber industry profits and/or agency staffing levels.

In *some* cases, following strict guidelines, the prudent and sparing use of small chainsaws can aid forest restoration — by removing certain understory trees that have grown so big that if they burn they will threaten the old-growth overstory. This rarely occurs in remaining roadless areas that, not having been logged or roaded, are in the most natural and ecologically balanced condition. Other forests that have been high-graded once, twice or three times are more likely to exhibit this problem. In general, newly established *small* young trees are the ones that pose the biggest problem in terms of fire danger — particularly where long-term fire suppression has been practiced. The *big* old trees need to be conserved because they provide shade, retain moisture and actually help reduce overall fire danger. Mostly because the agency has always managed public forests almost solely for, and most often in the context of, timber sales, the Forest Service is now repackaging timber sales as "ecological restoration projects." Ecological restoration costs money, so the agency often tries to raise the money by offering enough big trees to bidding timber companies to cover the cost of "treating" the small trees in the project area. (The industry term for this "treatment" is "punishment acres" where they are required to cut down little trees in order to get at the big ones).

The problem with this strategy is two-fold. First, the big trees should be conserved for ecological purposes (including fire resiliency). Second, there is no money in logging small trees. The Forest Service has offered many restoration sales over the past decade that almost always serve up more trees for logging than conservationists would prefer — only to discover that no timber companies are interested in bidding. The usual practice is to then reconfigure the sale so it includes even more big trees to attract industry bids. Removing the big trees not only degrades the ecosystem but actually increases the risk of future fire. This is because the shade provided by big trees helps maintain cool moist fuel conditions, helps reduce wind speeds during a fire and suppresses the growth of "ladder fuels." Sometimes, even well-intentioned thinning can make things worse instead of better, while careful use of prescribed fire almost always moves things in the right direction. The Forest Service could learn much from the National Park Service, an agency that routinely burns all kinds of forest ecosystems without first resorting to timber sales and chainsaws.

Currently, there is no real money in forest conservation and certainly not the amount available from forest exploitation. (What has posterity ever done for a corporation's bottom line?) Past mismanagement has created an ecological debt that we cannot pay down by going still further into hock.

Unroading the Wild

While the TV ads would have us believe that a four-wheel drive can take us to a wild place, it really can't. Wherever the engine takes us, real wildness will be just out of hearing over the next ridge. If we insist on driving into the wilderness, we're likely to destroy what we came to find.

−Chris Madson[3]

Some federal forest roads should be maintained to provide access to recreation areas and scenic viewpoints. However, scientific studies show most forest roads to be extremely damaging to nature, expensive to maintain and of little public value. These should be abandoned for reclamation by nature. The resulting smaller road system would be better — for public use and to minimize environmental harm — than the current overly large and under-maintained system. Many roads are ticking time bombs waiting for the next torrential rains to set them off — sliding down steep slopes into stream bottoms or human communities. The backlog of minimum road maintenance on the National Forest System is $8 billion.

The Forest Service should proactively close all unneeded roads and not just by constructing gates at the road's entrance. Problem roads should be made "hydrologically invisible" by installing water bars at appropriate intervals to divert surface water back to its natural flow and keep it out of ditches. Roadside ditches tend to collect water and deliver it quickly to streams, so that during a storm the pulse of water causes erosion and scours fish eggs from their nests. Water bars on the other hand tend to dissipate water and redirect it to vegetated surface areas and ultimately to subsurface channels. This helps filter the water and slow the delivery of water to streams.

Located where roads cross streams, culverts are often not big enough to handle large flood flows so they tend to get plugged, back up and cause large landslides. All the fine grained fill material used to bridge the stream then smothers fish nests downstream. In addition, culverts often create barriers for migrating fish and amphibians. Water bar construction and culvert removal work is very cost-effective and can provide transitional jobs in the woods for out-of-work loggers and equipment operators.

The Siuslaw National Forest once produced a lot of salmon. As logging and roads

increased, salmon numbers decreased. Today, coho salmon is listed as threatened under the Endangered Species Act, and chinook salmon, steelhead and cutthroat trout qualify for protected status. The Forest Service is slowly beginning to realize that the Siuslaw National Forest is more valuable for salmon, water, wildlife and recreation than for logging. The President's Northwest Forest Plan dropped the timber cut on the Siuslaw more than 90 percent. Consequently, two-thirds of the Siuslaw's road system is now being closed and restored. The Siuslaw's example should, and will likely be, followed by other national forests.

The vast majority of Forest Service roads are low-speed roads built for log trucks. As logging decreases, so do the taxpayer dollars that maintain these roads. As Congress reduces the Forest Service budget, many national forests are closing ranger district offices and cutting staff positions. Given these trends, a coalition of environmentalists and fiscal conservatives may finally be able to persuade Congress to cut the Forest Service road-building budget and allocate money to watershed restoration, thus benefiting taxpayers, the environment and local economies.

More Public Forestlands

Only public ownership can reliably, certainly, durably allow certain natural processes the room they need.

—Carl Pope, Executive Director, Sierra Club[4]

In the West, we have extraordinary landscapes but they are not complete. When many of the boundaries of our national parks and forests were established years ago, we didn't have the science to tell us more land was needed. Now we have the science and we need to act on it.

—Bruce Babbitt, former Secretary of Interior[5]

Not long ago, the giant timber company Weyerhaeuser sold its extensive holdings in the Klamath Basin. International Paper has also sold 200,000 acres in Oregon's central Coast Range. Other multinational corporations have sold other forested tracts around Oregon. Still more timber companies will sell and run. In capitalism, making a killing always takes precedence over making a living. In these days of global competition — and especially since trees grow more slowly than money — capital that had been invested in *standing* timber is now moving elsewhere to reap greater returns on investment than are available from *growing* timber. However, if these large private timber holdings remain in corporate ownership, even greater economic pressures will result, causing even more ecological destruction.

Most of Oregon's industrial timberland has now been heavily logged at least twice.

◄ After clearcutting, some forests may recover on their own. However dense artificial plantations can often benefit ecologically from careful thinning to reduce tree density and help restore natural variability.

ELIZABETH FERYL, ENVIRONMENTAL IMAGES

Where huge trees once stood are now stunted monoculture plantations more ecologically akin to a cornfield than a forest.

The chainsaw, the bulldozer and the chemical pulping process have allowed efficient mining of forests. However, the era of forest mining is ending and more of our fiber for paper and construction products will come from the nation's expansive farmlands, which are far more productive for growing fiber than forestlands.

History has shown we cannot rely on the private sector to restore Oregon's forests and protect our drinking water. If the public wants to preserve and restore salmon and other forest species, and protect sources of drinking water (and it does), then these conservation responsibilities should be borne mostly by the public, not the private, sector.

There are at least six million acres of private corporate timberland (roughly the size of the Deschutes, Mount Hood, Willamette, Winema, Rogue River and Umpqua National Forests) that could be reconverted to public forestland. The State of Oregon should acquire it from willing sellers and give it to the United States to be managed as national forests. This should be done because it is ecologically necessary, socially desirable, economically rational and fiscally feasible. Oregon must reinvest in and maintain its natural infrastructure just as does its other infrastructure.

If population grows, we will need more real forests. Oregon enjoys many of the state parks it has today because Sam Boardman, Oregon's first superintendent of State Parks, had the vision to convince Oregonians to buy park land when it was cheap, though not yet needed. Today, most politicians cannot even convince Oregonians to pay for what is needed now, let alone in the future. Private timberland is not inexpensive now; it will not get any cheaper.

Among the ecological and recreational achievements that could be realized with the acquisition of more public forestland is a Willamette Valley Greenbelt — equivalent to a band of Silver Falls State Parks surrounding the Willamette Valley in the foothills of the Cascade and Coast ranges — envisioned by former Oregon State Parks Director Dave Talbot to complement the Willamette River Greenway. A protected forest corridor running from Portland's Forest Park to the Pacific Ocean could also become a reality.

In 1977, I visited Klootchie Creek in Clatsop County near where the nation's largest known Sitka spruce now stands and where the largest known Douglas-fir once stood. A Crown Zellerbach executive described what had been a magnificent old-growth Douglas-fir forest of 12-foot diameter trees, where there are now only clearcuts and plantations, by saying, "We knew in the 1950s we had to log it then, or it would be a national park by now."

In the 1920s the Commonwealth of Virginia acquired some cut-over, burned-off, mined-out, grazed-down, plowed-up mountains and gave them to the United States in order to, as the National Park Service said, "invite nature back." It was a radical idea, but the creation of Shenandoah National Park is now considered a very reasonable

◄ Nature reclaiming what was once an all-weather gravel road.

thing to have done. Since it takes several hundred years to regrow 12-foot diameter Douglas-firs, even in the Oregon Coast Range, we must start reconverting private timberland to public forestland immediately.

The state could finance this proposed conservation effort. At $500 per acre of cutover timberland (a fair price for large acreages), the purchase cost of six million acres is $3 billion. Borrowing at 6 percent for 200 years — about the length of time we have been cutting down Oregon's forests and the minimum time required grow a decent old-growth forest — servicing the debt would cost $15 million per month. A 4¢/gallon increase in the state fuels tax and equivalent increases in the weight-mile tax could easily pay the debt. This would be a logical exchange, because Oregonians would mitigate the climate change impacts of burning gasoline, while conserving and restoring the state's forests. The carbon from burning the fossil fuels would be removed from the air and sequestered in what will eventually again become old-growth forests.

Here is another way to look at it. With (at the moment) three million Oregonians, the cost is less than $5/month per Oregonian — or less than the price of a six-pack of decent Oregon microbrew — to acquire six million acres of public forestlands. Here's to restoring Oregon's forests!

Self-Restraint for the Betterment of All

Humans are orders of magnitude more successful than any other species. Humans also now determine whether any species or ecosystem lives or dies. We (currently) have no serious predators, save ourselves. To date we have successfully outmaneuvered all the major environmental checks and balances that keep other species within limits. Our population continues to grow despite diseases like AIDS. Even a loss in our species' fertility hasn't slowed our population growth. Due to environmental stresses, human sperm counts are down 50 percent over the last thirty years. But what do we do about it? Rather than address the underlying causes we learn to make babies in test tubes.

We have — for the short-term at least — transcended any limits. But nature bats last. In the end, humans must learn to live within our means or Earth will no longer support us. Finding another suitable planet is as impractical as it is improbable. The evolutionary challenge is whether humans will acquire the wisdom to do something no other species has ever done or had to do — practice willful self-restraint. We must learn to live within both our economic and environmental means. Will we as a species learn that our long-term survival, as well as our short-term real comfort, depends upon a healthy, clean and biologically diverse planet? Protecting and restoring Oregon's forest wildlands is an important step toward that goal. ◆

GARY BRAASCH

Public forestland in Saddle Mountain State Park surrounded by private timberland.

Notes

[1] Soulé, Michael and Reed F. Noss. 1998. *Rewilding and biodiversity: complementary goals for continental conservation.* Wild Earth 8(3): 26.

[2] Leopold, Aldo. 1970. A SAND COUNTY ALMANAC: WITH ESSAYS ON CONSERVATION FROM ROUND RIVER. Ballantine Books. New York, NY: 197.

[3] Madson, Chris. 1997. *Dismount.* Wyoming Wildlife 61(10): 4 ("Land Ethic" column).

[4] Pope, Carl. 1998. *Downpayments on the rewilding of America.* Wild Earth 8(4): 37.

[5] Wilkinson, Todd. *To protect land, Uncle Sam buys more.* Christian Science Monitor (Sept. 14, 1999).

Home to Oregon's Rainforests
Coast Range Ecoregion

Extending from the Lower Columbia River south to the California border, and east from the northeastern Pacific Ocean to the interior valleys of the Willamette, Umpqua and Rogue Rivers and to the Klamath Mountains, the 5.8 million acres in Oregon's portion of the Coast Range Ecoregion rarely exceed 2,500 feet in elevation. Yet these mountain slopes are steep and interlaced and incised with countless trickles and streams. The highest point, Marys Peak (4,097 feet), is visible from much of the mid-Willamette Valley. Beyond Oregon, the Coast Range Ecoregion extends north into far western Washington (and includes Vancouver Island in British Columbia) and south to northwestern California. In Oregon, only two rivers cross through the Coast Range: the Umpqua and the Rogue. Rain-soaked, the Coast Range is highly productive for coniferous forests that once covered the entire region. Sitka spruce dominated the fog belt along the immediate coastline, while inland was a mosaic of Douglas-fir, western hemlock and western redcedar. Unfortunately, a great many of the original forests have been clearcut and are now dominated by Douglas-fir plantations and alder stands.

The Coast Range climate is maritime with cool and very wet winters and mild, dry summers. The lack of harsh weather ensures a long growing season, allowing trees to grow most of the year. Consequently, coastal temperate rainforests often contain more biomass per acre than even tropical rainforests. Annual rainfall ranges from 60 to 80 inches along the coast and up to 200 inches in inland areas. With such a wet climate, the natural fire frequency is very low, between 90 and 250 years on average.

Major wildlife species include Roosevelt elk, black-tailed deer, coyote, cougar, bobcat, black bear, northern spotted owl, marbled murrelet, silverspot butterfly, numerous species of salmon, a great variety of amphibians, reptiles and slugs and over 7,000 species of arthropods.

Located next to the Pacific Ocean, the Coast Range ecoregion contains Oregon's wettest forests. Precipitation, which is related to elevation and distance from the ocean, is the most significant factor in determining forest types in this ecoregion.

Sitka Spruce is the most common type of Oregon coastal forest and is often intermingled with western hemlock and Douglas-fir groves. The species is most often found in windy, foggy sites and on wet, north-facing slopes.

Far less common along the coast are **Shorelands**. These open beaches, dunes and spits sometimes harbor dense shrub communities that include shore pine.

Douglas-fir/Western Hemlock forests — the most common forest type in western Oregon — dominate the interior of the ecoregion. After a disturbance (such as fire or a blowdown), Douglas-fir will dominate a site for centuries. If no additional major disturbance occurs, the shade-tolerant western hemlock will eventually overtake the Douglas-fir and achieve stand dominance on the wettest sites. Grand fir and western redcedar are occasionally found in these forests. Red alder and bigleaf maple are common along watercourses, and noble fir can be found at the highest snowy points in the Coast Range. Toward the southern end of the Oregon Coast Range, coastal **Redwood** trees range into Oregon up to twelve miles north of the California border and are usually found on slopes rather than in river bottoms. Nearby, in a narrow band south from Coos Bay into California, Port Orford-cedar can also be found.

Douglas-fir/Broadleaf Deciduous forests are found in relatively drier parts of the Coast Range. There the predominant broadleaf trees are red alder, bigleaf maple and — toward the southern end of the ecoregion — Oregon white oak, tan oak and Pacific madrone.

On the eastern edge of the Coast Range ecoregion one will find little pockets of **Douglas-fir/Oregon White Oak**, **Oregon White Oak/Douglas-fir** or **Oregon White Oak/Ponderosa** forest. The first is more commonly found where the Coast Range meets the Willamette Valley and is a result of the historic fire-clearing regimes practiced by Native Americans and early European settlers. Unless fire intervenes, the Douglas-fir will eventually dominate. The latter two forest types are usually found on the edges of the Upper Willamette, Umpqua and Rogue Valleys, often in association with ponderosa pine and incense cedar. Another variant of these forest types is **Oregon White Oak/Pacific Madrone,** usually found in the drier Umpqua Valley.

At some time in their existence, most forest communities will be set back to early successional forest and are classified as **Cutover/Burned** forest. This can occur naturally — from lightning-caused wildfires, native insect or disease events, or blowdown by wind — or unnaturally, by way of logging, human-caused fire, human-caused blowdown (due to unnatural and vulnerable forest edges caused by clearcuts), non-native disease and insects, or aggressive fire-fighting. Particularly troubling are "backburns," where firefighters intentionally burn the forest in front of an oncoming wildfire. In many cases, the backburns are far more intense and destructive than the natural burn would have been.

Providing scale for this giant Sitka spruce (*Picea sitchensis*) are ONRC staffers Erin Fagley, Chandra LeGue and Jeremy Hall. ▶

Ecoregions of Oregon's Coast Range

The low mountains of the Coast Range Ecoregion are covered by highly productive, rain-drenched evergreen forests. Sitka spruce forests originally dominated the fog-shrouded coast, while a mosaic of western redcedar, western hemlock and seral Douglas-fir blanketed inland areas. Today, Douglas-fir plantations are prevalent on the intensively logged and managed landscape. Lithology influences land management strategies; slopes underlain by sedimentary rock are more susceptible to failure following clear-cutting and road building than those underlain by volcanic rocks.

Further refining the ecoregion, scientists divide Oregon's Coast Range Level III Ecoregion into seven Level IV ecoregions:

The **Coastal Lowlands** ecoregion contains beaches, dunes and marine terraces below 400 feet elevation. Wet forests, lakes, estuarine marshes and tea-colored (tannic) streams are characteristic features of the landscape. Wetlands have been widely drained and converted to dairy pastures. Residential, commercial and recreational developments are expanding in the coastal corridor.

The **Coastal Uplands** includes headlands and low mountains surrounding the Coastal Lowlands. The climate of the Coastal Uplands is marine influenced with an extended winter rainy season and minimal seasonal temperature extremes. Abundant fog during the summer dry season reduces vegetation moisture stress. This ecoregion includes much of the historic distribution of Sitka spruce. Today, its Douglas-fir forests are managed for logging.

The lower, more coastal parts of the mountainous **Volcanics** ecoregion are affected by fog. This ecoregion is underlain by fractured basaltic rocks. As a result, summer stream flows are more consistent than on the sedimentary rocks of surrounding ecoregions, and streams still support runs of spring chinook salmon and summer steelhead. Its Douglas-fir plantations are intensively logged. Sediment delivery rates to streams following disturbance are lower than in the Mid-Coastal Sedimentary Ecoregion.

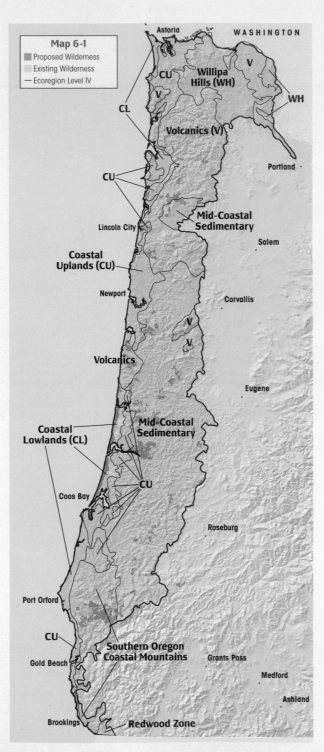

Map 6-1
■ Proposed Wilderness
Existing Wilderness
— Ecoregion Level IV

WASHINGTON

Astoria
CU — Willipa Hills (WH)
V
CL — V
WH
Volcanics (V)
Portland
CU
Mid-Coastal Sedimentary
Lincoln City
Salem
Coastal Uplands (CU)
Newport
Corvallis
V
V
Volcanics
Eugene
Coastal Lowlands (CL)
Mid-Coastal Sedimentary
CU
Coos Bay
Roseburg
Port Orford
CU
Southern Oregon Coastal Mountains
Gold Beach
Grants Pass
Medford
Ashland
Brookings — Redwood Zone

The **Willapa Hills** ecoregion is more rolling and has a lower drainage density than other upland areas in the Coast Range. Logging is relatively easy and less expensive in this accessible terrain. Industrial timberland has almost completely replaced the historic forests of the Willapa Hills. When disturbed, the silt- and clay-textured soils are easily eroded, thereby degrading stream quality. Large herds of Roosevelt elk winter in this ecoregion.

The mountainous **Mid-Coastal Sedimentary** ecoregion lies outside of the coastal fog zone and is typically underlain by massive beds of sandstone and siltstone in contrast to the Volcanics Ecoregion. This ecoregion is more rugged than the geologically similar Willapa Hills. Its Douglas-fir forests are intensively managed for logging. Slopes are prone to failure when disturbed, particularly south of the Siuslaw River. Stream sedimentation is higher than in the Volcanics ecoregion.

The **Southern Oregon Coastal Mountains** is a geologically and botanically diverse ecoregion that is a transition zone between the Coast Range and the Siskiyou Mountains. This ecoregion has the climate of the Coast Range and the varied lithology of the higher, more dissected Siskiyou Mountains (in the Klamath Mountains). Distributions of northern and southern vegetation blend together here and species diversity is high. Douglas-fir, western hemlock, tanoak, Port Orford cedar and western redcedar occur.

The low mountains of the **Redwood Zone** lie entirely within the coastal fog zone and are characteristically covered by coast redwood and Douglas-fir. Historically, unbroken redwood forests occurred and moderated local climate by trapping coastal fog and producing shade. Remnants of unlogged redwood forest still survive east of Brookings.

Text gratefully adapted from Thor D. Thorson, Sandra A. Bryce, Duane A. Lammers, Alan J. Woods, James M. Omernik, Jimmy Kagan, David E. Pater, Jeffrey A. Comstock. 2003. Ecoregions of Oregon (color poster with map, descriptive text, summary tables and photographs). USDI-Geological Survey. Reston, VA (map scale 1:1,500,000).

Today, 28 percent of the Oregon Coast Range Ecoregion is publicly owned by the federal government. The major federal holdings include the Siuslaw National Forest and the western margin of the Siskiyou National Forest managed by the Forest Service and the Bureau of Land Mangement's Coos Bay District, along with the western portions of the BLM Roseburg, Eugene and Salem Districts.

Currently, only four small areas of Oregon's Coast Range are protected as Wilderness (Drift Creek, Cummins Creek, Rock Creek and Grassy Knob), comprising a mere 0.7 percent of the ecoregion.

Conservationists are proposing Wilderness protection for three multi-unit areas: Coast Range, Elk River and Oregon Dunes. If designated, together they would comprise a total of 5 percent of the ecoregion.

Proposed Coast Range Wilderness
Temperate Rainforest

The abundant rain and fertile soils of the proposed Coast Range Wilderness combine to grow big trees and big salmon. The diversity of fish, wildlife and plants is incredible. The area is home to 26 species of amphibians and reptiles, 235 species of birds, over 200 species of fish and 69 species of mammals. Threatened species include the bald eagle, northern spotted owl, marbled murrelet and Oregon silverspot butterfly. Other wildlife species of special concern include the Northwest pond turtle, peregrine falcon, big-eared bat, Alsea micro caddisfly, wolverine, common loon, white-footed vole, Haddock's caddisfly, long-billed curlew and red-legged frog. Among the plethora of Coast Range plant species, conservationists are particularly concerned about adder's tongue, philia moss and western red avens.

Today, only a small amount of virgin forest remains in Oregon's temperate rainforest. Much of the Coast Range is privately owned and has been logged over multiple times. Most of the big old trees are now big old stumps — but some vitally important remnants still remain. And most of them are tucked away in the publicly-owned Siuslaw National Forest, where most of the Coast Range Wilderness is proposed.

This archipelago of wildlands stretches from the Pacific Ocean on the west, to Mount Hebo in the north, Marys Peak on the east and Wasson Creek on the south. Many units of the proposed Wilderness coincide with key aquatic diversity areas identified by the American Fisheries Society. Salmon species here include coho, spring and fall chinook, and chum in the lower rivers, along with summer and winter steelhead.

A few units of the proposed Wilderness also lie within the Oregon Biodiversity Project's Tillamook Bay Watershed Conservation Opportunity Area and are adjacent to

Old-growth Douglas-fir (*Pseudotsuga menziesii*) in the Valley of the Giants Unit of the proposed Coast Range Wilderness. While this unit is small in size, the very large trees project a Wilderness mystique. ▶

Proposed Coast Range Wilderness

LEVEL IV ECOREGIONS
Mid-Coastal Sedimentary (66%), Volcanics (27%)
Coastal Uplands (6%), Coastal Lowlands (<0.1%);
Klamath Mountains Level III Ecoregion: Inland
Siskiyous (<1%)

VEGETATION TYPES
Douglas-fir/Western Hemlock (81%), Sitka
Spruce (13%), Douglas-fir/Broadleaf Deciduous
(5%), Siskiyou Mixed Conifer (<1%), Siskiyou
Jeffrey Pine (<1%), Cutover/Burned (<1%)

DRAINAGE SUBBASINS
Alsea, Coos, Coquille, Nestucca, Lower Umpqua,
Middle Willamette, Siletz, Siuslaw, Upper
Willamette, Wilson, Yamhill, Yaquina

ELEVATION RANGE
59-4,090 feet

UNITS
Arnold Creek, Bailey Ridge, Barclay Creek, Baxter
Creek, Bear Creek, Big Creek, Billie Creek, Bills
Creek, Blue Ridge, Cape Horn, Cascade Head,
Cedar Creek, Cougar Creek, Crazy Creek, *Cummins
Creek Additions* (North Additions, South Additions),
Deadwood Creek, Deerhead Point, Dick's Ridge,
Doerner Fir, *Drift Creek Additions* (Boulder Creek,
Butler Creek, Cougar Creek, Lloyd Collette, Trout
Creek [North], Trout Creek [South]), Fairview
Mountain, Fiddle Creek, George Creek, Green
Mountain, Greenleaf Creek, Gwynn Creek, Haney
Creek, Hoffman Creek, Karnowsky Creek, Lind
Peak, Little Wolf Creek, Lower Drift Creek, Lower
Tioga Creek, Marys Peak, McKinney Creek, Middle
Fork of the North Fork Smith River, Miles Mountain,
Moon Creek, Morris Creek, Mount Hebo, Mount
Popocatepetl, North Fork Alsea River, North Fork
Smith River, North Prong Creek, Palmer Mountain,
Parker Creek, Randall Hill, Rock Creek, *Rock Creek
Additions* (East Additions, West Additions), South
Fork Smith River (South), South Fork Smith River
(North), Swamp Creek, Sweet Creek Falls, Table
Creek, Table Mountain, Tenmile Ridge, Three
Buttes, Toketa Creek, Trask River, Upper Drift Creek,
Upper Tioga Creek, Valley of the Giants, Vingie
Ridge, Wasson Creek, Windy Peak, Yellow Creek

EXISTING WILDERNESSES INCORPORATED
Cummins Creek, Drift Creek, Rock Creek

SIZE
144,495 acres (226 square miles, not including
22,457 acres of currently protected Wilderness)

COUNTIES
Benton, Coos, Douglas, Lane, Lincoln, Tillamook,
Washington, Yamhill

FEDERAL ADMINISTRATIVE UNITS
Siuslaw National Forest; BLM Coos Bay, Eugene,
Roseburg and Salem Districts

CONGRESSIONAL DISTRICTS
1st, 4th, 5th

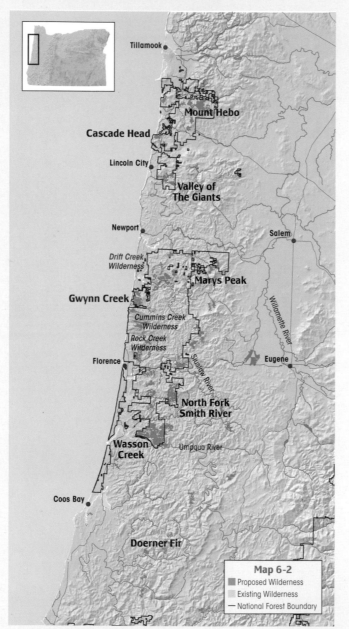

Map 6-2
- Proposed Wilderness
- Existing Wilderness
- National Forest Boundary

Some of the individual units in the proposed Wilderness are highlighted below.

Cascade Head includes incredible old-growth Sitka spruce forest and is a focus of scientific research.

Doerner Fir is a very small area, but hosts the world's largest known Douglas-fir tree.

The Sitka spruce old-growth forest of **Gwynn Creek** near Cape Perpetua is awesome to walk through and surrounds one of the most extensive trail systems in the Coast Range.

The remaining old-growth forest on **Marys Peak** exists today only because the Forest Service was reluctant to log all of Corvallis' drinking water supply too rapidly. Marys Peak is the highest point in the Coast Range. Here one can find old-growth noble fir, which is very rare in the Oregon Coast Range.

Mount Hebo is featured on page 89.

North Fork Smith River includes the nearly 90-foot high Kentucky Falls and spectacular old-growth forest with trees over twice as tall as the falls.

The Valley of the Giants is a very small area with very large trees, many over 450 years old. The hellish 30-mile drive through ravaged industrial timberlands to the giants makes one appreciate the importance of this refuge.

Wasson Creek extends from near sea level to 1,600 feet in elevation and is truly a forest primeval. Along the creek are rarely visited waterfalls known as the Devil's Staircase. Dense vegetation and steep slopes make visiting the unit a major challenge. The difficulties associated with logging steep slopes and unstable soils are the only reasons that Wasson Creek remains roadless and unlogged. The high density of spotted owls in the unit testifies to the abundance of old-growth forest. One can easily get to Wasson Lake (full of wild cutthroat trout) where, in the spring, one can witness a fantastically massive congregation of rough-skinned newts all looking for sex.

ERIK FERNANDEZ

The Nestucca State Scenic Waterway flows through the Mount Hebo Unit of the proposed Coast Range Wilderness.

Douglas-fir with some western hemlock, western redcedar and red alder mixed in. Understory plant species include trillium, sword and bracken fern and sourgrass.

Numerous streams arise on the north slope of Mount Hebo and drain into the Nestucca River. Wildlife species here include deer, elk, cougar, black bear, great blue herons, bald eagles, salmon and steelhead.

Winter snow lingers briefly on the open grass-covered balds and subalpine meadows at the summit of Mount Hebo. These balds and meadows are home to the endangered Oregon silverspot butterfly, a species that was once found in many locations. The host plant to the butterfly is the early blue violet, which is also declining due to habitat alteration. Wildflowers, which are abundant on Mount Hebo in the early summer, include several botanically interesting species. Two 80-foot waterfalls, spectacularly misnamed Niagara Falls, are easily accessible by trail. The "Pioneer-Indian" Trail was originally used by indigenous people and developed in 1854 to bring settlers from the Willamette Valley to Tillamook Bay. One can also drive a paved road to the summit that once hosted a radar station. Views from Mount Hebo are panoramic and include the Pacific Ocean, the Nestucca River Valley and far too many clearcuts. However, the steep terrain and the dense vegetation keep all but a few visitors from reaching the heart of this proposed Wilderness unit.

PROPOSED WILDERNESS
Coast Range

LOCATION
5 miles east of Hebo

LEVEL IV ECOREGIONS
Volcanics (66%), Mid-Coastal Sedimentary (34%)

VEGETATION TYPES
Douglas-fir/Western Hemlock (98%), Sitka Spruce (2%)

TERRAIN
Steeply rugged.

DRAINAGE SUBBASIN
Nestucca

ELEVATION RANGE
400-3,154 feet

SIZE
11,203 acres

COUNTIES
Tillamook, Yamhill

FEDERAL ADMINISTRATIVE UNITS
Siuslaw National Forest (Hebo Ranger District); BLM Salem District (Tillamook Resource Area)

USGS 7.5' QUAD MAPS
Beaver, Blaine, Hebo, Niagara Creek, Springer Mountain

FEATURED UNIT
Mount Hebo

At 3,154-feet, the flat-topped basalt Mount Hebo is the second highest point in Oregon's Coast Range.

Although it receives over 180 inches of precipitation annually, Mount Hebo did burn in 1910. Following those fires, the south slope of Mount Hebo was replanted with non-local Douglas-fir. The north slope, that remains roadless, reforested naturally and has relic older trees which can be seen popping through the younger canopy. The old trees, often covered in moss, are mainly

Wasson Lake in the Wasson Creek Unit of the proposed Coast Range Wilderness.

temperate rainforests of the Tillamook State Forest that are recovering from logging. More proposed Wilderness units are located in the Nestucca River Watershed Conservation Opportunity Area, which includes the north slope of Mount Hebo. This watershed is a stronghold for chum, coho, spring chinook and winter steelhead, and includes about a dozen aquatic diversity areas. Other proposed Wilderness units coincide with the Alsea-Siuslaw Conservation Opportunity Area and include twelve aquatic diversity areas and some of the highest concentrations of what are called "salmon core areas," considered vital by salmon habitat biologists to the survival of the species.

Major tree species in the proposed Wilderness are Sitka spruce, Douglas-fir, bigleaf maple, western redcedar, western hemlock and red alder. The highest points in the proposed Wilderness are grass balds — uniquely grassy areas with no trees — and rock outcroppings.

Recreational opportunities throughout the proposed Wilderness are virtually endless and include hiking, fishing, hunting, backpacking, birding and measuring the circumference of old-growth trees with outstretched arms (the original form of tree-hugging).

Many, but not all, of the roadless units in this proposed Wilderness are located in the Northwest Forest Plan's "Tier 1 Key Watersheds." The Tier 1 designation offers

some protection against road building, but little against logging. Other threats include off-road vehicles.

To protect numerous threatened and endangered species and salmon stocks, the Forest Service — beginning with the Clinton administration — has been aggressively removing roads from the forest landscape here, while thinning only the young tree plantations (generally a good thing). The current administration under George W. Bush is less inclined to remove roads and more inclined to log the last big trees. Designating the Coast Range Wilderness can prevent logging of old growth and help preserve all the ecological components of a coastal temperate rainforest.

Proposed Elk River Wilderness
Most Productive Salmon Watershed Remaining in the Lower 48 States

The proposed Elk River Wilderness encompasses all the remaining wildlands in the Elk River watershed and the roadless lands in the headwaters of the Sixes and Coquille Rivers. The proposed Wilderness is near the southern end of Oregon's Coast Range. It extends inland from where the Elk and Sixes Rivers reach the Pacific — just south and north of Cape Blanco, respectively. Over 170 inches of rain falls in the Elk River basin each year, but only 12 inches fall between May and September. Given its proximity to the ocean, summer fogs often extend inland to elevations approaching 1,500 feet.

Besides the usual tree species, such as Douglas-fir, western hemlock, tanoak, Pacific yew, western redcedar, Jeffrey pine, madrone, bigleaf maple, red alder, sugar pine, knobcone pine, western white pine and lodgepole pine, extensive stands of Port Orford-cedar grace this proposed Wilderness. Some Douglas-fir specimens here exceed 300-feet in height and 10-feet in diameter, as do some Port Orford-cedar. Understory species include rhododendron and manzanita on the drier south slopes and evergreen huckleberry on the wetter north slopes. The area's vast old-growth forest is some of the best remaining low elevation coastal temperate rain forest in Oregon.

Endemic to southwestern Oregon and northwestern California, Port Orford-cedar is threatened by a non-native root disease. The exotic Asian, water-borne pathogen is spread primarily by spores in the mud attached to and thrown around by logging and road building equipment. If Port Orford-cedar trees are in the path of water draining off a

Proposed Elk River Wilderness

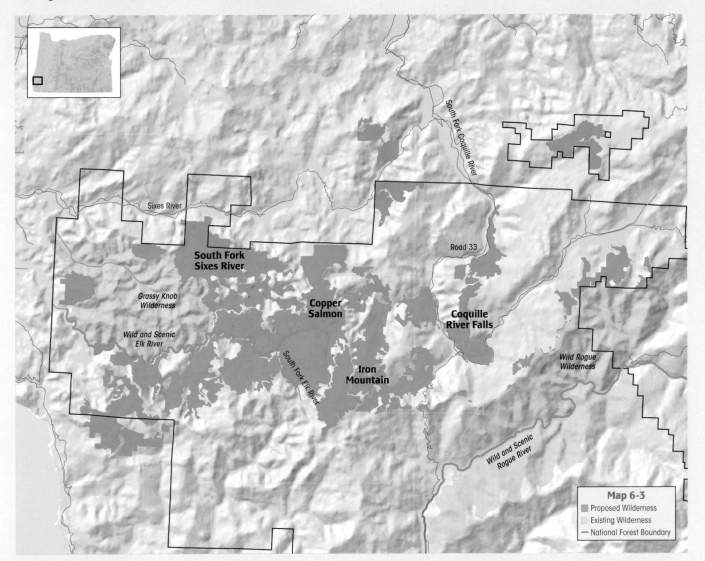

Map 6-3
■ Proposed Wilderness
□ Existing Wilderness
— National Forest Boundary

LEVEL IV ECOREGIONS
Southern Oregon Coastal Mountains (84%), Mid Coast Sedimentary (14%); Klamath Mountains Level III Ecoregion: Inland Siskiyous (2%)

VEGETATION TYPES
Douglas-fir/Western Hemlock (65%), Siskiyou Mixed Conifer (32%), Oregon White Oak/Ponderosa (4%), Cutover/Burned (<1%)

DRAINAGE SUBBASINS
Coquille, Elk, Sixes

ELEVATION RANGE
203-4,026 feet

UNITS
Bald Mountain, Coal Falls Creek, Copper Salmon, Coquille River Falls, *Grassy Knob Additions* (North Fork Dry Creek, Rock Creek, South Fork Sixes River), Hall Creek, Iron Mountain, Jim Hayes Creek, Milbury Mountain, Mud Lake, Panther Creek, Purple Mountain, Riggs Creek, Two by Four Creek, *Wild Rogue Additions* (Panther Ridge)

EXISTING WILDERNESS INCORPORATED
Grassy Knob

SIZE
55,041 acres (86 square miles, not including 17,200 acres of currently protected Wilderness)

COUNTIES
Coos, Curry

FEDERAL ADMINISTRATIVE UNITS
Siskiyou National Forest; BLM Coos Bay and Medford Districts

CONGRESSIONAL DISTRICT
4th

Highlights of some of the proposed Wilderness units are listed below.

Copper Salmon is featured on page 92.

Iron Mountain has a nice hiking trail along the summit.

The hillsides, stream banks and wetlands of the **Coquille River Falls** unit are thick with Port Orford-cedar. To protect important salmonid spawning and rearing habitat, the stream is closed to angling.

The **South Fork Sixes River** includes several miles of pristine spawning habitat for several species of anadromous fish.

PROPOSED WILDERNESS
Elk River

LOCATION
12 miles east of Port Orford

LEVEL IV ECOREGION
Southern Oregon Coastal Mountains

VEGETATION TYPES
Douglas-Fir/Western Hemlock (87%),
Siskiyou Mixed Conifer (13%)

TERRAIN
Extremely rugged and steep.

DRAINAGE SUBBASINS
Coquille, Sixes, Elk

ELEVATION RANGE
801-3,579 feet

SIZE
11,207 acres

COUNTIES
Coos, Curry

**FEDERAL
ADMINISTRATIVE UNIT**
Siskiyou National Forest (Powers Ranger
District)

USGS 7.5' QUAD MAPS
Barklow Mountain, Father Mountain, Ophir
Mountain

FEATURED UNIT
Copper Salmon

N amed for Copper and Salmon Mountains, this proposed
Wilderness unit is characterized by very steep slopes with
very unstable soils.

The area encompasses eighteen miles of salmon spawning
streams. The dense network of waterways is home to sea-run
cutthroat trout and coho salmon, both of which are listed under
the Endangered Species Act. The streams also contain lampreys,
resident coastal rainbow trout, winter steelhead, as well as spring
and fall chinook salmon.

The North Fork of the Elk River in the heart of this unit is
possibly the most productive salmon stream in the lower 48
states. Due to its amazing productivity, scientists study the North
Fork of the Elk River as a benchmark for conditions that support
an especially high diversity and abundance of native fish species.
A natural fire and large landslide, which occurred some time in the
past century, deposited huge amounts of large woody debris
(once large living trees) and sediment in the valley, contributing to
the conditions that make the watershed so rich in salmon and
other fishes.

The area also has some of the highest densities of marbled
murrelets left in the lower 48 states. The high concentration of
spotted owls found here may be evidence of "packing" that occurs
when birds move from destroyed habitat nearby to old trees still
left standing, which include large groves of very large Port
Orford-cedar.

A federal species of concern, the Del Norte salamander
(*Plethodon elongates*), has been seen near Copper Mountain in
this unit.

Approximately 300 species of plants can be found on Iron
Mountain along the Copper Salmon unit boundary, including the
northernmost Brewer's Spruce. Rare plants in the unit include
Oregon Bensonia (*Bensonia oregana*), Bolander's hawkweed
(*Hieracium bolanderi*), Piper's bluegrass (*Poa piperi*) and hairy
manzanita (*Arctostaphylos glandulosa*).

Wilderness designation can help scientists better understand
watershed conditions that create excellent salmon habitat and

Old growth Port Orford-cedar (*Chamaecyparis lawsoniana*) in the Copper Salmon
unit of the proposed Elk River Wilderness.

improve the chances of restoring salmon runs elsewhere.

Much of the Elk River is part of the Wild and Scenic Rivers
and/or Oregon Scenic Waterways systems, recognizing the natural
and recreational values both inside and outside the protected river
corridor and associated tributary streams.

road, their chances for survival are not good. Wilderness designation — which prohibits road building and logging — provides the best protection against the disease.

Much of the proposed Elk River Wilderness is critical habitat for the northern spotted owl, bald eagle, marbled murrelet and various runs of Pacific salmon. Black-tailed deer, Roosevelt elk, black bear and mountain lion are common here, as is the ringtail cat. Elusive marten have been sighted here and fisher are suspected to inhabit the area.

The watersheds encompassed by the proposed Wilderness contain highly productive salmon streams, most notably the Elk River. The mostly intact Elk River watershed (i.e., relatively few roads and clearcuts) allows the river and its feeder streams to clear twenty-four hours after a big storm. Clean, clear, cold water is ideal for spawning and hatching salmon.

The Elk River is the most productive salmon-producing watershed remaining in the lower 48 states. Because of their importance to coho, spring and fall chinook salmon, as well as winter steelhead, the American Fisheries Society has identified several aquatic diversity areas that coincide with many units of this proposed Wilderness. The Elk River also contains sea-run cutthroat trout, chum salmon, Pacific lamprey, Western brook lamprey, prickly sculpin, Pacific staghorn sculpin and three-spine stickleback. The Sixes River hosts winter steelhead, both resident and sea-run cutthroat trout, as well as spring and fall chinook salmon. The Coquille River watershed is home to coho and chinook salmon, sea-run cutthroat trout and steelhead.

The Oregon Biodiversity Project's Cape Blanco Conservation Opportunity Area includes the entire Elk River watershed, which is highly valued for both its terrestrial and aquatic biological diversity — including old-growth conifer forests. The area is home to more than twenty-five "at-risk" species and the increasingly rare Port Orford-cedar.

To protect its numerous natural and recreational values, portions of the Elk River has been designated a national Wild and Scenic River and an Oregon Scenic Waterway. However, these natural values are dependent upon the quality of upland and tributary streams that lie outside the protected river corridor.

Recreation here centers on the fantastic fishing which is a direct product of the landscape's wilderness quality. Hiking and hunting are also popular, as is simply enjoying the magnificent old-growth Port Orford-cedar.

While nearly 45,000 acres of the proposed Wilderness is not currently scheduled for timber cutting, the area remains vulnerable to logging.

The North Fork Elk River is the most productive stretch of salmon habitat in the lower 48 states. ▶

Proposed Oregon Dunes Wilderness
Largest Coastal Sand Dunes on Earth

From the North Spit of Coos Bay to Heceta (pronounced HEC-ah-ta) Head (which is directly adjacent to Heceta [pronounced Heh-SEA-ta] Beach), the Coos Bay Dune Sheet covers 54 miles of shoreline and ranges inland up to three miles. Much of the area is within the Oregon Dunes National Recreation Area (NRA) and is suitable for Wilderness designation. Starting at sea level and not rising far above it, the dunes are the lowest elevation wildlands in Oregon.

Depending on the winds and whims of nature, the dunes can reach more than 500 feet above sea level. The dunes change constantly as they have for the past 7,000 years, so their height varies continually. Early offshore European explorers mistook the white dunes for snow. The extremely pale sand is about one-third quartz, one-third feldspar and the rest a combination of chert, agate, some magnetite and other dark minerals.

There are three distinct types of dunes. Closest to the beach are the transverse dunes, a common dune form found in desert regions. These low-profile wave-like structures run almost parallel to the beach. Just inland are the oblique ridges. Some run over a mile in length and are hundreds of feet tall. Oblique ridges are found nowhere else in the world. Until they are stopped by higher ground, the dunes advance three to five feet annually and bury everything in their path, including forests, lakes and streams. The parabola (or crescent) dunes originate in vegetated areas. The wind creates a "blow-out" that allows these dunes to advance. The sand can build to a 33-degree angle of repose. If it gets any steeper, the sand begins to flow.

Vegetation contributes to both the creation and destruction of dunes. The combination of temperate rain forest "islands" in the huge desert-like dune fields result in an ecosystem found nowhere else on earth.

The first or "pioneer" species to vegetate open sand include prostrate lupine, seashore bluegrass, dunegrass, large-headed sedge, gray beach peavine, beach silver top and beach morning glory. The shrubs that follow include salal, rhododendron and evergreen huckleberry. Then come the trees, primarily shore pine and Sitka spruce, along with western hemlock, western redcedar and wax myrtle. In long-stabilized areas, Douglas-fir will take root and can last a half millennium.

Several coastal lakes and streams penetrate the dunes. The lakes were formed by sand dams on streams or by sand that moved in to block ocean inlets. Steelhead, coho salmon and other fish species inhabit these beautiful white sand bottom streams.

At least twenty-six distinct wildlife habitats have been identified in the Oregon Dunes. The dunes and associated estuaries and their offshore waters host 426 species,

Islands of forest are found in a sea of sand. ▶

Proposed Oregon Dunes Wilderness

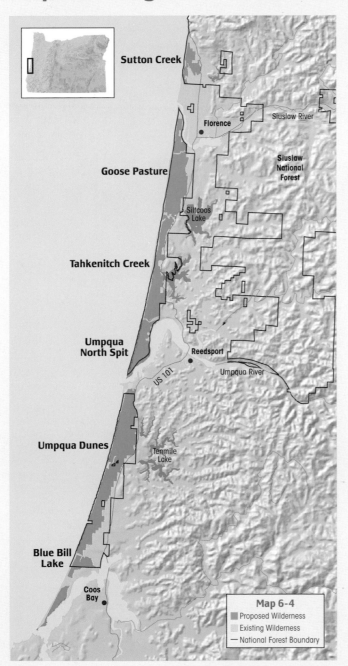

Some of the proposed Oregon Dunes Wilderness units are summarized below.

A rewarding little loop trail can be found at **Bluebill Lake** on the northern end of the North Spit of Coos Bay.

Goose Pasture lies between the Siuslaw River and Siltcoos River and includes some small dunal lakes.

Umpqua North Spit unit includes the spit on the north side of the Umpqua River and many small wetlands.

Sutton Creek is north of the Siuslaw River outside of the Oregon Dunes NRA and is a unique ribbon of riparian habitat in a dune-forest woodland.

Takenitch Creek lies between the Siltcoos River and Sparrow Park Road and includes Threemile Lake, Butterfly Lake and a few other unnamed small lakes.

The **Umpqua Dunes** are featured on page 96.

LEVEL IV ECOREGION
Coastal Lowlands

VEGETATION TYPES
Shorelands (65%), Sitka Spruce (35%), Douglas-fir/Western Hemlock (<1%)

DRAINAGE SUBBASINS
Coos, Siltcoos, Siuslaw, Umpqua

ELEVATION RANGE
0-500+ feet

UNITS
Bluebill Lake, Goose Pasture, North Spit Coos Bay, Siuslaw Dunes, Sutton Creek, Tahkenitch Creek, Umpqua Dunes, Umpqua North Spit

EXISTING WILDERNESS INCORPORATED
None

SIZE
27,722 acres (39 square miles)

COUNTIES
Coos, Douglas, Lane

FEDERAL ADMINISTRATIVE UNIT
Oregon Dunes National Recreation Area, Siuslaw National Forest

CONGRESSIONAL DISTRICT
4th

PROPOSED WILDERNESS
Oregon Dunes

LOCATION
6 miles south-southwest of Winchester Bay

LEVEL IV ECOREGION
Coastal Lowlands

VEGETATION TYPES
Shorelands (72%), Sitka Spruce (28%)

TERRAIN
Vast expanses of open sand.

DRAINAGE SUBBASINS
Umpqua, Tenmile

ELEVATION RANGE
0-500+ feet

SIZE
10,290 acres

COUNTIES
Coos, Douglas

FEDERAL ADMINISTRATIVE UNIT
Siuslaw National Forest (Oregon Dunes National Recreation Area)

USGS 7.5' QUAD MAPS
Lakeside, North Bend, Winchester Bay

DOMINIC DEFAZIO

While often narrow in width, the solitude in proposed Oregon Dunes Wilderness is very real. When walking in dunes, it feels much larger than it is as one takes one step back for every two forward.

FEATURED UNIT

Umpqua Dunes

One of the most magnificent and vast expanses of open sand in the Oregon Dunes lies in the Umpqua Dunes, south of the Umpqua River. This roadless unit is bounded on the north by Umpqua Lighthouse State Park and on the south by the Horsefall Beach Road.

A three-mile "trail" (actually a series of guide posts, only visible if they haven't been swallowed by the sand) leads visitors across the open sand, through the foredune and onto the beach. Along the way, one will see towering sculpted dunes, tree islands and freshwater ponds. Unfortunately, most of the unit is now open to off-road vehicles. A portion of the unit, which runs from the Douglas-Coos County line south to Tenmile Creek, however, is closed to the motorized monsters. Violations of the closure by scofflaws are common.

Tenmile Creek flows out of Tenmile Lake to the ocean through three miles of sand. In late summer, shifting sand can choke off the creek. Fall rains allow the creek to again find its way to the ocean, opening up passage for migrating steelhead and coho salmon. The city of Coos Bay would like to dewater Tenmile Creek to facilitate industrial growth. One would think that one of the state's wettest regions would not have a water shortage. That assumption is correct. It is the present wasteful use of water and fantasies of a major industrial port that create Coos Bay's potential "shortage." Tenmile Lake and its tributaries are home to 20 percent of the remaining coho salmon on Oregon's south coast. The salmon's only path to the sea is by way of Tenmile Creek.

Lakes and wetlands add important habitat diversity to the sand dunes.

beach grass.

The ever-shifting sands of the Oregon Dunes are dying and will be completely stabilized — hence rendered inert — within a half-century unless drastic action is taken to control European beach grass, an exotic species intentionally planted in the dunes to facilitate settlement and development. This pernicious weed prevents beach sand from replenishing the dunes and the grass is now covering the dunes themselves. It is also forcing out the area's native species, including American dune-grass and pink sand verbena.

Since European beach grass was established in the 1920s, an unnatural stabilized foredune has been established parallel to the beach, choking off the dunes' sand supply. As the wind passes eastward over the foredune in summer, when the water table is low, it scoops out a depression, called a deflation plain, immediately to the east of the foredune. In winter, the water table rises to form wetlands full of small orchids, insect-eating sundew plants and salamanders. Over time, the deflation plain can become impenetrable, overrun with dense vegetation. Aerial photography from the 1930's show that 80 percent of the dunes were open sand. Today, only about 20 percent remain open.

The Forest Service has been timid in its response to this threat, because the attempted solutions have been expensive and not very productive. Herbicides, mechanical disturbance, fire, irrigating with salt and grazing have all been tried with mixed results. The agency needs to redouble its efforts.

Without intervention, the dunes' demise is inevitable. If nothing else, the Oregon National Guard should be dispatched periodically to bulldoze a breach in the foredune that would allow sand to flow inward and replenish the dunes. The Wilderness Act and subsequent management policy provides for such actions as necessary to protect wilderness values.

Wilderness designation for the Oregon Dunes can conserve, protect and restore one of the world's most unique ecosystems. ◆

including 247 birds, 79 mammals (50 on land, 29 in the ocean), 83 fish, twelve amphibians, three reptiles and two shellfish species. Forest creatures here include black-tailed deer, white-footed vole, coyote, raccoon and black bear. Beavers, otters, sea lions and seals are found in the estuaries, along with Canada geese, bald eagles, osprey, cormorants, as well as gull and egret species. Beetle tracks can be seen in the smooth sand. The threatened western snowy plover also nests here in open sand where vehicles, dogs and humans can easily disturb it.

The most popular form of recreation at the Oregon Dunes is roaring up and down the sand in dune buggies, all-terrain vehicles and motorcycles. Such activities are annoying to every other dunes visitor and harmful to plants and wildlife, not to mention dangerous for the riders.

Hiking here is best from June through October, as four-fifths of the 80 inches of annual rainfall occurs during the other months. If one is on foot, the Oregon Dunes always seem bigger than they are, because the leeside loose sand usually results in one step slipping back for every two steps forward. The windward side, however, can be a remarkably firm walking surface. Horseback riding is also popular here. So is jumping off the steep side of dunes and trying to keep your head above the rest of one's body all the way to the bottom.

The Oregon Dunes are eminently suitable for Wilderness designation that would eliminate the damage caused by off-road vehicles. The entire area, however, will need some aggressive and periodic management to curtail the threat posed by European

World-Class Biodiversity
Klamath Mountains Ecoregion

The 3.9 million acres of the Klamath Mountains Ecoregion in Oregon (most of the ecoregion lies in California) extend from the California border to the southern end of the Willamette Valley, and from the Cascade foothills to the Coast Range. They encompass what the International Union for the Conservation of Nature calls an area of "global botanical significance" and the World Wildlife Fund terms the "Galapagos of North America." The region's highest point, Mount Ashland, rises to 7,533 feet in the Siskiyou Mountains.

Defining the region's geography can be as knotty as its geology and botany. The Siskiyou Mountains run generally east-west, roughly parallel to the Oregon-California border, which they cross three times. In the western portion of the region, the Siskiyou Mountains divide with one flank ranging northward along the Illinois Valley and the other southward to the Siskiyou Wilderness in California. In Oregon, the Siskiyou Mountains lie primarily within the Rogue River and Klamath National Forests, as well as the Medford District of the Bureau of Land Management. Only a small fraction of the Siskiyou Mountains is actually in the Siskiyou National Forest. Most of the Siskiyou National Forest is located in Oregon and is almost entirely composed of the Klamath Mountains. The Klamath Mountains, however, do not drain south into the Klamath River — most of which flows through California — but into the Chetco, Illinois, lower Rogue and other Oregon rivers and streams that flow into the Pacific Ocean.

The Klamath Basin is located in the East Cascades Slopes and Foothills Ecoregion. The Klamath River itself begins in Oregon below Upper Klamath Lake, then cuts through the California portion of the Cascades Ecoregion, flowing from the east side of the Cascades through the Klamath Mountains and California's Coast Range, before emptying into the Pacific Ocean. This confounded geography is why the region is often called the "Klamath Knot" — and why we appreciate maps.

Due to the great diversity and age of the underlying geology and soils, the Klamath Mountains Ecoregion is extremely diverse. The ecoregion was not shaped by volcanoes, but is made up of a jumble of igneous (mostly basalt), metamorphic (mostly granite) and sedimentary rock formations. Monadnock formations (an isolated rock mass above a plain) are also found here. The topography ranges — and often changes abruptly — from valley bottoms, to gentle foothills, to very steep, dissected and folded mountains. The varied topography is home to botanically rich forests, riparian zones, bogs, grasslands, savannas and alpine meadows.

Perhaps most interesting of the region's geological features are the serpentine formations which are made up of "an unusual metamorphic rock rich in magnesium and some other minerals but deficient in calcium and others."[1] The serpentine soils found here are low in silica and high in heavy metals such as zinc, iron, chromium, nickel, magnesium and cobalt. Several unusual plant and insect species co-evolved with the unique chemistry of these lands.

The Klamath Mountains Ecoregion hosts some of the most diverse conifer forests in the world. Over thirty species of conifers are found here. The region is a botanic crossroads, hosting species common to the Sierra Nevada Mountains, Sacramento Valley, Cascade Mountains, Coast Ranges and the Great Basin. Of the 4,000 plant species found in Oregon, about half are found in the Klamath Mountains Ecoregion, including 115 at-risk plant and animal species. Many of these species are endemic to the region and are on official state or federal conservation lists.

Many of the Klamath Mountains roadless wildlands proposed for Wilderness protection have been identified by The Nature Conservancy as vital to the protection of the region's biodiversity.

The region's sub-humid climate is mild, but distinguished by an extended summer drought. Up to 140 inches of precipitation can fall in the mountains, but as little as 20 inches in the valleys, where temperatures in the summer can exceed 100 degrees.

All of the region's habitats have been sculpted by fire, usually frequent low-level surface fires with the infrequent, high intensity, stand-replacing fires.

Major charismatic animal species include Roosevelt elk, mountain lion, coyote, black-tailed deer, coyote, ringtail cat, fisher, marten, river otter, eagles, hawks, osprey, peregrine falcon, ruffed grouse, numerous species and stocks of Pacific salmon (including some of the most productive runs outside of Alaska) and the well-known northern spotted owl.

The Klamath Mountains Ecoregion has been called a mollusk mecca. With 235 native species and subspecies, mollusks outnumber the numerous breeding bird species found in the region. Well over half these mollusks are endemic to the Klamath Mountains, meaning that they are found nowhere else on earth.

In addition to precipitation and elevation, the significant variables that determine forest types in the Klamath Mountains Ecoregion are soil and aspect. North-facing

The currently protected Kalmiopsis Wilderness needs to be tripled in size to ensure the enduring resource of wildness. ▶

KLAMATH MOUNTAINS ECOREGION

Ecoregions of Oregon's Klamath Mountains

This ecoregion encompasses the highly dissected ridges, foothills and valleys of the Klamath and Siskiyou mountains. It was unglaciated during the Pleistocene epoch, when it served as a refuge for northern plant species. Its mix of granitic, sedimentary, metamorphic and extrusive rocks contrasts with the predominantly volcanic rocks of the Cascades. The mild, subhumid climate of the Klamath Mountains is characterized by a lengthy summer drought. It supports a mosaic of both northern Californian and Pacific Northwestern conifers and hardwoods.

Scientists have further subdivided Oregon's Klamath Mountains Level III Ecoregion into seven Level IV ecoregions:

The **Rogue/Illinois Valleys** ecoregion supports Oregon white oak and California black oak woodland, ponderosa pine and grassland. As in other highly developed valleys, little original vegetation remains. Remnants of oak savanna, prairie vegetation and seasonal ponds persist on the mesa tops of the Table Rocks north of Medford. Elsewhere, land uses include orchards, cropland and pastureland. Climate, vegetation and resulting land use are more similar to northern California's inland valleys than to the Willamette Valley.

The **Oak Savanna Foothills** border the Rogue and Illinois river valleys ecoregion, sharing their Mediterranean-type climate. The driest area east of Medford is dominated by oak woodlands, grassland — savanna, ponderosa pine and Douglas-fir. The wetter foothills flanking the Illinois Valley support Douglas-fir, madrone and incense cedar. This ecoregion is lower and less dissected, with more oak woodland and less closed-canopied forest than the Inland Siskiyous.

Unlike the purely mountainous terrain of the Inland Siskiyous or the broader Rogue/Illinois Valleys, the **Umpqua Interior Foothills** ecoregion is a complex of foothills and narrow valleys containing fluvial terraces and floodplains. This ecoregion is drier than the foothills of the Willamette Valley partly because the summer Pacific high pressure system arrives earlier and remains longer than in ecoregions to the north. Summers are hot and dry, and soils have a xeric moisture regime in contrast to the udic soils of the Mid-Coastal Sedimentary ecoregion in the Coast Range to the west. Oregon white oak woodland, Douglas-fir, ponderosa pine, madrone and an understory chaparral community cover the slopes and intermingle with pastureland, vineyards, orchards and row crops.

The **Serpentine Siskiyous** ecoregion is lithologically distinct from the rest of the Klamath Mountains. Many plants have difficulty growing in its serpentine soils due to a shortage of calcium and high levels of magnesium, nickel and chromium. As a result, vegetation is often sparse and composed of specialist species. Jeffrey pine and endemic oak and ceanothus species have evolved to grow in the potentially toxic and nutrient-poor serpentine soils. Historic mines and associated water quality problems occur.

The forested **Inland Siskiyous** ecoregion is higher and more mountainous than neighboring foothill and valley ecoregions Rogue/Illinois Valleys, Oak Savanna Foothills

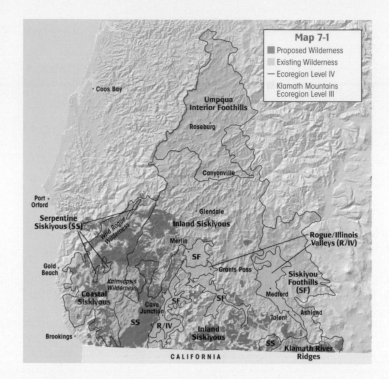

and Umpqua Interior Foothills. This ecoregion has a higher fire frequency, less annual precipitation and longer summer droughts than the Coastal Siskiyous. Forest cover is a diverse and multi-layered mix of conifers, broadleaf evergreens, deciduous trees and shrubs in contrast to the predominantly coniferous forests that occur in the Coast Range or Cascades.

The **Coastal Siskiyous** ecoregion has a wetter and milder maritime climate than else-where in the Klamath Mountains. Productive forests composed of tanoak, Douglas-fir and some Port Orford cedar cover its mountainous landscape; tanoak is more common than elsewhere in Oregon. Broadleaf evergreens, such as tanoak and madrone, quickly colonize disturbed areas, making it difficult to regenerate conifer forest growth. Xeric soils derived from Siskiyou rock types are characteristic. Udic soils which support western hemlock and Sitka spruce are much less common than in the wetter Coast Range.

The **Klamath River Ridges** have a dry, continental climate. Vegetation varies with slope, aspect and elevation. Higher altitudes and north-facing slopes have Douglas-fir and white fir; lower elevations and south-facing slopes are covered in ponderosa pine and western juniper, species that are more drought resistant than other vegetation types found in the Klamath Mountains.

Text gratefully adapted from Thor D. Thorson, Sandra A. Bryce, Duane A. Lammers, Alan J. Woods, James M. Omernik, Jimmy Kagan, David E. Pater, Jeffrey A. Comstock. 2003. Ecoregions of Oregon (color poster with map, descriptive text, summary tables and photographs). USDI-Geological Survey. Reston, VA (map scale 1:1,500,000).

slopes are much wetter than south-facing ones, while certain soil types favor specific tree species.

The most common forest type in the ecoregion is the **Siskiyou Mixed Conifer** with its varying and abundant mixes of Douglas-fir, sugar pine, ponderosa pine, incense cedar and white fir. Bigleaf maple, Pacific madrone and western white pine are also common here. Western red cedar and western hemlock can be found in the area's wetter sites. A variant of this forest type is the **Siskiyou Mixed Conifer-High Elevation** forest with more white fir and less Douglas-fir, sugar pine, ponderosa pine and western white pine. The lower-elevation variant is the **Siskiyou Mixed Evergreen** forest, which has more of Pacific madrone, tanoak and other broadleaf trees.

Oregon White Oak/Ponderosa, **Oregon White Oak/Douglas-fir**, **Oregon White Oak/Juniper** and **Oregon White Oak/Pacific Madrone** forests are found at the edges of the Rogue and Umpqua Valleys. The latter of these four forest types is also found in the drier parts of the Rogue and Chetco River drainages, where incense cedar may also be present.

Many species of trees cannot tolerate the serpentine soils that characterize the region's Siskiyou Jeffrey Pine forests. On drier sites, the Jeffrey pines are widely spaced among sparse grass cover. On higher, wetter sites, Douglas-fir grows along with incense cedar and knobcone pine, sugar pine and western white pine.

Adding to the diversity of the Klamath Mountains Ecoregion forests are small pockets of **Douglas-fir/Ponderosa/True Fir** and **Mountain Hemlock/Red Fir** forest. The former is much more common east of the Cascade crest and the latter more commonly found in the Cascades Ecoregion, along with **Douglas-fir/Western Hemlock** forests. Widely scattered on drier sites are stands of **Douglas-fir/Ponderosa/Incense Cedar** and small stands of pure **Ponderosa**.

One of Oregon's — and the world's — rarest forest types is the **Redwood** forest. Redwoods are found primarily in California, but Oregon does have particularly rare and magnificent stands in the Coast Range Ecoregion (described here because the Oregon Redwood Units are in the proposed Kalmiopsis Wilderness Additions).

At some time in their existence, most forest communities will be set back to early successional forest and are classified as **Cutover/Burned** forest. This can occur naturally — from lightning-caused wildfires, native insect or disease events, or blow-down by wind — or unnaturally, by way of logging, human-caused fire, human-caused blowdown (due to unnatural and vulnerable forest edges caused by clearcuts), non-native disease and insects, or aggressive fire-fighting. Particularly troubling are "backburns," where firefighters intentionally burn the forest in front of an oncoming wildfire. In many cases, the backburns are far more intense and destructive than the natural burn would have been.

About half — 52 percent to be exact — of Oregon's Klamath Mountains Ecoregion

The Illinois River in the proposed Kalmiopsis Wilderness Additions. The majority of the half-million acres within the perimeter of the infamous 2002 Biscuit Fire only burned lightly or not at all. Some areas burned more heavily, but nature has been healing herself from fires far longer than Smokey Bear has been around.

is federally owned. The major federal holdings in this Ecoregion include most of the Siskiyou National Forest, a sizeable portion of the Rogue River National Forest, a small part of the Klamath National Forest that is in Oregon, the western part of the BLM Medford District and the eastern portion of the BLM Coos Bay District.

There are presently three Wilderness areas (Kalmiopsis, Wild Rogue and Red Buttes) comprising only 5.7 percent of the Oregon portion of this ecoregion.

Conservationists propose four additional multi-unit Wilderness areas: the Kalmiopsis Additions, Siskiyou Crest, Soda Mountain and Wild Rogue Additions. If designated, these areas would increase Wilderness protection to 23.9 percent of the ecoregion.

SANDY LONSDALE

Proposed Kalmiopsis Wilderness Additions
Largest and Most Ecologically Diverse Wildland in Oregon

One of Oregon's largest remaining wildlands, the proposed Kalmiopsis Wilderness Additions include lands in the Hunter Creek, Illinois, North Fork Smith, Chetco, Winchuck and Pistol River watersheds. (Segments of the Illinois, North Fork Smith and Chetco Rivers are part of the National Wild and Scenic Rivers System.) The rugged, steep and deep canyons and ridges are covered with dense old-growth forests, grassy prairies, serpentine barrens, serpentine fens (also called darlingtonia fens), talus, sparse open forests, savannas, sphagnum bogs and hardwood forests. These wildlands continue into California.

The proposed Wilderness additions, especially in the south, can appear both hostile and inviting. The ruggedness and occasionally sparse vegetation can be off-putting to some, but the region's geologic and botanic wonderland is irresistibly enticing. The current Kalmiopsis Wilderness is named after *Kalmiopsis leachiana*, a tiny rhododendron-like flower that is one of the rarest plants in North America.

The area's extraordinary botanical diversity stems from its geological diversity. Several major geologic formations dominate the landscape. Underneath the redrock rainforest are serpentine soils (created on the sea floor 200 million years ago), which form a unique substrate chemically unsuited for most plant species common to the ecoregion. In some places where standing water meets the serpentine, there are fens (alkaline bogs) that are characterized by the carnivorous darlingtonia plant. Interspersed with the peridotite serpentine is a granite-like rock, which gives a Sierra-like feel to the landscape. Nearby volcanic and sedimentary formations give rise to the area's lush forests.

Precipitation here ranges from 90 to 140 inches annually. During summer droughts, temperatures can rise to over 100 degrees.

The region's major tree species include Douglas-fir, Port Orford-cedar, Jeffrey pine, Oregon white oak, canyon live oak, knobcone pine, incense cedar, western white pine, white fir, Pacific madrone, bigleaf maple, western redcedar and the endemic Brewer's spruce. The serpentine soils produce much stunted vegetation; however, Jeffrey pine and numerous endemic species can tolerate the soils' unique chemistry that is toxic to other plants.

The rivers and streams within the proposed Wilderness are noted for their exceptional water quality. They clear quickly even after the heaviest storms. Coho, spring and fall chinook salmon, as well as winter steelhead are abundant here, as are

Western azalea (*Rhododendron occidentale*) is but one of the multitude of wildflower species in the proposed additions to the Kalmiopsis Wilderness. ▶

Proposed Kalmiopsis Wilderness Additions

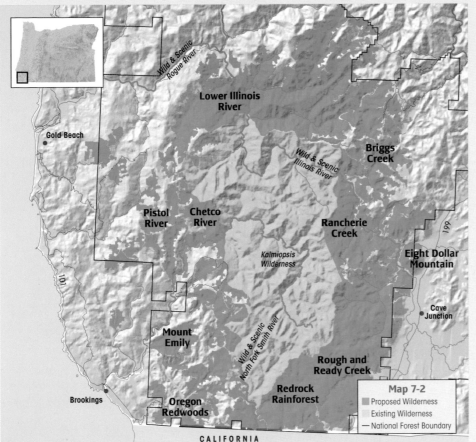

Map 7-2
■ Proposed Wilderness
▨ Existing Wilderness
— National Forest Boundary

herb (*Epilobium oreganum*) and Howell's mariposa-lily (*Calochortus howellii*).

The **Lower Illinois River** unit is terrific for whitewater boating. It also includes Indigo, Silver and Lawson Creeks, which are refuges for endangered salmon stocks.

Mount Emily was the target of a lone Japanese incendiary bomb during World War II and now has a memorial trail to the summit with fine views of nearby mountains, the coast and ocean. Emily Creek has fall chinook salmon, winter steelhead, resident trout and coho salmon.

Although located at the northern edge of the species' range, the **Oregon Redwoods** units include a *Sequoia sempervirens* that is 11-feet in diameter. These units also include Peavine Ridge, the only known location of Kellogg's Lily (*Lillium kelloggii*) in Oregon, and are home to other sensitive species such as Andrew's bead lily (*Clintonia andrewsiana*). Scientists suspect that Kurabayashi's wake robin (*Trillium angustipetalum*) is also here.

Some of the units in the proposed Wilderness are highlighted below.

The **Briggs Creek** units features knobcone pine, Oregon white oak and canyon live oak interspersed with the darlingtonia pitcher plant. It is also important spawning habitat for anadromous fish.

The **Chetco River** units include several streams of pristine water quality that support important fisheries, including unusually large fall chinook salmon.

Eight Dollar Mountain is a cone-shaped peak with grasslands interspersed with fens and forests. The serpentine soils here host such rare plants as Waldo or elegant gentian (*Gentiana setigera [bisetaea]*), large-flowered rush-lily (*Hastingia bracteosa*), western senecio or Siskiyou butterweed (*Senecio hesperius*), Oregon willow-

The **Pistol River** units include several interesting plant species, as well as chinook salmon and steelhead runs.

The **Rancherie Creek** unit includes Pearsoll Peak (the highest point in the proposed Wilderness), where fourteen conifer species have been identified in one little pocket that sits among open ridges, springs and wetlands.

The **Redrock Rainforest** is named for its reddish peridotite soils. It also contains the world's largest expanse of exposed serpentine rock and supports one of the world's four most diverse types of temperate forest.

Rough and Ready Creek is featured on page 104.

LEVEL IV ECOREGIONS
Coastal Siskiyous (40%), Serpentine Siskiyous (38%), Inland Siskiyous (18%), Rogue/Illinois Valleys (<1%); Coast Range Level III Ecoregion: Redwood Zone (2%), Southern Oregon Coastal Mountains (<1%)

VEGETATION TYPES
Siskiyou Mixed Conifer (51%), Siskiyou Jeffrey Pine (26%), Oregon White Oak/Ponderosa (10%), Douglas-fir/Western Hemlock (8%), Siskiyou Mixed Evergreen (2%), Siskiyou Mixed Conifer-High Elevation (1%), Cutover/Burned (<1%), Oregon White Oak/Douglas-fir (<1%), Oregon White Oak/Pacific Madrone (<1%), Redwood (<1%). *These figures are pre-2002 burns. In most cases, especially where less than completely burned, the same vegetation type remains. In other cases, the fire reset certain lands to "cutover/burned."*

DRAINAGE SUBBASINS
Chetco, Illinois, Smith, Winchuck

ELEVATION RANGE
200-5,034 feet

UNITS
Bear Ridge, Bravo Ransom Creek, Briggs Creek, Buck Creek, Dutchy Creek, Eagle Creek, East Fork Pistol River, Eight Dollar Mountain, Hog Mountain, Hunter Creek, Jack Creek, Josephine Creek, *Kalmiopsis Additions* (Redrock Rainforest, Lower Illinois River, Rancherie Creek), Mineral Rock Fork, Mount Emily, Myrtle Creek, North Fork Pistol River, North Fork Smith River, Peavine Ridge, Pebble Hill, Quail Prairie Creek, Quail Prairie Mountain, Signal Buttes, Six Mile Creek, Snow Camp Meadow, Soldier Creek, Sunrise Creek, Upper Wheeler Creek, Wheeler Creek

EXISTING WILDERNESS INCORPORATED
Kalmiopsis

SIZE
343,711 acres (537 square miles, not including 179,655 acres of currently protected Wilderness)

COUNTIES
Curry, Josephine

FEDERAL ADMINISTRATIVE UNITS
Siskiyou National Forest; BLM Coos Bay and Medford Districts

CONGRESSIONAL DISTRICT
4th

SANDY LONSDALE

PROPOSED WILDERNESS
Kalmiopsis Additions

LOCATION
3 miles west of O'Brien

LEVEL IV ECOREGIONS
Serpentine Siskiyous (100%), Rogue/Illinois Valleys (<1%)

VEGETATION TYPES
Siskiyou Jeffrey Pine (95%), Siskiyou Mixed Conifer (5%), Oregon White Oak/Ponderosa (<1%). *These figures are pre-2002 burns. In most cases, and especially where less than completely burned, the same vegetation type remains. In other cases, the fire reset certain lands to "cutover/burned."*

TERRAIN
Mountainous with both broad valleys and deep canyons.

DRAINAGE SUBBASIN
Illinois

ELEVATION RANGE
1,598-4,597 feet

SIZE
20,603 acres

COUNTY
Josephine

FEDERAL ADMINISTRATIVE UNIT
Siskiyou National Forest (Illinois Valley Ranger District)

USGS 7.5' QUAD MAPS
Buckskin Peak, O'Brien

Darlingtonia californica is a carnivorous plant found along Rough and Ready Creek in the Redrock Rainforest Unit of the proposed Kalmiopsis Wilderness Additions.

FEATURED UNIT

Rough and Ready Creek

Rough and Ready Creek has been a tributary of the Illinois River since the lands rose from the ocean floor some forty million years ago. This untamed stream is of incomparable beauty as it bends and braids across a rugged and superficially stark landscape. The water's clarity is an indication of the watershed's integrity.

Intact and uncompromised, Rough and Ready Creek is eligible for protection in the National Wild and Scenic Rivers System, as well as home to at-risk steelhead and cutthroat trout. Nearby springs feed surrounding wetlands that support lilies, orchids and carnivorous plants.

Only one-tenth of the watershed has been surveyed, but over 300 vascular plant species have been identified, of which at least 45 are considered rare. Of Oregon's 1,400 watersheds, Rough and Ready Creek has the highest concentration of rare plant species. Along the creek, one can find phlox, paintbrush and rare willows. In the creek's floodplain grow rock cress and Waldo buckwheat. Up slope, ancient and twisted Jeffrey pine and Port Orford-cedar forests are interspersed with openings of native bunch-grasses and western azalea. The rare Sadler oak (*Quercus sadleriana*) thrives here along-side the insectivorous pitcher plant (*Darlingtonia californica*). While the area qualifies as a rainforest that receives 60 to 100 inches of annual precipitation, the landscape also retains a desert-like character. In this portion of the Redrock Rainforest region are pockets of greenish serpentine soils, which are full of heavy metals that are toxic to many plants. However, some species can survive here, an adaptation that makes them both rare and tough!

Although the unit's botanical and geologic importance has been recognized in a variety of administrative land classifications, the unit remains blanketed by mining claims. A large mining operation has been proposed to extract nickel, iron and other miner-als from the red soils. It would require 25-ton ore trucks to rumble back and forth on fifteen miles of new or reconstructed roads — crossing the creek numerous times — up to 14,000 trips per year! A new, toxic smelter would also be constructed in the area. Rare plant colonies, Port Orford-cedar, spawning fish, all those who drink the local water and breathe the local air (not to mention human skinny-dippers) would be but a few of the victims of this greed.

The mining claimant wants to exercise a provision of the Mining Law of 1872 that would convert approximately 4,000 acres of public land into private property for $2.50/acre (a total of $10,000.00). Thus far, the mining corporation has been thwarted, but Wilderness designation and a public buyout of any valid claims are needed to prevent the inevitable and utter destruction of Rough and Ready Creek. With such protection, this rare community of life could continue to function naturally for at least another 40 million years.

sea-run cutthroat and coastal rainbow trout. Pacific lamprey, three-spined stickleback and assorted sculpin can also be found in the area's streams. This wealth of aquatic life has led the American Fisheries Society to identify several aquatic diversity areas here.

Birds of particular interest in the area include the northern spotted owl, osprey, bald eagle and peregrine falcon. Major mammal species include black-tailed deer, Roosevelt elk, black bear and possibly even Bigfoot (a.k.a. Sasquatch). Amphibians of particular interest include the Del Norte and California slender salamanders.

The Oregon Biodiversity Project's Upper Illinois River Conservation Opportunity Area, which includes Rough and Ready Creek, encompasses the southeast quadrant of the proposed Kalmiopsis Wilderness Additions. The area was designated to bring attention to a variety of unique plant communities and older forests, as well as over thirty "at-risk" species that live there.

Recreation here includes fishing, hunting, hiking, camping, horseback riding, whitewater boating, photography, botanizing, birding, sightseeing and swimming — not to mention gazing in wonderment at the ecological diversity.

Over 310,000 acres of the proposed Wilderness additions are nominally off-limits to logging, but that could change under the current or future administrations. Other threats include off-road vehicle abuse and mining. Where there is serpentine soil, there is nickel, chromite and cobalt. Gold and copper are also present in the area and miners enjoy dredging the streams for gold, an activity extremely harmful to salmonid fish species. A high percentage of the area is actively unstable and prone to landslides.

Proposed Siskiyou Crest Wilderness
Ecological Land Bridge between the Klamath and Cascades Mountains

The high mountain wildflower meadows, lakes that lie at the base of craggy peaks, magnificent and mossy old-growth forests, and streams and waterfalls on the slopes of the Siskiyou Mountains all offer outstanding opportunities for human recreation and solitude. For wildlife species, the Siskiyou Mountains crest is a land bridge between the mountains of the Coast and Cascade ranges.

The Siskiyou Mountains crest's eastern terminus is Soda Mountain in the Cascade-Siskiyou National Monument. Soda Mountain is actually in the Cascades Ecoregion. The north slope of the main Siskiyou Mountains crest drains into the Bear Creek, Applegate River and Illinois River watersheds, all of which flow into the Rogue River. The south slope drains into the Klamath River. Sixty-two miles west as the crest turns,

The Brewer spruce (*Picea brewerana*), found only in the Siskiyou Mountains, "weeps" to cope with heavy snowfall.

the Siskiyou Mountains divide near the California border where the headwaters of the Klamath, Applegate and Illinois rivers begin. One flank ranges north 22 miles, past Oregon Caves National Monument and peters out at Roundtop Mountain. The other flank of the Siskiyous ranges southwest another 22 miles to Youngs Peak in the Siskiyou Wilderness in California, where it dead-ends at the north-south Coast Range. Youngs Peak is a triple watershed divide. Its western side drains into the Smith River Basin, its south side drains into the Klamath River Basin and its north side flows into the Rogue River Basin.

Interstate 5 crosses the Siskiyou Mountains at Siskiyou Pass (4,310'). A few miles west is Mount Ashland (7,533'), the highest point along the crest. The crest continues into California, staying mostly above 7,000-feet in elevation until Condrey Mountain (7,112'). From there it descends gradually through several peaks to Sucker Creek Gap (back in Oregon) that is just over one mile high. The northern crest rises again to over 7,000 feet at Grayback Mountain (7,055') and then declines gently to Roundtop Mountain (4,693').

The Siskiyou Mountains crest crosses the Oregon-California border three times. A sizable portion of the proposed Wilderness is in California and won't be dealt with further here. Most of the crest has a great trail along the top of it, including part of the Pacific Crest National Scenic Trail.

The crest is made up of distinctly-colored meta-sedimentary, metavolcanic rocks, granite (*Gray*back Mountain) and peridotite (*Red* Butte). At 425 million years old, the rocks comprising the Siskiyou Mountains are estimated to be Oregon's oldest. The climate, the underlying geology, soils, slopes and aspects together create a botanical wonderland that includes numerous species found here and nowhere else. Due to the habitat diversity, overall species diversity, especially butterflies, is very high.

The crest and its slopes are important habitat for cougar, fisher, wolverine, marten, black bear, elk, fox, bobcat and coyote. The gray wolf, grizzly bear and

Proposed Siskiyou Crest Wilderness

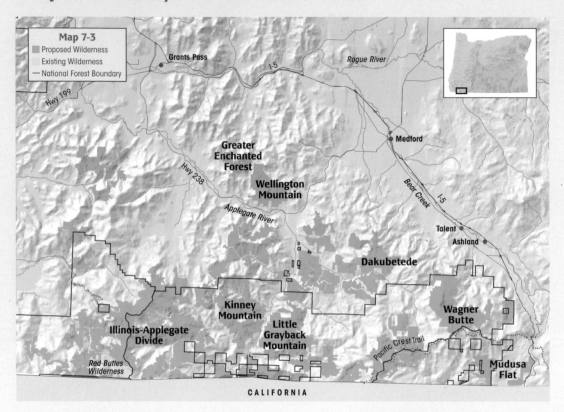

Map 7-3
- Proposed Wilderness
- Existing Wilderness
- National Forest Boundary

Some of the units of the proposed Wilderness are highlighted below.

Dakutubede is featured on page 107.

The **Greater Enchanted Forest** includes a unique riparian area dominated by old-growth Douglas-fir and numerous ancient bigleaf maples. Along with spotted owls, another species of concern here is the northern goshawk.

The **Illinois-Applegate Divide** ranges northward from the existing Red Buttes Wilderness and includes a portion of Oregon Caves National Monument.

Kinney Mountain has an old "bigfoot trap" — mute testimony to the hope that the species exists. Local wildlife that no one doubts the existence of include grouse, quail, deer and bear.

Little Grayback Mountain has steep slopes of mixed conifer forests and open grassy slopes that are favored by bears and bear hunters.

Mudusa Flat is geologically interesting and has several caves, as well as meadows and old-growth sugar pine.

Wagner Butte includes the headwaters of the city of Ashland's watershed and has spotted owls in mixed stands of ponderosa pine, Douglas-fir and white fir. It contains the only Engelmann spruce stands in the Klamath Mountains and one of three local stands of quaking aspen. The higher elevations include Shasta red fir and sugar pine. A rare flower, the Henderson's horkelia (*Horkelia hendersonii*) is found here, as is the rare and endemic Mount Ashland lupine (*Lupinus aridus*) that is now threatened by ski area expansion.

Wellington Mountain is located within the Applegate Watershed, but away from the high Siskiyou Mountains crest. It contains a very rare low-elevation (1,800-3,000') old-growth forest and is home to the northern spotted owl and a rare lily, the Gentner's fritillary (*Fritillaria gentneri*). It also contains spawning habitat for steelhead.

CHANT THOMAS

The Dakubetede Unit of the proposed Siskiyou Crest Wilderness is a complex mosaic of deciduous woodland, conifer forest, diverse shrubland and steep grasslands that evolved in the arid rain shadow of the Siskiyou's highest peaks. It receives only about 15 inches of precipitation annually, making it one of the driest locations in western Oregon.

FEATURED UNIT

Dakubetede

Many of the wildlands in the proposed Siskiyou Crest Wilderness are located far downslope from the high crest of the Siskiyou Mountains. The low-elevation Dakubetede ("dah-KU-be-TE-de") Unit is north of the Little Applegate River, which is an important spawning stream for coho salmon and steelhead.

Here local rainshadows and microclimates can give one the impression of being east of the Cascade Mountains. Klamath Knot geology is on full display here. The landscape is a mosaic of plant communities dictated by the varied soil types.

Conifer and hardwood forests inhabit the deep canyons.

Meadows, oak woodlands and white-leaf manzanita, ceanothus and birch-leaf mountain mahogany cover the steep ridges. Deciduous hardwood species here include red-osier dogwood, western madrone, Oregon white and California black oak, Oregon ash, bigleaf maple and Pacific willow. Coniferous softwood species include Douglas-fir, Pacific yew, knobcone and ponderosa pine and incense cedar.

Other species of note include both tall and dwarf Oregon grape, rabbitbrush (a staple of eastern Oregon landscapes), elderberry, serviceberry, creeping snow-berry, osoberry, blackberry, Klamath plum, hazel, black hawthorn, buckbrush, rose, cascara and — last, but not least — poison oak, a species that many people do not notice until it's too late.

The westernmost stands of western juniper are found here, as is the only known Oregon population of the endemic Siskiyou water birch. The area is also home to Gentner's fritillary (*Frilillaria gentneri*), a gorgeous red lily that is extremely rare and found only in Jackson and Josephine Counties, and the Applegate stonecrop (*Sedum oblanceolatum*), which is only found in the Applegate drainage. Many species living here along the Siskiyou Mountains crest are at the edge of their respective ranges.

The Muddy Gulch drainage has excellent examples of rare tufa and travertine geomorphological formations (also called "limestone" benches), which create several large, flat bottoms in otherwise steep V-shaped canyons.

Originally built to divert water for mining, the historic Sterling Ditch traverses Dakubetede. But the scar is healing well and now serves as the backbone of a good walking trail system.

PROPOSED WILDERNESS
Siskiyou Crest

LOCATION
13 miles west-southwest of Ashland

LEVEL IV ECOREGION
Inland Siskiyous

VEGETATION TYPES
Siskiyou Mixed Conifer (62%), Cutover/Burned (29%), Siskiyou Mixed Evergreen (9%).

TERRAIN
Steep south-facing slopes dissected by steep canyons.

DRAINAGE SUBBASIN
Applegate

ELEVATION RANGE
1,998-5,197 feet

SIZE
6,651 acres

COUNTY
Jackson

FEDERAL ADMINISTRATIVE UNIT
BLM Medford District (Ashland Resource Area)

USGS 7.5' QUAD MAP
Sterling Creek

California bighorn sheep have been extirpated from the area, but could be reintroduced. A population of white-headed woodpeckers, more common in eastside forests, is found southwest of Mount Ashland.

The rarest amphibian in western North America, the Siskiyou Mountains salamander (*Plethodon stormi*), lives only in the Upper Applegate and Seiad Creek drainages. Three subspecies have been identified, one north and two south of the crest. Unlike most salamanders that are aquatic by nature, this species lives in mossy talus (large rocks with lots of sheltering spaces in-between) shaded by thick forests. The crest is also the northern edge of the black salamander's range.

Over three-quarters of the 35 known species of coniferous tree species in the Klamath Mountains Ecoregion of Oregon and California are found in the proposed Siskiyou Crest Wilderness. Species more common to the Cascade Range but found along the Siskiyou Mountains crest include Engelmann spruce, Pacific silver fir, Alaska yellow cedar, subalpine fir and quaking aspen. Other species found here include Douglas-fir, ponderosa pine, madrone, manzanita, California black and Oregon white oak, bigleaf maple, ash and mountain mahogany. The last major tree species to be identified by science in the United States, the weeping or Brewer's spruce is endemic to the region, as are the Baker cypress and Sadler oak. One will also find lots of ponderosa, Jeffrey and knobcone pines, incense cedar, mountain hemlock and Shasta red fir.

The Applegate gooseberry (*Ribes marshallii*), which grows only on the slopes of the Applegate Valley, is one example of a variety of rare and unique species found along the Siskiyou Mountains crest.

The Oregon Biodiversity Project's (OBP) Upper Illinois River Conservation Opportunity Area encompasses the northern extension of the Siskiyou Mountains crest. The area was designated to bring attention to a variety of unique plant communities and old forests, as well as over 30 "at-risk" species that live here. OBP's Upper Applegate Conservation Opportunity Area, which also encompasses a portion of the proposed Wilderness, is recognized for its critical aquatic habitats. It also includes rare inland Port Orford-cedar habitats.

The American Fisheries Society has identified several aquatic diversity areas within the proposed Wilderness because of their importance to coho salmon, spring and fall chinook salmon, as well as summer and winter steelhead runs.

Recreation opportunities in the proposed Wilderness include hiking, backpacking, hunting, fishing, botanizing and amphibianizing.

Nearly 50,000 acres of the proposed Siskiyou Crest Wilderness are outside the currently programmed timber base, but that doesn't guarantee a stump-free future. Other serious threats include livestock grazing, ski area expansion, road building, off-road vehicles and wildfire suppression.

The views never end in the proposed Siskiyou Crest Wilderness. ▶

Proposed Soda Mountain Wilderness[2]
Ecological Crossroads

Ecologically, the Soda Mountain area is the nexus in Oregon where east meets west meets north meets south.

The western limits of the arid and sunny Oregon desert mingle here with the towering temperate forests of the west Cascades and Siskiyou ranges, the eastern limits of vegetation dependent on the moist and cool Pacific Ocean and the northern limits of the drier, sunnier California chaparral.

Depending on the aspect, elevation and soil-type (as determined by the under lying geology), one may find oneself in a true fir forest, a montane wildflower meadow, a pine-oak/fescue grassland, a maple-black oak riparian forest, an Oregon white oak savanna, a juniper-cedar/bunchgrass bald or a chaparral brushland — and several of these diverse ecological communities are often within a few steps of each other. The Oregon white oak/ponderosa pine plant community is uncommon and little of it is currently included in Oregon's Wilderness areas.

Ten rare, threatened or endangered species have been identified in this mosaic of habitats. Roosevelt elk, mountain quail, cougar, black bear, bobcat, golden eagle, goshawk, bald eagle and prairie falcon are also found here. The lower elevations are critical black-tailed deer winter range. The diversity of butterflies is one of the highest in North America; over 120 species have been identified in the vicinity. The mollusk diversity is astounding as well, with as many as twenty new species recently described, including nine endemic to the area within the 53,000-acre Cascade-Siskiyou National Monument.

The monument includes all of the proposed 23,138-acre Soda Mountain Wilderness in Oregon. An additional 9,000 acres of roadless lands in California are also proposed for Wilderness protection.

The desert influence is obvious here: big sagebrush, low sagebrush, Idaho fescue, bluebunch wheatgrass, western juniper, rabbitbrush, desert parsley, Indian paintbrush and wild rose occur in the area.

Prominent wildflower species include lavender calypso orchid, purple larkspur, golden tower butterweed, blue flax, Tolmie's cat's ear, Klamath fawn-lily, western trillium, Indian paintbrush, several species of lomatium, Pursh's milk-vetch, Shelton's violet, western buttercup, Sierra snakeroot and the phantom orchid.

Plant species of special concern include the Ashland thistle (*Cirsium ciliolatum*), pygmy monkey flower (*Mimulus pygmaeus*), clustered lady's slipper (*Cypripedium fasciculatum*), green-flowered wild ginger (*Asarum wagneri*) and the Siskiyou fritillary (*Fritillaria glauca*). In spring and summer, clouds of butterflies visit these wildflower meadows.

The American Fisheries Society has identified several aquatic diversity areas

Proposed Soda Mountain Wilderness

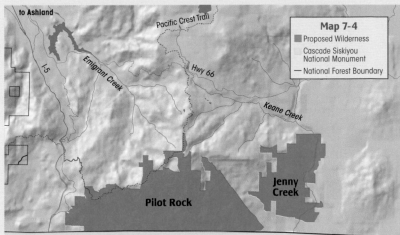

Map 7-4
■ Proposed Wilderness
Cascade Siskiyou National Monument
— National Forest Boundary

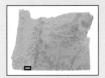

The proposed Wilderness has two units.

Jenny Creek is featured on page 110.

The **Pilot Rock** unit includes the most striking feature of the area: a very large volcanic plug of columnar basalt (hornblende andesite). Pilot Rock is visible for miles around, including from Interstate 5. Several miles of the Pacific Crest National Scenic Trail traverse the unit.

LEVEL IV ECOREGIONS
Klamath River Ridges (98%); East Cascades Slopes and Foothills
Level III Ecoregion: Southern Cascade Slope (<2%); Cascades
Level III Ecoregion: Southern Cascades (<1%)

VEGETATION TYPES
Siskiyou Mixed Conifer (32%), Siskiyou Mixed Evergreen (26%), Oregon White Oak/Ponderosa (20%), Oregon White Oak/Douglas-fir (8%), Ponderosa (7%), Cutover/Burned (3%), Oregon White Oak/Pacific Madrone (2%), Oregon White Oak/Juniper (1%)

DRAINAGE SUBBASINS
Middle Rogue, Upper Klamath

ELEVATION RANGE
2,979-5,910 feet

UNITS
Jenny Creek, Pilot Rock

EXISTING WILDERNESS INCORPORATED
None

SIZE
23,138 acres (36 square miles)

COUNTY
Jackson

FEDERAL ADMINISTRATIVE UNIT
BLM Medford District (Ashland Resource Area [Cascade-Siskiyou National Monument])

CONGRESSIONAL DISTRICT
2nd

PROPOSED WILDERNESS
Soda Mountain

LOCATION
5 miles south of Pinehurst

LEVEL IV ECOREGIONS
Klamath River Ridges (95%), Southern
Cascades (1%); Cascades Level III
Ecoregion: Southern Cascade Slope (4%)

VEGETATION TYPES
Siskiyou Mixed Evergreen (53%), Oregon
White Oak/Ponderosa (24%), Ponderosa
(23%)

TERRAIN
A prominent ridge, steep canyons and
creeks.

DRAINAGE SUBBASIN
Upper Klamath

ELEVATION RANGE
3,199-5,378 feet

SIZE
6,043 acres

COUNTY
Jackson

**FEDERAL ADMINISTRATIVE
UNIT**
BLM Medford District (Ashland Resource
Area [Cascade-Siskiyou National
Monument])

USGS 7.5′ QUAD MAPS
Parker Mountain, Soda Mountain

PEPPER TRAIL

Jenny Creek in the unit of the same name in the proposed Soda Mountain Wilderness.

FEATURED UNIT

Jenny Creek

*"I like those kind of places where I can lie in my bunk and dream of
the days gone by, and listen to the breezes making music in the
treetops. The sounds of the forest bring peace to the soul and I like
to hear the owls calling to one another, the barking of a coyote on
some far off hill, the scream of a cougar along with the noisy tale of
a rattlesnake singing its war song. I would not trade a place like that
for any of the things that can be found in the cities with all their
bright lights and glare."*

—George Wright (lifelong local resident) [3]

The Jenny Creek Unit is located on the eastern side of the
proposed Wilderness and is dominated by Keene Creek
Ridge. Plant communities here include a relatively rare
mixed conifer forest with a sugar pine overstory. Incense cedar
and Douglas-fir are common. Western juniper/Oregon white oak,

Oregon white oak/wedgeleaf
ceanothus and mixed
conifer/California black oak
are other interesting plant
communities in the unit. Other
major tree species include
Douglas hawthorn, bigleaf maple,
shining and arroyo willows,
Douglas spirea, mock-orange,
Oregon ash, white alder, black
cottonwood, birch leaf mountain
mahogany and quaking aspen.

Jenny Creek provides
important habitat for aquatic
species, including the Jenny
Creek redband trout and Jenny
Creek sucker, which are found
nowhere else. Other rare species
include the speckled dace and
Klamath small-scale sucker.

The unit is important deer
and elk winter range, as well as
home to at least six species of
bats, the western pond turtle,
the yellow-legged frog and at
least 43 species of butterflies.

Rare plant species here include Greene's mariposa lily
(*Calochortus greenei*), Howell's yampa or false-caraway (*Perideridia
howellii*) and Bellinger meadow-foam (*Limnanthes floccosa* ssp.
bellingeriana) which is often associated with Biscuit Scablands,
a rare mound and swale topography with patterned ground and
vernal pools. The unit contains the Oregon Gulch Research Natural
Area, designated to allow for the continued scientific study of two
ecological communities: (1) a mixed conifer forest dominated by
Douglas-fir and ponderosa pine with large scattered sugar pine
and incense cedar prominent in the overstory and (2) a manzanita-
wedgeleaf ceanothus/bunchgrass chaparral both at the eastern
boundary of the Klamath River Ridges of the Klamath Mountains
Ecoregion.

At Agate Flat are deposits of petrified wood and many colors
of agate.

Numerous archeological sites have been found in the area.

Many unmarked trails provide outstanding hiking and
horseback riding throughout the unit.

within the proposed Wilderness.

There are many trails here, but most are unmarked, except for the Pacific Crest National Scenic Trail. Views of Mount Shasta can be seen throughout the area. In addition to hiking, recreational opportunities here include hunting, fishing, horseback riding, botanizing and lepidopterizing.

In June 2000, President Bill Clinton designated 52,947 acres of federal land as the Cascade-Siskiyou National Monument, which included all of the proposed Wilderness. All monument lands are withdrawn from mineral exploitation and most logging is prohibited (though the level of protection depends on definitions to be included in the final management plan). Clinton proclaimed the national monument to protect the area's unparalleled biological diversity. However, this extraordinary landscape is still threatened by livestock grazing and off-road vehicles.

Proposed Wild Rogue Wilderness Additions
The Wildest Stretch of the Wild Rogue River

From its confluence with Grave Greek to its confluence with Quosatana Creek, the incomparable lower Rogue River defines the proposed additions to the Wild Rogue Wilderness. In 1968 Congress first recognized the ecological and recreational importance of the Lower Rogue when it designated the free-flowing segment from the confluence with the Applegate River downstream to the Lobster Creek Bridge as one of the original segments of the National Wild and Scenic Rivers System.

The Rogue River rises near Crater Lake in Oregon's Cascade Range (see the proposed Rogue-Umpqua Wilderness). After leaving the Cascades, the Rogue flows through the pastoral Rogue Valley before entering deep, forested canyons of the Klamath Mountains. Finally, 215 river miles from its source, the Rogue River meets the Pacific Ocean at Gold Beach.

The 33.6-mile stretch of the Rogue that flows from the confluence of Grave Creek to Illahe is classified as "wild" under the Wild and Scenic Rivers Act. The classification is the most protective under the law. The Rogue River is famous for its steelhead and salmon fishing, outstanding whitewater boating and wildlife viewing. (It's very likely that one will see at least one black bear if one floats or walks the Rogue River.)

In recognition that the narrow management corridor along the river cannot fully protect the values for which the Lower Rogue River was designated a Wild and Scenic River, Congress acted further in 1978 to designate the Wild Rogue Wilderness, which

◀ Waterfall in the Pilot Rock Unit of the proposed Soda Mountain Wilderness.

ELIZABETH FERYL, ENVIRONMENTAL IMAGES

LEVEL IV ECOREGIONS
Inland Siskiyous (48%), Coastal Siskiyous (33%), Serpentine Siskiyous (6%), Rogue/Illinois Valleys (<1%), Oak Savanna Foothills (<1%); Coast Range Level III Ecoregion: Southern Oregon Coastal Mountains (10%), Mid-Coastal Sedimentary (2%)

VEGETATION TYPES
Siskiyou Mixed Conifer (52%), Oregon White Oak/Ponderosa (41%), Douglas-fir/Broadleaf Deciduous (3%), Siskiyou Jeffrey Pine (2%), Siskiyou Mixed Evergreen (1%), Cutover/Burned (<1%), Oregon White Oak/Douglas-fir (<1%)

DRAINAGE SUBBASIN
Lower Rogue

ELEVATION RANGE
200-5,298 feet

UNITS
Ash Gulch, Bonanza Basin, Buckhorn Mountain, Cedar Mountain, Centennial Gulch, Colvig Gulch, East Sardine Creek, Fall Creek, Foster Creek, Greens Creek, Horn Gulch, Horse Creek, Iron Gulch, Iron Mountain, Lake of the Woods Mountain, Little Savage Creek, Lobster Creek, Lone Tree Ridge, Lost Valley, Maple Gulch, Monson Valley, Nine Mile Spring, Onion Mountain, Ophir Mountain, Pickett Creek, Potato Illahe Mountain, Quosatana Creek, Reuben Creek, Sexton Mountain, Shan Creek, Shasta Costa Creek, Slate Creek, Stair Creek, Whiskey Creek, *Wild Rogue Additions* (Billings Creek, Mule Creek, South Additions, Stair Creek, West Fork Cow Creek, Zane Grey), Wilson Creek, Wolf Creek

EXISTING WILDERNESS INCORPORATED
Wild Rogue

SIZE
172,470 acres (269 square miles, not including 35,818 acres of currently protected Wilderness)

COUNTIES
Curry, Douglas, Jackson, Josephine

FEDERAL ADMINISTRATIVE UNITS
Siskiyou National Forest; BLM Coos Bay and Medford Districts

CONGRESSIONAL DISTRICT
4th

Proposed Wild Rogue Wilderness Additions

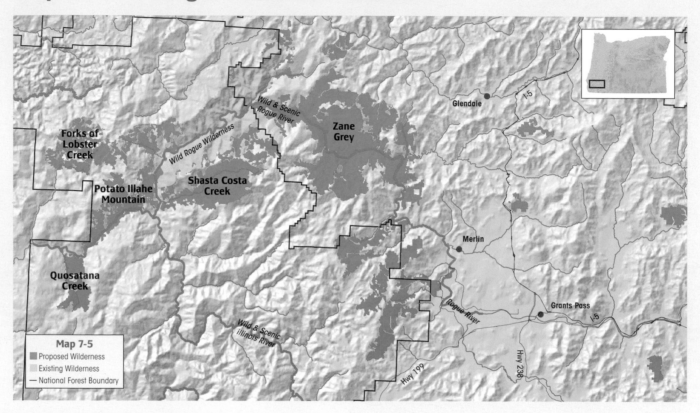

Map 7-5
■ Proposed Wilderness
  Existing Wilderness
— National Forest Boundary

Some of the units of the proposed Wilderness are highlighted below.

The **Forks of Lobster Creek** units don't have lobster, but they do have crayfish, crawfish or crawdads, however you call them. While not lobster, they're not bad.

Potato Illahe Mountain varies from rolling, hummocky terrain to steep slopes and deeply incised drainages where hardwood stands and conifers are interspersed with meadows, prairies and cliffs. It also includes several miles of trail along the river, which is part of the greater Rogue River Trail system.

Quosatana Creek is a copious producer of salmon and a study area for macroinvertebrates. It is also nesting habitat for endangered marbled murrelets. The natural openings that occur in the forest here increase the diversity of wildlife habitat.

Shasta Costa Creek flows through an area of transition between the Klamath Mountains and the Coast Range ecoregions. Both chinook salmon and steelhead spawn in the creek.

Zane Grey is featured on page 113.

FEATURED UNIT
Zane Grey

The largest roadless wildland along the Rogue River is named after the American writer of western novels who owned a miner's cabin at Winkle Bar where he came to fish and write.

The unit includes 24 miles of the Rogue, as well as numerous tributaries including Howard, Windy, Bunker, Kelsey and Whisky Creeks. An aural and visual testimony to the steep terrain, waterfalls abound here, especially during spring run-off. Because most visitors are focused on the mainstem of the Rogue, these tributary streams are rarely visited. Those who do visit can see waterfalls cascading into mossy green pools and other displays of stunning beauty. The surrounding hillsides are either thickly forested with old growth conifers or canyon live oak, or are covered with rocky talus.

A rare species of stonecrop (*Sedum moranii*), a hearty wildflower that appears to grow right out of the rock, can be spotted here.

The wildest part of the Rogue River Trail and the wildest section of the Rogue Wild and Scenic River traverse the unit. If one doesn't want to rough it overnight in this Wilderness, one can stay in lodges along the way, located just outside of the proposed Wilderness. The river is a challenge for boaters (which is why they flock to the Rogue every summer), but hikers find the Rogue River Trail generally easy going.

A short trail to Rainie Falls along the south bank of the Rogue is used by fishermen and those who come to observe migrating salmon and steelhead and the numerous foundering and flounderings of watercrafts that fail to properly negotiate Rainie Falls.

This unit is visited by hordes of people, mostly by boat. Boating is increasingly regulated to maintain both a wild recreational experience for visitors and a wild home for the area's permanent residents — fish and wildlife.

After several days of floating the very wild Rogue River a visitor may eventually encounter an infamous Rogue River "Mail" boat, loaded with tourists and propelled by a very powerful and loud motor. Motorized craft are currently allowed too far upstream into the wild section of the river. A common reaction of many rafters — still on a wilderness high — has been spontaneous (and First Amendment-protected) mooning of the noisy power craft. If done in close enough proximity — and deep enough water — the boat pilot invariably feigns an attempt to ram the boatload of mooners. No one gets hurt, but the mooners often get wet from the wake and spray.

A forest threatened by logging in the Zane Grey Unit of the proposed Wild Rogue Wilderness Additions.

PROPOSED WILDERNESS
Wild Rogue

LOCATION
20 miles west-northwest of Agness

LEVEL IV ECOREGIONS
Inland Siskiyous (79%), Coastal Siskiyous (21%)

VEGETATION TYPES
Oregon White Oak/Ponderosa (78%), Siskiyou Mixed Conifer (20%), Cutover/Burned (2%)

TERRAIN
Major river canyon, steep with cascading tributaries.

DRAINAGE SUBBASIN
Lower Rogue

ELEVATION RANGE
400-3,852 feet

SIZE
46,645 acres

COUNTIES
Curry, Josephine

FEDERAL ADMINISTRATIVE UNIT
BLM Medford District (Glendale and Grants Pass Resource Areas)

USGS 7.5' QUAD MAPS
Bunker Creek, Galice, Kelsay Peak, Mount Peavine, Mount Rueben

includes the river from its confluence with Mule Creek to near Illahe. It also includes many of the side canyons and ridges of the river canyon that provide important habitat for fish and wildlife. The Wild Rogue included the first Bureau of Land Management holdings in Oregon to be designated Wilderness.

The proposed Wild Rogue Wilderness Additions include all the remaining wildlands in the Lower Rogue Canyon and its tributaries, which are vital to keeping the Wild Rogue wild. Spring and fall runs of chinook salmon, as well as winter and summer steelhead spawn in the tributaries and also linger in the cooler water found at the mouths of these creeks when the mainstem of the Rogue is too warm for salmonids. Other aquatic species found here include sea-run cutthroat trout, lamprey, sculpin, stickleback, dace, sturgeon, coastal rainbow trout and western pond turtle. The Lower Rogue is known for the "half-pounders," immature summer steelhead that return to the river after less than a year at sea.

Wildlife here includes water ouzel, cliff swallow, kingfisher, great blue heron, osprey, beaver, ringtail, cougar, Roosevelt elk, black-tailed deer, peregrine falcon, bald eagle and the northern spotted owl. The Rogue River canyon is an essential wildlife migration corridor between inland and coastal habitats. One may also encounter poison oak that grows to human height here, along with yellowjackets and ticks. (No Eden is perfect.)

Most of the rain that falls here (up to 110 inches) does so between September and May. As one descends the Lower Rogue, moving from east to west, the vegetation changes to reflect the increased precipitation. Major tree species include Douglas-fir, sugar and ponderosa pine, incense cedar, white fir, bigleaf maple, madrone, myrtle-wood, western white pine, western hemlock, western red cedar, tanoak, Oregon white oak, red alder and grand fir. Divergent species sometimes occur in close proximity as the microclimates in this diverse landscape can change dramatically.

Most recreation in the proposed Wilderness is associated with either whitewater rafting or walking the Rogue River Trail.

Nearly 109,000 acres of the proposed Wilderness additions are not currently slated for logging. Unfortunately, the rest of the acreage is at risk and the other 109,000 acres could be if administrative policies change. Off-road vehicles, roading and mining are the other major threats to this landscape. ◆

Notes

[1] Noss, Reed and Allan Cooperrider. 1994. Saving Nature's Legacy. Island Press. Washington, DC: 180.

[2] Text adapted with permission of the publisher of Oregon Desert Guide: 70 Hikes, by Andy Kerr, The Mountaineers Books, Seattle, WA. © 2000 by The Larch Company, LLC.

[3] Prevost, Marc and Steve Mark (eds.). undated. Siskiyou Naturalist: Natural History Guide to the Soda Mountain and Pilot Rock Region. Northwest Nature Shop. Ashland, OR: 5.

◄ While an original unit of the National Wild and Scenic Rivers System, the wildness of the Lower Rogue River extends far beyond what is protected in the narrow Wild and Scenic corridor.

Young Volcanoes and Old Forests
Cascades Ecoregion

The Oregon portion of the Cascades Ecoregion encompasses 7.2 million acres and contains the highest mountains in the state. The Cascades Ecoregion is the backbone of Oregon, stretching lengthwise from the Columbia River Gorge almost to the California border. Its width is defined by the Willamette Valley and Klamath Mountains Ecoregions on the west and the Eastern Cascade Slope and Foothills Ecoregion on the east. The highest peak is Mount Hood (11,239'). This ecoregion also extends northward into Washington and has three unusual outlier terrestrial "islands:" Paulina Mountains southeast of Bend, Black Butte near Sisters and Mount Shasta in California.

Geologically, the ecoregion consists of two mountain ranges: the High Cascades and the Western (sometimes called "Old") Cascades. Both are parallel north-south ranges, but they are geologically distinct, as one is much older than the other.

The High Cascades are long ridges and plateaus with steep slopes and wide glaciated valleys that retain heavy winter snowpacks, especially in the north. Numerous snow-capped volcanic peaks, both active and dormant, range from 7,000 to 11, 239 feet in elevation. The High Cascades are about eight million years old. About 85 percent of the range is basalt.

Can you name the Oregon High Cascades volcanic peaks from north to south? How about their elevations? The Oregon Cascade peaks above 7,000-feet in elevation that are *not* protected in national parks or designated Wilderness are: Mount Bachelor (9,065'), Mount Bailey (8,363'), North Paulina Peak (7,686'), Pelican Butte (8,036'), Paulina Peak (7,984'), Maiden Peak (7,818'), Tumalo Mountain (7,775'), Cowhorn Mountain (7,664') and Olallie Butte (7,215').

The Western Cascades have steep ridges and river valleys, and peaks that average 4,000 to 5,600-feet in elevation. Although a combination of erosion and vegetative cover makes their origins less apparent than that of the High Cascade peaks, the Old Cascades were also shaped by volcanism.

The moist temperate climate here is supported by 50 to 150 inches of precipitation annually. These mountains and high valleys were once covered by old-growth forests. Today 95 percent of the ecoregion's remaining old growth is above 2,000 feet elevation and is generally fragmented by logging. Subalpine meadows are also found at the higher elevations.

Some 10,000 species of plants, animals and fungi are associated with these old-growth forests. These include Roosevelt elk, black-tailed deer, beaver, black bear, coyote, marten, fisher, cougar, raccoon, rabbits, squirrels and (probably) lynx. Bird species include the northern spotted owl and other owls, blue and ruffed grouse, band-tailed pigeon, mountain quail, hawks, numerous songbirds, pileated woodpecker and other woodpeckers, bald eagle, golden eagle, osprey and peregrine falcon. Fish species include Pacific salmon stocks, bull trout and rainbow trout. Five of the eleven species endemic to the ecoregion are amphibians: Pacific giant salamander, Cascade seep salamander, Oregon slender salamander, Larch Mountain salamander and the Cascades frog.

The effects of latitude on forest type are obvious in the Cascades as they range from the Columbia River to the California border. The effects of elevation are dramatic as well.

Beginning at the Willamette Valley margin and heading both eastward and upward, one finds **Douglas-fir/Oregon White Oak** forests that are typical of the valley margins that were once shaped by fires set by Native Americans and early settlers.

Just up slope from the Douglas-fir/Oregon White Oak forests are **Douglas-fir/Broadleaf Deciduous** forests where, on the wetter sites, red alder and bigleaf maple are also found.

As the elevation continues to rise, **Douglas-fir/Western Hemlock** — Oregon's most common forest type — dominates the western or Old Cascades. Grand fir, red alder and bigleaf maple are important components, the latter two especially along streams. Western redcedar also occurs in many areas.

Silver Fir/Western Hemlock/Noble Fir forests represent a transition between Douglas-fir/Western Hemlock and Mountain Hemlock forests (described next). This forest type extends south to the Rogue-Umpqua Divide, but is mostly found north of Diamond Peak to south of Mount Hood in the Warm Springs and Clackamas River drainages.

Higher still, **Mountain Hemlock** forests dominate the High Cascades from Mount Hood south to the California border. Pure stands of mountain hemlock are often found North of Willamette Pass, in some places mixed with whitebark pine.

On the highest slopes of the High Cascades the forest opens toward timberline and is characterized by **Mountain Hemlock/Parklands** and on the mountain ridges, whitebark pine. Trees here take on a dwarf scrub form, shaped by the wind. Although **Subapline Fir/Engelmann Spruce Parklands** are more common in Oregon's Blue Mountains, a few patches of this Rocky Mountain forest type are found in the Cascades.

Ecoregions of Oregon's Cascades

The mountains of the Cascades are widely underlain by Cenozoic volcanic rocks and have been affected by alpine glaciation. Maximum elevations of up to 11,239 feet occur on active and dormant volcanic peaks in the eastern part of the ecoregion. The western Cascades are older, lower and dissected by numerous, steep-sided stream valleys. The Cascades have a moist, temperate climate that supports an extensive and highly productive coniferous forest that is intensively managed for logging. Subalpine meadows occur at high elevations.

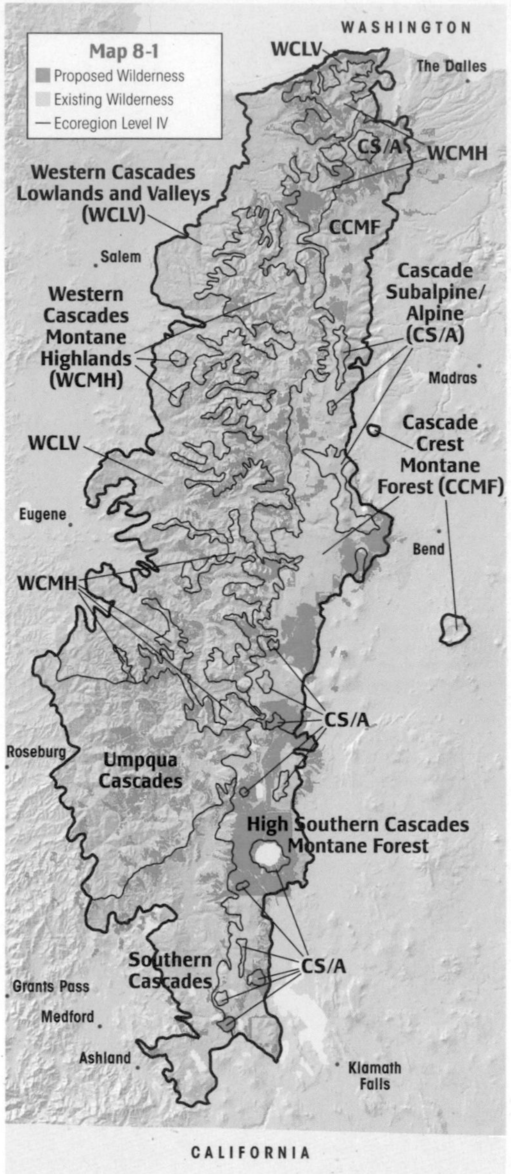

Further refining the ecoregion, scientists divide Oregon's Cascade Range Level III Ecoregion into seven additional Level IV ecoregions:

The **Western Cascades Lowlands and Valleys** ecoregion includes the lower slopes of the Cascades. Its mild, wet climate promotes lush western hemlock — Douglas-fir forests. Soils are warmer than in higher elevation ecoregions. The steep valleys contain high gradient rivers and streams that support cold water salmonids, including the threatened chinook salmon, steelhead and bull trout. Reservoirs store winter snow melt for irrigation and municipal water supply in the Willamette Valley.

The **Western Cascades Montane Highlands** are composed of steeply sloping, dissected mountains between about 3,000 and 6,500 feet elevation. The western Cascades are older and more eroded than the lava plateau and prominent snow-covered cones of the High Cascades (the Cascade Crest Montane Forest and Cascades Subalpine/Alpine Ecoregions); they are composed of dark basalt in contrast to the gray andesite of the High Cascades. The Western Cascades Montane Highlands has lower temperatures and receives more winter snow than the Western Cascades Lowlands and Valleys. Soils have frigid or cryic temperature regimes, in contrast to the mesic temperature regime of soils in the Western Cascades Lowlands and Valleys. Abundant precipitation supports forests dominated by Douglas-fir, western hemlock, noble fir and Pacific silver fir.

The **Cascade Crest Montane Forest** ecoregion consists of an undulating plateau punctuated by volcanic mountains and lava flows. Volcanism in the Pliocene epoch over-topped the existing Miocene volcanics of the Western Cascades Montane Highlands. Later Pleistocene glaciation left numerous naturally-fishless lakes. Today, this ecoregion contains forests dominated by mountain hemlock and Pacific silver fir. It has a shorter summer

drought and fewer intermittent streams than the High Southern Cascades Montane Forest.

The **Cascades Subalpine/Alpine** ecoregion contains the prominent volcanic peaks of the High Cascades. Pleistocene glaciation reshaped the mountains above 6,500 feet, leaving moraines, glacial lakes and U-shaped glacial canyons. Glaciers and permanent snowfields still occur on the highest peaks. The vegetation is adapted to high elevations, cold winter temperatures, short growing season and deep winter snow pack. Herbaceous subalpine meadow vegetation and scattered patches of mountain hemlock, subalpine fir and whitebark pine occur near timberline.

The **High Southern Cascades Montane Forest** ecoregion is an undulating, glaciated, volcanic plateau containing isolated buttes, cones and peaks. The terrain is less dissected than the Southern Cascades. At 4,000 to 8,200 feet, maximum elevations are intermediate to those in the Southern Cascades and the Cascades Subalpine/Alpine ecoregions. Cryic soils support mixed coniferous forests dominated by mountain hemlock, lodgepole pine and Pacific silver fir; they are colder than the mesic and frigid soils of the Southern Cascades. Grand fir, white fir and Shasta red fir also occur and become more common toward the south and east. The High Southern Cascades Montane Forest has a longer summer drought and more intermittent streams than the Cascade Crest Montane Forest.

The **Southern Cascades** ecoregion is lower in elevation and less rugged than the more highly dissected Western Cascades Montane Highlands to the north. Mt. McLoughlin, at 9,500 feet, is the highest peak in this ecoregion. The climate is drier than in the Western Cascades Lowlands and Valleys and the Western Cascades Montane Highlands and the vegetation reflects it. Western hemlock and western red cedar, which are indicator species of the Western Cascades Lowlands and Valley and the Western Cascades Montane Highlands Ecoregions, decline southward in the Southern Cascades Ecoregion and are replaced by Sierra Nevada species such as incense cedar, white fir and Shasta red fir that tolerate prolonged summer drought. Overall, river and stream discharge is also significantly lower than in systems to the north.

Text gratefully adapted from Thor D. Thorson, Sandra A. Bryce, Duane A. Lammers, Alan J. Woods, James M. Omernik, Jimmy Kagan, David E. Pater, Jeffrey A. Comstock. 2003. Ecoregions of Oregon (color poster with map, descriptive text, summary tables and photographs). USDI-Geological Survey. Reston, VA (map scale 1:1,500,000).

Map 8-1
- Proposed Wilderness
- Existing Wilderness
- — Ecoregion Level IV

WASHINGTON

WCLV · The Dalles · CS/A · WCMH · Western Cascades Lowlands and Valleys (WCLV) · Salem · CCMF · Western Cascades Montane Highlands (WCMH) · Cascade Subalpine/Alpine (CS/A) · Madras · WCLV · Cascade Crest Montane Forest (CCMF) · Eugene · Bend · WCMH · Roseburg · Umpqua Cascades · CS/A · High Southern Cascades Montane Forest · Grants Pass · Southern Cascades · CS/A · Medford · Ashland · Klamath Falls · CALIFORNIA

Sometimes even photographers put down their cameras and just take in the old-growth forest. ▶

Above timberline are **Alpine Barren Fell Fields** where low herbaceous, dwarf shrub and cushion plant communities grow, but which are snow-covered most of the year. Also usually covered with snow is the **Open Lava** found along the high crest, which is mostly bare rock, except for lichens and the occasional mountain hemlock, Douglas-fir and vine maple.

Over the crest and moving down the eastern slope, one will find **Subalpine Lodgepole** and **Lodgepole** forests. Both are naturally occurring monocultures, with the latter occurring on poorly drained and very coarse soils. If the **True Fir/Lodgepole** forests that grow at this altitude are undisturbed for long enough, the true fir will eventually overtop the lodgepole pine.

Farther downslope are varying mixes of forest types that feature ponderosa pine, true firs, Douglas-fir and the occasional western larch. **Ponderosa/Douglas-fir/True Fir** is common in the eastern part of the northern Cascades. Lower in elevation are **Ponderosa/Douglas-fir/Western Larch/Lodgepole** (western larch is minor and scattered in this forest type) and **True Fir/Lodgepole/Western Larch/Douglas-fir** forests. Along the lowest edges of the eastern side of the Cascades Ecoregion are some nearly pure stands of **Ponderosa** pine forest and **Ponderosa on Pumice**. **Ponderosa/Lodgepole** forest stands are often a sharp mosaic of the two species, as lodgepole is more tolerant of pumice soils and frost pockets.

The southern Cascades and northern Cascades in Oregon differ significantly. **Mountain Hemlock/Red Fir** forests — which may be intermingled with Douglas-fir, western white pine and white fir — are common from Three Sisters south to Aspen Butte. On the lower western slopes of the southern Cascades (south of the Rogue-Umpqua Divide) are stands of **Siskiyou Mixed Conifer** with varying combinations of Douglas-fir, sugar pine, ponderosa pine, incense cedar and white fir. Also common here are bigleaf maple, Pacific madrone and western white pine. On wetter sites grow western redcedar and western hemlock. **Siskiyou Mixed Evergreen** forest, similar to the Mixed Conifer variety, except with a greater broadleaf tree component, is also found here. Another variant is the **Siskiyou Mixed Conifer-High Elevation** type that grows along the Rogue-Umpqua Divide and has more white fir and less Douglas-fir, sugar, ponderosa pine and western white pine. One will also find Shasta red fir and lodgepole pine in the Cascades variant of this Klamath Mountains Ecoregion forest type.

Between Mount Hood and the lower Deschutes River (but also in the southern Oregon Cascades) are stands of **Oregon White Oak/Ponderosa**, a variant of the **Oregon White Oak/Douglas-fir** and **Oregon White Oak/Pacific Madrone** forest-types, where incense cedar may also occur. Even more rare is the **Ponderosa/Oregon White Oak** combination that grows in this region. Moving east toward the Blue Mountains Ecoregion, below timberline or interspersed as stringers with other forest

The Upper Clackamas River in the proposed Clackamas Wilderness. ▶

types, one will find **Big Sage/Shrub**, **Big Sagebrush** and **Grasslands/ Bunchgrass** communities.

Throughout the Cascades, tufted hairgrass and sedge typically dominate the **Marsh/Wet Meadow** areas.

At some time in their existence, most forest communities will be set back to early successional forest and are classified as **Cutover/Burned** forest. This can occur naturally — from lightning-caused wildfires, native insect or disease events, or blowdown by wind — or unnaturally, by way of logging, human-caused fire, human-caused blowdown (due to unnatural and vulnerable forest edges caused by clearcuts), non-native disease and insects, or aggressive fire-fighting. Particularly troubling are "backburns," where firefighters intentionally burn the forest in front of an oncoming wildfire. In many cases, the backburns are far more intense and destructive than the natural burn would have been.

Presently, 74 percent of the Oregon's Cascades Ecoregion is federally owned public land. Major federal holdings include the Willamette, Umpqua, most of the Mount Hood, Rogue River and portions of the Deschutes and Winema National Forests; the eastern parts of the BLM Medford, Roseburg, Eugene and Salem Districts; and Crater Lake National Park.

To date there are eleven Wilderness areas (Mark. O. Hatfield, Mount Hood, Salmon-Huckleberry, Table Rock, Bull-of-the-Woods, Opal Creek, Middle Santiam, Menagerie, Waldo Lake, Boulder Creek and Rogue-Umpqua Divide) and portions of eight others (Badger Creek, Mount Jefferson, Mount Washington, Three Sisters, Diamond Peak, Mount Thielsen, Sky Lakes and Mountain Lakes) designated in Oregon's Cascades, comprising 13.7 percent of the ecoregion.

Conservationists propose eleven new multi-unit Wilderness areas: Clackamas, Columbia River Gorge, McKenzie, Mount Hood Additions, North Umpqua, Rogue-Umpqua, Santiam, South Cascades, Three Sisters Additions, Upper Deschutes and Upper Willamette. If designated, these areas would protect a total 34.1 percent of the ecoregion as Wilderness.

Proposed Clackamas Wilderness
Very Large Trees, Pacific Salmon and Clean Drinking Water

Roads, clearcuts and dams have decimated much of the once pristine Clackamas River Watershed. Yet wildlands (both large and small) and wild rivers (both rapid and

Old growth Douglas-fir (*Pseudotsuga menzeisii*) in the Big Bottom Unit of the proposed Clackamas Wilderness.

slow) persist here despite the surrounding development and devastation. Together, these wild areas maintain the ecological function of the upper Clackamas River Basin. Protecting these areas, and the judicious restoration of the roaded and logged forests nearby (and removal of some unnecessary dams), will allow the Clackamas River Basin to once again provide a full compliment of ecosystem goods and services to human and fish and wildlife communities, including clean, plentiful water, biological diversity, abundant habitat and endless forms of sustainable recreation.

The Clackamas River arises on Olallie Butte at 6,000 feet elevation. Although the headwaters receive 130 inches of precipitation annually, these streams are dry at their source in late fall. The headwaters are eventually joined by springs downstream to create an annual flow that joins the Willamette River at Oregon City. Along the way, major tributaries entering the Clackamas within the boundaries of the Mount Hood National Forest include the Collawash River, Oak Grove Fork of the Clackamas River, Roaring River, Fish Creek and South Fork Clackamas River. The North Fork Clackamas River and Eagle Creek join the mainstem Clackamas downstream from the forest boundary. A segment of the Clackamas River is protected as part of the National Wild and Scenic Rivers System, from its source at Big Springs to Big Cliff near the national forest boundary. It is also the primary source of drinking water for 190,000 Clackamas County residents.

At lower elevations (which receive 60 inches of precipitation annually), the forests are dominated by dense, lush Douglas-fir with some western hemlock found in the understory. As the elevation increases, the forest changes to Pacific silver fir, lodgepole

LEVEL IV ECOREGIONS
Western Cascades Montane Highlands (49%),
Cascade Crest Montane Forest (25%), Western
Cascades Lowlands and Valleys (25%)

VEGETATION TYPES
Douglas-fir/Western Hemlock (58%), Silver
Fir/Western Hemlock/Noble Fir (18%), Subalpine
Lodgepole (12%), Mountain Hemlock (10%),
Cutover/Burned (1%), Douglas-fir/Broadleaf
Deciduous (<1%)

DRAINAGE SUBBASINS
Clackamas, Molalla

ELEVATION RANGE
801-6,358 feet

UNITS
Big Bottom, Black Wolf Meadows, Bob Meadow,
Bull-of-the-Woods/Opal Creek Additions (Elk
Lake, Dickey Peak, East Fork Collawash River, Hot
Springs Fork, Nasty Rock, North Whetstone
Creek), Bump Creek, Burnt Granite, Cottonwood
Meadows, Ed's Meadow-Clackamas River, Fish
Creek, Hawk Mountain, Memaloose Lake,
Mistletoe-Clackamas River, Molalla Headwaters,
Monon Lake, North Pinhead Butte, Oak Grove
Fork, Olallie Meadow-Lemiti Butte, *Olallie Lakes*,
Pyramid Lake, Roaring River, *Salmon-Huckleberry
Additions* (Eagle Creek, North Fork Clackamas
River Headwaters), Scorpion Mountain, Sisi
Butte, Slow Creek, South Fork Clackamas River,
Summit Lake, Summit Lake, *Table Rock Additions*
(North Additions, South Additions), West Pinhead
Butte

**EXISTING WILDERNESSES
INCORPORATED**
Bull-of-the-Woods, portion of Salmon-
Huckleberry, Table Rock

SIZE
107,617 acres (168 square miles, not including
42,339 acres of currently protected Wildernesses)

COUNTIES
Clackamas, Jefferson, Marion, Wasco

**FEDERAL
ADMINISTRATIVE UNITS**
Mount Hood and Willamette National Forests;
BLM Salem District

CONGRESSIONAL DISTRICTS
2nd, 3rd, 5th

Proposed Clackamas Wilderness

Some of the units in the proposed Wilderness are highlighted below.

Big Bottom features some of the most extensive and impressive stands of large trees in Oregon. The area's Douglas-fir, western hemlock, grand fir and western redcedar (including Oregon's largest at nearly 12-feet in diameter at the base) are simply awe-inspiring. Pacific yew is also common here. Big Bottom is both low in elevation and flat, a landform that very rarely has any virgin forest left (because it's so easy to log). The old-growth forest protects the forest floor from accumulating three to four feet of snow, as the adjacent clearcuts do, thereby providing critical wintering habitat for deer and elk. At least two pairs of northern spotted owls make their home in Big Bottom. Four pristine miles of the Clackamas River flow through the unit in braided channels full of large woody debris. The large logjams and numerous beaver dams provide perfect habitat for fish. The holding pools and deep troughs of spawning gravel make this stretch of the river the most productive, complex and diverse fish habitat on the Clackamas. The largest remaining concentration of the cold water corydalis (*Corydalis aquae-gelidae*) on the Clackamas River is found here, thriving in the cold water and shade.

Eagle Creek has been the site of a major logging controversy. The Forest Service sold timber sales here, proudly noting that their logging plans were a model of the Northwest Forest Plan's "new forestry." However, when Congress enacted the "salvage rider" in 1995 the courtroom door was closed to citizens seeking to hold the Forest Service accountable to the law and parts of the area were logged. Citizens responded by personally occupying trees ("tree sitting") in the remaining unlogged sale units for three years. Eventually, even the timber company that had purchased the sales became convinced that it would cause too much ecological damage to log it and requested release from their contract. An independent scientific panel also raised serious questions about the sales. Finally, under pressure from citizen activists, scientists and decisionmakers — including six members of Congress led by Senator Ron Wyden — the Forest Service withdrew the sales, including those planned for this roadless area.

Ed's Meadow-Clackamas River and **Mistletoe-Clackamas River** both include roadless habitats along the Clackamas River.

The **East Fork of the Collawash River**, **Hot Springs Fork** and **Nasty Rock** units all should have been included in the Bull-of-the-Woods Wilderness when it was designated in 1984, but were left out due to timber conflicts.

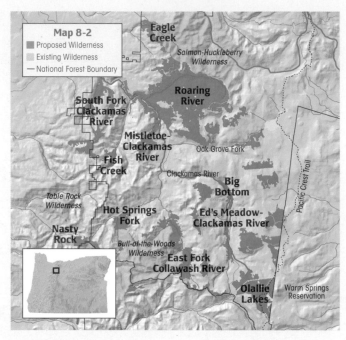

Fish Creek supports more wild steelhead than any other tributary of the Clackamas River.

Olallie Lakes contains the headwaters of the Clackamas, Warm Springs (Deschutes Basin) and Breitenbush (Santiam Basin) Rivers, as well as over 200 lakes and ponds in an extensive system of wetlands. It is a high elevation plateau dotted with several cinder cones and other unique geological landforms. Otter, eagle and mink can often be seen here. The unit is optimal habitat for black-backed and three-toed woodpeckers and, potentially, the great grey owl. The Pacific Crest National Scenic Trail passes through the unit.

Roaring River is featured on page 121.

The **South Fork Clackamas River** unit includes Memaloose Creek. For centuries, these steep, wet and rocky slopes have protected hundreds of acres of old-growth forest from fire. Beneath the overstory of old-growth Douglas-fir, western hemlock and western redcedar are 400-year old Pacific yew trees. The astounding quantity of moss and lichens on trees, logs and rocks is evidence of the area's long period of stream, soil and forest stability.

Shellrock Lake in the Roaring River Unit of the proposed Clackamas Wilderness.

FEATURED UNIT

Roaring River

The Roaring River watershed is the largest unprotected oasis of wildlands on the Mount Hood National Forest.

The Roaring River begins on Signal Buttes at 5,000 feet in elevation, falls over 4,000 feet and flows for fifteen miles before joining the Clackamas River. The upper watershed is a broad glacial valley with slopes covered with a mosaic of forest, talus meadows and lakes. The lower four miles of the river flow through a narrow gorge past basalt cliffs and more talus slopes, while the lowest portion of the river flows through a nearly flat valley bottom.

Much of the Roaring River watershed is covered with snow for five to seven months each year. Several prominent Old Cascades peaks offer sweeping views of the area, including distant High Cascades peaks. The peaks tower over numerous jewel-like (and trout-filled) lakes including Huxley, Rock, Shining and Serene Lakes and their associated wet meadows. The lakes here are so numerous that many are unnamed.

The lowest elevation canyon bottoms are forested with old-growth Douglas-fir, bigleaf maple, western redcedar and red alder with vine maple in the understory. As elevations increase, the forest changes to mountain hemlock, Pacific silver fir and noble fir with some Engelmann spruce, western white pine and lodgepole pine. Sitka alder can be found along the upper river. Interspersed among the higher elevation forests are wet and dry mountain meadows, talus, hardwood shrub thickets and rocky cliffs with bear grass, rhododendron and huckleberry in the understory.

Wildlife species abound and include badger, fisher, cougar, marten, northern spotted owl, beaver, pika, Townsend's chipmunk, brush rabbit, golden-mantled ground squirrel, Douglas squirrel, porcupine, mink, weasel, mountain lion, bald eagle, osprey, black bear, coyote and pileated woodpecker. The lower portions of the watershed are winter range for black-tailed deer and Roosevelt elk.

The pristine watershed with its cool, clean water supports strong runs of coho salmon, spring chinook salmon, winter and summer steelhead, as well as populations of resident cutthroat trout, coastal rainbow trout, mountain whitefish, dace, coarse-scale sucker and sculpin. Intact watersheds like the Roaring River serve as scientific control areas for restoring abused watersheds elsewhere.

The Roaring River watershed contains several unique botanical features, including an unusual combination of plant communities in the talus habitats along the ridgeline and in the river's braided stream channels below.

The entire mainstem of the Roaring River, from its source to its confluence with the Clackamas River, is a unit of the National Wild and Scenic Rivers System. The 4.6 miles of South Fork Roaring River has been found eligible for Wild and Scenic River status — but has not yet received this official designation.

Recreation opportunities here include hiking, camping, fishing, hunting, cross-country skiing, snowshoeing, horseback riding and cross-country exploration. While one can also kayak upstream from the lower end of the river, it is impossible to do so from the upper end. While trails allow access to much of the area, there are many places the trails don't go and few people have ever seen.

PROPOSED WILDERNESS
Clackamas

LOCATION
17 miles southeast of Estacada

LEVEL IV ECOREGIONS
Western Cascades Montane Highlands (66%), Western Cascades Lowlands and Valleys (34%)

VEGETATION TYPES
Douglas-Fir/Western Hemlock (59%), Silver Fir/Western Hemlock/Noble Fir (20%) Mountain Hemlock (16%), Subalpine Lodgepole (4%)

TERRAIN
Very steep canyons.

DRAINAGE SUBBASIN
Clackamas

ELEVATION RANGE
991-5,159 feet

SIZE
35,704 acres

COUNTY
Clackamas

FEDERAL ADMINISTRATIVE UNIT
Mount Hood National Forest (Clackamas River Ranger District)

USGS 7.5' QUAD MAPS
High Rock, Three Lynx

pine, western larch and mountain hemlock. On wetter sites, western redcedar is common. Bigleaf maple, red alder and black cottonwood are found on riparian flats, while some of the drier and higher sites feature Oregon white oak and ponderosa pine. Some of the Cascades' largest Pacific yews are found in the Oak Grove Fork watershed.

Species of special concern found in the proposed Wilderness include the bald eagle, pileated woodpecker, marten, river otter, beaver, peregrine falcon, wolverine, sandhill crane, Pacific western big-eared bat, white-footed vole, harlequin duck, red-legged frog, Cope's giant salamander, painted turtle, western pond turtle, fisher, spotted frog and Cascade frog. Also found here are black-tailed deer and Roosevelt elk.

The American Fisheries Society has identified several aquatic diversity areas within the proposed Wilderness which recognize this important habitat for coho salmon (the last remaining late-run coho in the Columbia River Basin), spring chinook salmon (one of the last two remaining runs in the Willamette Basin), winter and summer steelhead, bull trout, resident cutthroat trout, sculpin, coastal rainbow trout, redside shiner, mountain whitefish and coarse-scale sucker.

Recreational opportunities in the proposed Wilderness abound and include whitewater boating, hunting, camping, fishing, hiking, cross-country skiing, snowshoeing sightseeing and tree-hugging.

Approximately 78,000 acres of the proposed Wilderness are now nominally off-limits to logging. Other threats to the area include off-road vehicles, mining and road building.

Horsetail Falls in the Gorge Face Unit of the proposed Columbia River Gorge Wilderness. Most of the gorge's waterfalls are not protected as Wilderness.

Proposed Columbia River Gorge Wilderness
Waterfalls and Wildflowers from Rainforest to Desert

In 1986 Congress established the Columbia River Gorge National Scenic Area (CRGNSA), in large part to protect scenic and natural resources on public and private lands, but also to provide a playground for the growing Portland-Vancouver metropolitan area. To date, environmental conservation and protection under the CRGNSA's unique land use regulations has been more effective on public lands than on private lands in the gorge. Private lands (not surprisingly) are where most management controversies have arisen. The proposed Columbia River Gorge Wilderness is intended to eliminate management controversies arising on roadless and undeveloped public forestlands in the area.

The Columbia River Gorge has the greatest concentration of waterfalls in North America. Most are located within the proposed Wilderness. People are drawn by the area's extraordinary scenery, where one can see cliffs, water or waterfalls and forest in almost every direction. In autumn, the fiery reds, yellows and oranges of bigleaf maple, cottonwood, Oregon ash, vine maple, red alder and the many leafy shrubs contrast with the dark green conifers.

Nearly 1,000 native species of wildflowers can be found in the Columbia River Gorge. This unparalleled assemblage of wildflowers is due to the precipitous 4,000-foot change in elevation from the river bottom to the mountain cliffs above, precipitation that diminishes from west to east along this 85-mile passage through the High Cascades and the varied soils of the area. Given the dramatic changes in terrain, it is not uncommon to find alpine flowers growing near sea level. Sixteen plant species are endemic to the Columbia River Gorge and vicinity, many of which are found within the proposed Wilderness. Forty-five of the area's plant species in the area are now listed by the state or federal government as endangered, threatened or sensitive.

While much of the proposed Wilderness burned in 1902, many pockets of residual old-growth forest exist at Tanner Creek, Multnomah Basin and Larch Mountain. If left

Proposed Columbia River Gorge Wilderness

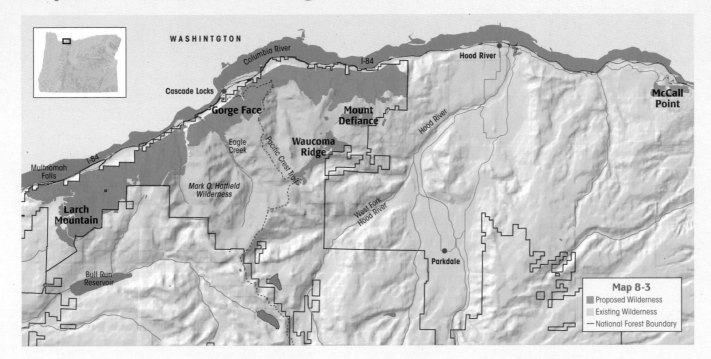

Map 8-3
■ Proposed Wilderness
▨ Existing Wilderness
— National Forest Boundary

Several of the proposed Wilderness units are highlighted below.

The **Gorge Face** is the largest unit in the proposed Wilderness. It contains the vast majority of the waterfalls on the Oregon side of the Columbia River Gorge.

Larch Mountain is featured on page 123.

McCall Point offers breathtaking views overlooking the Columbia and contains over 300 species of wildflowers, including at least four that exist only in the gorge. Adjacent holdings by Oregon State Parks and The Nature Conservancy increase the importance of this unit.

Mount Defiance contains the highest elevation lands in the gorge.

Waucoma Ridge provides a wildlands buffer for the Pacific Crest National Scenic Trail.

LEVEL IV ECOREGIONS
Western Cascade Lowlands and Valleys (60%), Western Cascade Montane Highlands (37%); Columbia Basin Level III Ecoregion: Oak/Conifer Foothills (3%)

VEGETATION TYPES
Douglas-fir/Western Hemlock (92%), Mountain Hemlock (4%), Ponderosa/White Oak (2%), Silver Fir/Western Hemlock/Noble Fir (2%) Cutover/Burned (<1%), Grasslands/Bunchgrass (<1%),

DRAINAGE SUBBASINS
Lower Columbia Basin, Mid Columbia Basin

ELEVATION RANGE
180-4,959 feet

UNITS
Larch Mountain, *Mark O. Hatfield Additions* (Gorge Face, Indian Mountain, Mount Defiance, Mount Talapus-Table Mountain, Waucoma Ridge), McCall Point

EXISTING WILDERNESS INCORPORATED
Mark O. Hatfield

SIZE
39,951 acres (62 square miles, not including 39,000 acres of currently protected Wilderness)

COUNTIES:
Hood River, Multnomah, Wasco

FEDERAL ADMINISTRATIVE UNITS
Mount Hood National Forest

CONGRESSIONAL DISTRICTS
2nd, 3rd

PROPOSED WILDERNESS
Mount Hood Additions

LOCATION
12 miles southwest of Cascade Locks

LEVEL IV ECOREGIONS
Western Cascades Lowlands and Valleys
(58%), Western Cascades Montane
Highlands (42%)

VEGETATION TYPE
Douglas-Fir/Western Hemlock (100%)

TERRAIN
Extremely steep and rugged.

DRAINAGE SUBBASIN
Lower Columbia Basin

ELEVATION RANGE
180-4,056 feet

SIZE
18,110 acres

COUNTY
Multnomah

**FEDERAL ADMINISTRATIVE
UNIT**
Columbia River Gorge National Scenic Area
(US Forest Service)

USGS 7.5′ QUAD MAP
Multnomah Falls

The view near the summit in the Larch Mountain Unit of the proposed Columbia River Gorge Wilderness. Mount Hood is in the background.
The middle ground is the Bull Run Watershed, the water supply for nearly one million Oregonians in the Portland metropolitan area.

FEATURED UNIT

Larch Mountain

There are no larch trees on Larch Mountain. The deciduous conifer is found on the other side of the Mount Hood National Forest, but not here. Larch Mountain is north of Mount Hood, just south of the Columbia River Gorge and is visible from Portland.

The forest on Larch Mountain is mostly Douglas-fir, western hemlock, Pacific silver fir and noble fir (early Oregon lumbermen marketed noble fir as "Oregon larch"). Much of it is old-growth forest, including a rare stand of old-growth western hemlock. The lower elevations contain mountain maple. A particularly rich understory of diverse shrubs and forbs (wildflowers) distinguishes this forest from those elsewhere in the area.

This unit contains the Multnomah Basin, which lies above famous Multnomah Falls and is where Multnomah Creek rises from numerous springs on Larch Mountain. Plunging 620 feet, Multnomah Falls are the second highest in the United States and are seen by over two million people annually, making them the number one natural attraction in Oregon. Besides the extensive old-growth forest, there are significant wetlands, meadows and rock gardens here.

The Oregon side of the gorge is spectacularly steep, with sheer cliffs and rocky outcroppings that expose numerous other waterfalls. Besides Multnomah Falls, other named waterfalls within the Larch Mountain unit include Oneonta, Horsetail, Elowah and Wake Falls. Numerous other falls remain unnamed on Tanner, Moffett, McCord, Tumalt, Horsetail, Oneonta, Wahkeena and Coopey creeks.

The topography makes for challenging hiking, but there are numerous trails in the unit for ease of access. Another high point in the unit includes Angel's Rest, an excellent example of basalt cliffs in the western end of the gorge. It is important habitat for rare plants and home to an outlier stand of quaking aspen.

Larch Mountain's old-growth forest provides habitat for the spotted owl, marten, pileated woodpecker and ruffed grouse. Bald eagles also nest in the unit. The lower elevations are critical winter range for deer and elk.

A few years ago the Forest Service proposed to log near the summit of Larch Mountain, but withdrew its plans upon hearing public outcry over the potential degradation of the drinking water supply for the town of Corbett.

The Larch Mountain salamander (*Plethodon larselli*) is endemic to a small portion of the Cascade Mountains in northern Oregon and southern Washington.

untouched by humans for another century, the remainder of these forests will likely become old growth again too. Major coniferous trees species in the proposed Wilderness include Douglas-fir, western hemlock, western redcedar, noble fir and Pacific silver fir. Major understory species include vine maple, huckleberry, salal, Oregon grape, oxalis, sword fern, bracken fern, trillium and vanilla leaf. In the higher elevations on Mount Defiance and Waucoma Ridge, Pacific silver fir is more common, along with mountain hemlock, noble fir and lodgepole pine. The understory contains species such as serviceberry, rhododendron and beargrass. Because the wide and deep Columbia River Gorge is such a definite break in the landscape, it serves as the southern limit of many typically northern plant and animal species, as well as the northern limit of many typically southern species.

The Columbia River Gorge is home to a concentration of rare and endemic animal species, as well as plants. The Oneonta Gorge is one of the few sites in Oregon where the Cope's giant salamander lives. The species requires very cold, very clean water. The Larch Mountain salamander (which ranges as far north as Snoqualmie Pass) favors talus habitat within these Douglas-fir forests. Other amphibian species of concern in the gorge include the western pond turtle, clouded salamander, Cascade frog, northern leopard frog, Oregon slender salamander, painted turtle, red-legged frog, spotted frog and the tailed frog.

Pacific lamprey, coho salmon and coastal cutthroat trout all spawn in the tributary streams that emerge from the gorge face. Other fish species found here include coastal rainbow trout and winter and summer steelhead.

The bald eagle, peregrine falcon and northern spotted owl are imperiled bird species of special concern found in the area. Other sensitive forest species include the acorn woodpecker, black-backed woodpecker, flammulated owl, great gray owl, harlequin duck, Lewis' woodpecker, northern goshawk, pileated woodpecker, purple martin, pygmy nuthatch, three-toed woodpecker, white-headed woodpecker and Williamson's sapsucker. Lewis and Clark noted California condors when they traveled this stretch of the Columbia. Perhaps these birds will again be seen soaring over the gorge someday.

Mammals of special concern here include pika, marten, wolverine, fisher and fringed myotis. Other mammal species include black bear, deer, elk, cougar, bobcat, coyote, fox, weasel and beaver.

Recreational activities in the proposed Wilderness include hiking, backpacking, botanizing, birding, hunting, fishing and waterfall watching.

Approximately 37,000 acres of the proposed Wilderness is nominally off-limits to logging under the Northwest Forest Plan. Otherwise, the Columbia River Gorge National Scenic Area Act discourages, but does not expressly prohibit, the degradation of natural and wildlands values in the area.

The wildlands of the proposed Columbia River Gorge Wilderness include most of the national forest lands on the Oregon side of the gorge. While logging is not expressly prohibited in the statute that created the CRGNSA, a political firestorm erupts every time the Forest Service attempts to log in the area. And while the agency too often seeks to "salvage" timber remaining after a natural wildfire or natural insect or disease infestation has occurred, another great threat to the Columbia River Gorge wildlands is from the increasing number of people who visit the area each year. Today, these lands need to be protected as Wilderness to ensure their protection *from* an ever-increasing human population living in the ever-larger and ever-closer Portland-Vancouver metropolitan area. A Wilderness designation would be an additional, protective overlay within the CRGNSA.

Proposed McKenzie Wilderness
Waterfalls, Bull Trout, Big Trees and Clean Water

Extending from the lava strewn high mountain crests to lowland old-growth forests, the proposed McKenzie Wilderness hosts a full complement of ecosystem types

GEORGE WURTHNER

and breathless Oregon Cascades scenery. Rock outcroppings rise above forests that give way to wildflower meadows. Roadless lands and intact old-growth forests contribute unmistakably to the water quantity and quality of the McKenzie River and provide important fish and wildlife habitat along the river corridor.

The McKenzie River begins at Clear Lake. Downstream, it is joined by the South Fork McKenzie River, Blue River (which could have just as well been called the North Fork of the McKenzie River) and the Mohawk River. Eventually the McKenzie empties into the Willamette River north of Eugene. Unfortunately, the Army Corps of Engineers dammed both the South Fork McKenzie River and Blue River. However, where the mainstem flows freely from its source at Clear Lake to Scott Creek (except for the relatively small Carmen and Trail Bridge Dams and resultant reservoirs), the upper McKenzie River is designated as a National Wild and Scenic River and is part of the Oregon Scenic Waterways System. This river segment is nationally renowned for its rolling cold, clear water that lures all sorts of whitewater rafters, kayakers and drift-boaters looking for a challenge.

Wildlife abounds in the proposed Wilderness. Bird species include the spotted owl, kestrel, red-tailed hawk, rough-legged hawk, sharp-shinned hawk, northern goshawk, osprey, golden eagle and bald eagle. Mammals of note include black-tailed deer, beaver, black bear, coyote, red tree vole, Roosevelt elk, beaver, cougar, bobcat and marten.

The river and its tributaries provide important habitat for bull trout, spring and fall chinook salmon, winter and summer steelhead, as well as coastal rainbow and cutthroat trout populations. The American Fisheries Society has identified several aquatic diversity areas that support these fisheries and coincide with several units of the proposed Wilderness.

The low elevation forests in the western part of the proposed Wilderness are predominantly Douglas-fir, along with western redcedar, western hemlock and some hardwoods such as bigleaf maple and alder. As the elevation increases, true firs such as Pacific silver fir dominate along with mountain hemlock. At the coldest and highest elevations, Engelmann spruce, subalpine fir and lodgepole pine dominate. Understory species here include beargrass, huckleberry, vine maple, ocean spray, salal, Oregon grape, rhododendron and golden chinquapin.

Recreational opportunities in the proposed Wilderness include hiking, backpacking, cross-country skiing, horseback riding, fishing, hunting, whitewater sports and hot springs soaking.

Approximately 34,000 acres of the proposed Wilderness are nominally off-limits to logging. Off-road vehicles and roading are the other major threats to the area.

Koosah Falls in the Tamolitch Falls Unit of the proposed McKenzie Wilderness. ▶

Proposed McKenzie Wilderness

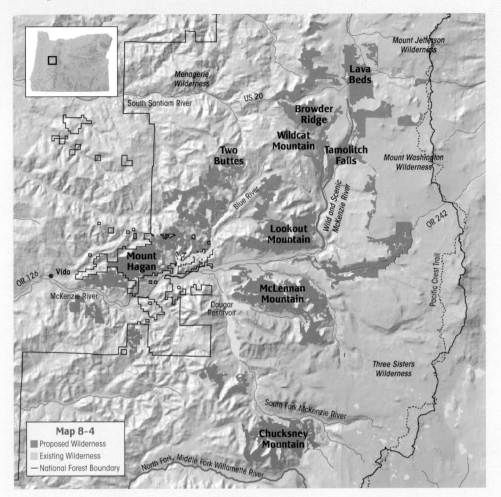

Map 8-4
■ Proposed Wilderness
■ Existing Wilderness
— National Forest Boundary

Some of the proposed Wilderness units are highlighted below.

Browder Ridge includes the secluded 12-acre Heart Lake that sits below a long high ridge that is often struck by lighting. Douglas-fir six feet in diameter and larger are present. Of special note is an impressive stand of old-growth Alaska yellow cedar.

Chucksney Mountain is featured on page 128.

The **Lava Beds** units contain relatively recent lava beds near the Santiam Pass.

Lookout Mountain features trails through significant old-growth forest.

McLennen Mountain is heavily forested with some open grass meadows and patches of alder trees.

Mount Hagan is a very low elevation Douglas-fir/western hemlock forest with salal and Oregon grape common in the understory.

Tamolitch Falls contains a segment of the McKenzie River that disappears and reappears as it flows through a lava labyrinth. It also includes a good portion of the 26-mile McKenzie River National Recreational Trail.

Two Buttes has numerous mountain lakes and ponds, some of which are half-in and half-out of the Mount Washington Wilderness.

Wildcat Mountain has Pacific silver fir communities of scientific interest.

PROPOSED WILDERNESSES
McKenzie, Upper Willamette

LOCATION
19 miles south of McKenzie Bridge

LEVEL IV ECOREGIONS
Western Cascades Montane Highlands (83%), Western Cascades Lowlands and Valleys (16%), Cascade Crest Montane Forest (1%)

VEGETATION TYPES
Douglas-Fir/Western Hemlock (43%), Mountain Hemlock (35%), Silver Fir/Western Hemlock/Noble Fir (22%)

TERRAIN
Long high ridge with steep flanks.

DRAINAGE SUBBASINS
McKenzie, Middle Fork Willamette

ELEVATION RANGE
2,398-5,760 feet

SIZE
16,632 acres

COUNTY
Lane

FEDERAL ADMINISTRATIVE UNIT
Willamette National Forest (McKenzie and Middle Fork Ranger Districts)

USGS 7.5' QUAD MAPS
Chucksney Mountain, Grasshopper Mountain

DAVID STONE, WILDLAND PHOTOGRAPHY

Due to the active exclusion of fire, young trees are encroaching on Grasshopper Meadow in the Chucksney Mountain Unit of the proposed McKenzie Wilderness.

FEATURED UNIT

Chucksney Mountain

Extensive wildflower meadows, talus and large cliffs are found along Hi Yu Ridge, a long high divide between the South Fork McKenzie and North Fork of the Middle Fork Willamette River drainages. The Chucksney Mountain unit encompasses part of the ridge and is part of the proposed McKenzie and Upper Willamette Wilderness areas.

The terrain is steep with sharp spur ridges and rocky outcroppings. Chucksney Mountain (5,760') and Grasshopper Mountain (5,642') are the highest points in the area, from which there are striking views of the Three Sisters and the densely forested canopy in the pristine watershed of the North Fork of the Middle Fork Willamette River.

Black-tailed deer and Roosevelt elk are plentiful in this popular hunting area. There are also high concentrations of black bear here. Both hunters and hikers use several miles of the Hi Yu and Chucksney Mountain trails in this unit.

On the lower slopes, patches of old-growth Douglas-fir forest (with some western hemlock) are found among younger forests. Vine maple and alder are scattered in the understory along with salal, Oregon grape and rhododendron. Further up the slopes, true firs and mountain hemlocks dominate and the understory changes to huckleberry and beargrass. On the highest slopes, Engelmann spruce, subalpine fir and lodgepole pine comprise a more open forest where dwarf huckleberry, beargrass and wildflowers form the understory.

The Chucksney Mountain unit has extensive wildflower meadows. Dry montane meadows such as those found here are in danger of disappearing from the Oregon Cascades due to fire suppression that allows conifers to gradually invade the meadows.

To restore meadows, on October 9, 1996 — just before the inevitable rain and snow season was to begin — the Forest Service set fire to 60 acres of meadows on Hi Yu Ridge. Because the ridge drops off precipitously, the risk of the fire spreading downward into the forest was minimized. The goal was to kill 50 to 100 percent of all the conifers smaller than 4 inches in diameter at the base that were invading the meadow. The fire succeeded in killing 50 to 70 percent of the lodgepole pine and 100 percent of the grand fir. Ecological succession was successfully reset, with four new native pioneer herbaceous species replacing five other native species that were present before the fire.

The cost of setting the fire was $400 ($6.67/acre) plus an additional $1,200 to establish and maintain a 20-acre unburned control area ($60/acre). The control was necessary for this particular scientific study, but wouldn't be necessary as an ongoing management activity. It was estimated that using mechanical treatment (chainsaws) to achieve the same result would have cost $1,500 ($25/acre). Fire was the most natural and inexpensive way to retain healthy meadows and surrounding forestlands. Yet that didn't stop the Forest Service from spending $1,300/acre in 2001 attempting to put out naturally caused wild fires that would have provided the same ecological benefits to dry montane meadows and other habitats as the prescribed burn.

Besides the aesthetic benefits (no stumps), fire is ecologically preferable to mechanical treatment for several reasons. The large standing dead trees left by fire provide important snag habitat; the palatability of forage increases under the newly opened canopy for deer, elk and other species; fire kills forest insect pests; and soils remain stable (much more so than when mechanical treatments are employed) and their productivity is maintained or enhanced. Between lightning strikes and Native American burning, these high mountain meadows once had a typical fire interval of five to 20 years.

Proposed Mount Hood Wilderness Additions
Portland's Backyard Play Land with Pacific Salmon, Mountain Meadows and Big Trees

The Mount Hood Wilderness Additions include all the remaining unprotected wildlands in the watersheds of the rivers that descend from Mount Hood: the Sandy, Salmon (a tributary of the Sandy), Hood and White Rivers. Another major tributary watershed of the Sandy is the Bull Run River. Being further west, the Bull Run does not originate on Mount Hood, but is still known throughout northwest Oregon as the primary water supply for the Portland metropolitan area. The Sandy and Hood Rivers flow directly into the Columbia River, while the White River flows into the Deschutes, which then joins the Columbia about a hundred miles east of Portland. Segments of the White, Sandy and Salmon Rivers are designated units of the National Wild and Scenic Rivers System.

The proposed Mount Hood Wilderness Additions include the entire spectrum of ecosystem types found in the northern Oregon Cascades. There are very low elevation lush old-growth forests, shrubby riparian areas, high elevation cold forests, alpine meadows, exposed rock, drier open forests and the edge of the Sagebrush Sea.

The rivers here generally have excellent water quality, though those fed from Mount Hood glaciers are naturally silt-laden during times of maximum glacial melt. In its upper reaches, the aptly named White River is laden with milky colored silt from the White River Glacier. The Sandy River flows either pale green or milky gray from the glacial flour of the Sandy and Reid Glaciers. The Salmon River, which rises below the Palmer Glacier, has the least amount of sediments, but probably the most salt because of artificial efforts to make the highest snowfields persist longer for summer downhill skiing. The Hood River rises from the Coe, Langille, Ladd, Eliot, Newton and Clark Glaciers. The generally steep mountain gradients create numerous waterfalls.

In the western lowlands, hardwoods such as bigleaf maple and red alder are most common. Rising in elevation, conifer species begin to dominate and include Douglas-fir, western hemlock and western redcedar. At the highest elevations that support trees, Pacific silver fir, noble fir, grand fir, subalpine fir, western larch, mountain hemlock, lodgepole pine and western white pine are prevalent. Understory species at middle to low elevations include vine maple, rhododendron, huckleberry, ocean spray, salal, golden chinquapin, beargrass and Oregon grape. Salmonberry and devil's club are found in very wet areas. As elevations decrease and the climate gets drier in the east, there are increasing numbers of ponderosa pine and Oregon white oak.

SANDY LONSDALE

Oregon white oak (*Quercus garryana*) and ponderosa pine (*Pinus ponderosa*) in the Lower White River Unit of the proposed Mount Hood Wilderness Additions.

Recognizing the area's importance to bull trout, coastal rainbow trout, redband trout, cutthroat trout, coho salmon, spring and fall chinook salmon, as well as winter and summer steelhead, the American Fisheries Society has identified several aquatic diversity areas within the proposed Wilderness additions.

Bird species found here are as diverse as the ecosystem types. In alpine areas, gray jay, mountain chickadee and gray-crowned rosy finch, Mountain bluebird, rufous hummingbird, Stellar's jay and band-tailed pigeon are found. Ruffed grouse occur in the small meadows, abundant springs and dense conifers of the subalpine zone. In the large meadow complexes, one finds wading birds such as the sandhill crane and great blue heron, as well as flycatchers, warblers and swallows. In the mature and old-growth forest, common species include flicker, hairy and pileated woodpeckers, red-breasted sapsucker, along with kingfisher, water ouzel, nuthatch and kinglet. Lower, wider river areas provide habitat for a variety of herons and waterfowl, including wood duck, merganser and mallard. Of special note are the imperiled bald eagle, peregrine falcon, northern goshawk and northern spotted owl that each specialize in their own niche habitats found in the area.

Mammal species here include bobcat, cougar, coyote, black bear, beaver, marten, wolverine, as well as ubiquitous deer and elk. The white-footed vole, the rarest vole in North America, lives only in Oregon's riparian forests west of the Cascade Crest where

LEVEL IV ECOREGIONS
Cascade Crest Montane Forest (37%), Western Cascades Montane Highlands (31%), Western Cascades Lowlands and Valleys (17%), Cascade Subalpine/Alpine (<2%); East Cascades Slopes and Foothills Level III Ecoregion: Grand Fir Mixed Forest (7%), Oak/Conifer Foothills (6%), Ponderosa Pine/Bitterbrush Woodland (1%); Columbia Basin Level III Ecoregion: Umatilla Plateau (<1%)

VEGETATION TYPES
Douglas-fir/Western Hemlock (46%), Mountain Hemlock (17%), Silver Fir/Western Hemlock/Noble Fir (10%), Ponderosa (7%), Ponderosa/Douglas-fir/True Fir (4%), Douglas-fir/Broadleaf Deciduous (4%), Douglas-fir/Ponderosa/True Fir (3%), Cutover/Burned (3%), True Fir/Lodgepole (2%), True Fir/Lodgepole/Western Larch/Douglas-fir (1%), Alpine Barren Fell Field (1%), Big Sagebrush (<1%), Mountain Hemlock/Parklands (<1%), Juniper/Bitterbrush (<1%), Open Lava (<1%)

DRAINAGE SUBBASINS
Hood, Lower Deschutes, Sandy

ELEVATION RANGE
801-9,412 feet

UNITS
Abbot Burn, *Badger Creek Additions* (East Additions, Eightmile Meadow, West Additions), Barlow Butte, Basin Point, Big Bend Mountain, Bonney Butte, Boulder Lake, Cedar Creek, Clear Fork Butte, Cougar Creek, Crow Creek, Fifteenmile Creek, Hellroaring Creek, Joes Point, Jones Creek, Jordan Creek, Little Clear Creek, Little Sandy River, Lost Lake Butte, Lower Badger Creek, Lower White River, Marco Creek, Mill Creek Buttes, *Mount Hood Additions* (Coe Branch, East Bunchgrass Ridge, Red Hill-Middle Fork Hood River Lava Beds, Sandy River, Tilly Jane Creek-Polallie Creek, Upper White River, Zigzag and Little Zigzag Rivers), North Boulder Creek, North Mountain, Roaring River, *Salmon-Huckleberry Additions* (Abbott Burn, Alder Creek, Linney Butte, Salmon River Meadows, West Hunchback Mountain), Salmon River Meadows, Shellrock Mountain, South Fork Bull Run River, Tom Dick and Harry Mountain, Township Meadow, Twin Lakes, Upper Salmon River.

EXISTING WILDERNESSES INCORPORATED
Badger Creek, Mount Hood and portion of Salmon-Huckleberry

SIZE
172,107 acres (269 square miles, not including 106,908 acres of currently protected Wildernesses)

COUNTIES
Clackamas, Hood River, Multnomah, Wasco

FEDERAL ADMINISTRATIVE UNITS
Mount Hood National Forest; BLM Prineville and Salem Districts

CONGRESSIONAL DISTRICTS
2nd, 3rd, 5th

Proposed Mount Hood Wilderness Additions

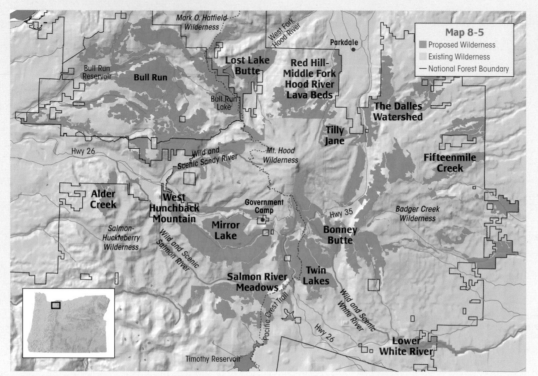

Some of the proposed Wilderness units are highlighted below.

Alder Creek provides pristine water to the town of Sandy.

Roadless units within the **Bull Run** Management Unit are closed to public access (save the Pacific Crest National Scenic Trail) to protect near-pristine drinking water supplies.

Every September and October, Hawkwatch International counts 2,500 to 4,000 migrant raptors, representing 18 species (including the relatively rare merlin) atop **Bonney Butte**. Landforms on the unit naturally constrict winged passage, creating a funnel for migratory birds on the Pacific Flyway.

Fifteenmile Creek is within the Oregon Diversity Project's North Wasco Conservation Opportunity Area, an area singled out for its two dozen at-risk plant and animal species. Most steelhead east of the Cascades are summer-run, but those in Fifteenmile Creek are winter-run.

There are many "Lost Lakes" in Oregon, but the picture postcard view of Mount Hood from Lost Lake is the familiar one. The old-growth forests that surround the lake (the **Lost Lake Butte** unit) are magnificent.

The **Lower White River** includes the White Wild and Scenic River and Oregon white oak and ponderosa pine forests that provide habitat for the bald eagle and peregrine falcon.

The **Red Mountain-Middle Fork Hood River Lava Beds** contains a low-elevation lava flow of unusual geological interest.

Both the Salmon River and the Pacific Crest National Scenic Trail cross the **Salmon River Meadows**. The diversity of riverine and forested habitats supports over 228 native fish and wildlife species in this unit — including 31 that are threatened, endangered or sensitive. Sandhill cranes nest here at the northern edge of their range. Of particular note is American scheuchzeria (*Scheuchzeria palustris* var. *americana*), a plant species very rarely found in Oregon, but more common in wetlands elsewhere.

Like the Bull Run Watershed, roadless units of The Dalles Watershed (**Mill Creek Buttes** and **Crow Creek**) are closed to public access to protect drinking water supplies.

A popular gateway to the Mount Hood Wilderness, **Tilly Jane** contains old-growth forest of mountain hemlock, subalpine fir and whitebark pine. Home to the historic Tilly Jane Trail, a popular cross country ski route, the area also cleans and recharges the ground water for Crystal Springs, from which a quarter of Hood River County residents receive their drinking water.

Twin Lakes is featured on page 131.

Hunchback Mountain is not in the Salmon-Huckleberry Wilderness, but the east half of the mountain is. From its summit, one can see from Mount Rainier to Three Fingered Jack. The unprotected half is a prominent landmark along US 26.

LINDA FOLKESTEAD

One of the Twin Lakes in the Twin Lakes Unit of the proposed Mount Hood Wilderness Additions.

FEATURED UNIT

Twin Lakes

South of Barlow Pass and north of Wapinitia Pass between the upper reaches of the Salmon and White Rivers lies a gem. Bordered by US 26 on the west, the historic Barlow Road (built in 1846 as an alternative to floating one's wagon through the Columbia River Gorge) on the east and a logging road on the south, the Twin Lakes unit is little known and even less protected.

The Twin Lakes were formed in glacial cirques. Other small lakes here include Green and Catalpa Lakes. There are also a number of wet meadows. The lakes empty easterly into Barlow Creek, which flows into the White River. The ephemeral streams in the western part of the unit flow toward the Salmon River Meadows. Sandy and silt loam soils predominate here and the steeply glaciated side-slopes exhibit potential for soil erosion. The terrain is quite steep if one tries to travel east to west, but rather gentle along the north-south divide.

The majority of the area is densely forested with Douglas-fir, noble fir, Pacific silver fir, mountain hemlock, Engelmann spruce, western white pine and lodgepole pine. The understory is quite diverse, with huckleberry, rhododendron, beargrass and a variety of other shrubs and wildflowers. Scattered throughout and associated with the higher points are barren or sparsely vegetated talus openings.

Wildlife species of special note here include the imperiled northern spotted owl and marten. Ruffed grouse are common, as are deer and elk. There are three miles of fish-bearing streams and a great blue heron rookery in the unit.

The Confederated Tribes of the Warm Springs Indian Reservation conducts an annual first huckleberry ceremony in the unit. However, forest encroachment onto the huckleberry patches caused by the lack of fire is resulting in a decline in huckleberry production.

Five miles of the Pacific Crest National Scenic Trail traverse the area and other trails connect the unit's major lakes.

PROPOSED WILDERNESS
Mount Hood Additions

LOCATION
6 miles south-southeast of Government Camp

LEVEL IV ECOREGION
Cascade Crest Montane Forest

VEGETATION TYPES
Mountain Hemlock (79%), True Fir/Lodgepole/Western Larch/Douglas-Fir (18%), Douglas-Fir/Western Hemlock (2%), Silver Fir/Western Hemlock/Noble Fir (1%)

TERRAIN
Generally steep with some plateaus.

DRAINAGE SUBBASINS
Lower Deschutes, Sandy

ELEVATION RANGE
3,199-5,200 feet

SIZE
7,301 acres

COUNTIES
Clackamas, Hood River, Wasco

FEDERAL ADMINISTRATIVE UNIT
Mount National Forest (Hood River Ranger District)

USGS 7.5' QUAD MAPS
Mount Hood South, Wapinitia Pass

its preferred food is red alder leaves.

The area's amphibian species of special concern include the Cope's giant salamander, red-legged frog, western pond turtle and painted turtle.

Recreational activities here include hiking, whitewater rafting, canoeing, cross-country skiing, snowshoeing, hunting, fishing, camping or just taking in the endless variety of views of Mount Hood.

Approximately 98,000 acres in the proposed Wilderness are presently nominally off-limits to logging. Other threats to the area including mining, off-road vehicles, roading, livestock grazing and downhill ski area expansion.

Proposed North Umpqua Wilderness
Parklands, River Canyons, Salmon, Old Trees and Wildflowers

The relatively free-flowing North Umpqua River and large amount of old-growth forest and roadless areas in the river's basin make it one of the best remaining salmon and steelhead streams on the West Coast. While lower sections of the North Umpqua Watershed have been heavily logged and the upper stretch of the river is dammed in several places, the remaining wildlands in between have managed to maintain the incredible biodiversity that characterizes the North Umpqua River Basin. These wildlands provide the high quality clean, cold water that sustains the North Umpqua River's world famous fish runs.

The North Umpqua River begins at Maidu Lake, less than a mile from the Cascade Crest, and flows freely until it reaches the first of several indignities at Lemolo Reservoir. Three dams divert much of the river into canals and pipes so it can produce power at a series of eight hydroelectric generators including facilities at Toketee and Soda Springs Reservoirs. After that point, the river again flows freely (save for the small and obsolete Winchester Dam near Interstate 5) and unimpeded to its confluence with the South Umpqua downstream of Roseburg. The Umpqua River then flows through the Coast Range to the Pacific Ocean. The 33.8-mile segment of the North Umpqua from Soda Springs Powerhouse to its confluence with Rock Creek (about 12 miles below the Umpqua National Forest boundary) is part of the National Wild and Scenic Rivers System.

The distinctive canyon country of the lower North Umpqua basin includes vast low elevation Douglas-fir forests with a mosaic of meadows, balds, cliffs, boulders, spires and other rock outcroppings. Higher up in the watershed, the forests are

UMPQUA WATERSHEDS

This Douglas-fir (*Pseudotsuga menzeisii*) in the Bunker Hill Unit of the proposed North Umpqua Wilderness is perhaps 1,000 years old. The only way to know for sure is to cut it down and count the rings. Counts on nearby stumps showed over 600 rings on trees that were three feet in diameter at their base. In the name of forest "health," the Forest Service is contemplating cutting down this tree to make more room for a younger (but still rather old) ponderosa pine (*Pinus ponderosa*) nearby.

predominantly mountain hemlock with more and larger open areas. Although it has been heavily logged, the North Umpqua Basin still has some of the largest concentrations of old-growth forest left in Oregon.

The river's deep and relatively straight east-west canyon exposes a cross-section of the region's geological history, including elements of both the more recent Mount Mazama-dominated High Cascades geology to the east and much older geology of the Western Cascades.

Prehistoric peoples used this area continuously since before the eruption of Mount Mazama about 7,700 years ago. Consequently, the area has some of the most abundant and rich archeological sites in the region.

Major wildlife species here include peregrine falcon, deer (white-tailed, black-tailed and mule), Roosevelt elk, black bear, cougar, bobcat, coyote, bald eagle, northern spotted owl, marten, fisher and wolverine.

The American Fisheries Society has recognized the important wild coho salmon,

Proposed North Umpqua Wilderness

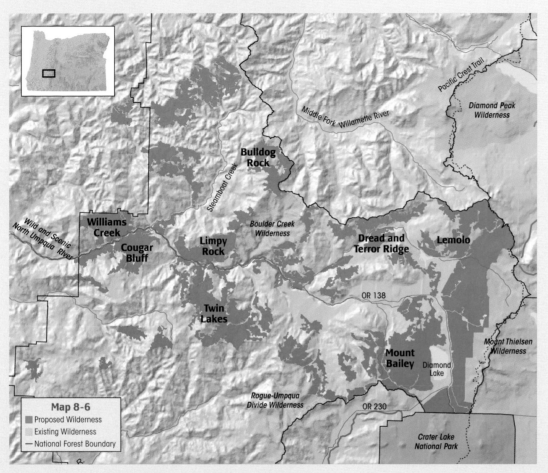

Map 8-6
- ▪ Proposed Wilderness
- ▫ Existing Wilderness
- — National Forest Boundary

habitat and is potential lynx habitat. It also happen to offer some of the most striking scenery along the North Umpqua River.

Geologically, **Limpy Rock** is an outlier of the Klamath Mountains Ecoregion. It has soils that support plants usually found in that ecoregion, the most well known of these being the Kalmiopsis (*Kalmiopsis leachiana*). Also worth noting are spring phacelia (*Phacelia verna*), grass fern (*Asplenium septentrionale*), branching montia (*Montia diffusa*) and woodland milk vetch (*Astragalus umbraticus*). Despite the steep and rugged terrain, botanists travel from afar to visit this unit.

Mount Bailey is featured on page 134.

The **Mount Thielsen Additions** unit contains some of the upper reaches of the North Umpqua River and lower stretches of Thielsen Creek. The current Oregon Cascades Recreation Area designation provides inadequate protection for these roadless forests (see the proposed Upper Deschutes Wilderness, pages 147-150.)

Twin Lakes unit on the North Umpqua-South Umpqua Divide not only contains these beautiful lakes and associated wet meadows, but also the headwaters of Calf Creek and Copeland Creek. The unit contains much old-growth Douglas-fir with an understory of rhododendron and vine maple and a few Alaska yellow cedar. The unit also has a number of important archaeological sites.

Williams Creek and **Cougar Bluff** are important for low-elevation big game winter range.

Some of the proposed Wilderness units are highlighted below.

Bulldog Rock is very scenic, with forests, meadows, wetlands and rock outcroppings. It also provides exceptionally cold, clean water to the world famous steelhead run in Steamboat Creek. The cold north-facing slopes harbor Pacific silver fir and Alaska yellow cedar, both uncommon in the southern Cascades.

Little is known about **Dread and Terror Ridge** unit, but the name does make one want to hike the trail along the ridge, one of the longer stretches of the North Umpqua Trail. The spectacular Lemolo Falls (169') are located at the eastern end of this ribbon-like roadless area.

The **Lemolo** unit contains some of Oregon's last, best wolverine

LEVEL IV ECOREGIONS
Western Cascade Montane Highlands (38%), High Southern Cascades Montane Forest (35%), Western Cascades Lowlands and Valleys (24%), Cascade Subalpine/Alpine (2%), Southern Cascades (<1%), Cascade Crest Montane Forest (<1%)

VEGETATION TYPES
Douglas-fir/Western Hemlock (54%), Mountain Hemlock/Red Fir (25%), Subalpine Lodgepole (5%), Oregon White Oak/Ponderosa (4%), Silver Fir/Western Hemlock/Noble Fir (3%), Siskiyou Mixed Conifer (3%), Cutover/Burned (2%), Mountain Hemlock (2%), Mountain Hemlock/Parklands (1%), Open Water (<1%), Ponderosa/Douglas-fir/True Fir (<1%), Siskiyou Mixed Conifer-High Elevation (<1%), Mountain Hemlock/Red Fir/Lodgepole (<1%), Douglas-fir/Broadleaf Deciduous (<1%)

DRAINAGE SUBBASIN
North Umpqua

ELEVATION RANGE
912-8,368 feet

UNITS
Bear Creek, *Boulder Creek Additions* (Balm Mountain, Illahee Rock, Medicine Creek), Bulldog Rock, Bunker Hill, Canton Creek, Cedar Creek, Chilcoot Mountain, City Creek, Clearwater Falls, Cougar Bluff, Cowhorn Mountain, Dread and Terror Ridge, Dumont Creek, Elbow Butte, Elephant Mountain, Fish Creek, Flat Rock, Garwood Butte, Grotto Falls, Horn Prairie, Horseshoe Bend, Kelsay Valley, Lake West, Lemolo, Lemon Butte, Limpy Creek, Limpy Rock, Mount Bailey, *Mount Thielsen Additions* (North Umpqua Headwaters, Thielsen Creek), North Crater, Oak Flats, Pass Creek Calapooya Mountains, Pig Iron, Red Cone, Rhododendron Ridge, *Rogue-Umpqua Divide Additions* (Rolling Grounds), Shadow Falls, Sherwood Butte, Skookum Lake, Spotted Owl Creek, Steamboat Creek, Steelhead Creek, Thorn Prairie, Thunder Creek, Twin Lakes, Warm Springs Creek, Williams Creek, Windy Creek

EXISTING WILDERNESSES INCORPORATED
Boulder Creek, portion of Rogue-Umpqua divide and portion of Mount Thielsen

SIZE
200,691 acres (314 square miles, not including 40,400 acres of currently protected Wildernesses)

COUNTIES
Douglas, Lane

FEDERAL ADMINISTRATIVE UNITS
Umpqua National Forest; BLM Eugene and Roseburg Districts

CONGRESSIONAL DISTRICT
4th

MIKE PIEHL

PROPOSED WILDERNESS
North Umpqua

LOCATION
5 miles West of Diamond Lake

LEVEL IV ECOREGIONS
High Southern Cascades Montane Forest
(89%), Cascade Crest Subalpine/Alpine
(11%)

VEGETATION TYPES
Mountain Hemlock/Red Fir (69%),
Oak/Ponderosa (18%), Mountain
Hemlock/Parklands (9%), Douglas-
Fir/Western Hemlock (2%), Siskiyou Mixed
Conifer (2%), Open Water (<1%)

TERRAIN
Volcanic peak.

DRAINAGE SUBBASINS
North Umpqua

ELEVATION RANGE
4,554-8,368 feet

SIZE
18,863 acres

COUNTY
Douglas

**FEDERAL
ADMINISTRATIVE UNIT**
Umpqua National Forest (Diamond Lake
Ranger District)

USGS 7.5' QUAD MAPS
Diamond Lake, Garwood Butte, Lemolo Lake

Mount Bailey in the proposed North Umpqua Wilderness.

FEATURED UNIT

Mount Bailey

If forlorn Mount Bailey was aligned with other well-known peaks of the Cascade Crest, it would already be protected as Wilderness. However, it has the geographic misfortune to be located about ten miles to the west of the crest. It is the largest roadless and unprotected wilderness tract in the Umpqua National Forest. From the summit, one can see from Mount Hood to Mount Shasta. It is also the highest point in Oregon's forested ranges that is accessible (for now) by snowmobile.

Mount Bailey is a classic High Cascades volcano, with steep slopes, cinder fields, lava flows and glacial washes. The highly porous soils — created by 35-foot deep ash deposits from ancient Mount Mazama — limit surface water (lakes and streams) in the area as precipitation and snowmelt immediately percolate deep underground. Those streams that do exist tend to appear fully formed from springs fed by the percolated ground water.

The trail to the summit begins in a relatively high-elevation Douglas-fir/western hemlock forest with some white fir. One then walks through a band of lodgepole pine, then through mountain hemlock and Shasta red fir (with a few Pacific silver fir and western white pine as well) and finally into a mix of mountain hemlock, subalpine fir and whitebark pine. The at-risk Whitney's Haplopappus (*Hazardia* [Haplopappus] *whitneyi* ssp. *discoideus*) grows on the rocky slopes above timberline.

Bald eagles nest on Mount Bailey above Diamond Lake. The mountain is summer range for deer and elk, and wolverine tracks have been sighted in the area.

Mount Bailey was (and is) a vision quest site for Native Americans who recognize the mountain as a source of spiritual power, calling it Medicine Mountain.

In 1886, President Grover Cleveland issued an executive order temporarily setting aside ten townships (each 36 square miles), including Mount Bailey, from sale, mining and logging, "pending legislation looking to the creation of a public park." The park that became Crater Lake National Park in 1902 was little more than seven townships and did not include Mount Bailey. Over the decades, the National Park Service has tried without success to gain control of nearby Mount Bailey, Diamond Lake and Mount Thielsen.

spring and fall chinook salmon and winter and summer steelhead runs associated with the North Umpqua — among the most productive in Oregon — by designating multiple aquatic diversity areas within the proposed Wilderness. The North Umpqua also has unique runs of sea-run cutthroat and rainbow trout and numerous tributary streams of the North Umpqua River below Toketee Falls are included in the Oregon Biodiversity Project's Umpqua Headwaters Conservation Opportunity Area.

Best known for its fly-fishing, and increasingly known for its whitewater rafting, the proposed North Umpqua Wilderness also provides excellent hiking, hunting, picnicking, horseback riding, swimming, sightseeing, photography, camping and botanizing.

Approximately 130,000 acres of the proposed Wilderness are somewhat off-limits to logging. However, current land use allocations have loopholes large enough to allow a convoy of log trucks to pass through. Off-road vehicles, roading and mining are other major threats to the area.

Proposed Rogue-Umpqua Wilderness
Old-Growth Forests, Salmon Streams, Mountain Meadows and Wonderful Rock Formations

The proposed Rogue-Umpqua Wilderness includes all federal roadless lands in the South Umpqua River drainage and in the upper Rogue River Basin west and north of the Rogue River, which is a federally protected Wild and Scenic River. The entire area is incredibly scenic. Its diverse terrain includes magnificent low-elevation dark forested valleys, high alpine meadows and lakes, as well as fascinating basalt outcroppings.

Much of the area has been designated as late successional reserve under the Northwest Forest Plan in recognition of its significant value as wildlife habitat. The varied landscape makes for diverse wildlife populations. Notable species include black-tailed deer, Roosevelt elk, black bear, blue grouse, mountain beaver, coyote, cougar, snowshoe hare, otter, mink, gray squirrel, ruffed grouse, spotted owl, marten, fisher, western pond turtle, yellow-legged frog and red-legged frog.

The American Fisheries Society has identified several aquatic diversity areas within the proposed Wilderness, recognizing the important runs of coho, spring Chinook salmon, as well as summer and winter runs of steelhead. The Oregon Biodiversity Project's Umpqua Headwaters Conservation Opportunity Area, which

A snag in the Donegan Prairie Unit of the proposed Rogue-Umpqua Wilderness. ▶

LEVEL IV ECOREGIONS
Southern Cascades (49%), Western Cascades Montane Highlands (29%), High Southern Cascades Montane Forest (4%); Klamath Mountains Level III Ecoregion: Oak Savanna Foothills (10%), Inland Siskiyous (8%), Umpqua Interior Foothills (<1%)

VEGETATION TYPE
Douglas-fir/Western Hemlock (45%), Siskiyou Mixed Conifer (30%), Mountain Hemlock/Red Fir (11%), Siskiyou Mixed Evergreen (5%), Silver Fir/Western Hemlock/Noble Fir (3%), Oregon White Oak/Ponderosa (2%), Siskiyou Mixed Conifer-High Elevation (2%), Cutover/Burned (1%), Douglas-fir/Broadleaf Deciduous (<1%), Oregon White Oak/Douglas-fir (<1%), Subalpine Lodgepole (<1%)

DRAINAGE SUBBASINS
Middle Rogue, Upper Rogue, South Umpqua

ELEVATION RANGE
997-6,930 feet

UNITS
Acker Rock, Bailey Ridge, Beaver Creek, Berry Creek, Bitter Lick Creek, Blue Gulch, Board Mountain, Buckhorn Mountain, Cedar Springs Mountain, Coffee Creek, Collins Ridge, Donegan Prairie, Drew Creek, Dumont Creek, Elkhorn Creek, Flood Rock, Hatchet Creek, Hawk Mountain, Horn Prairie, Last Creek, Morine Creek, Mount Stella, Pipestone Creek - Beaver Creek, Pass Creek-Calapooya Mountains, Point Nance, Poole Creek, Quartz Creek, *Rogue-Umpqua Divide Additions* (Abbott Creek, Castle Rock Fork, Fish Lake Creek, Jackson Creek Headwaters, Log Creek, Mosquito Camp, Paul Pearson I, Paul Pearson II, Muir Creek, Rabbit Ears, Travail Creek), Sherwood Butte, Snowshoe Springs, South Fork Cow Creek, Straight Creek, Surveyor Creek, Tatouche Peak, Yellow Jacket, Yellow Jacket Spring, Yellow Rock

EXISTING WILDERNESS INCORPORATED
portion of Rogue-Umpqua Divide

SIZE
121,972 acres (191 square miles, not including 33,200 acres of currently protected Wilderness)

COUNTIES
Douglas, Jackson

FEDERAL ADMINISTRATIVE UNITS
Rogue River and Umpqua National Forests; BLM Medford and Roseburg Districts

CONGRESSIONAL DISTRICTS
2nd, 4th

Proposed Rogue-Umpqua Wilderness

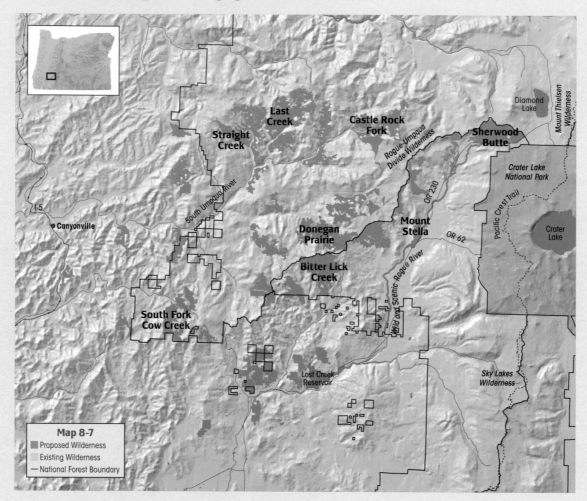

Map 8-7
- Proposed Wilderness
- Existing Wilderness
- National Forest Boundary

Last Creek includes trees over 800 years old and great views from atop Big Squaw Mountain.

Mount Stella hosts segments of the Rogue River and the Upper Rogue River Trails.

The **Rogue-Umpqua Divide Additions** include numerous wildlands "appendages" that should have been included in the original Rogue-Umpqua Divide Wilderness designated by Congress in 1984. The proposed additions contain significant low elevation old-growth forest and numerous interesting rock formations, including Rabbit Ears, two spires that can be seen from many vantage points in the Upper Rogue River Basin.

Sherwood Butte has pumice soils and steep ridges covered with mountain hemlock and Shasta red fir. Sitting atop the Rogue-Umpqua Divide, this unit also has some relatively flat moist meadows. There is good habitat for the rare marten here.

South Fork Cow Creek contains some mature, picture-perfect old-growth forest and an easy trail by which to see it.

From the vantage point of Smith Ridge, one can look into **Straight Creek** where big old pines are scattered amongst giant old firs that support the endangered northern spotted owl.

Some of the units in the proposed Wilderness are highlighted below.

Bitter Lick Creek is featured on page 137.

Castle Rock Fork includes habitat for the endangered peregrine falcon. The Castle Rock Fork provides one quarter of the late summer flows to the upper South Umpqua River and has unusually cold water.

Donegan Prairie hosts a variety of habitats from wet meadows and dry prairies to old-growth sugar pine and incense cedar forest. For many species, including northern spotted owls, the unit is a link in a crucial low-elevation wildlife corridor along the Rogue-Umpqua Divide.

KEN CROCKER

Old-growth forest along Bitter Lick Creek in the unit of the same name in the proposed Rogue-Umpqua Wilderness.

FEATURED UNIT
Bitter Lick Creek

Bitter Lick Creek is named for a couple of "salt" licks in the heart of the unit. (They are quite bitter, with a strong hint of sulfur.). The watershed is generally intact and contains a vast low-elevation old-growth forest. The uppermost portions include talus, cliffs, outcroppings, dry open meadows and brush. The highest point in the unit is Butler Butte along the Rogue-Umpqua Divide.

The area's old growth is not particularly large in diameter (most of these trees are four- to five-feet in diameter, but one seven-foot specimen has been seen), but there is an unusually high number of large trees per acre. Species include Douglas-fir, sugar pine, grand fir, incense cedar and western hemlock. To walk through this magnificent ancient forest is an impressive experience.

Other tree species here include lodgepole pine and golden chinquapin in the drier sites and alder along the streams and at higher elevations. Pacific yew is also quite abundant, as is bigleaf maple in the riparian corridors. Understory species include Oregon grape, sword fern, huckleberry and vine maple.

The upper reaches of Bitter Lick Creek flow through steep terrain that creates countless pools and riffles. As the creek continues south to the lower end of the unit, it pours into a wide valley with a gentle gradient. Bitter Lick Creek is a tributary of Elk Creek (partially blocked by the half-baked, then half-constructed and now mostly-dead Elk Creek Dam). The Elk Creek watershed has much of the remaining wild coho salmon habitat left in the upper Rogue River.

The unit is excellent habitat for spotted owls and other old-growth dependent species.

A trail leading from the bottom of the creek to the top is lightly maintained and easily passable for a few miles, but the further one goes, the more likely one will get blocked by thick vegetation. A few years ago, the Forest Service placed a clearcut directly on the trail's path to discourage recreational use and as an attempt to disqualify the unit from future wilderness consideration. Though it is quite annoying to tread through the (temporary) devastation (on a hot day, the clearcut can be 30 degrees warmer than the adjoining old-growth forest), the clearcut will eventually grow back and the old-growth forest up the trail is well worth the annoyance.

PROPOSED WILDERNESS
Rogue-Umpqua

LOCATION
12 miles northwest of Prospect

LEVEL IV ECOREGIONS
Southern Cascades (62%), Western Cascades Montane Highlands (38%)

VEGETATION TYPES
Mountain Hemlock/Red Fir (42%), Siskiyou/Mixed Conifer (20%), Siskiyou Mixed Conifer-High Elevation (19%), Oregon White Oak/Ponderosa (18%), Silver Fir/Western Hemlock/Noble Fir (1%), Douglas-Fir/Western Hemlock (<1%)

TERRAIN
Steeply incised canyons.

DRAINAGE SUBBASIN
Upper Rogue

ELEVATION RANGE
2,398-5,401 feet

SIZE
8,028 acres

COUNTY
Jackson

FEDERAL ADMINISTRATIVE UNITS
Rogue River and Umpqua National Forests (Prospect and Tiller Ranger Districts)

USGS 7.5' QUAD MAPS
Abbot Butte, Butler Butte, Sugarpine Creek, Whetstone Point

includes the headwaters of the South Umpqua River and some of the Cascades Ecoregion's most important salmon and steelhead habitat, is also located within the proposed Wilderness. The area's rivers and streams are home to cutthroat trout. Such streams within the proposed Wilderness contribute significantly to domestic drinking water supplies downstream.

Numerous species of rare plants have been located in the proposed Wilderness, including California sword fern (*Polystichum californicum*), spring phacelia (*Phacelia verna*), Columbia lewisia (*Lewisia columbiana*) and Umpqua swertia (*Frasera umpquaensis*).

Major tree species here include Douglas-fir, sugar pine, incense cedar, subalpine fir, western hemlock, mountain hemlock, Pacific yew, vine maple, lodgepole pine, grand fir, bigleaf maple, golden chinquapin, alder, Shasta red fir and western white pine.

There are many trails in the proposed Wilderness, including one that follows much of the Rogue-Umpqua Divide. Other recreational opportunities here include hunting, fishing, horseback riding and salt licking.

Native Americans have long used areas in the proposed Wilderness for gathering huckleberries and other fruit and plants, and continue to do so today.

As many as 89,000 acres of the proposed Wilderness are not currently slated for logging, but plans can change. Other threats to the area include off-road vehicles, livestock grazing and road building.

Proposed Santiam Wilderness

Very Big and Very Old Trees with Lots of Wildflowers

Some of the oldest, largest trees remaining in Oregon are found in the Santiam Basin (as well as some of the largest and ugliest clearcuts). Extensive stands of old-growth forest characterize most of the roadless units in the proposed Santiam Wilderness. Rock outcroppings, wildflower meadows, lakes, waterfalls, streams and marshes add to the diversity of these wildlands. The roadless units tend to be steep, which is often the only reason they have not been roaded and logged yet.

The North, Middle and South Santiam Rivers all arise in the Willamette National Forest. The Middle Santiam joins the South Santiam in what is currently Foster Reservoir near Sweet Home. The Little North Santiam River empties into the North Santiam, which along with the South Santiam forms the Santiam River a few miles east of Interstate 5. The mountain streams in the area often have spectacular little

◀ A northern spotted owl in an old-growth forest near the Breitenbush River in the proposed Santiam Wilderness.

Proposed Santiam Wilderness

Some of the units in the proposed Wilderness are highlighted below.

Bachelor Mountain features several miles of ridgeline and canyon trails. It is a haven for songbirds and wildflowers and may be habitat for the critically endangered lynx. It also contains very large Engelmann spruce and sugar pine. Cascade peaks visible from here range from Mount Hood to Diamond Peak.

Managed by the Bureau of Land Management, **Crabtree Valley** is an island of pristine forest surrounded by a sea of industrial clearcuts. The valley's old-growth Douglas-fir and western redcedar are perhaps 1,000 years old.

Elkhorn Creek contains magnificent old-growth forests and a creek that is home to steelhead and cutthroat trout and flows through one of the most rugged and remote forested gorges in Oregon. The unit contains nearly all of upper Elkhorn Creek and portions of the Cedar Creek watershed.

Gordon Meadows contains lakes and meadows in various stages of succession. Towering over the lakes and meadows is Soapgrass Ridge. Here one will find the Millennium Grove, a unique stand of 700 to 900 year-old – and older – old-growth Douglas-fir interspersed with other younger, 400 to 500 year-old trees.

The **Hoover Ridge** unit is a scenic backdrop for anglers and boaters on Detroit Reservoir and is home to nesting bald eagles.

Iron Mountain is featured on page 140.

Jumpoff Joe is an impressive rock outcropping that is easily seen from US 20. The Old Santiam Wagon Road traverses the unit.

Located between the Middle Santiam Wilderness and the Quartzville Creek Wild and Scenic River, **McQuade Creek** contains some massive old-growth forests.

Moose Creek qualifies for federal Wild and Scenic River status and hosts runs of spring chinook salmon and winter steelhead that are facing extinction. The unit's intact low-elevation forest is very rare in the Oregon Cascades.

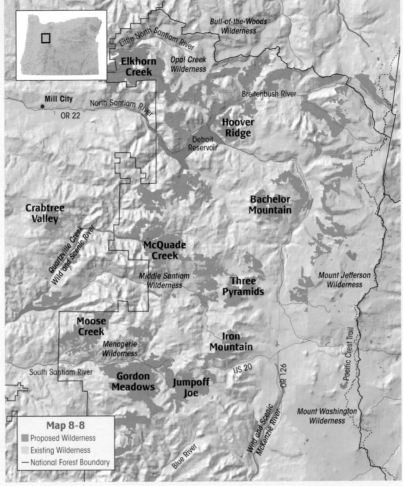

Map 8-8
■ Proposed Wilderness
■ Existing Wilderness
— National Forest Boundary

The **Mount Jefferson Additions** units are numerous roadless and undeveloped areas adjacent to the Mount Jefferson Wilderness. Located downslope from the current Wilderness boundary, these units usually contain larger trees. They were not protected as part of the previous Wilderness designation due to the commercial value of the forest.

Three Pyramids contains a true "cathedral forest" hidden in a remote valley with towering ridges above. The soils in this unit are so unstable that landslides regularly occur in this virgin forest, even without the prodding of roading and logging. Above the forest are wildflowers usually not found in the vicinity, suggesting an ice-age refuge.

LEVEL IV ECOREGIONS
Western Cascades Montane Highlands (72%), Western Cascades Lowlands and Valleys (20%), Cascade Crest Montane Forest (8%), Cascade Subalpine/Alpine (<1%)

VEGETATION TYPES
Douglas-fir/Western Hemlock (70%), Silver Fir/Western Hemlock/Noble Fir (20%), Mountain Hemlock (5%), Cutover/Burned (3%), Douglas-fir/Broadleaf Deciduous (2%), Open Water (<1%), Subalpine Lodgepole (1%), Alpine Barren Fell Field (<1%)

DRAINAGE SUBBASINS
North Santiam, South Santiam

ELEVATION RANGE
984-6,001 feet

UNITS
Bachelor Mountain, Blowout Creek, Box Canyon, Browder Ridge, *Opal Creek Additions* (Byars Rock, Elkhorn Creek, Marten Butte), Byars Creek, Cliffs Creek, Crabtree Valley, Daley Lake, Eagle Canyon, Gordon Meadows, Hall Ridge, Hoover Ridge, Iron Mountain, Jumpoff Joe, Lower Quartz Creek, *Menagerie Wilderness Additions* (Moose Mountain, West Additions), *Middle Santiam Additions* (Gordon Peak, McQuade Creek), Minniece Point, Moose Creek, Mount Bruno, *Mount Jefferson Additions* (Big Meadows, Devils Peak, Grizzly Creek-Puzzle Creek, Lower Triangulation Peak, North Additions, North Breitenbush River, Pine Ridge, Woodpecker Ridge), Olallie Lakes, Pyramid Creek, Sardine Mountain, Scorpion Mountain, Slate Rock, Three Pyramids, Tidbits Mountain-Owl Ridge, Two Girls, Upper Quartzville Creek, Upper Soda, White Bull Mountain, Wildcat Mountain

EXISTING WILDERNESSES INCORPORATED
Menagerie, Middle Santiam, portions of Mount Jefferson and Opal Creek

SIZE
120,095 acres (188 square miles, not including 106,901 acres of currently protected Wildernesses)

COUNTIES
Clackamas, Jefferson, Linn, Marion

FEDERAL ADMINISTRATIVE UNITS
Mount Hood and Willamette National Forests; BLM Salem District

CONGRESSIONAL DISTRICTS
4th, 5th

PROPOSED WILDERNESS
Santiam

LOCATION
16 miles east of Cascadia

LEVEL IV ECOREGIONS
Western Cascades Montane Highlands
(94%), Cascade Crest Montane Forest (6%)

VEGETATION TYPES
Silver Fir/Western Hemlock/Noble Fir (29%),
Douglas-Fir/Western Hemlock (28%),
Mountain Hemlock (24%), Cutover/Burned
(11%), Douglas-Fir/Broadleaf Deciduous (8%)

TERRAIN
Rugged and seasonally covered with either
snow or wildflowers.

DRAINAGE SUBBASIN
South Santiam

ELEVATION RANGE
3,398-5,795 feet

SIZE
8,803 acres

COUNTY
Linn

**FEDERAL
ADMINISTRATIVE UNIT**
Willamette National Forest (Sweet Home
Ranger District)

USGS 7.5' QUAD MAPS
Echo Mountain, Harter Mountain

GEORGE WUERTHNER

Wildflowers in the Iron Mountain Unit of the proposed Santiam Wilderness.

FEATURED UNIT

Iron Mountain

Over 300 species of flowering plants belonging to 18 distinct plant communities are found on Iron Mountain, one of many mountains in this unit. Crescent and Echo Mountains, as well as North, South and Cone Peaks are comparably diverse, though not as well known. From the various summits, one can see from Mount Jefferson to Diamond Peak. This unit contains the headwaters of the North, Middle and South Santiam Rivers.

A good trail system that links most of the unit's distinct habitats makes exploring the area easy and enjoyable. Deep, dark forest stands, alpine meadows, rock spires, cliffs and bare volcanic rock contribute to the landscape's diversity.

The area's varied microclimates (dry to wet and warm to cold — all in close proximity), soil types and elevations provide diverse habitats for numerous plant and animal species. The highlands were spared glacial scouring and/or inundation during the last ice age, which contributes to the remarkable geography. Over 60 species found here are unusual or rare for the western Cascade Mountains, including one species of sagebrush (*Artemisia ludoviciana*).

On a mere quarter section (160 acres) on Echo Mountain Ridge, one can find 80 percent of all the Oregon conifer species found at that elevation. The fifteen species of conifers (along with Pacific yew) that have been identified in the unit are:

- Pacific silver fir
- white fir
- noble fir
- dwarf juniper
- western white pine
- lodgepole pine
- western redcedar
- mountain hemlock
- grand fir
- subalpine fir
- Alaska yellow cedar
- Engelmann spruce
- ponderosa pine
- Douglas-fir
- western hemlock

There are, in fact, sixteen species, if one counts the grand fir-white fir hybrid. Surprisingly, sugar pine is not found here, although it is found elsewhere in the proposed Wilderness. This may be because this area is located near the northern edge of the sugar pine's range, or perhaps there just wasn't room for it here.

waterfalls, cataracts and crystalline pools.

Recognizing the area's notable spring chinook and winter steelhead, the American Fisheries Society has identified a Little North Santiam aquatic diversity area that includes significant roadless lands. Other fish species found here include native cutthroat and coastal rainbow trout.

The city of Salem collects its water from the North Santiam River and has requested that Congress "enact legislation to increase the protection of forests on federal lands in the North Santiam Watershed." Lebanon, Sweet Home and Albany depend on water from the South Santiam River, while Jefferson drinks from the mainstem Santiam River.

The forests in this proposed Wilderness are mostly dominated by Douglas-fir, especially at lower elevations, but also include numerous other species. As the elevation increases, so does the number of true firs in the mix. At the highest elevations are mountain hemlock. The area also contains alder and other hardwoods, with an understory of rhododendron, Pacific yew, vine maple, salmonberry, salal and Oregon grape.

Mammal species here include beaver, black bear, coyote, cougar, black-tailed deer, Roosevelt elk, marten, coyote, mink, bobcat, red tree vole and possibly lynx. Small game birds include ruffed grouse, blue grouse and mountain quail. Waterfowl include teal and wood ducks. Other notable bird species include northern spotted owl, peregrine falcon, osprey and bald eagle. The rough-skinned newt, Cascades frog, long-toed salamander and boreal toad may be found in the wettest habitats created by fog drip, rain and/or snow.

Recreational opportunities include hiking, horseback riding, hunting, fishing, botanizing, birding and tree identification.

Approximately 66,000 acres of the proposed Wilderness are nominally off-limits to logging. Other threats to the area include off-road vehicles, road building and mining.

Proposed South Cascades Wilderness
High-Elevation Parklands and Lower-Elevation Forests

From Crater Lake to the southern end of the Cascade Range in Oregon, the proposed South Cascades Wilderness includes several unprotected Cascade Crest peaks, low elevation forests and critical fish habitat. Much, but not all, of the region's high elevation forests are already protected in Wilderness areas. The unprotected high elevation forests, and those at low elevations, dominated by Douglas-fir on the west side and by ponderosa pine on the east, remain vulnerable to logging and are threatened with

The National Park Service is carefully reintroducing fire onto their lands within the proposed South Cascades Wilderness. ▶

LEVEL IV ECOREGIONS
High Southern Cascades Montane Forest (63%), Southern Cascades (15%), Cascade Subalpine/Alpine (11%); East Cascades Slopes and Foothills Level III Ecoregion: Pumice Plateau (6%), Klamath/Goose Lake Basins (1%), Southern Cascade Slope (<1%); Klamath Mountains Level III Ecoregion: Oak Savanna (3%)

VEGETATION TYPES
Mountain Hemlock/Red Fir (50%), Siskiyou Mixed Conifer-High Elevation (11%), Subalpine Lodgepole (11%), Siskiyou Mixed Conifer (8%), Mountain Hemlock/Parklands (6%), Marsh/Wet Meadow (4%), Cutover/Burned (2%), Ponderosa on Pumice (2%), Mountain Hemlock/Red Fir/Lodgepole (1%), Lodgepole on Pumice (1%), Ponderosa/Douglas-fir/True Fir (1%), Open Water (1%), Douglas-fir/Western Hemlock (1%), Douglas-fir/Ponderosa /True Fir (<1%), Mountain Hemlock (<1%), Oregon White Oak/Pacific Madrone (<1%), Oregon White Oak/Ponderosa (<1%), Ponderosa/Lodgepole (<1%), Siskiyou Mixed Evergreen (<1%)

DRAINAGE SUBBASINS
Upper Klamath, Upper Klamath Lake, Upper Rogue

ELEVATION RANGE
2,080-8,929 feet

UNITS
Brown Mountain, Crater Lake Rim, Dead Soldier Meadow, Deer Creek, Dunlop Meadows, Farlow Hill, Forked Horn Springs, Ginkgo Creek, Green Springs Mountain, Grizzly Peak, Heppsie Mountain, Lake West, Mill Creek, Mount Scott, *Mount Thielsen Additions* (Cottonwood Creek, Miller Creek, Red Cone Spring), *Mountain Lakes Additions* (Clover Creek Headwaters, Little Aspen Butte, Varney Creek, West Additions), North Crater, Poole Hill, Red Blanket Mountain, Red Cone, Service Glades, *Sky Lakes Additions* (Beaver Creek, Big Meadows, Black Bear Swamp, Cedar Spring, Cherry Creek, Crane Creek Headwaters, Dole Spring, Imnaha Creek-Sumpter Creek, Lower Mount McLoughlin, Pelican Butte, Red Blanket Creek, Rye Spur, Sevenmile Creek), Slinger Rock, Sun Creek, Union Creek, West of Corral Springs, Wheeler Creek

EXISTING WILDERNESSES INCORPORATED
portion of Mount Thielsen, Mountain Lakes, Sky Lakes

SIZE
299,703 acres (468 square miles, not including 165,029 acres of currently protected Wilderness)

COUNTIES
Douglas, Jackson, Klamath

FEDERAL ADMINISTRATIVE UNITS
Rogue River and Winema National Forests; BLM Medford District; Crater Lake National Park

CONGRESSIONAL DISTRICTS
2nd, 4th

Proposed South Cascades Wilderness

Some of the units of the proposed Wilderness are highlighted below.

Brown Mountain straddles the Cascade Crest and includes several miles of the Pacific Crest National Scenic Trail. It's a scramble over fresh talus to bag this peak (7,311'). Brown Mountain is a small shield volcano capped with a cinder cone. Large boulder fields dominate the upper slopes. Vegetation is sparse with some Shasta red fir dotting the slopes. Alder and willows grow in the wetter spots where snowmelt accumulates. Streams are non-existent.

The Crater Lake National Park units include **Mount Scott** and other notable high points on and near the Cascade Crest such as **Red Cone** and **Union Peak**. They also include the head of the Rogue River and the beginning of the Rogue River Trail. While logging and mining do not threaten these park units, the National Park Service could revert to its road-building and over-development past and open these pristine areas to the abuses of the outside world. Protecting the park backcountry as Wilderness will ensure that the park's front-country development doesn't expand any further.

Sun Creek, in the southeast corner of the park, is critical habitat for the endangered bull trout. The park and surrounding areas were once the site of the late Mount Mazama, which, through a series of erup-tions, built itself to about 12,000 feet elevation (higher than Mount Hood). Then about 7,700 years ago, Mount Mazama blew its top, scat-tering a layer of ash over eight states and three Canadian provinces. The eruption was 42 times greater than that of Mount Saint Helens in 1980. The magma chamber collapsed and eventually filled with rain and snowmelt, forming Crater Lake, the deepest lake (1,932') in the United States and the seventh deepest lake in the world. If one takes the time to leave the crowds along Crater Lake's rim road, one will find oneself in some of the wildest and least visited forestlands in Oregon.

The Pacific Crest National Scenic Trail traverses the **Green Springs Mountain** unit.

Grizzly Peak is a small unit, but the 5,920-foot peak dominates the view from nearby Ashland.

The **Mount Thielsen Additions** units include small but important sections that were left out of the original Wilderness because they might have had a commercially valuable log or two. Unprotected wildlands near Miller Lake are also included. Miller Lake was once home to the Miller Lake lamprey, thought to be extinct after being intentionally poisoned by state fish "biologists" to make room for exotic, more sporting fish species in the lake. Fortunately, some Miller

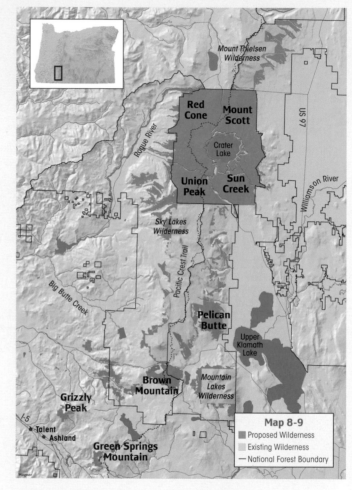

Map 8-9
■ Proposed Wilderness
■ Existing Wilderness
— National Forest Boundary

Lake lamprey survived in the creek below the lake where they have been recently rediscovered. It is hoped that, in this more enlightened time, they will be protected and conserved.

The **Mountain Lakes Additions** units would round out a perfect square township (Township 37 South, Range 6 East, Willamette Meridian) protected as Wilderness, while adding some lower elevation areas and associated ecosystem diversity, including spotted owl and wolverine habitat.

Pelican Butte is featured on page 143.

The **Sky Lakes Additions** units also include lower elevation lands, more diverse forests and larger trees.

SANDY LONSDALE

Pelican Butte has been and will always be threatened with ski area development and logging until protected as Wilderness.

FEATURED UNIT

Pelican Butte

There are no pelicans on Pelican Butte. It was named after nearby Upper Klamath Lake's Pelican Bay, where pelicans are numerous. Pelican Butte should have been included in the Sky Lakes Wilderness, designated by Congress in 1984. However, fantasies of a downhill ski area and the big timber on the lower slopes prevented its inclusion.

The cone-shaped Pelican Butte is an andesite shield volcano located east of the Cascade Crest and entirely within the Klamath River Basin. The lower three-fifths of the butte is forested with mature and old-growth ponderosa pine, white fir, Shasta red fir, mountain hemlock and quaking aspen. The upper two-fifths is open, often exposed lava and rocky terrain that also supports whitebark pine. There are some lakes, meadows and a few streams with associated riparian areas in the unit.

The plant communities here include mixed conifer/snowbrush-bearberry, white fir/chinquapin-boxwood-prince's pine, Shasta red fir-white fir/chinquapin-prince's pine/sedge, mountain hemlock/grouse huckleberry and white fir-alder/shrub meadow.

The Klamath Basin is home to the largest wintering population of threatened bald eagles in the lower 48 states. In the winter, up to 100 bald eagles can be found roosting near the lake, at the northern base of Pelican Butte. As many as 34 endangered, threatened, sensitive or indicator species may be found on the butte, much of which is critical habitat for the threatened northern spotted owl and a stronghold for pileated and white-headed woodpeckers. Both bald eagles and spotted owls are protected under the Endangered Species Act. Pelican Butte is also excellent habitat for wolverine, lynx, marten and fisher. Its streams are home to redband trout and endemic mollusk species.

The 30 to 40 inches of annual precipitation (which is mostly snow that is gone by July) on the butte disappears into the very porous soils. The water re-emerges downslope as springs that feed into the lake, supplying pristine water to Pelican Bay, itself a critical source of fresh water in one of the most polluted (nutrient rich) lakes in Oregon. Farther out in the lake the water pH can become as alkaline as dishwashing detergent by late summer. The endangered Qapdo and C'wam (a.k.a. Lost River and shortnose suckers), along with redband trout, find a seasonal refuge in Pelican Bay.

Much of the Pelican Butte unit has been designated a late successional reserve under the Northwest Forest Plan. Although lands in the unit are also designated for semi-primitive recreation, the Forest Service has entertained fantasies (and will likely again) of creating a $34 million resort ski area on the butte (hardly "semi-primitive"). In addition to disturbing and displacing the native wildlife and degrading water quality, a ski facility would disturb Native Americans' use of Pelican Butte for vision quests and prayer.

One year, guerrilla conservationists allegedly reopened an old trail up the butte to Francis Lake. The trail was long abandoned by the Forest Service, a common practice when the agency is seeking to log an area. Today the only scar that defiles the upper reaches of Pelican Butte's otherwise roadless lands is a rough jeep trail to the butte's summit to service some electronics facilities and a fire lookout.

PROPOSED WILDERNESS
South Cascades

LOCATION
20 miles south-southwest of Fort Klamath

LEVEL IV ECOREGIONS
High Southern Cascades Montane Forest (57%), Cascade Subalpine/Alpine (43%)

VEGETATION TYPES
Mountain Hemlock/Red Fir (47%), Mountain Hemlock/Parklands (38%), Siskiyou Mixed Conifer-High Elevation (14%), Cutover/Burned (2%), Marsh (1%), Wet Meadow (<1%), Subalpine Lodgepole (<1%)

TERRAIN
Fujiama-like Cascade peak.

DRAINAGE SUBBASIN
Upper Klamath Lake

ELEVATION RANGE
4,200-8,036 feet

SIZE
14,705 acres

COUNTY
Klamath

FEDERAL ADMINISTRATIVE UNIT
Winema National Forest (Klamath Ranger District)

USGS 7.5' QUAD MAPS
Crystal Bay, Lake of the Woods North, Pelican Butte, Pelican Bay

development.

The size and quality of the wilderness habitat and healthy populations of prey species (deer and elk) in Oregon's South Cascades have led wildlife biologists to identify the area as suitable for wolf reintroduction. The area also provides abundant habitat for other sensitive predator species, including lynx, marten, fisher and wolverine.

The mighty Rogue River begins in the South Cascades, as do numerous tributary streams that drain into Upper Klamath Lake and the Klamath River.

The American Fisheries Society has identified several aquatic diversity areas within the proposed Wilderness. Both coastal rainbow and redband trout are found in the area, as are the diminishing Klamath River and Pacific lamprey. The proposed Wilderness is a certain source of clean water for endemic and endangered species of lake fish (some that are pejoratively called "suckers") and lamprey. The proposed Wilderness also supplies drinking water to Medford.

Recreational opportunities in the area include hiking, backpacking, horseback riding, hunting, fishing, cross-country skiing and sucker watching. The proposed Wilderness would protect several miles of the Pacific Crest National Scenic Trail.

Approximately 72,000 acres of the proposed South Cascades Wilderness is not currently scheduled for logging. The remainder is at risk. Off-road vehicles and downhill ski developments are the other major threats to the area.

Proposed Three Sisters Wilderness Additions
Magnificent Lower-Elevation Forests on both sides of the Cascade Crest

The current Three Sisters and Waldo Lake Wilderness complex constitutes the largest protected contiguous wildland in the Oregon Cascades. It could be even larger. The contiguous Waldo "Lake" Wilderness was established separately in 1984, though it was a logical addition to the long-established Three Sisters Wilderness. When Congress finally did create Waldo Lake Wilderness, it yielded a political benefit to the Oregon Congressional delegation who were perceived as "saving Waldo Lake," although the designation fell short of actually including the lake (see Featured Unit: *Waldo Lake* on page 146).

The proposed Three Sisters Wilderness Additions encompasses portions of the headwaters of the North Fork of the Middle Fork Willamette, Middle Fork Willamette,

Lower Rosary Lake in the Maiden Peak Unit of the proposed Three Sisters Wilderness Additions. ▶

GEORGE WUERTHNER

Proposed Three Sisters Wilderness Additions

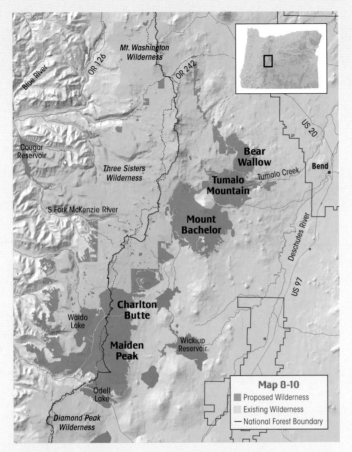

Map 0-10
- ■ Proposed Wilderness
- ▨ Existing Wilderness
- — National Forest Boundary

Some of the units in the proposed Wilderness are highlighted below.

Bear Wallow is important elk summer range. Willows are common along the creeks with occasional pockets of bog birch or quaking aspen. Major tree species here are lodgepole pine and mountain hemlock with some mixed conifer species at the lower elevations.

Charlton Butte contains mostly mountain hemlock and lodgepole pine forest with little apparent understory. Much of the unit burned in 1996 and is recovering well. Several trails, including the Pacific Crest Trail are available. A trail from Charlton Lake passes through lush meadows just before reaching Found Lake. From there, Hidden Lake is a cross-country climb uphill.

Maiden Peak includes several miles of the Cascade Crest, paralleled by the Pacific Crest National Scenic Trail. Maiden Peak (7,818') and The

Twins (7,362') are the highest points, with 360° panoramic views. Four-fifths of the forest is an unbroken swath of mature and old-growth mountain hemlock interspersed with scattered meadows. Lodgepole pine predominates most of the other fifth, along with some western white pine, subalpine fir, grand fir, Engelmann spruce and ponderosa pine. There are seven major lakes in the unit (including Rosary and Bobby Lakes) and numerous minor lakes and ponds. Gold Lake Bog Research Natural Area on the east end of Gold Lake is suspected breeding habitat for solitary sandpipers. If true, it is the only known nesting site for this variety of sandpiper in the lower 48 states.

Mount Bachelor includes most of Mount Bachelor, though it does not include any lands within the permit area of the Mount Bachelor Ski Area. While a good portion of this Cascade peak has been sacrificed for downhill skiing, not all of it should be. The headwaters of the Deschutes River and water for Lava Lake and Little Lava Lake come from this unit, and the very rare pumice grape fern (*Botrychium pumicola*) is found in the unit's alpine and montane habitats.

Tumalo Creek is the water supply for the city of Bend, which benefits from the well-developed riparian ecosystems along Tumalo Creek and its tributaries that contribute to both the quality and quantity of water in the creek. Though generally a high elevation forest of mountain hemlock, lodgepole pine and Engelmann spruce, ponderosa pine is also found at lower elevations in this unit. Wet meadows and springs are plentiful here. Coastal rainbow trout are found in Bridge Creek. The unit is also an important elk calving area.

The **Three Sisters Additions** and **Waldo Lake Additions** are those numerous roadless areas on the borders of the existing Wilderness areas that were not included in earlier Wilderness legislation, usually because timber interests prevented it. They are mostly forested lower elevation areas that add diversity to the Wilderness, but also include the south faces of Fuji Mountain (7,144') and Mount Ray (7,002').

Waldo Lake is featured on page 146.

LEVEL IV ECOREGIONS
Cascade Crest Montane Forest (73%), Western Cascades Montane Highlands (15%), Western Cascades Lowlands and Valleys (5%), Cascade Subalpine/Alpine (2%); East Cascades Slopes and Foothills Level III Ecoregion: Ponderosa Pine/Bitterbrush Woodland (5%), Pumice Plateau Basins (<1%), Pumice Plateau (<1%)

VEGETATION TYPES
Mountain Hemlock/Red Fir (19%), Subalpine Lodgepole (16%), Mountain Hemlock (15%), Lodgepole on Pumice (15%), Douglas-fir/Broadleaf Deciduous (9%), Mountain Hemlock/Red Fir/Lodgepole (5%), Mountain Hemlock/Parklands (4%), Silver Fir/Western Hemlock/Noble Fir (4%), Ponderosa on Pumice (4%), Open Water (3%), Ponderosa/Douglas-fir/True Fir (2%), Ponderosa/Lodgepole (1%), Cutover/Burned (1%), Subalpine Fir/Engelmann Spruce Parklands (<1%), True Fir/Lodgepole/Western Larch/Douglas-fir (<1%) Lodgepole/True Fir (<1%), Alpine Barren Fell Field (<1%), Open Lava (<1%)

DRAINAGE SUBBASINS
McKenzie, Middle Fork Willamette, Upper Deschutes

ELEVATION RANGE
1,332- 8,957 feet

UNITS
Bear Wallow, Charlton Butte, Cultus Mountain, Maiden Peak, Mount Bachelor, Skyliner, *Three Sisters Additions* (French Pete Addition, Gold Creek, Huckleberry Lake, Lava Camp, Mount David Douglas, Roaring River Headwaters, White Branch Creek), Tumalo Creek, *Waldo Lake Additions* (North Bank, Salmon Creek, South Fugi Mountain, South Lucky Lake, Three Prairies, Waldo Lake)

EXISTING WILDERNESSES INCORPORATED
Three Sisters, Waldo Lake

SIZE
196,214 acres (307 square miles, not including 325,908 acres of currently protected Wilderness)

COUNTIES
Deschutes, Klamath, Lane

FEDERAL ADMINISTRATIVE UNITS
Deschutes and Willamette National Forests

CONGRESSIONAL DISTRICTS
2nd, 4th

SANDY LONSDALE

Waldo Lake in the Waldo Lake Unit of the proposed Three Sisters Wilderness Additions.

PROPOSED WILDERNESS
Three Sisters Additions

LOCATION
20 miles east of Oakridge

LEVEL IV ECOREGION
Cascade Crest Montane Forest (100%)

VEGETATION TYPES
Open Water (59%), Mountain Hemlock/Red Fir (29%), Subalpine Lodgepole (11%), Mountain Hemlock (1%)

TERRAIN
Mostly perfectly flat.

DRAINAGE SUBBASIN
Middle Fork Willamette

ELEVATION RANGE
5,410-5,971 feet

SIZE
9,990 acres

COUNTY
Lane

FEDERAL ADMINISTRATIVE UNIT
Willamette National Forest (Middle Fork Ranger District)

USGS 7.5' QUAD MAPS
Irish Mountain, Waldo Lake, Waldo Mountain

FEATURED UNIT
Waldo Lake

The present Waldo "Lake" Wilderness does not actually include Waldo Lake. The public clamor for protection for the area was sufficient in 1984 for Congress to designate the lands around the lake as Wilderness, but the lake itself was left out of the designation because of perceived conflicts with Wilderness management.

Oregon's 13th largest lake, Waldo Lake sits in the Oregon Cascades at 5,414-feet elevation, is 6,298 acres in size and has a shoreline of 21.7 miles. The drainage area of the lake watershed is 19,840 acres. Maximum lake depth is 420 feet, with an average depth of 128 feet. Natural replacement of all the water in the lake takes 32 years.

The lake's water quality exceeds that of laboratory-grade distilled water. Waldo Lake as one of the most ultraoligotrophic (meaning "damn few nutrients") lakes in the world. Several factors make this so. No perennial streams enter the lake. The surrounding geology is so stable that little sediment reaches the lake. The unproductive soils that do exist there are thin and only support the shortest of growing seasons due to the long snow cover. A large percentage of precipitation received in the watershed falls directly on the lake. There is relatively little development in the watershed.

The lake's extraordinary cobalt blueness is due to the depth and clarity of the water. There are very few suspended particles and plankton in the lake. To observe the water's clarity, scientists drop a Secchi (black and white) disk into the lake. In Waldo Lake, disks are still visible at depths of 66 to 100 feet and have been seen at 140 feet. A Secchi disk in a typically eutrophic lake might not be visible much beyond two to six feet. (I once canoed at midnight under a full moon on Waldo Lake and finally figured out that the dark moving thing at the bottom of the lake was my shadow.)

Eutrophication happens. Natural eutrophication is one thing (all lakes eventually fill with sediment), but cultural (human-caused) eutrophication is quite another. Core samples of sediment have shown very low rates of eutrophication for several millennia. However, waterborne phytoplankton (plants) production is up, as are the number and kinds of tiny zooplankton (animals). The amount of nitrogen and phosphorus in the water limit a lake's primary biological productivity. Both are at naturally low levels in Waldo Lake. Nitrogen enters the lake from mats of cyanobacteria,

formerly called blue-green algae, which are fed by the deep penetrating sunlight. They in turn fix the nitrogen at the bottom of the lake. However, studies have shown that phosphorus (not nitrogen) is stimulating algal growth in Waldo Lake.

Fish stocking has been discontinued because fish are not native to Waldo Lake and they hasten eutrophication. Unfortunately, the increased nutrients, sediments and phosphorus (and silica) in the lake are coming from increased human use and are degrading water quality.

The Forest Service tried to take steps to reduce human impact and pollution in the lake, including limiting camping around the lake, restricting motorized boating to electric motors, closing or replacing leaking toilets, requiring the use of porta-potties and encouraging "leave no trace" camping techniques (including contemporaneous removal of any human-generated phosphorus-containing deposits). However, a rich timber baron who wanted unlimited access for his powerboat appealed the decision.

Waldo Lake is an Oregon Scenic Waterway and empties into North Fork of the Middle Fork of the Willamette River, a unit of the National Wild and Scenic Rivers System. Both designations were useful in preventing a hydroelectric project that would have reopened an abandoned underwater dam at Klovdahl Bay on the lake, but neither designation adequately protects Waldo Lake from other sorts of madness in the future. Amazingly, despite the fact that the lake is thought to be the purest large water body in the world, it has not been designated an Outstanding Resource Water by the Oregon Department of Environmental Quality — a designation which could help protect its water quality from degradation.

It is not too much to ask that the purest large body of water in the world be protected as Wilderness. Power boating should end immediately. Numerous comparably sized lakes and reservoirs (many nearby) are open to motorized use. Wind and human-powered boating on this unique lake are both adequate and preferred.

Relatively extreme measures are necessary to protect the extraordinary lake. Waldo Lake is not your average high mountain lake to lounge on deck with a fishing pole in one hand and a beer in the other. Experiencing Waldo Lake should not be casual and transient, but rather cosmic and transcendent.

GEORGE WUERTHNER

Maiden Peak in the Maiden Peak Unit of the proposed Three Sisters Wilderness Additions.

McKenzie and Deschutes Rivers.

The forests range from low-elevation old-growth Douglas-fir and western redcedar on the west, up through true-fir forests, and then to high elevation forests of lodgepole, mountain hemlock and Engelmann spruce. As the elevation drops on the east side of the crest, there are more true firs (though not always the same kind) and eventually ponderosa pine. Understory species include beargrass, huckleberry, vine maple, ocean spray, salal, Oregon grape, rhododendron, golden chinquapin, grouse huckleberry, manzanita, sedge, needlegrass, snowbrush, penstemon and lupine.

The area is not entirely forested. There are also wet meadows, dry prairies, bare basalt outcroppings, cascading streams, a few large lakes (one of which, Waldo, is very large), numerous small lakes and countless ponds in terrain that varies from deep, steep canyons, rocky ridges and volcanic peaks, to pumice flats.

The varying elevations in this unit are home to over 200 fish and wildlife species. Mammal species include both black-tailed and mule deer, Roosevelt and Rocky Mountain elk, coyote, cougar, marten, fisher, wolverine and quite possibly lynx. Bird species of special significance include the northern spotted owl, peregrine falcon and bald eagle.

Recognizing the important bull and coastal rainbow trout habitat here, the American Fisheries Society has identified several aquatic diversity areas in parts of the proposed Wilderness.

Recreational opportunities include short hikes, long hikes and even much longer hikes by way of the Pacific Crest National Scenic Trail. Cross-country skiing, snowshoeing, birding, fishing, hunting, photography, horseback riding and canoeing are also popular.

Approximately 119,000 acres of the proposed Wilderness is nominally protected from logging. The remainder is not. Off-road vehicles and roading are the other major threats to the area.

Proposed Upper Deschutes Wilderness
Cool Mountain Lakes and Old-Growth Mountain Hemlock

Most — but not quite all — of the Upper Deschutes River Basin has been roaded and logged. The proposed Upper Deschutes Wilderness includes all the remaining wildlands in the Upper Deschutes River Basin, the vast majority of which are located on and near the Cascade Crest between the Diamond Peak and Mount Thielsen Wilderness areas.

Most of the forest in the Upper Deschutes consists of vast amounts of high elevation mountain hemlock with a grouse huckleberry understory. Vegetation connoisseurs can further distinguish distinct plant communities by the other minor species in the understory. Other major tree species here include Engelmann spruce, lodgepole pine and whitebark pine. Some ponderosa pine and other mixed conifer species are found at the lowest elevations. Other understory species include manzanita, ceanothus, snowbrush and golden chinquapin. At mid-elevations, stringer meadows and sedge wetlands or blueberry/forb wetlands provide diversity to the vast lodgepole forests. However, almost none of the forest qualifies as "commercial" timber.

Within the proposed Wilderness, the Cascade Crest is a long high divide with only one major peak, Cowhorn Mountain, which used to be known as Little Cowhorn Mountain to distinguish it from a larger cowhorn-shaped peak nearby (one has to stretch one's imagination), now known as Mount Thielsen. The "cowhorn" on Cowhorn Mountain fell off naturally during the nineteenth century.

The Upper Deschutes River drainage is a center of rarity and endemism for both plants and animals. Over 110 species of wildlife are found in the proposed Wilderness.

Proposed Upper Deschutes Wilderness

LEVEL IV ECOREGIONS
Cascade Crest Montane Forest (50%), High Southern Cascades Montane Forest (11%), Cascade Subalpine/Alpine (10%); East Cascade Slopes and Foothills Level III Ecoregion: Pumice Plateau (21%), Pumice Plateau Basins (6%), Ponderosa Pine/Bitterbrush Woodland (2%)

VEGETATION TYPES
Lodgepole on Pumice (18%), Mountain Hemlock/Red Fir (17%), Subalpine Lodgepole (16%), Ponderosa/Douglas-fir/True Fir (15%), Ponderosa/Lodgepole (11%), Ponderosa on Pumice (8%), Mountain Hemlock/Red Fir/Lodgepole (5%), Douglas-fir/Ponderosa/True Fir (2%), Mountain Hemlock/Parklands (2%), Ponderosa (2%), Cutover/Burned (1%), Open Lava (1%), Open Water (1%)

DRAINAGE SUBBASINS
Little Deschutes, Upper Deschutes

ELEVATION RANGE
4,340-7664 feet

UNITS
Black Rock, Cowhorn Mountain, Crane Prairie, Davis Lake Lava Flow, Davis Mountain, Deer Creek, *Diamond Peak Additions* (Whitefish Creek), *Mount Thielsen Additions* (Little Deschutes River-Big Marsh Creek, Upper Deschutes River), Odell Creek, Siah Butte, Snow Creek, Walker Rim, West of Corral Springs

EXISTING WILDERNESSES INCORPORATED
portions of Diamond Peak, Mount Thielsen and Mount Washington

SIZE
59,150 acres (92 square miles, not including 55,412 acres of currently protected Wildernesses)

COUNTIES
Deschutes, Klamath

FEDERAL ADMINISTRATIVE UNITS
Deschutes and Winema National Forests

CONGRESSIONAL DISTRICT
2nd

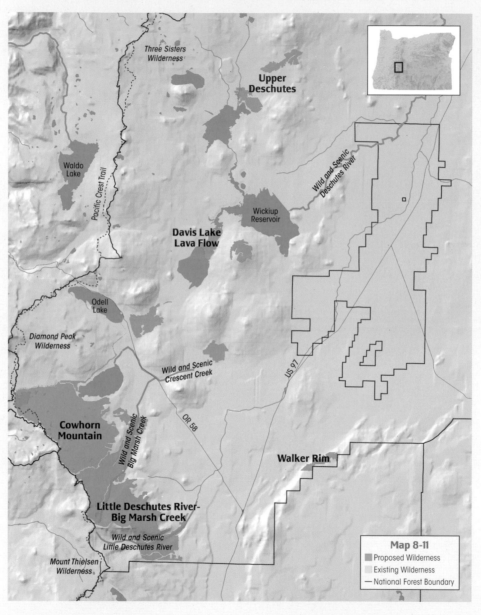

Some of the units in the proposed Wilderness are highlighted below.

The **Cowhorn Mountain** unit straddles the crest of the Cascades and includes lands in both the proposed North Umpqua and Upper Willamette Wilderness areas. The unit has a relatively high concentration of small mountain lakes, many with native redband trout.

Davis Lake Lava Flow is a relatively recent and quite stark lava flow.

The **Little Deschutes River-Big Marsh** unit is featured on page 149.

The **Upper Deschutes** includes several miles of the free-flowing Deschutes River above Crane Prairie Reservoir.

Walker Rim contains part of the most northern and western example of basin and range geology.

Map 8-11
Proposed Wilderness
Existing Wilderness
— National Forest Boundary

USDA FOREST SERVICE

Big Marsh in the proposed Upper Deschutes Wilderness. As the natural water regime is restored, conifers that encroached during the ranching era die off.

Big Marsh Creek begins as a trickle near the Cascade Crest. It is named for the big marsh it flows through on its way to its confluence with Crescent Creek. Both creeks are designated Wild and Scenic Rivers. Big Marsh, a unique high-elevation marsh, was long abused as a cattle ranch, but was eventually acquired by the Forest Service with the goal of restoring the marsh to natural conditions. Much of the marsh was diked and drained for the convenience of livestock. Now some of these dikes have been breached so Big Marsh can be a big marsh again.

Big Marsh Creek once had bull trout and can again, if stream temperatures downstream of the marsh become cold enough to accommodate them. This cooling will occur as the marsh regains its natural reservoir function and the majority of the creek's flow moves through the marsh subsurface — away from the sun. The overhanging banks of the creek and marsh are excellent habitat for native redband trout. The entire Big Marsh Creek is a thriving riparian community with a high diversity of sedges and willow species.

Several pairs of sandhill cranes nest in the marsh. It is unusual to find sandhill cranes this far west. It is unforgettable when one hears the cranes' call and see its dance while within sight of the snow-capped crest of the Cascade Range. The marsh is also popular with Roosevelt elk and northern harrier.

FEATURED UNIT

Little Deschutes River- Big Marsh Creek

The Little Deschutes River arises in a spectacular and unique narrow U-shaped glacial valley in the Mount Thielsen Wilderness, appropriately called the Little Deschutes Canyon. However, the river quickly leaves the protected Wilderness and meanders for several miles through lower elevation and picturesque wildlands. The Little Deschutes features a well-developed riparian system with healthy stringer meadows. The surrounding forest is primarily lodgepole pine, with some sugar pine. Roosevelt elk are numerous. A narrow corridor along the entire Little Deschutes River is a unit of the National Wild and Scenic Rivers System.

PROPOSED WILDERNESS
Upper Deschutes

LOCATION
14 miles southwest of Crescent

LEVEL IV ECOREGIONS
High Southern Cascades Montane Forest (46%), Cascade Crest Montane Forest (12%); East Cascades Slopes and Foothills Level III Ecoregion: Pumice Plateau (42%)

VEGETATION TYPES
Ponderosa/Douglas-Fir/True Fir (33%), Ponderosa/Lodgepole (27%), Subalpine Lodgepole (10%), Mountain Hemlock/Fir/Lodgepole (10%), Lodgepole on pumice (6%), Cutover/Burned (4%), Douglas-Fir/Ponderosa/True Fir (4%), Mountain Hemlock/Red Fir (4%), Ponderosa (2%)

TERRAIN
Rocky Cascade Crest and terraces.

DRAINAGE SUBBASINS
Little Deschutes, Upper Deschutes

ELEVATION RANGE
4,698-7,434 feet

SIZE
23,287 acres

COUNTY
Klamath

FEDERAL ADMINISTRATIVE UNITS
Deschutes and Winema National Forests (Crescent and Chemult Ranger Districts)

USGS 7.5' QUAD MAPS
Burn Butte, Cowhorn Mountain, Crescent Lake, Tolo Mountain

Major mammal species include cougar, black bear, marten, mink, beaver, weasel, snowshoe hare, fisher, wolverine and Roosevelt elk, as well as both black-tailed and mule deer. The area may also be suitable lynx habitat.

Major bird species found in the area include bald eagle, osprey, northern goshawk, Cooper's hawk, sharp-shinned hawk, blue grouse, ruffed grouse and numerous species of woodpeckers.

The Pacific Crest National Scenic Trail traverses the area, as do portions of the older and lower-elevation Oregon Skyline Trail. Numerous other trails offer easy access to this wilderness. Hiking, hunting, fishing, canoeing, horseback riding, wildlife watching and other recreational opportunities are plentiful. Summit Lake is on the edge of the area. Human- and wind-powered boating should replace motor boating on the waters in this area to preserve its wilderness character. (There is better motor-boating on Crescent and Odell Lakes, two larger lakes nearby.)

Some of the proposed Wilderness has been designated for protection and restoration as a late successional reserve under the Northwest Forest Plan.

Most, but not all, of the proposed Wilderness is within the Oregon Cascades Recreation Area (OCRA). In 1984, Congress established the OCRA at the insistence of then-Senator Mark Hatfield. Hatfield had long sought an alternative designation to Wilderness, which he often believed was too restrictive on agency managers, certain recreational activities and certain resource extraction. He wanted the political benefits of having "saved" an area by affording it some form of congressional designation, but did not wish the area to be managed as Wilderness. While the legislation creating the "recreation" area withdrew the area from further mining claims, according to the statute the OCRA is to be managed to:

(1) *provide a range of recreation opportunities from primitive to full service developed campgrounds;*
(2) *provide access for use by the public;*
(3) **to the extent practicable,** *maintain the natural and scenic character of the area; and*
(4) *provide for the use of motorized vehicles. (emphasis added)*[1]

The legislation further provides that logging, dams, grazing, power lines and other developments can be permitted in the OCRA by the managing agency. Unfortunately, while the creation of the Oregon Cascades Recreation Area changed the area's color on the map, it did little to change its actual management on the ground.

◄ Sawtooth Mountain is in the Cowhorn Mountain Unit, which is within the proposed Upper Deschutes, North Umpqua and Upper Willamette Wilderness.

Wildfire burned a mosaic in the Warner Creek Unit of the proposed Upper Willamette Wilderness.

Proposed Upper Willamette Wilderness
Lower Elevation and Very Scenic Old-Growth Forests

Located in the backyard of Eugene-Springfield (Oregon's second largest metropolitan area), the Upper Willamette Basin contains some extensive stands of pristine old-growth Douglas-fir forest.

The proposed Upper Willamette Wilderness includes roadless lands encompassing the upper tributaries of the Willamette River. Although early western cartographers drew the Willamette River coming from the Great Salt Lake (yes, Utah), it actually begins at Timpanogas Lake a few miles west from the Cascade Crest. Downstream of Oakridge, it is joined by the North Fork of the Middle Fork of the Willamette River (a.k.a. "North Fork of the Willamette") that flows from Waldo Lake (see the proposed *Three Sisters Wilderness Additions*, pages 144-147). Further downstream, a major tributary, Fall Creek, joins the Middle Fork before its confluence with the Coast Fork of the Willamette River just south of Eugene. There it forms the mainstem of the mighty Willamette River. Yet, because the Army Corps of Engineers has dammed the river in six places, the Upper Willamette River Basin is now a disconnected watershed of pools

and slack water.

Although logging in the Upper Willamette Basin has been extensive, the amount and proximity of the remaining roadless areas and old-growth forest make for a relatively intact terrestrial ecosystem.

The North Fork of the Middle Fork of the Willamette River is a federal Wild and Scenic River and an Oregon Scenic Waterway for 43.2 miles from Waldo Lake to the town of Westfir. The American Fisheries Society has designated the North Fork of the Middle Fork of the Willamette River watershed an aquatic diversity area because of its importance for native fish, including cutthroat trout. A relic bull trout population exists in the Upper Middle Fork Willamette watershed where active restoration efforts are underway.

Forests in the proposed Wilderness are predominantly old-growth Douglas-fir/western hemlock as is common throughout much of the Western Cascades. However, as one travels south through the area, incense cedar, sugar pine and even ponderosa pine — the last being more common in drier forests — join the Douglas-fir. Common understory species here include vine maple, rhododendron and Oregon grape.

Wildlife species include the northern spotted owl, peregrine falcon, osprey, bald eagle, pileated woodpecker and northern goshawk. Small game birds include ruffed and blue grouse, along with mountain quail. Black-tailed deer and Roosevelt elk are common, as are cougar, beaver, coyote and black bear.

Recreational opportunities include hunting, fishing, hiking, backpacking, horseback riding and enjoying naturally regenerated young forests (the rarest age class of forests).

Much of the proposed Wilderness has been designated for protection and restoration as a late successional reserve under the Pacific Northwest Forest Plan. Approximately 73,000 acres are generally off-limits to logging, but the remainder is not. Other threats to the area include road building and off-road vehicles. ◆

Notes

[1] 16 U.S.C. § 46000(c).

LEVEL IV ECOREGIONS
Western Cascades Lowlands and Valleys (45%), Western Cascades Montane Highlands (45%), Cascade Crest Montane Forest (8%), Cascade Subalpine/Alpine (2%)

VEGETATION TYPES
Douglas-fir/Broadleaf Deciduous (67%), Mountain Hemlock (11%), Silver Fir/Western Hemlock/Noble Fir (8%), Mountain Hemlock/Red Fir (8%), Cutover/Burned (2%), Mountain Hemlock/Parklands (2%), Cleared Grasslands (1%), Open Water (<1%), Subalpine Lodgepole (<1%)

DRAINAGE SUBBASINS
Coast Fork Willamette, Middle Fork Willamette

ELEVATION RANGE
997-7,664 feet

UNITS
Bear Bones Mountain, Bear Mountain, Bedrock Creek, Big Swamp, Brice Creek, Buffalo Peak, Bulldog Rock, Canton Creek, Cat Mountain, Cedar Creek, Chalk Creek, Chucksney Mountain, City Creek, Clover Patch Butte, Cowhorn Mountain, Deception Butte, *Diamond Peak Additions* (Salt Creek, Upper Hills Creek, West Additions), Dome Rock, Fairview Peak, Fall Creek, Groundhog Creek, Hardesty Mountain, Heckletooth Mountain, Huckleberry Mountain, Kitson Ridge, Larison Creek, Larison Rock, McClean Mountain, Monterica Creek, Moss Mountain, Mule Mountain, Noonday Ridge, North Fork- Middle Fork Willamette, Packard Creek, Puddin Rock, Tire Mountain, Too Much Bear Lake, Tumblebug Creek, Warner Creek, Windfall Creek, Wolf Mountain, Youngs Rock

EXISTING WILDERNESS INCORPORATED
portion of Diamond Peak

SIZE
136,468 acres (213 square miles, not including 19,183 acres of currently protected Wilderness)

COUNTIES
Douglas, Klamath, Lane

FEDERAL ADMINISTRATIVE UNITS
Umpqua and Willamette National Forests; BLM Eugene and Roseburg Districts

CONGRESSIONAL DISTRICT
4th

Proposed Upper Willamette Wilderness

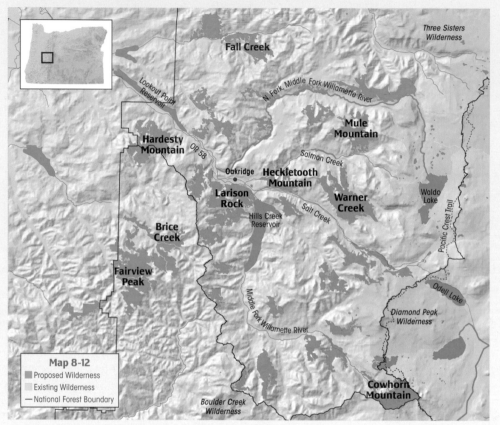

Map 8-12
- Proposed Wilderness
- Existing Wilderness
- National Forest Boundary

Some of the units in the proposed Wilderness are highlighted below.

Brice Creek contains a stream with numerous rocky bluffs and waterfalls, and is important to the city of Cottage Grove's water supply. Along a hiking trail in the unit, one can find old-growth Douglas-fir, western hemlock and even some sugar pine, with an understory of vine maple, rhododendron and golden chinquapin. The spring wildflower displays here are outstanding.

Cowhorn Mountain, along the Cascade Crest, is on a triple divide between the Willamette, Deschutes and Umpqua watersheds. Timpanogas Lake is on the edge of the unit and the Pacific Crest Trail passes through the unit.

The **Fairview Peak** units are in the Row (pronounced "row" as in a fight, not "row" as in a boat) River Watershed, a tributary of the Coast Fork Willamette River. On a clear day, one can see the Pacific Ocean

from atop Fairview Peak. A nearby trail served as an Indian trade route from the Upper Willamette Valley to eastern Oregon. The units contain several wet and "moist" meadows; the latter are a type uncommon in the region.

The **Fall Creek** units include some of the lowest elevation old-growth forest on the Willamette National Forest and are linked by the Fall Creek National Recreational Trail.

Hardesty Mountain is featured on page 153.

The **Heckletooth Mountain** and **Warner Creek** units include a trail linking Eugene to the Pacific Crest Trail and contain some very large, old (and now singed) Alaska yellow cedar, outstanding views, high waterfalls and unusual plant communities. The latter unit is the site of the infamous Warner Fire, an arson fire within spotted owl habitat "protected" from logging. (See Warner Creek Fire, page 42.) The area is now healing naturally and has yet to be logged, but is also yet to be adequately protected.

Larison Rock is not only important spotted owl habitat, but serves as the scenic pristine forest backdrop on the south side of the town of Oakridge.

Blair Meadow in the **Mule Mountain** unit has over 80 species of wildflowers.

FEATURED UNIT

Hardesty Mountain

I n an attempt to confuse the public and confound efforts to protect this roadless area, the Forest Service originally named this unit after the second highest point within its boundaries: Hardesty Mountain (4,273'). At the time, the area was better known for the highest peak in the area: Mount June (4,616'). (Folks from Cottage Grove more often refer to it as June Mountain.) One can see the Cascade peaks from Mount Hood to Mount Thielsen from atop either rocky summit, as well as large parts of the Coast Range and Willamette Valley.

Hardesty Mountain is a wild island in a sea of surrounding clearcuts. Only a half-hour drive from Eugene, the 20 miles of trails through ancient forests, wildflower meadows and high ridges in this unit are popular for low elevation backcountry recreation. Most recreation occurs on the Willamette National Forest (Middle Fork Willamette River watershed) side of the unit. The Umpqua National Forest (Coast Fork Willamette River watershed) side supplies drinking water to the city of Cottage Grove. The Forest Service prevents the public from swimming and camping in the municipal watershed to protect water quality, but has refused to end its own roading and logging in the watershed.

The unit is generally steep with a few gentle benches. The lowland old-growth forests below 4,000-feet elevation are comprised of Douglas-fir, incense cedar, Pacific madrone, western hemlock, western redcedar, bigleaf maple, Pacific yew, golden chinquapin and red alder, with occasional rock outcroppings poking through the forest canopy. Understory species include rhododendron, vine maple, salal, Oregon grape and an assortment of wild berries and ferns (sword, deer, licorice, bracken and maidenhair). Above 4,000-feet elevation, grand, noble and Pacific silver fir are common, with the occasional subalpine fir. Oregon white oak is found along the high divide.

The unit is winter range for black-tailed deer and Roosevelt elk and the cougars that depend upon them. Bald eagles and spotted owls nest on the slopes. Black bear are also present. Resident cutthroat trout are found in most creeks in the unit. Sixteen species of moths have been noted here. The Washington lily (*Lilium washingtonianum*) and calypso orchid or fairy slipper (*Calypso bulbosa*) may be seen amid the dense understory. Hardesty Mountain is also home to the rare Pacific giant salamander.

KURT JENSEN

A hiker in the Hardesty Mountain Unit of the proposed Upper Willamette Wilderness.

PROPOSED WILDERNESS
Upper Willamette

LOCATION
10 miles southeast of Lowell

LEVEL IV ECOREGIONS
Western Cascades Lowlands and Valleys (62%), Western Cascades Montane Highlands (38%)

VEGETATION TYPES
Douglas-Fir/Western Hemlock (100%), Douglas-Fir/Broadleaf Deciduous (<1%)

TERRAIN
Steeply forested slopes and rocky ridges.

DRAINAGE SUBBASINS
Coast Fork Willamette, Middle Fork Willamette

ELEVATION RANGE
1,181-4,266 feet

SIZE
8,077 acres

COUNTY
Lane

FEDERAL ADMINISTRATIVE UNITS
Umpqua and Willamette National Forests (Cottage Grove and Middle Fork Ranger Districts); BLM Eugene District (McKenzie Resource Area)

USGS 7.5' QUAD MAP
Mount June

Dry Open Forests
East Cascades Slopes and Foothills Ecoregion

From the snowline in the High Cascades to the Oregon portion of the Sagebrush Sea, the 6.8 million acres of the East Cascades Slopes and Foothills Ecoregion in Oregon are defined by their location within the rainshadow of the Cascade Mountains. The highest point in the ecoregion is Crane Mountain, which rises to 8,456 feet in the Warner Mountains. Beyond Oregon, this ecoregion extends north into Washington and south into California.

The East Cascades Slopes and Foothills Ecoregion is characterized by volcanism in the form of lava flows, cinder cones and volcanic buttes, with some basin and range topography mixed in. Much of the ecoregion's western portion is covered with a layer (from 2 inches to 50 feet thick) of pumice ash from the cataclysmic eruptions of the late Mount Mazama, the remnant of which is Crater Lake.

The dry continental climate in this area has greater temperature extremes than the Cascades Range. Rainfall varies from 20 to 120 inches annually. Summers are very dry.

Open lodgepole pine and ponderosa pine forests are common here. Both species are highly adapted to wildfire. Ponderosa pine tends to resist fire, while lodgepole seeds prolifically after being killed by a fire.

Wildlife in this ecoregion includes mule deer, Rocky Mountain elk, black bear, beaver, river otter, skunk, marten, raccoon, coyote, cougar, numerous species of songbirds, hawks, owls and increasing numbers of peregrine falcon. Although bald and golden eagles are uncommon in the ecoregion as a whole, the largest wintering population of bald eagles in the lower 48 states is found in the Klamath Basin. Fish species include rainbow and bull trout, as well as several Pacific salmon stocks.

A major distinguishing feature of the East Cascades Slopes and Foothills Ecoregion is the abundance of ponderosa pine. Ponderosa is found west of the Cascade Crest, but nowhere in such abundance as here.

Descending eastward out of the hemlock forest types of the High Cascades, there are a variety of forest types associated with ponderosa pine.

Ponderosa/Douglas-fir/True Fir is commonly found in the eastern portion of the northern Cascades in Oregon. Lower in elevation are the **Ponderosa/Douglas-fir/Western Larch/Lodgepole** and **True Fir/Lodgepole/Western Larch/Douglas-fir** forest types, where western larch is really just a minor component.

Following fire, **Subalpine Lodgepole** and **Lodgepole** grow in near monoculture

conditions. The same is true of **True Fir/Lodgepole** until true fir eventually overtops the lodgepole.

Mountain Hemlock is often found in pure stands at high elevations. **Mountain Hemlock/Red Fir/Lodgepole** is found south of the Three Sisters and on Newberry Crater.

Some **Subalpine Fir/Engelmann Spruce Parklands** are found at higher elevations in the Fremont National Forest. Such occurrences are the far western outliers of this Rocky Mountain forest type.

At lower elevations, especially east of US 97, one can find predominantly park-like stands of **Ponderosa**, as well as **Ponderosa on Pumice** that are characterized by low understory plant cover.

At even lower elevations, one will find **Ponderosa/Oregon White Oak** localized south of The Dalles and **Oregon White Oak/Ponderosa** in the lower Klamath Basin.

Further east and approaching Oregon's portion of the tree-free Sagebrush Sea, the ponderosa forests give way to a variety of juniper woodlands, including **Juniper/Ponderosa**, **Juniper/Mountain Big Sage**, **Juniper/Big Sage**, **Juniper/Bitterbrush**, **Juniper/Low Sage** and **Juniper/Grasslands**.

South of Bend, the ecoregion widens to the east and includes **Ponderosa/Lodgepole** where the latter species predominates in cold pockets and wetter sites.

Near the California border where the Cascade Crest is lowest, one finds **Douglas-fir/Ponderosa/True Fir**. This same association is common on the face of the Warner Mountains. Also on the slopes of the Warner Mountains are stands of **Douglas-fir/Ponderosa/Incense Cedar**, where incense cedar is as prevalent as the other tree species.

Yamsay Mountain and Gearhart Mountain are relatively cooler islands of **True Fir/Douglas-fir** surrounded by drier ponderosa pine forests.

Quaking Aspen grows widely but in small stands on the eastern slopes of the Cascades (and is almost nonexistent west of the Cascade Crest). However, it is delightfully the dominant species in a small band of forest southwest of Silver Lake. Larger stands of quaking aspen are also found on Steens Mountain and Hart Mountain in the Northern Great Basin Ecoregion.

Recent geologic activity has created **Open Lava,** where the vegetation is often

The open country of the East Cascades Slopes and Foothills Ecoregion often allows one to see where one is going. ▶

Ecoregions of Oregon's East Cascades Slopes and Foothills

The East Cascades Slopes and Foothills is in the rainshadow of the Cascade Range. It experiences greater temperature extremes and receives less precipitation than ecoregions to the west. Open forests of ponderosa pine and some lodgepole pine distinguish this region from the higher ecoregions to the west where hemlock and fir forests are common and the lower, drier ecoregions to the east where shrubs and grasslands are predominant. The vegetation is adapted to the prevailing dry, continental climate and frequent fire. Historically, creeping ground fires consumed accumulated fuel and devastating crown fires were less common in dry forests.

Further refining this ecoregion, scientists classify Oregon's East Cascades Slopes and Foothills Level III Ecoregion into nine additional Level IV ecoregions:

The **Grand Fir Mixed Forest** ecoregion is mostly outside the limit of maritime climatic influence. It is characterized by high, glaciated plateaus and mountains, frigid soils and a snow-dominated, continental climate. Grand fir, Douglas-fir, ponderosa pine and larch occur. This ecoregion is higher and moister than the Oak/Conifer Foothills Ecoregion, but the boundary between them is not sharp.

The **Oak/Conifer Foothills** ecoregion is more diverse than other parts of the East Cascade Slopes and Foothills. Marine weather enters this ecoregion via the Columbia River Gorge, moderating its otherwise continental climate. As a result, soil, climate and vegetation share characteristics of both eastern and western Oregon. Grasslands, oak woodlands and forests dominated by ponderosa pine and Douglas-fir occur. This ecoregion is lower and drier than the Grand Fir Mixed Forest ecoregion.

The undulating volcanic plateaus and canyons of the **Ponderosa Pine/Bitterbrush Woodland** have well-drained, frigid soils that are often derived from ash. Ponderosa pine is common; lodgepole pine is largely absent unlike in the Pumice Plateau. Understory vegetation varies with elevation; at lower elevations, antelope bitterbrush is important winter browse for deer.

The **Pumice Plateau** ecoregion is a high volcanic plateau. This ecoregion is characteristically covered by thick deposits of pumice and volcanic ash. Soils are very deep, highly permeable and droughty. Spring-fed creeks and marshes occur. Ponderosa pine forests are

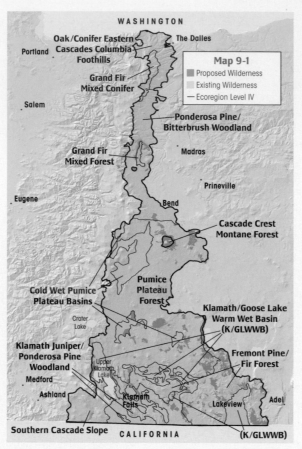

common on slopes; colder depressions and flats are dominated by lodgepole pine and higher elevations have white fir. Freezing temperatures are possible any time of year.

The **Pumice Plateau Basins** ecoregion includes Sycan Marsh, Klamath Marsh and La Pine Basin. All three areas function as catch-basins for cold air during the winter and have lower minimum temperatures than the Pumice Plateau ecoregion. Soils in this ecoregion have water tables at or near the surface for significant periods of the year in contrast to the Pumice Plateau Ecoregion. Marshes and forested wetlands provide important habitat for migratory waterfowl.

The **Klamath/Goose Lake Basins** ecoregion covers river floodplains, terraces and lake basins. A variety of wildrye, bluegrass and wheatgrass species once covered the basins, but most of the wet meadows and wetlands have been drained for agriculture. Several marshland wildlife refuges are key to preserving regional biodiversity, particularly at-risk bird and fish species.

The **Fremont Pine/Fir Forest** ecoregion contains mid-elevation mountains and high plateaus that rarely exceed timberline. Closed canopy forests contrast with the savanna of the Klamath Juniper Woodland. Ponderosa pine is widespread, but white fir, sugar pine and incense cedar also grow above 6,500 feet and on north slopes. Residual soils are common in contrast to the Pumice Plateau Ecoregion, where residual soils have been deeply buried by pumice and ash. This ecoregion has a high density of lakes and reservoirs.

The **Southern Cascades Slope** ecoregion is a transitional zone between the Cascades and the drier Eastern Cascade Slopes and Foothills. This ecoregion is higher and moister than the Fremont Pine/Fir Forest and it has a greater mix of forest types. Ponderosa pine woodland becomes mixed with white fir, incense cedar, Shasta red fir and Douglas-fir at higher elevations.

The **Klamath Juniper Woodland** ecoregion is composed of undulating hills, benches and escarpments covered with a mosaic of rangeland and woodland. Western juniper grows on shallow, rocky soils with an understory of low sagebrush, big sagebrush, bitterbrush and bunchgrasses. Other shrubland/grasslands include shrub species uncommon in eastern Oregon, such as woolly wyethia, Klamath plum and birchleaf mountain mahogany. The diverse shrublands provide important wildlife habitat.

Text gratefully adapted from Thor D. Thorson, Sandra A. Bryce, Duane A. Lammers, Alan J. Woods, James M. Omernik, Jimmy Kagan, David E. Pater, Jeffrey A. Comstock. 2003. Ecoregions of Oregon (color poster with map, descriptive text, summary tables and photographs). USDI-Geological Survey. Reston, VA (map scale 1:1,500,000).

Besides all those rims, the proposed Fremont Rims also has abundant Stringer Morrows.

limited to lichens and scattered trees that have found small pockets of soil that have collected in the lava flow. **Scrub**, characterized by black greasewood and shadscale, is found on the ever-fluctuating shallow inland lake basins that have high salinity and alkaline conditions. **Marsh/Wet Meadow** communities, characterized by bullrush, cattail and burr reed are common in the lower, tree-free wetlands.

The lowest elevations of the Eastern Cascades Slopes and Foothills are below timberline and are often comprised of **Big Sage/Shrub**, **Big Sagebrush**, **Bitterbrush Scrub** and **Low Sagebrush**.

At some time in their existence, most forest communities will be set back to early successional forest and are classified as **Cutover/Burned** forest. This can occur naturally — from lightning-caused wildfires, native insect or disease events, or blow-down by wind — or unnaturally, by way of logging, human-caused fire, human-caused blowdown (due to unnatural and vulnerable forest edges caused by clearcuts), non-native disease and insects or aggressive fire-fighting. Particularly troubling are "backburns," where firefighters intentionally burn the forest in front of an oncoming wildfire. In many cases, the backburns are far more intense and destructive than the natural burn would have been.

Fifty-four percent of Oregon's East Cascades Slopes and Foothills Ecoregion is federal public lands. Major federal holdings include all of the Fremont National Forest,

much of the Deschutes and Winema, and a portion of the Mount Hood National Forests. The western halves of the BLM Lakeview and Prineville Districts are also located in the ecoregion.

Currently, only one entire Wilderness area (Gearhart Mountain) and portions of eight other Wilderness areas (Badger Creek, Mount Jefferson, Mount Washington, Three Sisters, Diamond Peak, Mount Thielsen, Sky Lakes and Mountain Lakes) are found in Oregon's East Cascades Slopes and Foothills, comprising but 0.7 percent of the ecoregion.

Conservationists are proposing four new multi-unit Wilderness areas for the region: Fremont Rims, Klamath Basin, Metolius and Newberry Volcano. If designated, Wilderness protection would increase to a total of 8.8 percent of the ecoregion.

Proposed Fremont Rims Wilderness
Old-Growth Ponderosa Pine, Shimmering Quaking Aspen and Rimrock

The Fremont National Forest is the least visited and thus the least known national forest in Oregon. Even local use is limited given the limited number of locals.

The variety of habitats — which include wildflower meadows, sagebrush flats, wet meadows, dense forests, open forests, mahogany covered ridges, glacially carved calderas, park-like stands of ponderosa pine, aspen groves, riparian zones and springs — conspire to provide a highly scenic, distinctive and varied landscape. The rims that define the Fremont are either volcanic in origin or caused by tectonic uplift. Average annual precipitation varies from 16 to 40 inches, usually with a long summer drought. Temperatures range from -30 to 100° F.

The proposed Wilderness encompasses all the remaining wildlands on the Fremont National Forest within the Great Basin. Vegetation ranges from sagebrush on the lower gentle flats, to whitebark pine forests on the North Warner Mountains, Gearhart Mountain and Dead Horse Rim. In between, one can find lush and not so lush conifer forests, meadows and scablands. The most prominent, if no longer dominant, species is ponderosa pine. White fir dominate on higher elevation, north-facing slopes. Western white pine, sugar pine, incense cedar, subalpine fir, quaking aspen, mountain mahogany, western juniper and lodgepole pine are the area's other major tree species.

Proposed Fremont Rims Wilderness

LEVEL IV ECOREGIONS
Fremont Pine/Fir Forest (64%), Pumice Plateau (32%), Klamath/Goose Lake Basins (<1%); Northern Basin and Range Level III Ecoregion: High Lava Plains (2%), Semiarid Uplands (<1%), High Desert Wetlands (<1%)

VEGETATION TYPES
Ponderosa (41%), Ponderosa on Pumice (24%), Lodgepole on Pumice (9%), Big Sagebrush (5%), Cutover/Burned (5%), True Fir/Douglas-fir (3%), Juniper/Low Sage (3%), Juniper/Grasslands (2%), Juniper/Mountain Big Sage (2%), Juniper/Big Sage (1%), Lodgepole (<1%), Low Sagebrush (1%), Bitterbrush Scrub (1%), Marsh/Wet Meadow (<1%), Quaking Aspen (1%), Rimrock Shrublands (<1%), Scrub (<1%), Subalpine Fir/Engelmann Spruce Parklands (<1%), Big Sage/Scrub (<1%), Douglas-fir/Ponderosa/Incense Cedar (<1%), Douglas-fir/Ponderosa/True Fir (<1%)

DRAINAGE SUBBASINS
Goose Lake, Lake Abert (Closed), Summer Lake (Closed), Warner Lakes

ELEVATION RANGE
4,196-8,456 feet

UNITS
Abert Rim, Bald Mountain, Barry Point, Basin Springs, Bear Creek, Benny Creek, Blue Mountain, Boulder Springs, Brattain Butte, Buck Mountain, Chewaucan River, Club Cliff, Coleman Rim, Cox Creek, Crane Mountain, Crooked Creek, Dead Horse Rim, Deep Creek, Devils Ball Diamond, Doe Mountain, Drake Peak, East Duncan Creek, Elder Creek, Fawn Creek, Fitzwater Point, *Gearhart Mountain Additions* (Brownsworth Creek-Camp Creek, Cougar Creek-Dairy Creek, Nottin Creek), Government Harvey Pass, Grasshopper Flat, Grizzly Peak, Guyer Creek, Hadley Butte, Hager Mountain, Hanan Trail, Hay Creek, Horseshoe Creek, Horseshoe Meadow, Jones Canyon, Juniper Creek, Little Honey Creek, Little Muddy Creek, Lower Sycan Butte, Mill Creek, Moss-Pass Butte, Mount Bidwell, Muddy Creek, Myers Canyon, Newell Creek, North Fork Deep Creek, Parker Hills, Pine Creek, Ring Corral Creek, Silver Creek, Skull Creek, Smoke Creek, South Fork Sycan River, Thomas Creek, Upper Lapham Creek, Wart Peak, Watson Peak, White Rock Creek, Winter Ridge

EXISTING WILDERNESS INCORPORATED
portion of Gearhart Mountain

SIZE
212,476 acres (332 square miles, not including 5,793 acres of currently protected Wilderness)

COUNTIES
Klamath, Lake

FEDERAL ADMINISTRATIVE UNITS
Fremont National Forest; BLM Lakeview District

CONGRESSIONAL DISTRICT
2nd

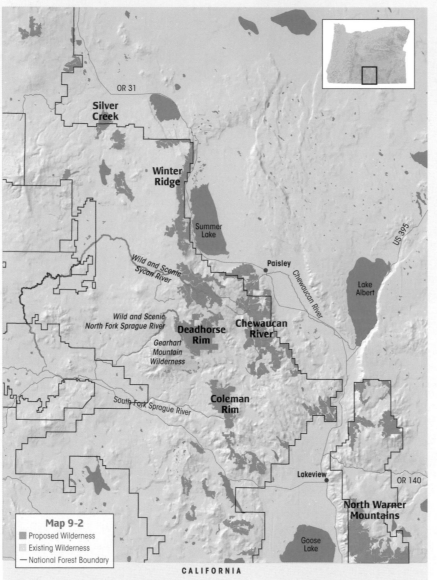

Map 9-2
- Proposed Wilderness
- Existing Wilderness
- National Forest Boundary

Some of the units in the proposed Wilderness are highlighted below.

The **Chewaucan River** units include portions of the river and vast highlands covered with mountain-mahogany, western juniper and sagebrush. Stands of quaking aspen and pockets of sugar pine are also present. The Chewaucan River is an important source of aquatic diversity in the area.

Coleman Rim contains the largest stand of ponderosa pine and mixed conifer old-growth forest remaining on the Fremont. Park-like stands of yellow-bellied ponderosa pine are interspersed with wet and dry meadows that are blanketed with wildflowers in the spring.

Dead Horse Rim is featured on page 159.

The **North Warner Mountains** units extend seamlessly into the South Warner Mountains in California and include the last refuge for cougar on the Fremont National Forest. California bighorn sheep, more common in the Sagebrush Sea to the east, are found here. The scarp of Crane Mountain (8,456-feet) is the highest point on the Fremont National Forest and contains some of the forest's largest pure stands of quaking aspen. At the northern end of these units is a center of concentration of rare and endemic plant species. Several streams in the North Warners contain native redband trout.

Over half of the **Silver Creek** unit is blanketed in pure stands of quaking aspen.

The **Winter Ridge** units include a massive fault scarp that towers over Summer Lake. The long views east out into the Sagebrush Sea (as far as Steens Mountain) are spectacular, as are the short views to nearby old-growth ponderosa pine and quaking aspen.

WENDELL WOOD

Dead Horse Rim in the Dead Horse Unit of the proposed Fremont Rims Wilderness.

PROPOSED WILDERNESS
Fremont Rims

LOCATION
20 miles northeast of Bly

LEVEL IV ECOREGION
Pumice Plateau (100%)

VEGETATION TYPES
Ponderosa on Pumice (64%), Lodgepole on Pumice (31%), Cutover/Burned (6%)

TERRAIN
A glaciated volcanic rim.

DRAINAGE SUBBASINS
Lake Abert, Sprague

ELEVATION RANGE
5,975-8,203 feet

SIZE
16,685 acres

COUNTY
Lake

FEDERAL ADMINISTRATIVE UNIT
Fremont National Forest (Bly and Paisley Ranger Districts)

USGS 7.5' QUAD MAPS
Coleman Point, Cougar Point

FEATURED UNIT
Dead Horse Rim

Standing on the summit of Dead Horse Rim on a clear spring day, one can peer outward into the Sagebrush Sea and see as far as the sky islands of Steens Mountain and Hart Mountain. Gazing downward, one overlooks extensive stands of virgin forest.

This is a landscape carved by uplift, eruption and glaciation. Dead Horse Rim is part of the eruptive volcanic center of Gearhart Mountain. West of the rim is a gentle downward slope, while to the east the drop is precipitous.

Nine-tenths of the unit is blanketed with forests. Whitebark pine grows at the highest elevations. At slightly lower elevations are vast stands of lodgepole pine. At the next level down are extensive stands of mixed-conifer old-growth forests. The very lowest elevations host extensive stands of almost pure ponderosa pine old-growth forests. These intact stands contain the rare green-tinged paintbrush (*Castilleja chlorotica*) and blue-leaved penstemon (*Penstemon glaucinus*).

Several perennial streams originate in the unit. Dead Cow Creek drains into the North Fork of the Sprague River, part of the National Wild and Scenic Rivers System. Augur, Dead Horse and Tamarack Creeks empty into the Chewaucan River.

The various conifer types contrast with stands of quaking aspen, rock outcroppings and moist meadows to create a memorable landscape. Walking up the lower stretch of Augur Creek is a stroll through a cathedral-like forest. Thus far conservationists have successfully halted Forest Service plans to road and log Augur Creek. The unit contains approximately 20 miles of maintained hiking trails.

Major shrub species here include bitterbrush, various sagebrush species and currant. Wildflower species include arrowhead balsamroot, aster, bleeding heart, fireweed, clarkia, penstemon, phacelia, spreading phlox, twinflower, lupine and western yarrow.

The Chewaucan is the only "river" (really a very small stream) that originates in the Fremont Rims country. Like the rest of creeks that drain this country, the Chewaucan flows into the Great Basin, its waters never reaching any ocean.

Over 300 species of fish and wildlife have been identified here. Major game species include Rocky Mountain elk, mule deer and pronghorn. Large predators include black bear, mountain lion and bobcat. Smaller animals of note include shrews, bats, pika, white-tailed and black-tailed jackrabbits, marmot, badger, mink, long-tailed weasel, marten, fisher and porcupine. Squirrel species include the California, Belding ground and golden-mantled.

Over 220 bird species have been identified on the Fremont Forest. Of these, the bald eagle and the peregrine falcon are most threatened. Other raptors include the northern goshawk, osprey, American kestrel, prairie falcon, golden eagle, merlin ("pigeon hawk") and several hawk species, including sharp-shinned, Cooper's, Swainson's, red-tailed, rough-legged and ferruginous. Waterfowl species include ducks and Canada geese. Numerous songbirds are found here, along with blue grouse (which are common) and the ruffed and sage grouse (less common). Owl species include barn, western screech, northern pygmy, long-eared, northern saw-whet, flammulated, great horned, great gray and short-eared. All of the region's woodpecker species are found in the proposed Wilderness: the northern flicker, Lewis', downy, white-headed, hairy, black-backed, three-toed and pileated woodpeckers, as well as the red-breasted, Williamson's and red-naped sapsuckers.

The American Fisheries Society has identified several aquatic diversity areas within the proposed Wilderness. Redband trout, although widely distributed, are in decline here due to roading, logging and grazing. The Pit-Klamath brook lamprey is endemic to the region, mostly found in the upper Klamath Basin, but also found in Crooked Creek and other drainages. Many of the streams within the proposed Wilderness are part of this species' historic and current range.

Rare plant species here include the pumice grape fern (*Botrychium pumicola*), which is generally found at much higher elevations in the Cascade Range. This fern grows in frost pockets in lodgepole pine forests in several locations on the Fremont.

The diversity of habitats in the proposed Wilderness accounts for the numerous butterfly species. Butterflies are excellent indicators of ecosystem health. Approximately 120 species and subspecies of butterflies are found in Klamath and Lake counties. Many units of the proposed Wilderness also have unusual concentrations of rare species and endemic animals. The Oregon Biodiversity Project has identified the Gearhart Mountain Conservation Opportunity Area as important habitat, which

SANDY LONSDALE

A little wetland in the Coleman Rim Unit of the proposed Fremont Rims Wilderness. ▶

encompasses both the Coleman Rim and Dead Horse Rim units.

Fishing (there are few lakes, but many streams) and hunting are the major recreational activities in this area, although opportunities for backpacking, horseback riding, hiking, cross-country skiing and dancing through park-like stands of ponderosa pine are plentiful.

The best way to see the proposed Wilderness is to escape two weeks and hike the 175-mile Fremont National Recreation Trail. Beginning in the Yamsay Mountain unit of the proposed Klamath Basin Wilderness, the trail heads eastward to Winter Ridge. It continues southward along Winter Ridge, then turns southeasterly to the Chewaucan River. The trail continues southeasterly to Crooked Creek along US 395, then heads east up Crooked Creek, where it forks in the North Warner Mountains. One spur heads northward to Vee Lake by Drake Peak and McDowell Peak and the other spur meanders southward along the North Warners over Crane Mountain, where it ends just across the California border.

Major threats to the proposed Wilderness include logging, roading, mining, livestock grazing and off-road vehicles.

Proposed Klamath Basin Wilderness
Upland Portion of the "Everglades of the West"

The Klamath River Basin stretches from Crater Lake National Park on the Cascade Crest in Oregon to Redwoods National Park on the Pacific Ocean in California. The upper river basin lies mostly in Oregon above Iron Gate Dam on the Klamath River and is known as the Klamath Basin. Much of the Klamath Basin was blanketed with pumice and ash by the explosion of Mount Mazama (now Crater Lake) 7,700 years ago.

Although 75 percent of the Klamath Basin's wetlands have been destroyed by agriculture and water diversions, the area remains immensely important to Pacific Northwest fish and wildlife. The Klamath Basin is both a stopover and breeding habitat for nearly 80 percent of ducks and geese and numerous other species of water birds migrating along the Pacific Flyway. It hosts the largest wintering bald eagle and wild redband trout populations in the lower forty-eight states. It has become known as the "Everglades of the West."

The Klamath was once the third largest salmon-producing river on the West Coast and remains a vital resource for riverine and coastal salmon-dependent

The Sycan River in the proposed Klamath Basin Wilderness. ▶

SANDY LONSDALE

Proposed Klamath Basin Wilderness

LEVEL IV ECOREGIONS
Pumice Plateau (41%), Klamath Juniper Woodland (24%), Fremont Pine/Fir Forest (17%), Klamath/Goose Lake Basins (9%), Pumice Plateau Basins (7%), South Cascade Slope (1%)

VEGETATION TYPES
Ponderosa (26%), Ponderosa on Pumice (15%), True Fir/Douglas-fir (15%), Juniper/Low Sage (13%), Juniper/Grasslands (9%), Marsh/Wet Meadow (8%), Juniper/Mountain Big Sage (4%), Lodgepole on Pumice (3%), Low Sagebrush (2%), Cutover/Burned (2%), Big Sagebrush (1%), Douglas-fir/Ponderosa/True Fir (1%), Juniper/Big Sage (1%), Open Water (<1%), Oregon White Oak/Ponderosa (<1%), Siskiyou Mixed Evergreen (<1%)

DRAINAGE SUBBASINS
Lost, Sprague, Summer Lake (Closed), Upper Klamath, Upper Klamath Lake, Williamson

ELEVATION RANGE
2,799-8,196 feet

UNITS
Abraham Flat, Adobe Flat, Arkansas Flat, Bad Lands, Barnes Valley Creek (mid), Barnes Valley Creek (upper), Barry Point, Box Springs, Brown Creek, Bryant Mountains, Chock toot Creek, Crystal Spring-Malone Springs, Devil Lake, Devils Garden, Dicks Spring, Fishhole Lakes, Fivemile Creek, Fourmile Creek, *Gearhart Mountain Additions* (Nottin Creek), Gerber Rim, Goodlow Rim, Haystack Draw, Horse Camp Rim, J Spring, Klamath River, Long Branch Creek, Lower Sycan River, Merritt Creek, Miller Creek, Modoc Mountain, Modoc Point, Norcross Springs, North Chiloquin Ridge, Paddock Butte, Paradise Creek, Pole Creek, Preacher Flat, RNA Spring, Rock Creek, Rogger Peak, Round Butte, Round Valley, Saddle Mountain, Shake Creek, Silver Dollar Flat, South Chiloquin Ridge, South Sycan Flat, Sprague River, Stump Pond, Swan Lake Rim, Sycan Flat, Sycan River, Three Creeks, Upper Dams Canyon, Upper Wildhorse Creek, Whiskey Creek, Wildhorse Creek, Wocus Bays, Ya Whee Plateau Rim, Yamsay Mountain, Yoss Creek Meadow, Yoss Ridge

EXISTING WILDERNESS INCORPORATED
portion of Gearhart Mountain

SIZE
199,533 acres (312 square miles, not including 17,016 acres of currently protected Wilderness)

COUNTIES
Klamath, Lake

FEDERAL ADMINISTRATIVE UNITS
Winema and Fremont National Forests; BLM Lakeview District; Upper Klamath Lake National Wildlife Refuge (US Fish and Wildlife Service)

CONGRESSIONAL DISTRICT
2nd

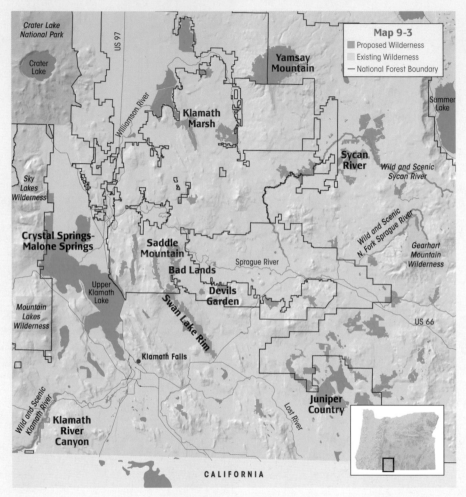

Some of the units in the proposed Wilderness are highlighted below.

The **Bad Lands** is an elevated rock formation surrounded by forest.

Crystal Spring-Malone Springs is a tule marsh where wocus and bullrush also grow. If the lake is not drained for irrigation, standing water covers the marsh for most of the growing season. This unit should be included in the adjacent Upper Klamath Lake National Wildlife Refuge. A canoe trail is the only access to the unit.

The **Devils Garden** is mostly barren rock with scattered brushy areas surrounding an elevated maar (a flat, generally circular, volcanic crater often filled with water). The maar formed from a volcanic eruptive

center on the floor of an ancient lake. It later filled in with sediments and then was re-exposed by erosion and uplift.

The various **Juniper Country** units near Gerber Reservoir contain a variety of western juniper communities variously associated with ponderosa pine, sagebrush and grasslands.

The **Klamath Marsh** units include both primary wetland habitats and adjacent forest edges of mature and old growth lodgepole and ponderosa pine.

Most of the steep canyons and cliffs of the **Klamath River Canyon** units are already protected within Wild and Scenic River and Oregon Scenic Waterway designations. However, maintenance of the wilderness experience of the canyon depends on the large adjacent roadless areas beyond the narrow river corridor also being protected as Wilderness. The units include some of the finest trout fishing in Oregon and are home to ringtail cats, river otter, ruffed grouse and many other species. Rafters love the Class IV (one thinks one may die) and Class V (one may well die) rapids.

Saddle Mountain, east of Upper Klamath Lake, is home to the most eastern occurrence of northern spotted owls.

Swan Lake Rim would make a tremendous national wildlife refuge if the adjacent Swan Lake was also acquired for public ownership.

The **Sycan River** units are critical habitat for the endangered bull trout. The nearby Sycan Marsh Preserve, owned by The Nature Conservancy, is a haven for bald eagles, waterfowl and sandhill cranes. It could be heaven for wildlife if water wasn't diverted for agricultural use and if livestock didn't graze the "preserve."

Yamsay Mountain is featured on page 163.

GEORGE WUERTHNER

Looking down the Buck Creek drainage in the Yamsay Mountain Unit of the proposed Klamath Basin Wilderness.

The soils are quite porous and most of the 25 to 30 inches of annual precipitation, which falls mainly in autumn and winter as snow, drains directly into the ground. The mountain's creeks — which often rise as springs — dissect the slopes and meander through the surrounding rolling hills and tablelands that are dotted by small buttes.

Jackson Creek begins in the caldera itself, escaping northward through the blown-out side and then westward to the Williamson River. Hoyt, Dry, Sheep, Aspen and Deep Creeks also contribute their waters to the Williamson. Long Creek flows south, then east toward the Sycan Marsh and Sycan Wild and Scenic River. The North and West Forks of Silver Creek, along with Guyer, Buck and Bridge Creeks, flow eastward into the Great Basin.

The larger creeks support riparian ecosystems. Long Creek is home to the endangered bull trout. Redband trout are found in Buck Creek. Dotting the streams are open wet meadows, where Rocky Mountain elk can often be seen.

The snow is usually gone from Yamsay's summit by late July. On top, one can see Cascade volcanoes (Mount Shasta to the Three Sisters) to the west and the Fort Rock Basin to the east. However, the view is marred to the south by severely logged private lands.

Yamsay Mountain is the northwestern terminus of the Fremont National Recreation Trail. A fire lookout once sat on the summit. A steep zigzagging former road to the summit has been closed and is being reclaimed by nature. Similarly, a jeep trail through the heart of the area has been converted to a hiking trail.

FEATURED UNIT

Yamsay Mountain

Ecologists classify Yamsay Mountain as a large block of relatively wet "True Fir/Douglas-fir forest," although presently there is not much, if any, Douglas-fir in the mix. The mountain rises above a drier landscape dominated by ponderosa pine. Yamsay's higher slopes present the easternmost example of the mountain hemlock/Shasta red fir ecotype, more commonly found along the Cascade Crest. Lodgepole pine is commonly found throughout and manzanita is common in the understory. Under the mixed conifers, one can also find snowbrush and grouse huckleberry.

A shield volcano, Yamsay Mountain was covered with 15 to 20 inches of ash from the explosions of the late Mount Mazama thirty miles due west. The north side of Yamsay's caldera then blew out and later glaciation created a gorgeous little valley in the remnant cone.

PROPOSED WILDERNESS
Klamath Basin

LOCATION
20 miles southwest of Silver Lake

LEVEL IV ECOREGION
Pumice Plateau (100%)

FOREST TYPES
True Fir/Douglas-fir (96%), Ponderosa on Pumice (4%), Cutover/Burned (<1%)

TERRAIN
Mountainous.

DRAINAGE SUBBASINS
Sprague, Summer Lake Closed, Williamson

ELEVATION RANGE
5,394-8,196 feet

SIZE
25,908 acres

COUNTIES
Klamath, Lake

FEDERAL ADMINISTRATIVE UNITS
Winema and Fremont National Forests (Chemult and Silver Lake Ranger Districts)

USGS 7.5' QUAD MAPS
Gordon Lake, Rodman Rock, Yamsay Mountain

commercial, recreational and tribal fisheries and associated communities. The growing ecological crisis in the Klamath Basin, combined with the chronic economic crisis in basin agriculture, presents both an unprecedented need and a new opportunity to conserve, protect and restore this incomparable ecosystem.

Most of the controversy in the Klamath Basin has centered on its wetlands — which are mostly privately owned or within national wildlife refuges. However, the proposed Klamath Basin Wilderness is comprised primarily (although not exclusively) of uplands — publicly owned and still roadless and undeveloped. Many species of fish and wildlife need both uplands and wetlands. Intact functioning uplands are necessary for intact functioning wetlands.

The Wood and Williamson Rivers, as well as many tributary streams that arise in the proposed South Cascades Wilderness (see pages 141-144), flow into Upper Klamath Lake. Before the damming of the Klamath River, spring, summer and fall chinook salmon and steelhead found their way through Upper Klamath Lake to spawn in streams above the lake. Salmon will not return to the Klamath Basin until six mainstem Klamath River hydroelectric dams are either modified to provide fish passage or are removed.

The American Fisheries Society has identified several "aquatic diversity areas" that include units of the proposed Wilderness, as does the Oregon Biodiversity Project's Upper Klamath Basin Wetlands Conservation Opportunity Area. The entire Klamath Basin is a concentration or "hotspot" of rare and endemic plants and animals, including many that are of special conservation concern.

The basin's roadless lands are refuges of cold, clean water, which provide spawning and rearing habitat for bull trout and redband trout — both native to the basin and widely distributed. Four (maybe five) lamprey species are found in the Klamath Basin, including three endemic ones: Klamath River, Pit-Klamath Brook and Miller Lake lamprey. Several species of mullet (pejoratively called "suckers" by some) are also found in the basin, including the C'wam and Qapdo (a.k.a. Lost River and shortnose "suckers").

Other species found in the Klamath River Basin and whose numbers are declining include the bald eagle, golden eagle, prairie falcon, peregrine falcon, western pond turtle and Townsend's big-eared bat.

The combination of elevation, aspect, uplands and wetlands creates a diversity of habitats and an abundance of wildlife in the proposed Klamath Basin Wilderness. After leaving the upper basin, the Klamath River cuts through the Cascade Range, something only one other river in Oregon does.

Recreational opportunities here include hunting, hiking, canoeing, fishing, backpacking, horseback riding, kayaking, rafting and lamprey watching.

Major threats to the proposed Klamath Basin Wilderness include roading, logging, mining, livestock grazing, water diversions for agriculture and off-road vehicles.

Proposed Metolius Wilderness

Green and Brown Bull Trout with Red Spots, Yellow-Bellied Ponderosas, Golden Larch and Aquamarine Waters

Gushing forth from springs at the base of Black Butte, the Metolius River is one of the largest spring-fed streams in the United States. A relatively constant 50,000 gallons per minute of pristine water flows out of the ground into a fully formed river at the Head of the Metolius. The view downstream toward Mount Jefferson is one of the most photographed scenes in Oregon. The Metolius River is both a State Scenic Waterway and a federal Wild and Scenic River.

Both the quantity and quality of the river's water depend upon protecting the remaining wildlands in the Metolius Basin. However, the Metolius Basin is special for more than just the river. From the Cascade Crest to Green Ridge, the Metolius Basin is noted for its unique ponderosa pine forests, extraordinary fish and wildlife populations, cool, clean streams and springs, outstanding views, mountain air and mountain views.

Among the Metolius's important tributary streams that begin high in the Cascade Range are Jefferson, Abbot, Brush, Roaring, Canyon, Jack, Spring, Lake, Candle and Cache Creeks. Alder, vine maple, serviceberry, snowberry and thimbleberry line their banks.

The Metolius Basin is known for its big yellow-bellied old-growth ponderosa pine with an open understory largely of bitterbrush and rabbitbrush. Some gnarled old western junipers can be found here as well, along with lodgepole pine, sugar pine, golden chinquapin, incense cedar, western larch, mountain hemlock, Douglas-fir and white fir. The mixed understory may also include snowbrush, pine-grass, sedge, bracken fern, snowberry and/or wildflowers.

The American Fisheries Society has identified several aquatic diversity areas within the proposed Wilderness. Similarly, the Oregon Biodiversity Project has identified the Metolius River Conservation Opportunity Area in recognition of the large population of bull trout and because it is a "hotspot" for many unique species of plants and animals. The federal government has also recognized the area as a center of concentration of species rarity and endemism for both plants and animals.

The endangered bull trout, declining throughout so much of its range, is doing well in the Metolius Basin, an argument for conserving and restoring cold, clean water within bull trout range. The species has been eliminated from much of its natural range

Proposed Metolius Wilderness

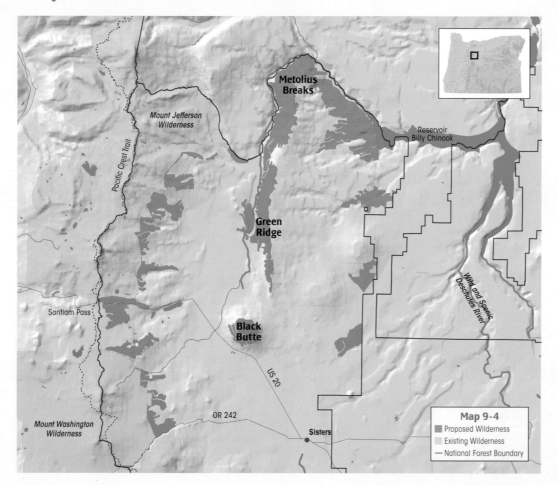

Map 9-4
■ Proposed Wilderness
□ Existing Wilderness
— National Forest Boundary

LEVEL IV ECOREGIONS
Ponderosa Pine/Bitterbrush Woodland (58%), Grand Fir Mixed Forest (11%); Cascades Level III Ecoregion: Cascade Crest Montane Forest (29%), Cascade Subalpine/Alpine (<3%)

VEGETATION TYPES
Ponderosa on Pumice (47%), Ponderosa/Douglas-fir/Western Larch/Lodgepole (15%), Ponderosa/Douglas-fir/True Fir (11%), Mountain Hemlock (10%), Ponderosa (4%), True Fir/Lodgepole/Western Larch/Douglas-fir (4%), True Fir/Douglas-fir (2%), Juniper/Mountain Big Sage (2%), Lodgepole on Pumice (2%), Open Lava (1%), Juniper/Bitterbrush (1%), Ponderosa/Lodgepole (1%), Alpine Barren Fell Field (<1%), Cutover/Burned (<1%), Subalpine Lodgepole (<1%)

DRAINAGE SUBBASIN
Upper Deschutes

ELEVATION RANGE
1,998-6,436 feet

UNITS
Black Butte, Cache Mountain, Circle Lake, Fly Creek, Green Ridge, Lower Canyon Creek, Metolius Breaks, *Mount Jefferson Additions* (Bear Valley, Brush Creek, Parker Creek Lava Flow, Round Lake), *Mount Washington Additions* (Dugout Lake), Squaw Back Ridge, Stevens Canyon

EXISTING WILDERNESSES INCORPORATED
portions of Mount Jefferson and Mount Washington

SIZE
39,411 acres (62 square miles, not including 47,488 acres of currently protected Wilderness).

COUNTIES
Deschutes, Jefferson

FEDERAL ADMINISTRATIVE UNIT
Deschutes National Forest

CONGRESSIONAL DISTRICT
2nd

Some of the units in the proposed Wilderness units are highlighted below.

Black Butte contains a major volcanic peak set off from the Cascade Crest. The distinctive form and color of Black Butte make it noticeable from long distances.

Green Ridge includes the Metolius Research Natural Area. An aggressive program of fire reintroduction is restoring the area's classic park-like stands of open ponderosa pine. Fire exclusion over the decades has resulted in thickets of young trees — both of ponderosa pine and other species — and dense brush growing on the forest floor. Much of the ponderosa pine forests in the developed portions of the Metolius Basin have been high-graded for timber. The result is that one very

rarely sees a snag — a standing dead tree — in the area. Snags are vital wildlife habitat for numerous bird species (including white-headed and pileated woodpeckers) and other wildlife. The research natural area hasn't been logged, so one sees many more snags here.

The Metolius Breaks is featured on page 166.

The **Mount Jefferson Additions** and **Mount Washington Additions** units are adjacent to the existing Mount Jefferson and Mount Washington Wildernesses. The current Wilderness boundaries were drawn to exclude forests that might be valuable for logging. Including these forests will protect these vulnerable areas and increase the ecological diversity of the basin.

PROPOSED WILDERNESS
Metolius

LOCATION
10 miles north of Camp Sherman

LEVEL IV ECOREGIONS
Ponderosa Pine/Bitterbrush Woodland (87%), Grand Fir Mixed Forest (12%)

VEGETATION TYPES
Ponderosa on Pumice (52%), Ponderosa/Douglas-Fir/Western Larch/Lodgepole (34%), Juniper/ Ponderosa (9%), Mountain Big Sage (5%), Ponderosa/Douglas-Fir/True Fir (1%)

TERRAIN
Deep river canyon.

DRAINAGE SUBBASIN
Upper Deschutes

ELEVATION RANGE
1,998-5,049 feet

SIZE
14,949 acres

COUNTY
Jefferson

FEDERAL ADMINISTRATIVE UNIT
Deschutes National Forest (Sisters Ranger District)

USGS 7.5' QUAD MAPS
Candle Creek, Fly Creek, Little Squaw Back, Metolius Bench, Prairie Farm Spring, Round Butte Dam, Shitike Butte

The Metolius River flowing through the Metolius Breaks Unit of the proposed Metolius Wilderness. The Castle Rocks can also be seen above the trees.

FEATURED UNIT

Metolius Breaks

Downstream from its confluence with Candle Creek until it empties into the stagnant backwater of Reservoir Billy Chinook, the Metolius River flows through a beautiful canyon that is in places up to 1,400 feet deep.

The fishing is outstanding, as is the whitewater rafting and kayaking with three long Class III rapids. A trail along the east/south bank provides for leisurely hiking and camping. The west/north bank is within the Warm Springs Indian Reservation where public access is prohibited.

Wildlife in the area is abundant and includes black bear, cougar and the western rattlesnake. Rocky Mountain elk and mule deer are very common here. The intact old-growth forest is habitat for many songbirds. Bald eagles and osprey nest along the river. Peregrine falcons may make their homes high in the cliffs above.

Moving west to east, the forest becomes progressively drier.

The western portion of the unit is a mixed conifer forest, with lots of ponderosa pine. The understory can include snowberry, snowbrush and pine-grass. Golden chinquapin can dominate the west- and north-facing slopes. Toward the east, the forests become almost purely ponderosa pine. Pine-grass, bitterbrush and bunchgrass dominate the dry forest understory. The wetter riparian zones along streams include mountain maple, bigleaf maple and Pacific dogwood. Even further east, the forest finally gives way to desert ecotypes: western juniper woodlands, big sagebrush and grass shrublands.

In the uplands near the northernmost Horn of the Metolius is a unique geological feature called Castle Rocks.

The 17.1 miles of the federally designated Metolius Wild and Scenic River in the Metolius Breaks Unit is classified as "scenic" under the law. "Scenic" is a more protective classification than "recreational," but less so than "wild." Congress applied the lesser "scenic" classification due to the presence of two old dead-end roads. However, the roads are now trails, thereby opening the way for this river segment to be classified as "wild."

where these conditions are lacking, including much of the "blue ribbon fishery" on the Deschutes River. Redband trout are also present in the Metolius. Before Round Butte Dam was constructed and blocked ocean migration, the Metolius was also a major salmon river. Its sockeye salmon runs were tremendous, but now only exist genetically in the form of kokanee, the landlocked variety of sockeye salmon.

The Metolius Basin is a refuge not only for fish and wildlife, but also for people. The river is popular for whitewater rafting, hiking and camping. Fly-fishers revere the Metolius' cold, clear water (although the water's clarity and glassy surface give fish a huge advantage over all but the most expert anglers). Other recreational opportunities include hunting, hiking and horseback riding, as well as marveling at the old-growth yellow-bellied ponderosa pine and the rare sight of a river that springs fully formed from a mountain. The lower river, adjacent to the Warm Springs Indian Reservation, is managed to prevent public motorized access.

Over 27,000 acres of the proposed Wilderness are not currently slated for logging. Due to constant and well-organized pressure from local permanent and seasonal residents, the Forest Service has dramatically — but not totally — scaled back its logging plans for the basin. However, a recent large fire of suspicious origin will cause some to want to log the burned trees. Other major threats to the proposed Wilderness include roading, livestock grazing and off-road vehicles.

Proposed Newberry Volcano Wilderness
Volcanic Wonderland

The Newberry Volcano is 630-square miles in size and features over 400 cinder cones. Rather than the classic steep-side stratovolcano shape common to High Cascades peaks, Newberry Volcano is a huge, gently sloping shield volcano. Extending from just south of Bend to just a few miles short of Oregon 31 southeast of La Pine, the volcano is approximately 34 miles north to south and 22 miles east to west at its widest point.

Rising steeply to over 4,000 feet above the surrounding volcanic butte-strewn plateau are the Paulina Mountains. At the center and highest part of the Paulina Mountains is Newberry Crater, a large rim that contains a 17 square-mile caldera.

The highest elevations in the Paulina Mountains are not actually part of the East Cascades Slopes and Foothills Ecoregion, but are instead an outlier of the Cascades Ecoregion.

Newberry Volcano is far from extinct, being both seismically and geothermally active. It is estimated that its magma chamber is merely two to five kilometers below the land surface. Eruptions have occurred over the last 600,000 years, the most recent

◄ Old-growth ponderosa pine (*Pinus Ponderosa*) in the proposed Metolius Wilderness. ONRC Eastern Field Representative Tim Lillebo provides scale.

Proposed Newberry Volcano Wilderness

LEVEL IV ECOREGIONS
Pumice Plateau (71%), Ponderosa
Pine/Bitterbrush Woodland (6%); Cascades Level
III Ecoregion: Cascade Crest Montane Forest
(20%); Northern Basin and Range Level III
Ecoregion: High Lava Plains (<2%), Pluvial Lake
Basins (<2%)

VEGETATION TYPES
Ponderosa on Pumice (30%), Lodgepole on
Pumice (24%), Mountain Hemlock/Red
Fir/Lodgepole (13%), Open Lava (12%),
Ponderosa/Lodgepole (10%), Juniper/Mountain
Big Sage (4%), Ponderosa/Douglas-fir/True Fir
(3%), Juniper/Big Sage (3%), Big Sagebrush
(2%), Bitterbrush Scrub (<1%), Open Water (<1%)

DRAINAGE SUBBASINS
Lower Crooked, Little Deschutes, Summer Lake
Closed, Upper Deschutes

ELEVATION RANGE
3,970-7,984 feet

UNITS
Aspen Flat, Benham Falls, Burnt Butte, Coyote
Flat, East Pine Mountain, Firestone Butte, Lava
Butte, Lava Cast Forest, Lava River Cave, Long
Butte, Lower Ground Hog Butte, Lower Sugar
Pine Butte, Mokst Butte, Nameless Lava, North
Paulina Peak, North Pot Holes, Paulina Creek,
Paulina Peak, Pine Mountain Summit, Pumice
Springs, Sand Butte, Scattered Lava, Stu Garrett,
Sugar Pine Ridge, Surveyor's Lava Flow, Topso
Butte, West Lava Cast Forest, West of Sand
Spring

**EXISTING WILDERNESS
INCORPORATED**
None

SIZE
99,307 acres (155 square miles)

COUNTIES
Deschutes, Lake

**FEDERAL
ADMINISTRATIVE UNITS**
Deschutes National Forest; BLM Prineville and
Lakeview Districts

CONGRESSIONAL DISTRICT
2nd

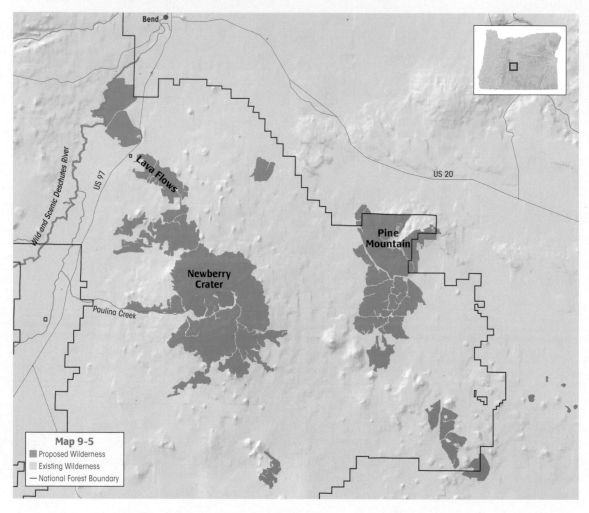

Map 9-5
■ Proposed Wilderness
■ Existing Wilderness
— National Forest Boundary

Some of the units in the proposed Wilderness are highlighted below.

The **Lava Flows** units consist mostly of relatively recent and basalt lava flows to the northwest of Newberry Crater. They include numerous ring fractures, cinder cones and tree casts. Tree casts formed in a matter of seconds as molten lava flowed around live trees. The trees were killed instantly, being reduced mostly to smoke, but not before the molten lava had cooled in the form of the tree. Several miles of the Upper Deschutes Wild and Scenic River flow through these units. One unit includes Benham Falls on the Deschutes River, which was created by the lava flow.

The **Newberry Crater** units are featured on page 169.

The **Pine Mountain** units are near the north end of Newberry Volcano. Pine Mountain is best known for the University of Oregon's astronomical observatory. The mountain contains several long, high ridges separated by broad valleys. The higher elevations contain a pure old-growth ponderosa pine forest.

One sees numerous Cascade peaks from Paulina Peak in the proposed Newberry Volcano Wilderness.

FEATURED UNIT

Newberry Crater

Four roadless units (North Paulina Peak, Paulina Creek, Paulina Peak and Sand Butte) are in Newberry Crater. It is possible to circumnavigate the entire Newberry Crater on 25 miles of trail. One will generally be between 6,500 and 7,500 feet in elevation, save for the Paulina Lake's outlet on the western edge at 6,331 feet. If one hikes after all the snow has melted, one must carry water. There is little open water in the crater's streams.

The views can be tremendous. At other times, however, one will travel through what appear to be monocultures of mountain hemlock or lodgepole pine. One will also walk across open flats and bare ridges. Much of the vegetation is dwarfed and stunted by the very long snow cover, very short growing season and poor soils.

While a geological gem, the unit is not a wildlife wonderland due the harshness of the landscape and climate.

If one begins at the lodge on the west edge of Paulina Lake and hikes clockwise, one will first climb gently and then more steeply on switchbacks to North Paulina Peak (7,720'). The trail does not go over the summit directly, so one has to pick a cross-country route to reach it. After bagging the peak, continue eastward and stay high on the caldera rim around the east side.

Eventually one will cross an all-weather road and now be heading west along the rim, above Pumice Flat (accurately described, if not originally named) and Big Obsidian Flow (ditto). The latter is one of the newest geologic features in central Oregon, the lava having last flowed around 650 AD. In 1964, NASA tested their moon suits on Big Obsidian Flow. At the lower end of the lava flow is Lost Lake, where an annual August migration of frogs hops across the flow. (Watch your step!)

Upon reaching Paulina Peak (7,984'), one may likely find hordes of tourists who have driven to the summit on a road. Descending steeply back to the lodge, it is time for that beer (or other cherished beverage) one has been dreaming about day and night.

PROPOSED WILDERNESS
Newberry Volcano

LOCATION
15 miles west-northwest of La Pine

LEVEL IV ECOREGIONS
Pumice Plateau (41%); Cascades Level III Ecoregion: Cascade Crest Montane Forest (59%).

VEGETATION TYPES
Mountain Hemlock/Fir/Lodgepole (41%), Lodgepole On Pumice (26%), Ponderosa on Pumice (17%), Ponderosa/Lodgepole (9%), Ponderosa/Douglas-Fir/True Fir (7%), Open Water (<1%)

TERRAIN
A steep, rugged caldera.

DRAINAGE SUBBASINS
Little Deschutes, Lower Crooked, Summer Lake Closed

ELEVATION RANGE
5,804-7,984 feet

SIZE
31,447 acres

COUNTY
Deschutes

FEDERAL ADMINISTRATIVE UNIT
Deschutes National Forest (Fork Rock Ranger District)

USGS 7.5' QUAD MAPS
East Lake, Fuzztail Butte, Lava Cast Forest, Paulina Peak

one being 1,300 year ago.

Inside the volcano's caldera are depressions that contain two little crater lakes: East Lake (170-feet deep) and Paulina Lake (250-feet deep). In times past, there may have been only one large lake some 1,600-feet deep.

Cinder cones, lava (basalt) flows, obsidian (rhyolite) flows, pumice flats and lava caves are just some of the unmistakable evidence of volcanism in this region.

In 1990, Congress established the 55,000-acre (86 square miles) Newberry National Volcanic Monument, covering about one-seventh of Newberry Volcano.

One can drive to the summit of Paulina Peak and view the entirety of Newberry Crater, the Big Obsidian Flow and the caldera's lakes. In the distance one can see other Cascade Peaks to the west and can look east into Oregon's Sagebrush Sea as far as Hart Mountain.

Precipitation falls mainly as snow here. Runoff into streams is minimal due to the very porous nature of the pumice soils. Redband trout may be found in the area's few streams.

This land is harsh, having been overlain with a generous helping of Mazama ash, a deep deposit of Newberry pumice or both. Basalt outcroppings poke through the terrain. As elevation increases, the vegetation becomes increasingly sparse. One will not find lush forests in this proposed Wilderness. The lower elevations have some dry open forests and some mixed conifer forest with an understory of snowbrush, manzanita or both. One may find a western white pine on the wetter north-facing slopes. Lupine grows on the pumice. At the lowest elevations, ponderosa pine, with bitterbrush, manzanita and/or needlegrass is common. Upslope, old-growth lodgepole pine is dominant in various associations with manzanita, needlegrass, lupine, grouse huckleberry and bitterbrush. Old-growth mountain hemlock is also found high up, often with grouse huckleberry underneath.

A rare endemic species known as pumice grape fern (*Botrychium pumicola*) is found in just three locations at Newberry Crater. Small and inconspicuous, the pumice grape fern favors high-silica pumice, very cold weather and full sun. It is also found in the High Cascades (from Broken Top to Crater Lake) and in frost pockets of lodgepole pine-covered pumice in several locations in the East Cascades Slopes and Foothills. At least 13,000 grape fern plants are known to exist. A perennial, it usually regrows annually to two to four inches in height. Reproduction occurs in underground darkness and is self-fertilizing at that. (Not really much of a social life.) The absence of fire to periodically clear out the lodgepole pine is hindering the grape fern's chances of survival, as does the relentless onslaught of human "progress" (roads, logging, fire suppression, etc.).

Bald eagles live near the two caldera lakes. Mule deer, Rocky Mountain elk and black bear may also be found here. The Clark's nutcracker is common in the lodgepole

◀ The Deschutes River in the Benham Falls Unit of the proposed Newberry Volcano Wilderness.

SANDY LONSDALE

The roadless land that surrounds Paulina Lake is the Newberry Crater Unit of the proposed Newberry Volcano Wilderness.

and whitebark pine forest.

Recreational opportunities include hiking, horseback riding, hunting and spelunking.

The major threats to the remaining wildlands in the proposed Newberry Volcano Wilderness are geothermal power development, the winter assault of loud, polluting snowmobiles and the summer onslaught of off-road vehicles.

Geothermal power development is a distinct possibility for the area as Newberry Crater is one of the hottest landscapes in North America. In the center of the caldera between the lakes, a test well showed a temperature of 509° F at 3,058 feet depth. Any geothermal development would require government subsidies, as power generation by this means is still more expensive than other methods. And any increase in demand for electrical power can easily be met by conservation measures. Compact fluorescent light bulbs, new efficient appliances and insulation are more worthy of subsidies and would allow the Newberry Crater to be protected as Wilderness. Besides, although geothermal is often advertised as "renewable energy," the optimal rate of exploiting the resource in order to maximize profit is more than the natural rate of reheating.

The other plagues upon the proposed Wilderness are logging, roading and ◆
livestock grazing.

Neither Cascades nor Rockies, but With Attributes of Both
Blue Mountains Ecoregion

Extending from Oregon's East Cascades Slopes and Foothills to the intersection of Oregon, Idaho and Washington, the 15.3 million acres of the Blue Mountains Ecoregion in Oregon are a conglomeration of mountain ranges, broad plateaus, sparse valleys, spectacular river canyons and deep gorges. The highest point is the Matterhorn that rises to 9,832 feet in the Wallowa Mountains. The ecoregion extends into southeastern Washington and west central Idaho.

Most of the mountain ranges in the Blue Mountains Ecoregion are volcanic. The Crooked River separates the Maury Mountains from the Ochoco Mountains, which are separated from the Aldrich Mountains by the South Fork John Day River. The Aldrich Mountains are separated from the Strawberry Mountain Range by Canyon Creek. These ranges generally run east-west. North of the Strawberry Range are the Blue Mountains themselves, which extend to the northern edge of the ecoregion. The Greenhorn Mountains are part of the Blue Mountains, but are sometimes described separately due to their unique geology. This is also true of the Elkhorn Range and the Wallowa Mountains, which are both ranges of intrusive granitic rocks that rise above the surrounding lava plains. Summit Ridge, over 50 miles long, is tall and rugged enough to be called a mountain range, but its precipitous drop into Hells Canyon causes one to think "canyon!" rather than "mountains." The ash from eruptions of Mount Mazama affected most of the ecoregion's soils.

Much of this ecoregion is tree-free. Most of its lower elevations are sagebrush-steppe and grasslands where the climate is too arid to support tree species. Where forests do occur at higher elevations, grand fir, lodgepole pine, Douglas-fir and ponderosa pine dominate, with Engelmann spruce and subalpine fir common at even higher elevations. The highest diversity of rare plants in the region is found in the Wallowa Mountains, an area generally unaffected by volcanism.

The region's various habitats are shaped by fire, with natural fire intervals ranging from frequent (ten to fifteen years) on the drier sites, to infrequent (100 to 300 years) in the cooler, wetter sites. Precipitation here ranges from nine to eighteen inches annually in the low valleys to 70 to 110 inches in the mountains. The growing season ranges from 30 to 130 days depending on elevation. The forests are home to Rocky Mountain elk, mule deer, black bear, cougar, bobcat, coyote, beaver, marten, raccoon, fisher, pileated woodpecker, golden eagle, chickadee and nuthatch, as well as various species of hawks, woodpeckers, owls and songbirds. Wolves, long absent from Oregon, are making their return to the state in this ecoregion. Individuals from packs reintroduced in nearby Idaho are dispersing into Oregon. Fish species include bull and rainbow trout, along with numerous stocks of Pacific salmon species.

Depending on precipitation, aspect, soil type, elevation, fire history and other factors, one generally finds various combinations of Douglas-fir, ponderosa pine, lodgepole, western larch, juniper and Engelmann spruce throughout the Blue Mountains.

Beginning approximately at the Lower Deschutes River and rising eastward, the lower elevations of the Blue Mountains Ecoregion are a jumble of **Juniper/Low Sage**, **Juniper/Big Sage**, **Juniper/Mountain Big Sage**, **Juniper/Grassland** and **Juniper/Bitterbrush** woodlands.

At the mid-elevations are vast forests of predominantly **Ponderosa** pine. These park-like stands are threatened by logging, livestock grazing and fire suppression. Also found throughout the Ochoco, Blue and Wallowa Mountains are various types of forests associated with ponderosa, such as **True Fir/Douglas-fir**, **Ponderosa/Douglas-fir/True Fir**, **Douglas-fir/Ponderosa/True Fir** and **True Fir/Lodgepole/Western Larch/Douglas-fir,** which are all typically at higher elevations than **Ponderosa/Douglas-fir/Western Larch/Lodgepole** forests.

Western Larch/Douglas-fir/Ponderosa/Lodgepole stands are found in the heart of the Blue Mountains and on the lower slopes of the Wallowa Mountains. Also found in the Blue Mountains, sometimes as monocultures, are **Lodgepole** and **Subalpine Lodgepole**.

Western Larch/Douglas-fir/True Fir is found in the lower Grande Ronde River drainage. A variant of the Western Larch/Douglas-fir/True Fir and Western Larch/Douglas-fir/Ponderosa/Lodgepole forest is the **Lodgepole/Western Larch** type, which is found in limited areas in the Blue Mountains and Wallowa Mountains.

Lodgepole/True Fir is found west of the Elkhorn Range. In the absence of fire,

the grand fir (of the true firs) will eventually replace the lodgepole.

At higher elevations in the Wallowas, Elkhorns and Strawberry Mountains is the **Subalpine Fir/Engelmann Spruce Parkland**, the western outlier of a Rocky Mountain forest type. At the highest elevations, **Alpine Barren Fell Fields** are often snow-covered and usually, but not always, devoid of vegetation.

In the Hells Canyon and Grande Ronde areas are **Ponderosa/Grasslands** where ponderosa pine are usually in a mosaic of stringers among the grasslands. Another mosaic of vegetation is formed by the **Ponderosa/Shrub** community, found along the northwest edge of the Blue Mountains. Also scattered throughout the region, but most common in Hells Canyon are **Montane Shrublands**, where mountain mahogany, snowberry and serviceberry are the dominant plants.

Where there are **Marsh/Wet Meadows** in the Blue Mountains, tufted hairgrass and sedge usually dominate.

At some time in their existence, most forest communities will be set back to early successional forest and are classified as **Cutover/Burned** forest. This can occur naturally — from lightning-caused wildfires, native insect or disease events, or blow-down by wind — or unnaturally, by way of logging, human-caused fire, human-caused blowdown (due to unnatural and vulnerable forest edges caused by clearcuts), non-native disease and insects, or aggressive fire-fighting. Particularly troubling are "backburns," where firefighters intentionally burn the forest in front of an oncoming wildfire. In many cases, the backburns are far more intense and destructive than the natural burn would have been.

Many of the roadless wildlands proposed for Wilderness protection in the Blue Mountain Ecoregion have been identified by The Nature Conservancy as vital to protect biodiversity in the area.

Currently, 51 percent of Blue Mountains Ecoregion in Oregon is publicly owned and managed by the federal government. All of the Ochoco, Malheur, Umatilla and Wallowa-Whitman National Forests, as well as the western portions of the BLM Vale, Burns and Prineville Districts lie within the region.

Currently there are ten Wilderness areas in Oregon's Blue Mountains: Mill Creek, Bridge Creek, Black Canyon, Strawberry Mountain, Monument Rock, North Fork John Day, North Fork Umatilla, Wenaha-Tucannon, Eagle Cap and Hells Canyon. These comprise 5.3 percent of the ecoregion.

Conservationists propose ten additional multi-unit Wilderness areas for the ecoregion: Blue Mountains, Grande Ronde, Hells Canyon Additions, Malheur Basin, Malheur Canyons, North Fork John Day-Elkhorns, Ochoco Mountains, South Fork John Day, Upper John Day and Wallowa Mountains. If designated, a total 17.8 percent of the ecoregion would be formally protected as Wilderness.

A July stroll in the proposed Ochoco Mountains Wilderness. ▶

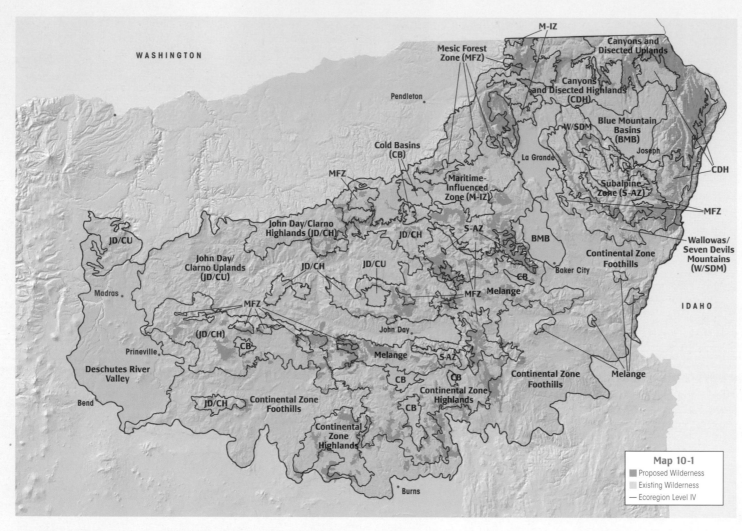

The map labels include: WASHINGTON, Pendleton, M-IZ, Mesic Forest Zone (MFZ), Canyons and Disected Uplands, Canyons and Disected Highlands (CDH), Cold Basins (CB), W/SDM, Blue Mountain Basins (BMB), Joseph, La Grande, CDH, MFZ, Maritime-Influenced Zone (M-IZ), Subalpine Zone (S-AZ), MFZ, John Day/Clarno Highlands (JD/CH), JD/CH, S-AZ, BMB, Wallowas/Seven Devils Mountains (W/SDM), JD/CU, John Day/Clarno Uplands (JD/CU), JD/CH, JD/CU, Continental Zone Foothills, Baker City, CB, Madras, MFZ, Melange, IDAHO, (JD/CH), CB, John Day, MFZ, Prineville, Deschutes River Valley, Melange, S-AZ, Melange, Bend, CB, CB, CB, Continental Zone Foothills, JD/CH, Continental Zone Foothills, CB, Continental Zone Highlands, Continental Zone Highlands, Burns.

Map 10-1
■ Proposed Wilderness
□ Existing Wilderness
— Ecoregion Level IV

The semiarid **John Day/Clarno Uplands** form a ring of dry foothills surrounding the western perimeter of the Blue Mountains. Highly dissected hills, palisades and colorful ash beds flank the valleys of the John Day and Crooked Rivers. This ecoregion has a continental climate moderated somewhat by marine influence. Juniper woodland has expanded markedly into the sagebrush-grassland during the 20th Century due to a combination of climatic factors, fire suppression and grazing pressure.

The low mountains of the **John Day/Clarno Highlands** are uniformly covered by ponderosa pine forest with a grass and shrub understory. The continental climate is tempered by a marine influence; it is not as dry, nor are temperature extremes as great, as in the Continental Zone

Oregon's Blue Mountains Ecoregion

The Blue Mountains Ecoregion is a complex of mountain ranges that are lower and more open than the neighboring Cascades and Northern Rockies. Like the Cascades, but unlike the Northern Rockies, the Blue Mountains are mostly volcanic in origin. However, the core of the Blue Mountains and the highest ranges, the Wallowa and Elkhorn Mountains, are composed of granitic intrusives, deep sea sediments and metamorphosed rocks. Much of the Blue Mountains Ecoregion is grazed by cattle, unlike the Cascades and Northern Rockies.

Further refining the ecoregion, scientists divide Oregon's Blue Mountains Level III Ecoregion into fourteen Level IV ecoregions:

Highlands. Historically, frequent low intensity fires reduced fuel loading in forests of widely spaced old-growth ponderosa pine. Today, after years of fire suppression and high grade logging, land managers attempt to emulate historical fire regimes to reverse the trend toward dense thickets of young growth that carry hot, stand-replacing fires.

The **Maritime-Influenced Zone** is the portion of the Blue Mountains ecoregion that directly intercepts marine weather systems moving east through the Columbia River Gorge. In addition, loess and ash soils over basalt retain sufficient moisture to support forest cover at lower elevations than elsewhere in the Blue Mountains. A dense and diverse shrub layer grows beneath the relatively open canopy of ponderosa pine and Douglas-fir which may delay tree regeneration following logging.

The **Melange** ecoregion has a complex geology, composed of ocean sediments, granitic intrusions and metamorphosed sediments. Soils are droughty and high in magnesium, creating a poor medium for plant growth; reforestation problems limit logging. Placer mining for gold altered the structure of many stream channels and left extensive tailings piles in riparian areas.

The **Wallowas/Seven Devils Mountains** ecoregion occupies the mid-elevation zone between the Subalpine-Alpine Zone and the Continental Zone Foothills. It is not as complex geologically as the Melange ecoregion, although it is also composed of ocean sediments. The character of its xeric forest of ponderosa pine and Douglas-fir varies between moister maritime-influenced and drier continental areas, particularly in the diversity and extent of the shrub understory. Streams following fault lines have eroded deep canyons and mountain water is diverted or impounded for irrigation and drinking water.

In the **Canyons and Dissected Highlands** ecoregion the uplifted Columbia Plateau basalt has been eroded to a series of knife-edge ridges flanked by deep canyons. This ecoregion occupies the elevational zone above the unforested Canyons and Dissected Uplands; it is drier than the marine-influenced Mesic Forest Zone that exists at similar elevations to the west. Moisture retaining loess and ash soils support Douglas-fir, larch and grand fir on relatively level benches and Douglas-fir in unstable colluvial soils on steep canyon slopes. The steep terrain limits human activities.

In Oregon, the **Canyons and Dissected Uplands** include the Snake, Grande Ronde and Imnaha river canyons that have cut 2,000 to 5,000 feet through the Columbia Plateau basalt and underlying metamorphic rocks. Stony colluvial soils retain little moisture and support bunch grasses and arid land shrubs. Grazing and recreation occur in Hells Canyon National Recreation Area. The canyons provide a refuge for elk, bighorn sheep, mountain goats and a concentration of wintering bald eagles. Of the major historic Snake River salmon stocks, the coho and sockeye are extinct, the chinook are threatened and summer steelhead are in decline.

The mountainous **Continental Zone Highlands** experience seasonal temperature extremes and low annual precipitation. The predominant forest cover is ponderosa pine with a shrub or bunchgrass understory. As in the John/Day Clarno Highlands, frequent fires once influenced the open character of the forest. This ecoregion lacks a zone of true firs found in other highland areas in the Blue Mountains. Many of its perennial streams flow south to end in the alkaline basins of the High Desert Wetlands in the Northern Basin and Range.

The **Continental Zone Foothills** lie in the rainshadow of the Cascade Range and Blue Mountains. Plants experience wide temperature variations, high evapotranspiration rates and high early-season moisture stress in the continental climate of this ecoregion. The distribution of desert shrubs varies with soil depth, texture and elevation. Mountain mahogany and bitterbrush provide winter cover and forage for mule deer. Rodents, songbirds and upland game birds also use the fruits of bitterbrush.

The **Blue Mountain Basins** ecoregion includes the Wallowa, Grande Ronde and Baker valleys. All three valleys are fault-bounded grabens or depressions filled with sediments. The Wallowa and Grande Ronde valleys have a marine-moderated climate and moisture retaining loess soils. The Baker Valley, located in the rainshadow of the Elkhorn Mountains, is drier and has areas of alkaline soil. All three valleys receive stream flow from the surrounding mountains. Most of the floodplain wetlands have been drained for agriculture, but a remnant exists in the Grande Ronde Basin at Ladd Marsh National Wildlife Refuge.

The disjunct **Mesic Forest Zone** includes the highest forested areas in the western Wallowas and the Blue Mountains. This ecoregion is marine-influenced with higher precipitation than other forested Blue Mountains ecoregions (such as the John Day/Clarno Highlands, Melange and Mesic Forest Zone). The ashy soil holds moisture during the dry season and supports a productive spruce-fir forest. The boundaries of this ecoregion correspond to the distribution of true fir forest before the modern era of fire suppression and high grade logging.

The **Subalpine-Alpine Zone** begins where the forest cover becomes broken by alpine meadows and continues through alpine meadowland to include the exposed rock and snowfields of the highest mountain peaks. Subalpine fir, Engelmann spruce and white-bark pine tolerate the cold soils, deep snowpack and extremely short growing season near timberline. Historically, green fescue and sedges covered high alpine meadows and ridges particularly in the Wallowas; but, following intense sheep grazing in the early 20th Century, many alpine plant associations reverted to seral or exotic species on rocky subsoil.

The **Deschutes River Valley** is a broad intermountain sagebrush-grassland. The climate of this ecoregion has a marine influence and is not as arid as in the botanically similar High Lava Plains of the Northern Basin and Range to the southeast. Because of the proximity of the High Cascades to the west, stream density and water availability are high. As a result, human population density is much higher than in the High Lava Plains. Canals carry river water to irrigated farms on floodplains and terraces.

The **Cold Basins** ecoregion contains high, wet meadows. The high meadows are often alluvial and have a high water table and silt or clay soils. Streams, if not channelized, are meandering and have a dynamic interaction with their flood plains. These unconstrained streams provide pool habitats that are important to salmonids. The short growing season and saturated soil make these basins unsuitable for most crops, except hay, but they are heavily grazed by cattle and elk.

Text greatefully adapted from Thor D. Thorson, Sandra A. Bryce, Duane A. Lammers, Alan J. Woods, James M. Omernik, Jimmy Kagan, David E. Pater, Jeffrey A. Comstock. 2003. Ecoregions of Oregon (color poster with map, descriptive text, summary tables and photographs). USDI-Geological Survey. Reston, VA (map scale 1:1,500,000).

GEORGE WUERTHNER

Proposed Blue Mountains Wilderness
Plateaus and Ridges, Canyons and Meadows, Elk and Fish

The proposed Blue Mountains Wilderness extends from near Fossil to the Washington border. The lands mainly drain northward and westward into the Umatilla River, Walla Walla River and Willow Creek basins. What doesn't drain into these three basins drains into the North Fork John Day River.

While this area includes some classic mountainous terrain, most of the proposed Wilderness is comprised of scenic narrow basalt ridges or plateaus that have been deeply incised and highly dissected by v-shaped stream valleys. Basalt outcroppings also dot the area. These dramatic elevational changes create dynamic microclimates that produce stringers of forests, brushfields and grasslands. Interstate 84 generally divides the drier southern from the wetter northern portion of the proposed Wilderness. In both parts, the cooler north-facing slopes include grand fir, Douglas-fir and other mixed conifers with some western larch. The warmer south-facing slopes feature open ponderosa pine, western juniper woodlands and grasslands. The higher elevations include subalpine fir. There are also occasional thick stands of lodgepole pine.

The Blue Mountains are centers of concentration of species rarity and endemism for both plants and animals. Numerous at-risk species live here, such as redband trout, wolverine, bull trout and several plant species, which prompted the Oregon Biodiversity Project to identify the Umatilla-Walla Walla Headwaters Conservation Opportunity Area as a priority for protection. In recognition of the important habitat for whitefish, bull trout, redband trout, spring chinook salmon and summer steelhead, the American Fisheries Society has also identified several aquatic diversity areas within the proposed Wilderness.

Almost 200 species of songbirds, birds of prey, wading birds and migratory birds can be found within the proposed Wilderness, including the three-toed woodpecker, black-backed woodpecker, pileated woodpecker, great gray owl, flammulated owl, western tanager, mountain bluebird, bald eagle and Steller's jay.

Rocky Mountain elk and mule deer are very common, as is the cougar that preys upon them. The proposed Wilderness contains large areas of both winter and summer range for these species. Other major mammal species include black bear, marten, bobcat and coyote. The proposed Wilderness is within a major wildlife corridor and contains habitat that could accommodate the return of lynx and wolf.

Recreational opportunities here include big game hunting, fishing, hiking, backpacking, birding, horseback riding, cross-country skiing or simply taking in the views.

The South Fork of the Umatilla River in the proposed Blue Mountains Wilderness. ▶

Proposed Blue Mountains Wilderness

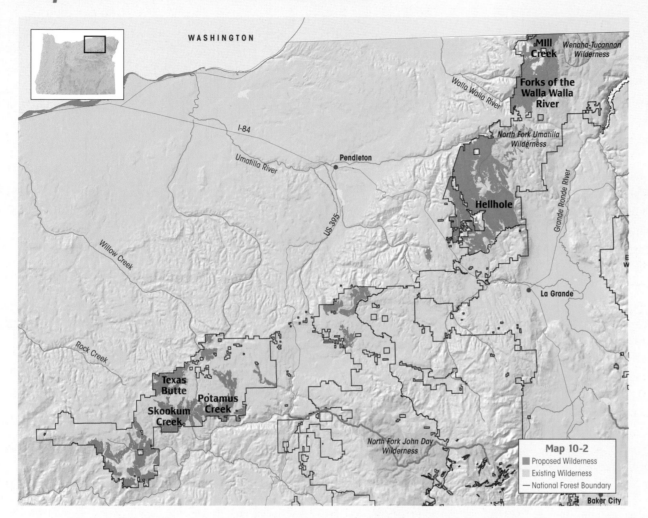

Map 10-2
- ■ Proposed Wilderness
- ▨ Existing Wilderness
- — National Forest Boundary

LEVEL IV ECOREGIONS

Maritime-Influenced Zone (41%), Mesic Forest Zone (36%), John Day/Clarno Highlands (17%), John Day/Clarno Uplands (4%), Canyons and Dissected Highlands (1%), Canyons and Dissected Uplands (<1%), Subalpine-Alpine Zone (<1%); Columbia Basin Level III Ecoregion: Deep Loess Foothills (<1%)

VEGETATION TYPES

Ponderosa (19%), Ponderosa/Douglas-fir/Western Larch/Lodgepole (16%), Western Larch/Douglas-fir/Ponderosa/Lodgepole (13%), True Fir/Douglas-fir (11%), True Fir/Lodgepole/Western Larch/Douglas-fir (9%), Ponderosa/Douglas-fir/True Fir (8%), Douglas-fir/Ponderosa/True Fir (7%), Juniper/Grasslands (5%), Ponderosa/Shrub (5%), Western Larch/Douglas-fir/True Fir (3%), Subalpine Fir/Engelmann Spruce Parklands (1%), Subalpine Lodgepole (1%), Big Sagebrush (<1%), Cutover/Burned (1%), Grasslands/Bunchgrass (<1%), Juniper/Mountain Big Sage (<1%), Lodgepole/Western Larch (<1%), Low Sagebrush (<1%), Montane Shrublands (<1%), Other Sagebrush (<1%), Ponderosa/Grasslands (<1%)

DRAINAGE SUBBASINS

North Fork John Day, Umatilla, Walla Walla, Willow

ELEVATION RANGE

1,798-5,780 feet

UNITS

Black Mountain, Blue Kettle Ridge, Bologna Basin, Crow Ridge, Dark Canyon, Doghouse, Dry Creek, Fivemile Creek, Forks of the Walla Walla, Happy Jack, Hellhole, Horse Heaven Ridge, Horseshoe Ridge, Indian Creek, Jones Canyon, Jussard Creek, Keith Canyon, Kelly Mountain, Klondike Springs, Lane Creek, Mahogany Butte, Mill Creek, *North Fork Umatilla Additions* (North Headwaters Additions, South Headwaters Additions), Owsley Creek, Potamus Creek, Skookum Creek, Short Canyon, Sugarloaf Mountain, Tamarack Creek, Texas Butte, Thompson Falls, Thorn Spring, Tiger Creek, Turner Mountain, Upper Potamus Creek, West Birch Creek, Wildhorse Springs, Willow Springs

EXISTING WILDERNESS INCORPORATED

North Fork Umatilla

SIZE

253,770 acres (397 square miles, not including 20,435 acres of currently protected Wilderness)

COUNTIES

Grant, Morrow, Umatilla, Union, Wallowa, Wheeler

FEDERAL ADMINISTRATIVE UNITS

Umatilla and Wallowa-Whitman National Forests; BLM Prineville and Vale Districts

CONGRESSIONAL DISTRICT

2nd

Some of the units of the proposed Wilderness are highlighted below.

The **Forks of the Walla Walla** unit is summarized on page 178.

Hellhole is far from being one, but one has to love the name. Rather, it is an oasis of "island-in-the-sky" forests and intimate enclosed canyons, and features magnificent views from its steep, grass-covered slopes. It includes the North Fork of Meacham Creek and the South Fork of the Umatilla River.

Mill Creek is closed to the public to protect the drinking water supply for the city of Walla Walla, except during elk hunting season. This unit extends into Washington.

Potamus Creek features bald eagles and is winter and summer range for big game. It is a center of concentration of species rarity and endemism for plants.

Skookum Creek contains the Utah thistle (*Cirsium utahense*), more common in the Great Basin desert.

Texas Butte is important summer range for Rocky Mountain elk and mule deer.

PROPOSED WILDERNESS
Blue Mountains

LOCATION
15 miles east-southeast of Milton-Freewater

LEVEL IV ECOREGIONS
Mesic Forest Zone (76%), Maritime-Influenced Zone (24%); Columbia Plateau Level III Ecoregion: Deep Loess Foothills (<1%)

VEGETATION TYPES
True Fir/Douglas-fir (56%), Western Larch/Douglas-fir/Ponderosa/Lodgepole (14%), Subalpine Lodgepole (8%), Ponderosa/Douglas-fir/Western Larch/Lodgepole (7%), Cutover/Burned (5%), Subalpine Fir/Engelmann Spruce Parklands (4%), Ponderosa/Douglas-fir/True Fir (3%), Western Larch/Douglas-fir/True Fir (2%), Douglas-fir/Ponderosa/True Fir (1%), Montane Shrublands (1%), Lodgepole/Western Larch (<1%)

TERRAIN
River canyons and high ridges.

DRAINAGE SUBBASIN
Walla Walla

ELEVATION RANGE
2,398-5,670 feet

SIZE
36,265 acres

COUNTIES
Umatilla, Wallowa

FEDERAL ADMINISTRATIVE UNITS
Umatilla National Forest (Walla Walla Ranger District); BLM Vale District (Baker Resource Area)

USGS 7.5' QUAD MAPS
Big Meadows, Bone Spring, Jubilee Lake, Tollgate

GEORGE WUERTHNER

The Forks of the Walla Walla Unit of the proposed Blue Mountains Wilderness.

FEATURED UNIT
Forks of the Walla Walla

A few miles upstream of Milton-Freewater, the North and South Forks of the Walla Walla River join to create the river's mainstem. About 12 miles up each fork is the boundary of the Umatilla National Forest, which is also the western boundary of the Forks of the Walla Walla unit.

The unit has deeply incised canyons with very steep slopes. The southern slopes include forested stringer draws interspersed with grasslands on the upper portions. Stands of ponderosa pine and mixed conifer dominate the lower elevations. On the north slopes are grand fir and mixed conifer at the lower elevations and subalpine fir at the higher elevations.

Mule deer and Rocky Mountain elk are numerous, as are hunters in the fall. White-tailed deer are also present. Upland game bird hunting is popular here. Streams support spring chinook salmon, summer steelhead, bull trout and redband trout, and also serve as the water supply for Milton-Freewater.

Classified as sensitive in Oregon and threatened in Washington, Sabin's lupine (*Lupinus sabinii*) probably grows in the unit, as it has been inventoried nearby.

There are over 35 miles of trails within the unit. A 30-mile multi-day backpacking trip is possible by descending from the headwaters of either the North or South Forks to near the western boundary where a connector trail crosses the ridge between them. After crossing a high divide, one then proceeds up the trail of the other fork. Unfortunately, at the end of this trip one must hike cross-country through some logged hillsides to return to one's point of departure.

Threats to the proposed Wilderness include off-road vehicles, mining, livestock grazing and the ever-present risk of logging.

Proposed Grande Ronde Wilderness

Wild Rivers, Beautiful Canyons, Elk-Filled Forests and Fish-Filled Streams

The proposed Grande Ronde Wilderness would protect stretches of the Grande Ronde River and its tributaries. Beginning at tiny Grande Ronde Lake at the north end of the Elkhorn Mountains, the Grande Ronde River cascades, twists and turns for 185 miles before joining the Snake River in Washington. After leaving the Blue Mountains, the river meanders through the pastoral Grande Ronde River Valley before entering the deep and rugged Grande Ronde Canyon with its dense coniferous forests and grasslands. Below the mouth of Wildcat Creek, the river canyon opens to exposed ridges and grasslands, then enters another rocky (and arid) canyon before reaching the Snake River. Along the way, the Wenaha (rhymes with "Imnaha") River joins the Grande Ronde. A segment of the Grande Ronde, from its confluence with the Wallowa River to the Washington border, is a unit of the National Wild and Scenic Rivers System.

Major tree species here include Douglas-fir, ponderosa pine, western larch, lodgepole pine, grand fir and Engelmann spruce. Riparian species include mock orange, cottonwood and alder.

Rocky Mountain elk, mule deer, Rocky Mountain bighorn sheep and the less common (in eastern Oregon) white-tailed deer are the major game species found in the proposed Wilderness. Other mammals include black bear, cougar, coyote, marten, mink, muskrat, beaver, river otter and raccoon.

Bird species include bald eagle, golden eagle, peregrine falcon, northern goshawk, Cooper's hawk, sharp-shinned hawk, great gray owl, blue grouse and ruffed grouse.

The Grande Ronde and tributaries is a center of concentration of species rarity and endemism for animals. The Oregon Biodiversity Project's Joseph-Imnaha Plateau Conservation Opportunity Area includes extensive grasslands in and around the Joseph Creek portion of the proposed Wilderness. At least ten at-risk plant species, as well as wolverine and possibly lynx, are found in the area.

Recognizing important bull trout, redband trout, summer steelhead and spring/summer chinook habitat, the American Fisheries Society has identified several

Grande Ronde Lake in the unit of the same name in the proposed Grande Ronde Wilderness. ▶

Proposed Grande Ronde Wilderness

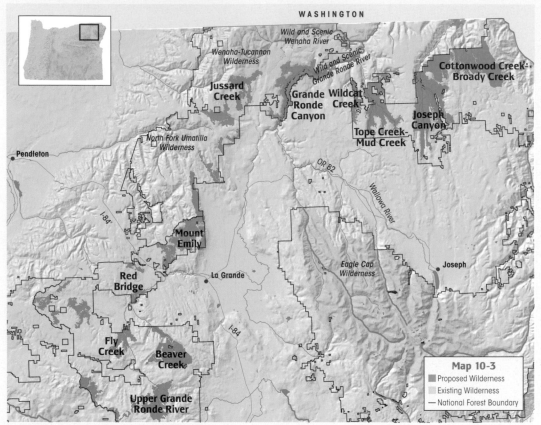

Map 10-3
■ Proposed Wilderness
□ Existing Wilderness
— National Forest Boundary

Some of the units in the proposed Wilderness are highlighted below.

Beaver Creek is a secondary water supply for the city of La Grande. The unit's northwest-facing slope allows it to receive more precipitation than the surrounding forestlands. Old Glory, an 800-foot high precipice, overlooks the watershed that is also excellent marten habitat. The area is closed to livestock grazing.

Grande Ronde Lake, **Fly Creek** and **Red Bridge** all include free-flowing segments of the Grande Ronde River, as well as small streams, spruce bogs, springs and meadows.

Grande Ronde Canyon is the centerpiece of the Grande Ronde federal Wild and Scenic River and Oregon Scenic Waterway. It is heavily boated in the spring until water levels recede to impassable levels.

Joseph Canyon is featured on page 181.

Mount Emily provides fantastic views of and from the Grande Ronde Valley and Wallowa Mountains. *Oregon Geographic Names* cites two possible sources for the naming of Mount Emily. It was either named for a married Emily of great mass or for a single — but very popular — Emily loved by masses of young males from La Grande who often went up to mount Emily.

Wenaha-Tucannon Additions units include roadless lands that should have been included in the adjacent Wilderness when it was designated in 1978. Although they are important habitat for spawning salmon and steelhead, as well as Rocky Mountain bighorn sheep, they were not included because they contained some commercially valuable timber. Some of the lower Wenaha River is also included in the additions.

The North End units (**Wildcat Creek**, **Tope Creek-Mud Creek** and **Cottonwood Creek-Broady Creek**) are important tributaries to the lower Grande Ronde River, providing both habitat for spawning fish and clean, cold water to the mainstem.

Joseph Creek in the Joseph Canyon Unit of the proposed Grande Ronde Wilderness.

FEATURED UNIT

Joseph Canyon

The 2,000-foot deep Joseph Canyon is a textbook example of Columbia River basalt being transformed by a down-cutting stream to create steep side slopes with exposed dikes and basalt layers.

Joseph Creek is a tributary to the Grande Ronde River. The portion of the creek that runs upstream for eight miles from the Wallowa-Whitman National Forest boundary is part of the National Wild and Scenic Rivers System. This management corridor, however, is narrow and does not adequately encompass — or protect — the unit's wildness. Spring and summer chinook salmon and summer steelhead spawn in the creek, where resident trout are also present.

On the wetter north- and east-facing slopes, the vegetation is classic stringer forests of Douglas-fir and ponderosa pine, which meets open native bunchgrass grasslands on the drier south- and west-facing slopes. Precipitation here averages just 15 inches annually and it gets quite hot in the summer.

Rocky Mountain elk, Rocky Mountain bighorn sheep, mule deer, white-tailed deer and cougar are all found in the unit. Mink, muskrat, beaver, river otter and raccoon are common small mammals. Birds of note include both golden and bald eagles, northern goshawk, both Cooper's and sharp-shinned hawks, great gray owl and both blue and ruffed grouse.

Chief Joseph of the Nez Perce was born in Joseph Canyon, most likely in one of several caves near the mouth of Joseph Creek. Petroglyphs are found on the steep canyon walls.

Most visitors view this unit from the very impressive Joseph Canyon overlook on Oregon Highway 3. Those with more time can hike deep into the canyon on one of several trails. Backpacking, birding, kayaking, sightseeing and photography are other popular activities. However one experiences Joseph Canyon, it is a memorable experience.

PROPOSED WILDERNESS
Grande Ronde

LOCATION
5 miles southeast of Flora

LEVEL IV ECOREGIONS
Canyons and Dissected Uplands (82%), Canyons and Dissected Highlands (18%)

VEGETATION TYPES
Ponderosa/Grasslands (87%), Ponderosa/Douglas-fir/Western Larch/Lodgepole (9%), Cutover/Burned (3%), Ponderosa (1%), Western Larch/Douglas-fir/Ponderosa/Lodgepole (1%)

TERRAIN
Deeply incised basalt canyons.

DRAINAGE SUBBASIN
Lower Grande Ronde

ELEVATION RANGE
2,497-4,968 feet

SIZE
39,884 acres

COUNTY
Wallowa

FEDERAL ADMINISTRATIVE UNITS
Wallowa-Whitman National Forest (Wallowa Valley Ranger District); BLM Vale District (Baker Resource Area)

USGS 7.5' QUAD MAPS
Roberts Butte, Shamrock Creek, Sled Springs, Table Mountain

LEON WERDINGER

aquatic diversity areas within the proposed Wilderness. Pacific lamprey also spawn in the area.

Recreational opportunities here include rafting, canoeing, big game and upland bird hunting, fishing, horseback riding, hiking, backpacking and sunning one's self at the edge of the river.

The proposed Wilderness is threatened by road building, logging, livestock grazing and mining. The Forest Service is currently using the "forest health" crisis as an excuse to road and log entire swaths of pristine, roadless forests.

Proposed Hells Canyon Wilderness Additions

Rocky Mountain Bighorn Sheep, Pacific Salmon, Deep Canyons and Long Trails

Hells Canyon is the deepest river gorge in North America.

Vast, rugged and stunningly beautiful, the landscape here is intoxicating. After visiting the Hells Canyon country, one is changed forever. More than merely picturesque, Hells Canyon is a landscape of critical ecological importance. Defined by the Snake and Imnaha (rhymes with "Wenaha") Rivers, the Hells Canyon country is one of Oregon's and the world's most wild, magical and remote places.

The proposed Wilderness features, in close proximity to one another, dense old-growth boreal forests, open bunchgrass slopes, lush stream zones with deciduous vegetation, alpine snowfields, desert lands with cactus, wildflower meadows and wet marshes.

Though much of these wildlands is included in the Hells Canyon National Recreation Area, established by Congress in 1985, the designation offers less than full protection for the area that has, in fact, been badly mismanaged by the Forest Service. While Wilderness designation protects some of Oregon's side of Hells Canyon, Congress stopped short of designating the river itself as Wilderness and skipped entirely much of the adjacent wildland plateaus and canyons that continue into Idaho.

The Oregon Biodiversity Project's Joseph-Imnaha Plateau Conservation Opportunity Area includes the lower and middle Imnaha Canyon in the proposed Hells Canyon Wilderness Additions. It includes extensive grasslands both on public and private land. At least ten at-risk species of plants, as well as wolverine and possibly

A Wild and Scenic River designation alone has not protected the Snake River from motorized intrusion. The current Hells Canyon Wilderness boundary begins where the Snake Wild and Scenic River boundary ends. The Wild and Scenic corridor itself needs to be designated Wilderness. ▶

Proposed Hells Canyon Wilderness Additions

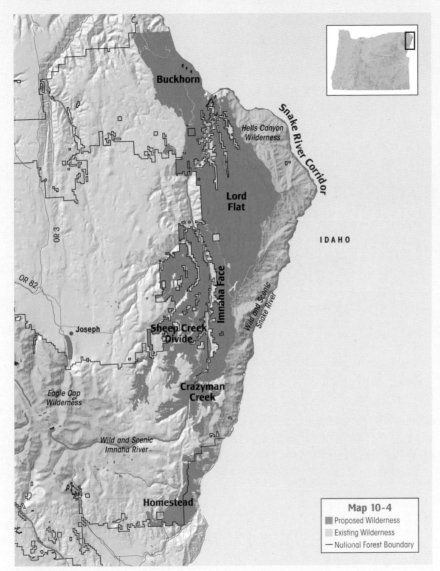

Some of the units in the proposed Wilderness are highlighted below.

Buckhorn includes over 20 miles of the free-flowing Snake River, four miles of the Imnaha River and several tributaries. It is now the state's only wildland that supports white sturgeon — some of which are 15 feet long.

At the south end of the 40-mile long Summit Ridge, tumbling **Crazyman Creek** feeds into the Imnaha River.

The **Homestead** unit has not one foot of hiking trail, but is home to beautiful old-growth Douglas-fir, ponderosa pine and bald eagles.

Imnaha Face lies between the Imnaha River and Summit Ridge and includes numerous tributaries that provide the river with very clean, cold water.

Lord Flat is featured on page 185.

When driving to Imnaha, many first time visitors mistake the knife-ridged and deep canyons of **Sheep Creek Divide** units for Hells Canyon or the Imnaha River Canyon.

The **Snake River Corridor** contains the wildlands within the Snake Wild and Scenic River corridor, adjacent to the existing Hells Canyon Wilderness. Wilderness designation for the river would finally end the use of loud, polluting jet boats.

Map 10-4
- ■ Proposed Wilderness
- ▨ Existing Wilderness
- — National Forest Boundary

LEVEL IV ECOREGIONS
Canyons and Dissected Uplands (69%), Canyons and Dissected Highlands (27%), Continental Zone Foothills (4%), Mesic Forest Zone (<1%), Blue Mountain Basins (<1%)

VEGETATION TYPES
Ponderosa/Grasslands (44%), Ponderosa/Douglas-fir/Western Larch/Lodgepole (20%), Grasslands/Bunchgrass (19%), Douglas-fir/Ponderosa/True Fir (10%), Western Larch/Douglas-fir/Ponderosa/Lodgepole (5%), Subalpine Lodgepole (1%), Cutover/Burned (<1%), Montane Shrublands (<1%), Ponderosa (<1%), Subalpine Fir/Engelmann Spruce Parklands (<1%)

DRAINAGE SUBBASINS
Asotin, Hells Canyon, Imnaha, Pine

ELEVATION RANGE
997-6,982 feet

UNITS
Bear Gulch, Big and Little Sheep Creeks, Buckhorn, Chesnimnus Creek Headwaters, Echo Canyon, Fish Creek, Gumboot Butte, *Hells Canyon Additions* (Buckhorn, Crazyman Creek, Homestead, Imnaha Face, Lord Flat, Snake River Corridor), Lake Fork Creek, Morgan Creek, North Cold Spring Mountain, North Fork Dry Creek, Stickney Gulch, Thomason Meadows

EXISTING WILDERNESS INCORPORATED
Hells Canyon

SIZE
313,017 acres (489 square miles, not including 131,133 acres of currently protected Wilderness)

COUNTIES
Baker, Wallowa

FEDERAL ADMINISTRATIVE UNITS
Wallowa-Whitman National Forest; BLM Vale District

CONGRESSIONAL DISTRICT
2nd

PROPOSED WILDERNESS
Hells Canyon Additions

LOCATION
2 miles east of Imnaha

LEVEL IV ECOREGIONS
Canyons and Dissected Uplands (78%),
Canyons and Dissected Highlands (22%)

VEGETATION TYPES
Ponderosa/Grasslands (56%), Douglas-
fir/Ponderosa/True Fir (29%),
Grasslands/Bunchgrass (11%), Subalpine
Lodgepole (4%), Montane Shrublands (<1%),
Ponderosa/Douglas-fir/Western
Larch/Lodgepole (<1%), Cutover/Burned
(<1%)

TERRAIN
Deeply dissected tablelands.

DRAINAGE SUBBASINS
Hells Canyon, Imnaha

ELEVATION RANGE
1,201-6,640 feet

SIZE
103,944 acres

COUNTY
Wallowa

**FEDERAL
ADMINISTRATIVE UNIT**
Wallowa-Whitman National Forest (Hells
Canyon Ranger District)

USGS 7.5' QUAD MAPS
Cactus Mountain, Deadhorse Ridge, Hat
Point, Fingerboard Saddle, Lord Flat, Sleepy
Ridge, Temperance Creek

ELLEN MORRIS BISHOP

The Lord Flat Unit of the proposed Hells Canyon Wilderness Additions.

FEATURED UNIT

Lord Flat

By Oregon standards, the Lord Flat Unit is huge. It extends from the Imnaha River on the west to Summit Ridge (the west rim of Hells Canyon) on the east, from Hat Point on the south and to the Dug Bar "road" on the north. Lord Flat is a large plateau that declines gently at first and then precipitously for over a mile in elevation. The unit features Columbia River basalt (dramatically incised by deep canyons), lush meadows, knife-edged ridges, rimrock canyons, forested benches, old-growth ponderosa pine forests, marshes, rock outcroppings and grassland slopes.

Cow, Horse and Lightning Creeks, and their tributaries, are awesome spectacles, dissecting the upland plateau and providing habitat for endangered spring and summer chinook salmon.

Rocky Mountain bighorn sheep, marten and peregrine falcon are a few of the rare species found in the unit. Rocky Mountain elk, mule deer and cougar are some of the area's other charismatic megafauna.

More than 100 miles of trails are available for horse and foot travel. The Western Rim National Recreation Trail follows Summit Ridge for over 30 miles. The Nee Mee Poo National Historic Trail is part of the route taken by Chief Joseph when he attempted to lead 400 of his people from the Wallowa Valley to Canada to escape the U.S. Army in 1877. After crossing the Snake River in spring flood (with horses, livestock, women, children and elders), fleeing 1,800 miles and engaging in 25 battles and skirmishes with up to 2,000 Army troops, the Nez Perce were finally captured within a mere 30 miles of the Canadian border in Montana.

From Jim Creek Butte in the Buckhorn Unit of the proposed Hells Canyon Wilderness Additions.

lynx, are found in the opportunity area.

The American Fisheries Society has identified several aquatic diversity areas within the proposed Wilderness, in recognition of the bull trout, redband trout, summer steelhead and spring/summer chinook salmon habitats. Pacific lamprey also spawn in the area.

Conservation biologists have identified Hells Canyon as one of the most critical areas for biodiversity in the western United States, linking the Northern Rockies with the Blue Mountains, the Cascades and Great Basin. Much of the proposed Wilderness addition along Summit Ridge is a center of concentration of species rarity and endemism for plants.

Major tree species here include ponderosa pine, subalpine fir, lodgepole pine, Engelmann spruce, Douglas-fir, western larch, grand fir, cottonwood and willow.

Over 350 species of wildlife, including 239 birds, 69 mammals and dozens of amphibians and reptiles can be found in the wildlands of Hells Canyon. Major predator species include cougar, black bear, bobcat, coyote, marten, fisher, lynx, river otter and occasionally wolf and grizzly bear.

The Hells Canyon ecosystem harbors the largest free-roaming Rocky Mountain elk herd in North America. (The Jackson Hole herd in Wyoming is human-fed.) Rocky Mountain bighorn sheep have been reintroduced, but are vulnerable to massive die-offs due to disease spread by domestic sheep that graze in the area.

Bird species of interest include both bald and golden eagles, northern goshawk, peregrine and prairie falcons, ferruginous hawk, great gray owl, western tanager, lazuli bunting, probably spruce grouse and an endemic subspecies of gray-crowned rosy finch (*Leucosticte tephrocotis wallowa*). (See the proposed *Wallowa Mountains Wilderness*, pages 204-207.) Ruffed grouse are faring well here. Spruce grouse are trying to hang on but are suffering from logging and roading. Sharp-tailed grouse are trying to come back but are hampered by livestock grazing.

Thirty at-risk plant species are found in the Hells Canyon country, including some that are found nowhere else. The botanically diverse landscape includes the legally protected (though still vulnerable to livestock grazing) Macfarlane's four-o'clock (*Mirabilis macfarlanei*) and Snake River goldenweed (*Pyrrocoma radiata*). Prickly pear cactus (*Opuntia polyacantha*) is found in the driest parts of Hells Canyon.

Recreational opportunities include river rafting, big game and upland bird hunting, fishing, birding, hiking, backpacking, horseback riding and staring down into one of the deepest gorges on earth.

Roading, logging, livestock grazing, invasive weeds and off-road vehicles threaten to defile this vast and unique natural landscape.

Proposed Malheur Basin Wilderness
Redband Trout, Old Forests and Wet Meadows

The proposed Malheur Basin Wilderness lies within the Silver Creek and Silvies River basins. Silver Creek drains into Harney Lake, while the Silvies River flows into Malheur Lake. During periods of high water, Malheur Lake subsumes Harney Lake to become Oregon's largest lake. The two basins are at the northern edge of the Great Basin, a huge expanse of the western United States that has no outlet to an ocean.[1]

The primary life zone of the proposed Wilderness is lower montane forest. At the highest elevations and on cooler north and east slopes are mixed conifer stands of Douglas-fir, western larch and grand fir. On the drier south- or west-facing slopes, ponderosa pine is the dominant species. Often lodgepole pine is also present. At middle to lower elevations, where the forest transitions to sagebrush-steppe, one finds open park-like stands of large ponderosa pine. This species is known for its distinctive orange-red (also known as "yellow-bellied"), jigsaw plate bark. The ponderosa pine understory is often bitterbrush, snowberry and/or bunchgrass. Where the pine gives way to the desert, western juniper is common. Large sagebrush prairies are also common, sometimes interspersed with wet meadows, mountain grasslands and scablands. Hardwoods such as willow, quaking aspen, black cottonwood and alder are

LEVEL IV ECOREGIONS
Continental Zone Highlands (65%), Continental Zone Foothills (28%), Cold Basins (5%), John Day/Clarno Uplands (2%); Northern Great Basin Level III Ecoregion: High Lava Plains (<1%)

VEGETATION TYPES
Ponderosa (66%), Ponderosa/Shrub (8%), Juniper/Grasslands (7%), Juniper/Mountain Big Sage (6%), Low Sagebrush (6%), Big Sagebrush (5%), Cutover/Burned (3%), Juniper/Big Sage (<1%), Juniper/Low Sage (<1%)

DRAINAGE SUBBASINS
Silvies, Silver Creek

ELEVATION RANGE
4,255-6,695 feet

UNITS
Badger Canyon, Black Rock, Bulger Creek, Calamity Butte, Chapin Table, Chickahominy Creek, Coffeepot Creek, Cow Creek, Devine Canyon, Dipping Vat Creek, Dry Mountain, Emigrant Creek, Garret Basin Spring, Gibbons Mill Canyon, Gradon Canyon, Green Butte, Hay Creek, House Creek, Hughet Valley, Johnnie Creek, King Mountain, Linda Driskil, Link Bar Spring, Lost Creek, Lower Buck Mountain, Lower Divine Canyon, Mineral Canyon, Myrtle Creek-Silvies River, Myrtle Park Meadows, Parasol Butte, Pine Spring Basin, Professor Spring, Rail Creek, Rice Spring, Sage Hen Creek, Sawtooth Creek, Scotty Creek, Sharff Cabin Creek, Silver Creek, Stancliffe Creek, Stinger Creek, Sundown Ridge, Upper Jump Creek, Upper Mill Creek, Upper Mountain Creek, West Fork Silvies River

EXISTING WILDERNESS INCORPORATED
portion of Strawberry Mountain

SIZE
143,191 acres (224 square miles, not including 1,794 acres of currently protected Wildernesses)

COUNTIES
Crook, Grant, Harney

FEDERAL ADMINISTRATIVE UNITS
Malheur and Ochoco National Forests; BLM Burns District

CONGRESSIONAL DISTRICT
2nd

Proposed Malheur Basin Wilderness

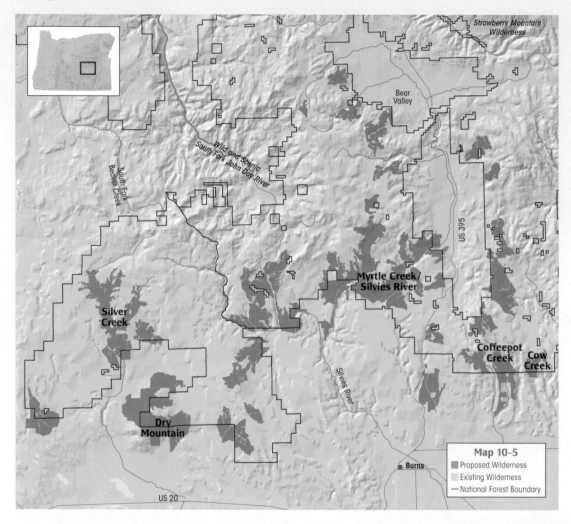

Map 10-5
- Proposed Wilderness
- Existing Wilderness
- National Forest Boundary

Some of the units in the proposed Wilderness are highlighted below.

The **Coffeepot Creek** and **Cow Creek** units support a wintering population of bald eagles. The eagles roost in old-growth ponderosa pine along the streams and hunt in the wetlands of the Malheur Lake Basin to the south.

Dry Mountain is of scientific interest for its various combinations of western juniper, big sagebrush, bitterbrush, ponderosa pine, mountain mahogany, bunchgrass, big sagebrush and bluebunch wheatgrass.

The **Myrtle Creek-Silvies River** unit is featured page 187.

Silver Creek features gently sloping plateaus dissected by steep canyons partially rimmed by rock outcrops. Eleven distinct plant communities are found in the unit, including moist meadows, various sagebrush communities, ponderosa pine and mixed conifer communities. Soda Spring is an interesting geological feature with algae growth that is greater than in other springs located throughout the Malheur National Forest. Patches of riparian vegetation in the unit are in excellent condition.

SANDY LONSDALE

The Silvies River in the Myrtle Creek-Silvies River Unit of the proposed Malheur Basin Wilderness.

FEATURED UNIT

FEATURED UNIT
Myrtle Creek-Silvies River

PROPOSED WILDERNESS
Malheur Basin

LOCATION
20 miles south-southwest of Seneca

LEVEL IV ECOREGIONS
Continental Zone Highlands (87%),
Continental Zone Foothills (13%)

VEGETATION TYPES
Ponderosa (82%), Low Sagebrush (14%),
Cutover/Burned (4%), Juniper/Grasslands
(<1%)

TERRAIN
Deep canyons.

DRAINAGE SUBBASIN
Silvies

ELEVATION RANGE
4,400-5,870 feet

SIZE
17,121 acres

COUNTIES
Grant, Harney

FEDERAL ADMINISTRATIVE UNITS
Malheur National Forest (Emigrant Creek
Ranger District); BLM Burns District (Three
Rivers Resource Area)

USGS 7.5' QUAD MAPS
Landing Creek, Mosquito Flat, Myrtle Park
Meadows, West Myrtle Butte

Myrtle Creek-Silvies River

This unit contains two 600-foot deep canyons that are approximately a mile wide at the top and 50 to 200 feet wide at the bottom. Some of the steep slopes are a series of benches, while others are smooth from top to bottom. Prominent rock outcroppings are abundant. The plateau tablelands atop the canyon rims are composed of a resistant 30- to 50-foot thick cap of welded tuff. Below the cap is a 40- to 60-foot layer of ash. Below that is a layer of hard basalt that forms ledges. And below that is another layer of welded tuff and another ash deposit. These layers are all water permeable, except the basalt. Wherever the water finally reaches an impermeable layer of basalt,

a spring forms. The remaining 400 to 500 feet of canyon wall is a series of tuffaceous layers. While geologically interesting, the unit is also very beautiful.

About seven-tenths of the unit is forested with old-growth ponderosa pine, including some specimens up to seven feet in diameter at the base. Douglas-fir and western juniper are the other prevalent tree species. Mountain mahogany is also present. Understory species include sagebrush, bunchgrass and wildflowers.

Rocky Mountain elk thrive in the area year-round. Mule deer use the unit in spring, summer and fall. Black bear and bobcat roam the forest, while Canada geese may be found along the streams. Prairie falcon and turkey vulture patrol the skies above.

Recreational opportunities here include fishing, big game hunting, picnicking and hiking. Trails are gently sloped and easy going. The Silvies River may be successfully boated at spring flood. In summer, the water levels drop and fishing or lounging along its banks are the best recreation.

BLUE MOUNTAINS ECOREGION

The Oregon Basin redband trout (*Oncorhynchus mykiss newberrii*) has strongholds in the proposed Malheur Basin Wilderness.

found in the riparian zones.

White-headed woodpecker, northern goshawk and pygmy nuthatch are common residents of the ponderosa pine forests. In the higher forests, three-toed woodpecker, snowshoe hare and golden-crowned kinglet are common. Vesper sparrow, Ord kangaroo rat and the Great Basin pocket mouse inhabit the juniper, sage and grassland plant communities. In the wetter open areas, one may see sandhill cranes, while in the open drylands, upland sandpipers may be found. Other major bird species include pileated woodpecker, black-backed woodpecker, flammulated owl and bald eagle.

Mule deer and Rocky Mountain elk are the most visible large mammals in the proposed Wilderness. Other mammals include black bear, cougar, marten, fisher, wolverine, bobcat, beaver and northern flying squirrel. Pronghorn numbers are increasing in the open sagebrush. Most of the units in the proposed Malheur Basin Wilderness are within a center of concentration of species rarity and endemism for animals.

The Oregon Biodiversity Project has identified an area of extensive wetlands located primarily on private lands as the Bear Valley Conservation Opportunity Area. Adjacent publicly owned roadless uplands in the proposed Wilderness contribute significantly to the water quality and quantity in these wetlands and to their continued function and restoration. In recognition of important redband trout habitat in the area, the American Fisheries Society has also identified several aquatic diversity areas that include portions of the proposed Wilderness.

Recreational opportunities include hunting, fishing, hiking, backpacking, horseback riding, cross-country skiing and birdwatching. On a crisp autumn afternoon, one

can doze against the sunny-side of an old-growth western larch that is just beginning to turn golden above the drying grass, while listening to the sound of rustling quaking aspen leaves. Some canoeing or kayaking is also possible during spring high water on certain streams.

Threats to the proposed Wilderness include logging, road building, livestock grazing and off-road vehicles.

Proposed Malheur Canyons Wilderness
Stunning Rimrock Canyons, Larch and Pine Forests and Trout-Filled Streams

The proposed Malheur Canyons Wilderness contains numerous springs, streams and river segments. Several streams rise on the slopes of the Strawberry Mountain Range and flow south to meet in the Logan Valley where they form the Malheur River. East of the Strawberries, the North Fork of the Malheur River forms and flows southward. After leaving the national forest, the North Fork is joined by the Little Malheur River, which begins in the Monument Rock Wilderness. The North Fork itself joins the mainstem Malheur at Juntura in the Oregon Desert (that has already been joined by the South Fork, which rises in the Sagebrush Sea), which eventually empties into the Snake River. Segments of the mainstem and North Fork Malheur rivers are units of the National Wild and Scenic Rivers System.

The Malheur River Basin ranges from high mountain peaks to high desert, from high-elevation Engelmann spruce and subalpine fir forests, to mid-elevation pine and larch forests, to low-elevation desert scrub. The wildest parts of the basin tend to be those lands with steep canyons. An additional 328,000 acres of the proposed Malheur Canyons Wilderness is within Oregon's portion of the Sagebrush Sea.[2]

Forest species include Engelmann spruce, subalpine fir, Douglas-fir, grand fir, western larch, ponderosa pine, lodgepole pine, western juniper, mountain mahogany, black cottonwood, quaking aspen and alder. Understory species include grouse or big huckleberry, currant bitterbrush, bunchgrass and sagebrush. Major bird species here include American pipit, white-crowned sparrow, Clark's nutcracker, Lincoln's sparrow, three-toed woodpecker, golden-crowned kinglet, pygmy nuthatch, white-headed woodpecker, vesper sparrow, osprey, golden eagle and bald eagle.

Major wildlife species here include Rocky Mountain elk, mule deer, pronghorn,

◀ Old-growth ponderosa pine (*Pinus ponderosa*) in the Silver Creek Unit of the proposed Malheur Basin Wilderness.

Proposed Malheur Canyons Wilderness

LEVEL IV ECOREGIONS
Continental Zone Highlands (41%), Continental Zone Foothills (40%), Mesic Forest Zone (14%), Subalpine-Alpine Zone (2%), Melange (2%), Cold Basins (<1%); Northern Great Basin Level III Ecoregion: High Lava Plains (<1%)

VEGETATION TYPES
Ponderosa (44%), Juniper/Grasslands (12%), True Fir/Douglas-fir (9%), Ponderosa/Douglas-fir/True Fir (7%), Ponderosa/Douglas-fir/Western Larch/Lodgepole (6%), Ponderosa/Shrub (4%), Low Sagebrush (4%), Subalpine Fir/Engelmann Spruce Parklands (3%), Big Sagebrush (2%), Cutover/Burned (2%), Juniper/Low Sage (2%), Lodgepole/Western Larch (2%), Marsh/Wet Meadow (1%), Other Sagebrush (1%), Subalpine Lodgepole (<1%), Juniper/Big Sage (<1%)

DRAINAGE SUBBASINS
Burnt, Upper Malheur, Willow

ELEVATION RANGE
3,629-8,032 feet

UNITS
Black Butte, Calamity Creek, Cottonwood Creek, Craft Point, Deardorff Creek, Deardorff Mountain, Duck Creek Headwaters, Elbow Canyon, Flag Creek, Gabe Spring, Glacier Mountain, Goodwater Spring, Gunbarrel Creek, Huckleberry Creek, Last Chance Creek, Little Bear Meadow, Little Muddy Creek, Logan Valley, Long Creek, Magpie Table, Malheur River Canyon, Middle Willow, *Monument Rock Additions* (Bullrun Creek, Camp Creek, Elk Flat, Little Malheur River, Lookout Spring), North Fork Malheur River, Pine Creek, Ragged Rock Spring, Reynolds Creek, Sheep Gulch, Schurtz Creek, Skull Springs, Spring Creek, *Strawberry Mountain Additions* (Meadow Fork), Summit Rock, Upper Blue Bucket Creek, Upper Malheur River, Van Gulch

EXISTING WILDERNESSES INCORPORATED
Monument Rock, portion of Strawberry Mountain

SIZE
168,442 acres (263 square miles, not including 19,686 acres of currently protected Wildernesses)

COUNTIES
Baker, Grant, Harney, Malheur

FEDERAL ADMINISTRATIVE UNITS
Malheur and Wallowa-Whitman National Forests; BLM Burns, Prineville and Vale Districts

CONGRESSIONAL DISTRICT
2nd

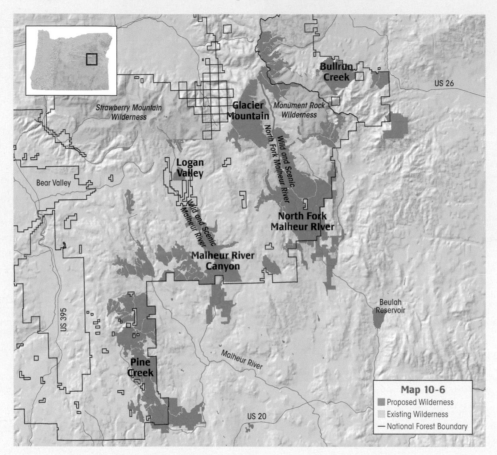

Map 10-6
- Proposed Wilderness
- Existing Wilderness
- National Forest Boundary

Some of the units in the proposed Wilderness are highlighted below.

Bullrun Creek and the adjacent Bullrun Mountain (part of the Burnt River Basin) should have been included in the Monument Rock Wilderness when it was designated in 1984. However, the low elevation old-growth forest here sits atop mineral deposits that were coveted by mining companies at the time.

Glacier Mountain has no glaciers now, but once did. Streams rising in the unit support redband and bull trout. In the alpine zone, one logically finds the alpine fleeceflower, alpine Idaho fescue, alpine big sagebrush and alpine sedge.

Logan Valley is part of a large montane wetland/wet meadow/upland habitat that features wildflowers in the spring and orange-yellow quaking aspen in the fall. It is one of four known nesting sites for long-billed curlew and upland sandpiper in Oregon. Bull trout and sandhill cranes are also present. Approximately 1,768 acres of the private land in Logan Valley was recently acquired for the Burns Paiute Tribe, which is restoring the area for ecological purposes.

Malheur River Canyon features outstanding trout fishing, virgin ponderosa pine forests and a 1,000-foot deep canyon. A segment of the Malheur River that flows through the unit is part of the National Wild and Scenic Rivers System.

The **North Fork Malheur River** is featured on page 191.

Pine Creek is a tableland with deeply incised canyons and slopes covered with ponderosa and mixed-conifer forests and native fish in the streams.

FEATURED UNIT

North Fork Malheur River

The North Fork Malheur River unit — from Elk Creek in the north to the North Fork's confluence with the Little Malheur River in the south and from Crane Creek in the west to Bear Creek in the east — includes both dense forest and open desert.

Huge old-growth ponderosa pines line the dry canyon bottoms that range in depth from 250 to 800 feet. The North Fork has cut through numerous layers of volcanic material, exposing rock outcroppings, talus and cliffs. Adjacent to the deep canyons are tablelands featuring a mosaic of conifer forest, quaking aspen, sagebrush and meadows. Western juniper and mountain mahogany become more prevalent as the land slopes southward and downward.

The river's exceptional water quality supports both endangered bull trout and declining redband trout. The entire length of the river within the proposed Wilderness unit is a component of the National Wild and Scenic Rivers System. However, the Wild and Scenic River management zone is far too narrow to adequately protect the surrounding wildness of the unit.

Big game hunting for Rocky Mountain elk and mule deer are major recreational activities. Fishing is also popular here. The twelve-mile North Fork Malheur River trail makes for easy access to the deep canyon. As one hikes the trail, the cry of osprey may often be heard above one's head and over the sounds of the river.

The North Fork Malheur River Unit of the proposed Malheur Canyons Wilderness.

PROPOSED WILDERNESS
Malheur Canyons

LOCATION
19 miles south-southwest of Unity

LEVEL IV ECOREGIONS
Continental Zone Foothills (60%), Continental Zone Highlands (40%)

VEGETATION TYPES
Juniper/Grasslands (49%), Ponderosa (48%), Low Sagebrush (3%)

TERRAIN
Tablelands dissected by canyons.

DRAINAGE SUBBASIN
Upper Malheur

ELEVATION RANGE
3,629-5,801 feet

SIZE
24,615 acres

COUNTIES
Baker, Grant

FEDERAL ADMINISTRATIVE UNITS
Malheur National Forest (Prairie City Ranger District); BLM Vale District (Malheur Resource Area)

USGS 7.5' QUAD MAPS
Castle Rock, Crane Prairie, Clevenger Butte, Flag Prairie

black bear and cougar. Some more enigmatic creatures include heather vole, pika, marten, snowshoe hare, Great Basin pocket mouse and Ord kangaroo rat.

Several dams currently block salmon from returning to the Malheur River Basin to spawn. However, in recognition of important populations of bull trout and redband trout, the American Fisheries Society has identified several aquatic diversity areas within the proposed Wilderness. These aquatic areas could again be prime salmon habitat if the dams were modified or removed.

The Oregon Biodiversity Project's Malheur River Conservation Opportunity Area includes three priority habitats in the area: ponderosa pine woodlands, grand fir forests and extensive mid-elevation wetlands.

Recreational opportunities include hunting, fishing, hiking, backpacking, cross-country skiing, horseback riding and dozing at the base of an old-growth ponderosa pine on a hot summer day.

Major threats to the proposed Wilderness include logging, road building, livestock grazing and off-road vehicles.

Proposed North Fork John Day-Elkhorns Wilderness

Rocky Mountain Elk, Salmon, Steelhead, Granite Ridges, Ponderosa Pine and Western Larch

The proposed North Fork John Day-Elkhorns Wilderness includes wildlands in the Burnt, Powder, North Fork and Middle Fork John Day (a tributary to the North Fork John Day) basins. Dams now block salmon runs in the Burnt and Powder rivers, but the John Day tributaries remain strongholds of anadromous fish populations. The proposed Wilderness includes the municipal drinking water supplies for Baker City and Long Creek.

Granite outcroppings, rolling benches, tablelands, deep canyons, alpine lakes, dark fir forests and open pine forests all characterize the area.

Major wildlife species here include Rocky Mountain elk, mule deer, black bear, cougar, coyote, bobcat, wolverine, mink, beaver, marten and possibly lynx. Major bird species include pileated woodpecker, northern goshawk, great gray owl, Clark's nutcracker, Lincoln's sparrow, white-crowned sparrow, golden-crowned kinglet, white-headed woodpecker, pygmy nuthatch and bald eagle. The Middle John Day River is the center of a concentration of species rarity and endemism for animals. Of particular note

◄ The Spring Creek Unit of the proposed Malheur Canyons Wilderness.

Proposed North Fork John Day-Elkhorns Wilderness

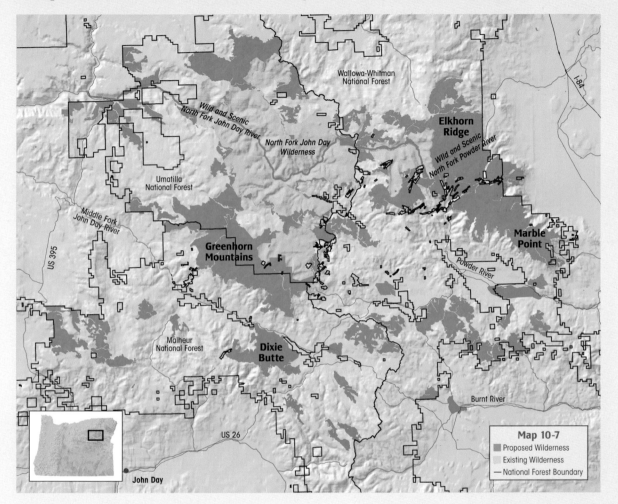

Map 10-7
- Proposed Wilderness
- Existing Wilderness
— National Forest Boundary

Some of the units of the proposed Wilderness are highlighted below.

Dixie Butte is the featured unit for the proposed Upper John Day Wilderness (see pages 201-204).

The **Elkhorn Ridge** is featured on page 194.

The **Greenhorn Mountains** units include a diverse landscape of glacially carved granite and Columbia basalt outcroppings surrounded by alpine and upland meadows, spruce bogs, cliffs and forests. They include Vinegar Hill, Indian Rock, Jumpoff Joe Peak and other landmarks along the divide between the North and Middle Forks of the John Day River. Views of the surrounding landscapes are spectacular.

Pine grosbeak and three-toed woodpecker can be found in this unique habitat. The area is suitable for the reintroduction of peregrine falcon. Most of the alpine flower types that grow west of the Rockies are found here.

Marble Point is located on the southern end of the Elkhorn Range and includes part of the watershed for Baker City. The water is so pure and the watershed so pristine that no filtering is required before the water is piped to the taps of over 10,000 Baker City residents. The municipal watershed is closed to public entry except during hunting season.

LEVEL IV ECOREGIONS
Mesic Forest Zone (47%), Melange (21%), Subalpine-Alpine Zone (19%), John Day/Clarno Highlands (12%), Cold Basins (<1%), Maritime-Influenced Zone (<1%), John Day/Clarno Uplands (<1%), Continental Zone Foothills (<1%)

VEGETATION TYPES
Ponderosa (44%), Juniper/Grasslands (12%), True Fir/Douglas-fir (9%), Ponderosa/Douglas-fir/True Fir (7%), Ponderosa/Douglas-fir/Western Larch/Lodgepole (6%), Low Sagebrush (4%), Ponderosa/Shrub (4%), Subalpine Fir/Engelmann Spruce Parklands (3%), Big Sagebrush (2%), Cutover/Burned (2%), Juniper/Low Sage (2%), Lodgepole/Western Larch (2%), Marsh/Wet Meadow (1%), Other Sagebrush (1%), Subalpine Lodgepole (<1%), Juniper/Big Sage (<1%)

DRAINAGE SUBBASINS
North Fork John Day, Middle Fork John Day, Powder

ELEVATION RANGE
2,979-9,106 feet

UNITS
Antone Creek, Arch Rock, Battle Creek, Bear Butte, Bear Wallow Springs, Beaver Dam Creek, Big Creek, Big Springs, Black Mountain, Bone Point, Bridge Creek, Case Ridge, China Creek, Clear Creek, Cornet Creek, Crawford Creek, Czar Springs, Davis Creek, Dean Creek, Deep Canyon, Desolation Creek, Dixie Butte, Fly Creek, Forks of Cable Creek-Hidaway Meadows, Fox Creek, *Greenhorn Mountain Unit Additions* (Greenhorn Mountains), Hinton Creek, Horse Canyon, Hunt Mountain, Idaho Creek, Indian Creek, Jumpoff Joe Peak, Keeney Meadows, Lamb Creek, Long Creek Municipal Watershed, Long Meadow, Lost Boy, Lunch Creek, Marble Point, *Middle North Fork John Day River Unit Additions* (Granite Creek Headwaters, Howard Creek, Martin Creek, Moon Meadow, Rabbit Creek Headwaters, Silver Butte, Upper North Fork John Day River), Mud Spring, Mulkey Springs, Nipple Butte, Pasture Creek, Patrick Creek, Pogue Mountain, Pole Bridge Creek, Resiliency Butte, Rock Creek Butte, Skinner Creek, South Fork Long Creek, Stices Creek, Thompson Gulch, Tope Spring, Trail Creek, Trout Creek, Twisted Rush, Upper China Creek, Upper Frosty Gulch, *Upper North Fork John Day River Unit Additions* (Cabell Meadow, Elkhorn Ridge, South Mount Ireland, South Columbia Hill), White Pine Knob

EXISTING WILDERNESS INCORPORATED
North Fork John Day

SIZE
283,474 acres (443 square miles, not including 121,352 acres of currently protected Wilderness

COUNTIES
Baker, Grant, Umatilla, Union

FEDERAL ADMINISTRATIVE UNITS
Malheur, Umatilla, Wallowa-Whitman National Forests; BLM Prineville and Vale Districts

CONGRESSIONAL DISTRICT
2nd

PROPOSED WILDERNESS
North Fork John Day-Elkhorns

LOCATION
8 miles west of Baker City

LEVEL IV ECOREGIONS
Subalpine-Alpine Zone (57%), Mesic Forest Zone (37%), Melange (7%)

VEGETATION TYPES
Subalpine Fir/Engelmann Spruce Parklands (39%), Ponderosa/Douglas-fir/True Fir (24%), Lodgepole/True Fir (16%), Western Larch/Douglas-fir/Ponderosa/Lodgepole (9%), Douglas-fir/ Ponderosa/True Fir (7%), Alpine Barren Fell Fields (3%), True Fir/Lodgepole/Western Larch/Douglas-fir (2%), Ponderosa (1%)

TERRAIN
Rugged granite and basalt.

DRAINAGE SUBBASINS
North Fork John Day, Powder

ELEVATION RANGE
4,734-9,106 feet

SIZE
51,569 acres

COUNTIES
Baker, Grant

FEDERAL ADMINISTRATIVE UNITS
Wallowa-Whitman National Forest (Baker Ranger District); BLM Vale District (Baker Resource Area)

USGS 7.5' QUAD MAPS
Anthony Lakes, Bourne, Elkhorn Peak, Rock Creek

The Elkhorns Unit of the proposed North Fork John Day-Elkhorns Wilderness.

FEATURED UNIT

Elkhorn Ridge

While cartographers and others differ as to whether the Elkhorns should be called a "ridge," "mountains" or a "range," there is no dispute that this formation of craggy peaks is the centerpiece of the proposed North Fork John Day-Elkhorn Wilderness. The highly scenic range of granite peaks runs northwest to southeast and includes the headwaters of the North Fork John Day, Grande Ronde (see *proposed Grande Ronde Wilderness*, pages 179-182) and Powder rivers.

The second largest geologic batholith in Oregon, the Elkhorns were carved by glaciers, leaving beautiful cirques and valleys. As the glaciers receded, the range remained high enough to support communities of whitebark pine. Elkhorn Ridge is a center of concentration of species rarity and endemism for plants.

Rocky Mountain elk can often be seen in the Elkhorns. Even if one doesn't see them, one may hear them bugling in autumn. Mountain goats, while highly charismatic megafauna, are nonetheless alien exotics to the range, having been transplanted decades ago. Even though mountain goats ranged the Elkhorns prior to the last ice age, they have not been native to the range since then.

Panoramic views of much of northeastern Oregon, from the Wallowa Mountains to the Strawberry Mountains, are visible from most sections of the Elkhorns crest. The 23-mile long Elkhorn Crest National Recreational Trail is the best way to enjoy the unit. Several other trails follow the area's rivers and creeks up to high alpine lakes.

Recreational opportunities include hunting, fishing, hiking, backpacking, horseback riding, cross-country skiing and sightseeing.

is an endemic subspecies of gray-crowned rosy finch that lives here (*Leucosticte tephrocotis wallowa*). (See the proposed *Wallowa Mountains Wilderness*, pages 204-207.)

The higher forests (above 6,000 feet in elevation) are dominated by lodgepole pine, subalpine fir and whitebark pine, interspersed with open slopes, low shrublands and rockslides. Below 6,000 feet, major tree species include western larch, Douglas-fir, grand fir, lodgepole pine, ponderosa pine and Engelmann spruce. Huckleberry is a common understory species. Riparian species include willow, quaking aspen, black cottonwood and alder. Fire is an active sculptor of this landscape.

Segments of the North Fork of the John Day and North Fork of the Powder River are units of the National Wild and Scenic Rivers System. However, the narrow protective corridors are not adequate to fully protect the adjacent wildlands.

Recognizing the critical importance of bull trout, redband trout, summer steelhead and spring chinook salmon habitat in the area, the American Fisheries Society has identified several aquatic diversity areas within the proposed Wilderness. Pacific lamprey also spawn in the North Fork John Day River. The North Fork John Day watershed now supports 70 percent of the total spring chinook and 43 percent of the summer steelhead runs in the John Day basin, the largest wild runs of these types left in the Columbia River system.

Hundreds of miles of hiking trails crisscross the proposed Wilderness. Hiking, camping, horseback riding, backpacking, hunting, cross-country skiing, fishing, birding, nature study, wildflower viewing and salmon watching are popular pursuits.

Major threats to the proposed Wilderness are logging, livestock grazing, mining and off-road vehicle use.

Proposed Ochoco Mountains Wilderness
Old Forests, Green Meadows and Wild Rivers

The Ochoco Mountains are a string of volcanoes, much older than those in the nearby High Cascades to the west. From near Prineville to near Dayville, the range runs 60 miles east-west. Much of the landscape has been roaded and logged, but a remarkable variety of wildlands still exists. The proposed Ochoco Mountains Wilderness contains "yellow-bellied" old-growth ponderosa pine (often more than 400 years old), thick mixed-conifer forests, high mountain sagebrush meadows full of wildflowers, lava flows, dry and wet meadows, cliffs, colorful rock outcroppings of welded tuff and small streams with native trout.

◄ Dutch Flat Lake in the Elkhorns Unit of the proposed North Fork John Day-Elkhorns Wilderness.

Proposed Ochoco Mountains Wilderness

LEVEL IV ECOREGIONS
John Day/Clarno Highlands (69%), John Day/Clarno Uplands (21%), Mesic Forest Zone (9%), Cold Basins (1%)

VEGETATION TYPES
Ponderosa (49%), Ponderosa/Douglas-fir/True Fir (19%), Big Sage (15%), Cutover/Burned (5%), Juniper/Mountain Low Sagebrush (4%), Juniper/Grasslands (4%), Ponderosa/Douglas-fir/Western Larch/Lodgepole (3%), Juniper/Big Sage (1%), Juniper/Low Sage (<1%), Marsh/Wet Meadow (<1%), True Fir/Douglas-fir (<1%) Big Sagebrush (<1%)

DRAINAGE SUBBASINS
Lower Crooked, Lower John Day, South Fork Crooked, Trout, Upper Crooked

ELEVATION RANGE
3,199-6,929 feet

UNITS
Ashley Ridge, Badger Creek, Begg Creek, Bellworm Canyon, *Bridge Creek Additions* (East Point, Maxwell Creek), Broadway Lava, Bull Mountain, Cottonwood Creek, Cougar Creek, Deer Creek, Dingus Springs, Dodds Creek, Dutchman Flat, Grassy Butte, Green Mountain, Hammer Creek, Hardscrabble Ridge, Hickey Creek, Indian Creek, Little Round Prairie, Lookout Mountain, *Mill Creek Additions* (Fintcher Creek, Wildcat Creek Headwaters), Mount Pisgah, North Bear Creek, North Fork Crooked River, Ochoco Divide, Peterson Lava, Rough Canyon, Round Mountain, Salt Butte, Steins Pillar, Tamarack Creek, Williams Prairie, Zany Fox

EXISTING WILDERNESSES INCORPORATED
Bridge Creek, Mill Creek

SIZE
110,192 acres (172 square miles, not including 22,800 acres of currently protected Wilderness)

COUNTIES
Crook, Grant, Wheeler

FEDERAL ADMINISTRATIVE UNITS
Ochoco National Forest; BLM Prineville District

CONGRESSIONAL DISTRICT
2nd

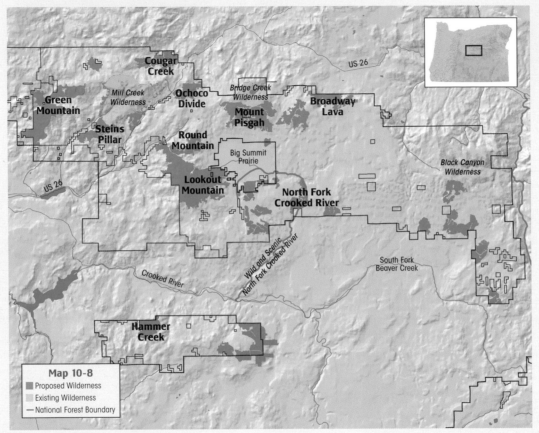

Map 10-8
- Proposed Wilderness
- Existing Wilderness
- National Forest Boundary

Lookout Mountain is featured on page 196.

Ochoco Divide is recognized for its Douglas-fir/pine-grass community.

The **Mill Creek Additions** units include wildlands directly adjacent to the Mill Creek Wilderness. These lands are primarily old-growth forests left out of previous Wilderness designations because the timber industry coveted them for logging.

Mount Pisgah features the highly scenic Indian Prairie dotted with wild flowers, quaking aspen, old-growth ponderosa pine and western larch. From the summit are spectacular views north to the John Day River country.

North Fork Crooked River flows through a high scenic canyon with rimrock cliffs, old-growth ponderosa pine forest and excellent trout fishing. A narrow strip on both sides the river (but not the entire canyon) is designated under the National Wild and Scenic Rivers System. The lower (Bureau of Land Management) portion of the unit lies in the Sagebrush Sea and is proposed as the Crooked River Wilderness of nearly 137,000 acres.[3]

Round Mountain offers scenic views to the north and is a wildlife corridor between Lookout Mountain and the main Ochoco Mountain divide.

Steins Pillar is a spectacular 200-foot high rock monolith that is wider at the top than at the base and towers above the surrounding forest.

Some of the units in the proposed Wilderness are highlighted below.

Broadway Lava contains one of the few visible lava flows in the forest. Since the lava flows in this area are relatively old geologically, most are covered by vegetation and mixed conifer forest.

Cougar Creek offers mountain meadows and many scenic vistas in a variety of forest types.

Green Mountain is excellent mule deer and Rocky Mountain elk range, has prominent, colorful, rock pillars and harbors the elusive wolverine.

Hammer Creek contains the largest remaining stands of unlogged forest in the Maury Mountains, a small east-west mountain range to the south of the Ochoco Mountains and an island in the desert Sagebrush Sea.

Old-growth ponderosa pine (*Pinus ponderosa*) in the Lookout Mountain Unit of the proposed Ochoco Mountains Wilderness.

LARRY N. OLSON

FEATURED UNIT

Lookout Mountain

Lookout Mountain stands out from the surrounding forested landscape because of its mountaintop meadows. The mountain is outstanding as the most ecologically diverse landscape with the largest intact old-growth forest on the Ochoco National Forest. It includes nearly all the ecological zones found in the larger proposed Wilderness and at least 28 distinct plant communities in a variety of successional stages.

Nearly two-thirds of the area is old-growth forest. Scenic meadows are found both at the lower elevations and on the mountain's summit. The unit contains one of the finest remaining park-like ponderosa pine forests left in the state and it is remarkably easy to enjoy. After hiking upward through the forest, one is rewarded at the summit with outstanding views of the Cascades from Diamond Peak to Mount Hood.

Notable wildlife species here include black bear, bobcat, ruffed grouse, marten, badger, wolverine, pronghorn, a variety of hawk species, pileated woodpecker and the occasional bald or golden eagle.

Dry and wet meadows exist here, both with tufted hair grass. The moist meadows contain ovalhead sedge and California catgrass. At lower elevations, plant communities include bluegrass scabland, bunchgrass, stiff sagebrush scabland and low sagebrush-bunchgrass. Western juniper woodlands are found in distinct association with bunchgrass, stiff sage, low sagebrush and big sagebrush.

The magnificent ponderosa pine forests are found in distinct associations with wheatgrass, fescue, bitterbrush, Ross sedge, blue wildrye and Douglas-fir-snowberry-oceanspray. As elevation increases, mixed conifer forests of ponderosa pine, grand fir, western larch and Douglas-fir are found in association with pine-grass on both ash and residual soils. The forests are found in association with grouse huckleberry, twinflower and/or Columbia brome. Even higher up, the forest becomes lodgepole pine, Engelmann spruce and subalpine fir, with grouse huckleberry and pine-grass in the understory. Near timberline, subalpine fir and Engelmann spruce dominate with a grouse huckleberry or big huckleberry understory. Groves of quaking aspen are found at various elevations. On the mountain's top are meadows of sagebrush, sedge and yarrow surrounding rock outcroppings.

A well-developed network of trails, including a seven-mile trail from the ranger station to the summit, provides easy access.

Trophy-sized mule deer and Rocky Mountain elk inhabit Lookout Mountain. Redband trout are found in the streams, making for great fishing. Other recreational opportunities include hiking, backpacking, cross-country skiing, snowshoeing, horseback riding and birding.

PROPOSED WILDERNESS
Ochoco Mountains

LOCATION
14 miles north-northwest of Post

LEVEL IV ECOREGION
John Day/Clarno Highlands

VEGETATION TYPES
Ponderosa/Douglas-Fir/True Fir (54%), Cutover/Burned (8%), Big Sagebrush (<1%)

TERRAIN
Gentle slopes, then rising steeply to a gentle broad summit.

DRAINAGE SUBBASINS
Lower Crooked, Upper Crooked

ELEVATION RANGE
3,199-6,929 feet

SIZE
19,220 acres

COUNTY
Crook

FEDERAL ADMINISTRATIVE UNITS
Ochoco National Forest (Lookout Mountain Ranger District); BLM Prineville District (Central Oregon Resource Area)

USGS 7.5' QUAD MAPS
Gerow Butte, Lookout Mountain, Whistler Point

Mixed conifer forests of predominantly ponderosa pine, Douglas-fir, grand fir and western larch dominate much of the landscape. Pure stands of park-like old-growth ponderosa pine occupy lower elevation south- and west-facing slopes. At higher elevations, major tree species include lodgepole pine, Engelmann spruce and subalpine fir. Stands of quaking aspen dot the forest. Western juniper is found both at the lowest elevations and at over 5,000 feet elevation, where it grows tall and thin, resembling fir trees. In the open prairies, you'll find blue-flag iris, Indian paintbrush, camas and various sunflower species.

The old-growth forest in the proposed Wilderness is critical habitat for several species including marten, pileated woodpecker and white-headed woodpecker. Both bald and golden eagles are present. Predators include black bear, cougar and coyote. Mule deer and Rocky Mountain elk are abundant, attracting hunters in the fall.

Summer steelhead spawn in the tributaries of the John Day River and native redband trout are found in numerous streams in the proposed Wilderness.

Recreational opportunities here include hunting, fishing, birding, hiking, backpacking, snowshoeing, cross-country skiing, horseback riding and just strolling through open old-growth forests.

Unfortunately, much of the remaining wildlands in the proposed Wilderness is slated for roading and logging. Other threats include livestock grazing and mining.

Proposed South Fork John Day Wilderness
California Bighorn Sheep, Pacific Salmon and Unique Wildflowers

In spite of the road that runs nearly its entire length, the South Fork of the John Day River — from where it begins in the Malheur National Forest to its confluence with the mainstem John Day River at Dayville — remains an ecological treasure. Much of the South Fork is included in both the Oregon Scenic Waterways and National Wild and Scenic Rivers Systems in recognition of its outstanding scenery, fisheries, hunting, hiking and camping. The high quality and quantity of these and other natural values in the watershed depend upon the associated wildlands upslope.

The Oregon Biodiversity Project has identified the South Fork John Day River Conservation Opportunity Area because the region is a center of concentration of species rarity and endemism for plants. The South Fork watershed includes eight aquatic diversity areas recognized by the American Fisheries Society for their important habitat for spring chinook salmon, summer steelhead, redband trout and Pacific

◄ The North Fork Crooked River Unit of the proposed Ochoco Mountains Wilderness.

Proposed South Fork John Day Wilderness

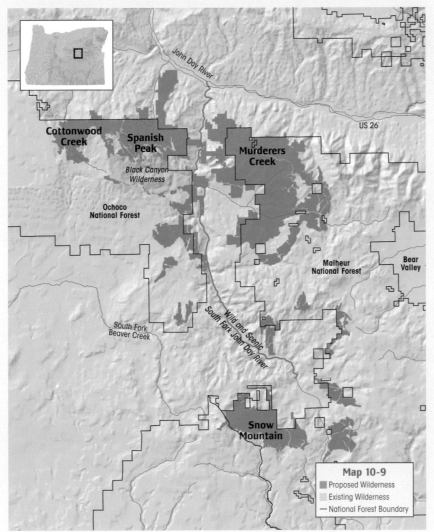

Map 10-9
- Proposed Wilderness
- Existing Wilderness
- National Forest Boundary

Some of the units in the proposed Wilderness are highlighted below.

Steelhead spawn in **Cottonwood Creek**.

Murderers Creek is featured on page 200.

Spanish Peak is immediately north of the Black Canyon Wilderness and contains a variety of conifer species. Wolverine and lynx are believed to inhabit the unit.

Snow Mountain, which features the highest elevation lands in the proposed Wilderness, is year-round elk habitat and spring, summer and fall range for mule deer. Mountain mahogany can be found under ponderosa pine and near western juniper on primarily south-facing slopes. Alder, willow and some mountain ash can be found along the streams.

LEVEL IV ECOREGIONS
John Day/Clarno Uplands (27%), Continental Zone Highlands (22%), John Day/Clarno Highlands (22%), Melange (17%), Mesic Forest Zone (10%), Continental Zone Foothills (2%)

VEGETATION TYPES
Ponderosa (49%), Ponderosa/Douglas-fir/True Fir (13%), True Fir/Douglas-fir (11%), Ponderosa/Shrub (9%), Low Sagebrush (9%), Big Sage (3%), Other Sagebrush (2%), Juniper/Low Sage (2%), Cutover/Burned (1%), Douglas-fir/Ponderosa/True Fir (<1%), Juniper/Big Sage (<1%), Juniper/Grasslands (<1%), Juniper/Mountain Marsh/Wet Meadow (<1%), Ponderosa/Douglas-fir/Western Larch/Lodgepole (<1%), Big Sage/Shrub (<1%), Big Sagebrush (<1%)

DRAINAGE SUBBASINS
South Fork John Day

ELEVATION RANGE
2,390-7,190 feet

UNITS
Antelope Creek, Ashley Ridge, Bear Tree Springs, Begg Creek, *Black Canyon Additions* (Bear Skull-Kelsey Spring, Cottonwood Creek, Wolf Mountain), Blue Ridge Spring, Burnt Mountain, Cougar Creek, Cougar Mountain, Devils Creek, Gilbert Ridge, Hardscrabble Ridge, Horse Mountain, Johnnie Creek, Lewis Officer Creek, Lower Murderers Creek, Murderers Creek, Sharff Cabin Creek, Snow Mountain, South Fork Deer Creek, Spanish Peak, Upper Murderers Creek, Venator Creek, Wildcat Gulch, Wind Creek

EXISTING WILDERNESS INCORPORATED
Black Canyon

SIZE
134,880 acres (211 square miles, not including 13,400 acres of currently protected Wilderness)

COUNTIES
Harney, Grant, Wheeler

FEDERAL ADMINISTRATIVE UNITS
Malheur and Ochoco National Forests; BLM Burns and Prineville Districts

CONGRESSIONAL DISTRICT
2nd

SANDY LONSDALE

PROPOSED WILDERNESS
South Fork John Day

LOCATION
10 miles south-southwest of Dayville

LEVEL IV ECOREGION
John Day/Clarno Highlands (39%), Melange (39%), Mesic Forest Zone (15%), Continental Zone Highlands (7%)

VEGETATION TYPES
Ponderosa (49%), True Fir/Douglas-fir (21%), Low Sagebrush (13%), Juniper/Mountain Big Sage (7%), Ponderosa/Douglas-fir/True Fir (5%), Juniper/Low Sage (3%), Big Sage/Shrub (<1%), Douglas-fir/Ponderosa/True Fir (<1%), Juniper/Grasslands (<1%)

TERRAIN
Generally steep and broken terrain.

DRAINAGE SUBBASIN
Upper John Day

ELEVATION RANGE
2,720-6,991 feet

SIZE
51,503 acres

COUNTY
Grant

FEDERAL ADMINISTRATIVE UNITS
Malheur National Forest (Blue Mountain Ranger District); BLM Prineville District (Central Oregon Resource Area)

USGS 7.5' QUAD MAPS
Aldrich Mountain North, Aldrich Mountain South, Big Weasel Springs

The Murderers Creek Unit of the proposed South Fork John Day Wilderness.

FEATURED UNIT

Murderers Creek

Murderers Creek is one of the most productive areas for wildlife in eastern Oregon. California bighorn sheep, mule deer and Rocky Mountain elk comprise the major big game species in the watershed. Cougar and black bear are also abundant.

Steelhead spawn and native redband trout live in the creek and its major tributaries: Cow, Cabin, Bark Cabin and Thorn Creeks. Murderers Creek's cool, clean water contributes significantly to the water quality and volume in the South Fork John Day River, which is especially important for salmon.

The lower portion of the Murderers Creek watershed is managed by the Oregon Department of Fish and Wildlife as the Phillip W. Schneider Wildlife Management Area. The upper portion of the watershed is Forest Service and Bureau of Land Management lands.

The roadless portions of the watershed are mostly forested with old-growth ponderosa pine and various fir species at the middle and higher elevations, sagebrush steppe at the lower elevations and western juniper in the transition zones. The varied elevations and diversity of vegetation support a diversity of wildlife species.

Scientists have recognized the importance of some natural combinations of vegetation found in the watershed's unforested areas. Among these are western juniper, low sagebrush, bunchgrass, Idaho fescue, sagebrush, Sandberg's bluegrass scabland and bitterbrush.

The unit contains a rare stand of Alaska yellow cedar, far disjunct from the rest of the species' range that generally occurs only in cold wet areas of the central Oregon Cascades and northward.

The steep and broken terrain is incredibly scenic. Big game hunting, fishing, hiking, horseback riding, game bird hunting and sightseeing are favorite recreational pursuits. Over 45 miles of trails lace the unit. A hiking trail has been proposed that would traverse the unit to connect the Pacific Crest National Scenic Trail along the Cascade Crest with the Desert Trail to the east (which is also under development).

As the name implies, the South Fork John Day milk-vetch (*Astragalus diaphanus* var. *diurnus*) is endemic to that watershed.

lamprey. Many of these areas lie within the proposed Wilderness.

The proposed South Fork John Day Wilderness spans both forest and desert, but the dividing line between these two different landscapes is not always clear. For example, desert-loving California (not Rocky Mountain) bighorn sheep are found in the area, even in the generally forested landscapes. Only the forested portion of the proposed Wilderness is discussed here. However, the proposed South Fork John Day Wilderness also includes nearly 77,000 additional acres of generally tree-free-wildlands within its borders to protect associated desert lands.[4]

Major tree species in the proposed Wilderness include ponderosa pine, western larch, Douglas-fir, grand fir and lodgepole pine. Understory vegetation can include huckleberry, pine-grass and Columbia brome. Subalpine fir, along with alpine sage, is found at the highest elevations. The drier slopes are covered with western juniper, sagebrush, mountain mahogany and some scattered ponderosa pine. Understory species include wheatgrass, fescue and bluegrass.

The signature big game animal here is California bighorn sheep. Rocky Mountain elk and mule deer are also quite abundant in the area, as are the cougar that prey upon them. Other mammals of note include black bear, wolverine, lynx, pronghorn, flying squirrel, vole, marmot and chipmunk.

Major bird species include pileated woodpecker, Lewis' woodpecker, northern goshawk, blue grouse, mountain quail, bald eagle and golden eagle.

The spotted bat, perhaps America's — and certainly Oregon's — rarest mammal, is found in the area. The western toad and Columbia spotted frog are local at-risk

amphibian species.

A unique plant species here is the South Fork John Day milk-vetch (*Astragalus diaphanus* var. *diurnus*) that occurs only in riparian and loose-soil exposed habitats.

The area is very scenic, with park-like stands of forest in a mosaic of shrub, grass and rock habitats. Recreational opportunities include big game and game bird hunting, fishing, hiking, backpacking and horseback riding. The most crowded time of the year is during big game hunting seasons.

The major threats to the proposed Wilderness include logging, roading and livestock grazing.

Proposed Upper John Day Wilderness
Westslope Cutthroat Trout, Salmon, Steelhead and Big Pines

At over 300 miles, the John Day River is the longest undammed river in Oregon. It also doesn't have any damn fish hatcheries. The river contains excellent fish habitat, primarily where there are adjacent roadless areas. The South Fork John Day (see pages 198-201) and North Fork John Day (see pages 192-195) are the major tributaries. The Middle Fork is a tributary to the North Fork.

The proposed Upper John Day Wilderness includes wildlands on both sides of the John Day Valley. On the south side are the east-west oriented Aldrich Mountains and Strawberry Mountains. The north side of the John Day Valley is mountainous as well, but has a less well-defined ridgeline than the high, long ridge on the south side. The varying elevations and aspects within the proposed Wilderness contribute to the area's significant ecological diversity. The area is also exceptionally scenic with vistas both awesome and sublime.

Tree species here include Engelmann spruce, subalpine fir, Douglas-fir, grand fir, western larch, ponderosa pine, lodgepole pine, western juniper, mountain mahogany, black cottonwood, quaking aspen and alder. Understory species include grouse huckleberry, bitterbrush, bunchgrass and sagebrush.

Of particular note is the occurrence of the rare silver colonial luina (*Luina serpentina*). Easily mistaken for rabbitbrush, it grows on the steeper talus corridors of upper Field Creek on the slope of Aldrich Mountain.

The area's major bird species include American pipit, white-crowned sparrow, Clark's nutcracker, Lincoln's sparrow, three-toed woodpecker, golden-crowned kinglet, pygmy nuthatch, white-headed woodpecker, vesper sparrow, osprey, sandhill crane,

LEVEL IV ECOREGIONS
Melange (52%), John Day/Clarno Highlands (29%), Mesic Forest Zone (15%) Subalpine-Alpine Zone (3%), John Day/Clarno Uplands (2%), Continental Zone Highlands (<1%)

VEGETATION TYPES
Ponderosa (53%), Douglas-fir/Ponderosa/True Fir (22%), Ponderosa/Douglas-fir/True Fir (11%), Cutover/Burned (2%), Juniper/Big Sage (<1%), Juniper/Grasslands (<1%), Juniper/Mountain Big Sage (<1%), Lodgepole/Western Larch (<1%), Marsh/Wet Meadow (<1%)

DRAINAGE SUBBASINS
Burnt, Upper John Day

ELEVATION RANGE
3,425-7,610 feet

UNITS
Belshaw Creek, Cottonwood Creek, Cummings Creek, Deardorff Creek, Dixie Butte, Fall Mountain, Grouse Creek, Hanscomb Mountain, Huckleberry Creek, Johnson Saddle, Keeney Meadows, Laycock Creek, McClellan Mountain, Nipple Butte, Reynolds Creek, Sagebrush Springs, South Fox Creek, *Strawberry Mountain Additions* (Crescent Creek, Frazier Nichol, Little Canyon Mountain, Little Indian Creek, Pine Creek, Sheep Gulch, Strawberry Creek), Vance Creek, Wickiup Creek, Wildcat Canyon

EXISTING WILDERNESS INCORPORATED
portion of Strawberry Mountain

SIZE
104,057 acres (163 square miles; not including 56,870 acres currently protected Wilderness)

COUNTIES
Baker, Grant

FEDERAL ADMINISTRATIVE UNITS
Malheur and Wallowa-Whitman National Forests; BLM Prineville District

CONGRESSIONAL DISTRICT
2nd

Proposed Upper John Day Wilderness

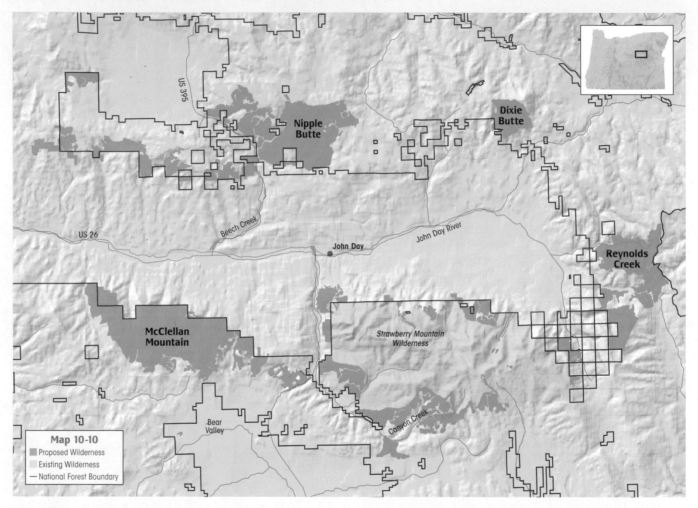

Map 10-10
- Proposed Wilderness
- Existing Wilderness
- National Forest Boundary

Some of the units in the proposed Wilderness are highlighted below.

Dixie Butte is featured on page 203.

McClellan Mountain has a growing population of California bighorn sheep, which are being returned after local extirpation in the last century.

Nipple Butte is heavily forested with ponderosa pine and contains steelhead and trout habitat.

Reynolds Creek has a beautiful trail (lined with mushrooms in the spring) that leads to a natural rock arch with Indian pictographs.

The **Strawberry Mountain Additions** include lower elevation forested areas left out of the Strawberry Mountain Wilderness expansion in 1984 due to timber conflicts.

FEATURED UNIT
Dixie Butte

One can drive to the summit of Dixie Butte and enjoy the panoramic views of two proposed Wilderness areas: the broad valley of the Upper John Day River and the narrower and more canyonesque Middle Fork John Day River. The road to the top of this prominent, cone-shaped landmark is generally passable in a high-clearance highway vehicle, but its precipitous route with a long, steep drop-off is not for the faint of heart. The Dixie Mountain unit is part of both the proposed Upper John Day and the North Fork John Day-Elkhorns Wilderness areas. Butte, Little Butte, Deerhorn and Davis Creeks flow northward through the unit into the Middle Fork of the John Day, while Standard and Dixie Creeks flow southward into the mainstem of the river.

The volcanic butte is covered with a thin (less than two-feet deep) layer of ash from the explosion of the late Mount Mazama. The top of the butte is steep terrain with subalpine and alpine habitats. Whitebark pine and subalpine fir are the major tree species. There is some mountain mahogany here and the ground cover is primarily mountain big sagebrush, elk sedge and fleece flower. Of particular interest are yellow and cream buckwheats, Richardson's penstemon, Lyall rockcress, Sierra-hare sedge and alpine prickly currant.

Skirting the lower slopes on more bench-like terrain is an old-growth Douglas-fir, true fir, western larch and ponderosa pine forest. Elk sedge and pine-grass are found in the understory.

The area's intact streams, with their clear, cold water, are important spawning and rearing areas for steelhead, trout and chinook salmon. Rocky Mountain elk, mule deer, cougar, bobcat and marten also thrive in this habitat.

A ten-mile recreation trail following the forested northern slopes of Dixie Butte is the best away to enjoy this unit. Cross-country skiing, hiking, horseback riding, hunting and fishing are other popular recreational pursuits.

SANDY LONSDALE

From the summit in the Dixie Butte Unit of the proposed Upper John Day Wilderness.

PROPOSED WILDERNESS
North Fork John Day-Elkhorns and Upper John Day

LOCATION
8 miles northeast of Prairie City

LEVEL IV ECOREGIONS
Melange (45%), Mesic Forest Zone (32%), John Day/Clarno Highlands (23%)

VEGETATION TYPES
Ponderosa/Douglas-fir/True Fir (62%), Ponderosa (20%), True Fir/Douglas-fir (11%), Cutover/Burned (7%), Willow Riparian (<1%)

TERRAIN
Steep and beautiful.

DRAINAGE SUBBASINS
Middle Fork John Day, Upper John Day

ELEVATION RANGE
3,799-7,592 feet

SIZE
18,387 acres

COUNTY
Grant

FEDERAL ADMINISTRATIVE UNITS
Malheur National Forest (Blue Mountain Ranger District); BLM Prineville District (Central Oregon Resource Area)

USGS 7.5' QUAD MAPS
Bates, Dixie Meadows

Paintbrush (*Castilleja* spp.) and other species on Fields Peak in the McClellan Mountain Unit of the proposed Upper John Day Wilderness.

golden eagle and bald eagle.

Rocky Mountain elk and mule deer are common. Other major wildlife species include black bear and cougar. More enigmatic residents include pika, bobcat, wolverine, marten, snowshoe hare and the occasional gray wolf.

The American Fisheries Society has identified several aquatic diversity areas within the proposed Wilderness in recognition of their importance for bull trout, redband trout, westslope cutthroat trout, spring chinook salmon and summer steelhead. Pacific lamprey also spawn in the headwaters of the Upper John Day basin.

Of particular note are the area's westslope cutthroat trout. The species is the native trout once common to the west slopes of the Rocky Mountains in Idaho, Montana, Alberta and British Columbia. In Oregon, westslope cutthroat trout are found only in the Upper John Day River Basin, perhaps left there 10,000-15,000 years ago after one of the many times ancient Lake Missoula drained itself during Pleistocene times. Unlike other subspecies of cutthroat trout, the westslope do not prey on other fish. This lack of predatory instinct probably evolved because the westslope co-evolved with two other fish-eating species: bull trout and northern pikeminnow. By specializing in the ingestion of invertebrates, the westslope has avoided direct competition with these

other species, which might otherwise be inclined to eat it for lunch. Sensitive to changes in water quality and temperature, the majority of westslope trout are now found in roadless areas. In the John Day Basin, westslope cutthroat trout are now absent from the North Fork and Middle Fork subbasins. The species resides in only 73 of the 179 miles of its original stream habitat in Oregon, a decline caused by competition from introduced exotic fish and habitat destruction.

Recreational opportunities here include hunting, fishing, backpacking, horseback riding, birding, cross-country skiing or just walking leisurely among some giant "pumpkins," also known as old-growth ponderosa pine.

Threats to the proposed Wilderness include roading, logging, livestock grazing, mining and off-road vehicle use.

Proposed Wallowa Mountains Wilderness
Lower-Elevation Old Forests, Mountain Meadows and Intact Streams

The unprotected wildlands of the proposed Wallowa Mountains Wilderness include open parklands, boulder-strewn meadows, dense forests, grassy slopes, wet and dry meadows, granite peaks, glaciated valleys, alpine lakes, basalt outcroppings, roaring creeks, towering cliffs and deep canyons.

The Wallowa Mountains are breathtakingly beautiful, even to area residents and frequent visitors. A sizable, but ecologically inadequate portion of the range is already protected in the highly popular Eagle Cap Wilderness. The area is so popular that some have taken to calling the mountain range the "Eagle Caps" in reference to the Wilderness, even though the Wilderness area was named after "Eagle Cap," the seventh highest peak in the range.

The Wallowa Mountains are a combination of granite and basalt. Granite dominates the higher elevations, basalt the lower. In between are combinations of both. Glaciation, volcanism, faulting, folding and erosion are all on full display in the Wallowa Mountains.

The waters that flow off the Wallowas end up in the Snake River, though by widely varying routes. The Wallowa River and its two major tributaries, the Lostine and Minam, drain the northern part of the range. Tributaries of the Grande Ronde River, which also includes the Wallowa, flow from the western slopes. Tributaries of the

Proposed Wallowa Mountains Wilderness

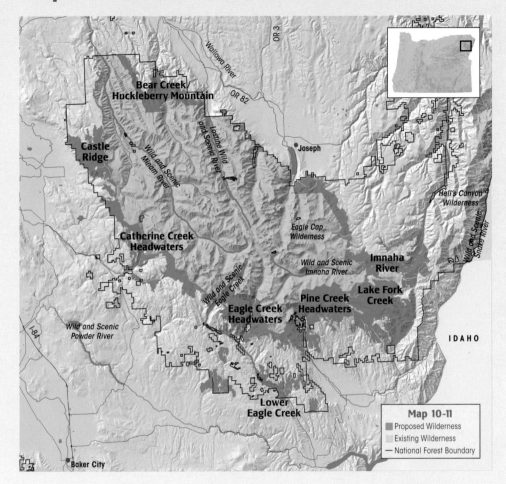

Map 10-11
- Proposed Wilderness
- Existing Wilderness
- National Forest Boundary

Some of the units in the proposed Wilderness are highlighted below.

Bear Creek-Huckleberry Mountain contains nearly four miles of trail in de facto wilderness before reaching the current Eagle Cap Wilderness boundary.

Castle Ridge features large outcroppings of monadnocks that rise above the surrounding forest. It is also a mountain hemlock research area.

Catherine Creek Headwaters is prime steelhead spawning habitat.

Eagle Creek Headwaters features several tributaries to the main Eagle and East Eagle Creeks. A steep, rugged and little-used trail traverses the unit.

Imnaha River includes a portion of the Imnaha Wild and Scenic River. The Imnaha River is one of the last strongholds of salmonids in the Snake River Basin.

Lake Fork Creek is featured on page 206.

Visitors can walk the length of the **Lower Eagle Creek** unit on a river-side trail near slopes with grassy openings, open parklands of ponderosa pine and unusual rock formations. The stream is of substantial volume and varies between deep pools, rapids, swift glassy-smooth stretches and pretty little waterfalls. This segment of Eagle Creek is designated as a unit of the National Wild and Scenic Rivers System.

Pine Creek Headwaters features granite outcroppings and glaciated valleys.

LEVEL IV ECOREGIONS
Mesic Forest Zone (49%), Wallowas/Seven Devils Mountains (21%), Canyons and Dissected Highlands (14%), Subalpine-Alpine Zone (13%), Continental Zone Foothills (3%), Blue Mountain Basins (<1%)

VEGETATION TYPES
Western Larch/Douglas-fir/Ponderosa/Lodgepole (38%), Ponderosa/Douglas-fir/Western Larch/Lodgepole (20%), Subalpine Lodgepole (11%), Ponderosa/Douglas-fir/True Fir (10%), Subalpine Fir/Engelmann Spruce Parklands (4%), Cutover/Burned (3%), Douglas-fir/Ponderosa/True Fir (3%), Lodgepole/Western Larch (2%), Ponderosa (2%), True Fir/Douglas-fir (2%), Ponderosa/Grasslands (2%), Big Sagebrush (1%), Western Larch/Douglas-fir/True Fir (1%), Alpine Barren Fell Field (<1%), Ponderosa/Shrub (<1%), Grasslands/Bunchgrass (<1%), Quaking Aspen (<1%)

DRAINAGE SUBBASINS
Imnaha, Pine, Powder, Upper Grande Ronde, Wallowa

ELEVATION RANGE
2,480-8,618 feet

UNITS
Castle Ridge, Cougar Creek, *Eagle Cap Additions* (Bear Creek-Huckleberry Mountain, Catherine Creek Headwaters, Eagle Creek Headwaters, Lick Creek, Lostine River, Lower McCully Creek, Northeast Additions, Northwest Additions, Pine Creek Headwaters, South Imnaha Slope), Goose Creek, Grave Creek-Deer Creek, Lake Fork Creek, Lick Creek, Lower Eagle Creek, Mount Howard, Mud Lake, Sawmill Creek, Skull Creek, South Fork Catherine Creek, Summit Creek, Upper Summit Creek

EXISTING WILDERNESS INCORPORATED
Eagle Cap

SIZE
173,786 acres (272 square miles, not including 349,897 acres of currently protected Wilderness)

COUNTIES
Baker, Union, Wallowa

FEDERAL ADMINISTRATIVE UNITS
Wallowa-Whitman National Forest; BLM Vale District

CONGRESSIONAL DISTRICT
2nd

PROPOSED WILDERNESS
Wallowa Mountains

LOCATION
12 miles north-northeast of Halfway

LEVEL IV ECOREGIONS
Mesic Forest Zone (52%), Canyons and Dissected Highlands (35%), Wallowa/Seven Devils Mountains (12%), Subalpine-Alpine Zone (<1%)

VEGETATION TYPES
Western Larch/Douglas-fir/Ponderosa/Lodgepole (43%), Ponderosa/Douglas-fir/Western Larch/Lodgepole (24%), Ponderosa/Douglas-fir/True Fir (17%), Subalpine Lodgepole (12%), Ponderosa/Grasslands (3%), Ponderosa (<1%)

TERRAIN
Enticingly rugged.

DRAINAGE SUBBASIN
Pine Creek

ELEVATION RANGE
2,799-6,824 feet

SIZE
32,153 acres

COUNTY
Baker

FEDERAL ADMINISTRATIVE UNIT
Wallowa Whitman National Forest (Pine Ranger District)

USGS 7.5' QUAD MAPS
Deadman Point, Duck Creek

FEATURED UNIT
Lake Fork Creek

Lying between the high Wallowa Mountains to the west and the high rim of Hells Canyon to the east, the mixed-conifer forests of the Lake Fork Unit receive more precipitation than anywhere else in Oregon east of the Cascade Crest. The land rises steeply in the lower elevations, sloping more gently higher up.

The unit is 90 percent forested with Douglas-fir, various true firs, western larch, ponderosa pine, lodgepole pine, quaking aspen and mountain maple. The rest is open grassy slopes. Since this is a wetter forest, the natural frequency of wildfire is comparably less than elsewhere in the region.

Lake Fork Creek is a tributary to North Pine Creek, which joins Pine Creek that flows into the Snake River. All of the streams in the unit are home to native redband trout. Lake Fork Creek and its major tributary, Elk Creek, are also strongholds for endangered bull trout.

Rocky Mountain elk and mule deer thrive in the alternately open and dense forests and their grass-shrub understory. The unit provides both summer and winter range for these species. Blue, ruffed and spruce grouse, along with black bear and cougar are found in the unit. Evidence of wolverine and lynx has also been documented.

The excellent fish and wildlife habitat is also visually pleasing to the human eye. Most recreation in the unit is big game hunting, followed by upland bird hunting, fishing and hiking. A portion of the unit is within the Hells Canyon National Recreation Area.

RIC BAILEY

Trail in the Lake Fork Unit of the proposed Wallowa Mountains Wilderness.

In Oregon, spruce grouse (*Falcipennis canadensis franklinii*) are found only in the proposed Wallowa Mountains Wilderness and Hells Canyon Wilderness Additions.

Powder River drain much of the southern end of the range, while Pine Creek and its tributaries flow from the southeastern corner. The Imnaha River drains the remainder of the range's eastern parts. The Powder River, Pine Creek, Imnaha River and Grande Ronde River all eventually empty into the Snake River.

Nearly all of the unprotected wildlands in the proposed Wallowa Mountain Wilderness are contiguous with the existing Eagle Cap Wilderness. Since establishing the area in 1964, Congress has expanded the Eagle Cap Wilderness twice. However, large expanses of both high and low elevation forestlands remain unprotected.

The northern additions to the proposed Wallowa Mountains Wilderness are centers of concentration of species rarity and endemism for plants and animals. The American Fisheries Society has identified several aquatic diversity areas within the proposed Wilderness in recognition of important bull trout, redband trout, spring/summer chinook salmon and summer steelhead populations that live and spawn in the area's many streams.

Major tree species here include Engelmann spruce, lodgepole pine, subalpine fir, whitebark pine, grand fir, Douglas-fir, western larch, ponderosa pine, quaking aspen and mountain maple.

Major bird species include bald eagle, prairie falcon, northern goshawk, red-tailed hawk, Cooper's hawk, osprey, ferruginous hawk, Clark's nutcracker, three-toed woodpecker and white-headed woodpecker. Of particular note is an endemic subspecies of the gray crowned rosy finch (*Leucosticte tephrocotis wallowa*), which is less tawny and

red-brown in color than *L. t. littoralis* found in the Cascades and Blue Mountains. During the breeding season, the subspecies can be found at the edges of receding snow.

The Wallowa Mountains (and perhaps the nearby Hells Canyon country) are home to the spruce grouse. Although it once ranged in the northern Oregon Cascades, the spruce grouse is now very rare in the state. The grouse is a more common resident of the northern boreal forests, mostly in Canada. The subspecies found in Oregon is *Dendragapus canadensis franklinii*. Spruce grouse favor mature conifer forests above 5,000 feet. While some of Oregon's habitat for this species is already protected in the Eagle Cap Wilderness, much of it is not. Many of the area's high elevation forests remain vulnerable to roading and logging. Closing certain roads and allowing logged forests to grow old again would provide more habitat for the bird. Given their limited distribution and natural unwariness of humans, spruce grouse are protected from hunting. However, often mistaken for blue grouse, many spruce grouse are still shot during hunting season.

Of the approximately 70 mammal species found in the Wallowa Mountains, the most notable are Rocky Mountain elk, mule deer, Rocky Mountain bighorn sheep, black bear, wolverine, fisher, river otter, cougar, lynx, beaver and coyote. A highly charismatic, but nonetheless alien exotic megafauna, is the mountain goat, which was transplanted by humans to the Wallowa Mountains a few decades ago. While mountain goats ranged the Wallowas before the last ice age, they have not been native to the range since the last glaciers receded.

Recreational opportunities include big game and upland bird hunting, fishing, hiking, whitewater boating, horseback riding, nature study, birding, berry picking, sightseeing and marveling at the alpine geology.

Major threats to the area are logging, livestock grazing, off-road vehicle use and mining.

◆

Notes

[1] The proposed Malheur Lake Wilderness of over 92,000 acres is described in Andy Kerr. 2000. OREGON DESERT GUIDE: 70 HIKES. The Mountaineers. Seattle, WA: 128-129.

[2] *For more information, see* Andy Kerr. 2000. OREGON DESERT GUIDE: 70 HIKES. The Mountaineers. Seattle, WA: 209-219.

[3] *For more information, see* Andy Kerr. 2000. OREGON DESERT GUIDE: 70 HIKES. The Mountaineers. Seattle, WA: 186-191.

[4] *For more information, see* Andy Kerr. 2000. OREGON DESERT GUIDE: 70 HIKES. The Mountaineers. Seattle, WA: 108-170.

Afterword

One final paragraph of advice: do not burn yourselves out. Be as I am — a reluctant enthusiast.... a part-time crusader, a half-hearted fanatic. Save the other half of your-selves and your lives for pleasure and adventure. It is not enough to fight for the land; it is even more important to enjoy it. While you can. While it is still here. So get out there and hunt and fish and mess around with your friends, ramble out yonder and explore the forests, climb the mountains, bag the peaks, run the rivers, breathe deep of that yet sweet and lucid air, sit quietly for awhile and contemplate the precious still-ness, the lovely mysterious and awesome space. Enjoy yourselves, keep your brain in your head and your head firmly attached to the body, the body active and alive and I promise you this much: I promise you this one sweet victory over our enemies, over those desk-bound men with their hearts in a safe-deposit box and their eyes hypnotized by desk calculators. I promise you this: you will outlive the bastards.

—Edward Abbey[1]

Edward Abbey.

Ed, take it from another Ed, not only can wilderness lovers outlive wilderness opponents, we can also defeat them.

The only thing necessary for the triumph of evil is for good men (sic) to do nothing.

—Edmund Burke[2]

Edmund Burke.

1 Van matre, Steve and Bill Weiler. 1983. THE EARTH SPEAKS. Institute for Earth Education. Greenville, WV: 57.

2 Andrews, Robert, Mary Biggs, Michael Seidel, et al. (eds.). 1996. THE COLUMBIA WORLD OF QUOTATIONS. Columbia University Press. New York, NY: (no. 9118) (available at www.bartleby.com/66/18/9118.html).

Footnotes and Sources

Many sources were consulted in writing this book. Individuals who provided information are recognized in the *Acknowledgements*. Many published and Internet sources consulted are listed in the *Bibliography*. A collection of hiking guides was also consulted to describe recreational opportunities in proposed Wilderness areas (see www.onrc.org/hikes).

Direct quotations are footnoted in the book text. However, the litany of facts and figures used in the book are not footnoted. An editorial decision was made to avoid burdening every fact and figure with a footnote. References consulted for such information are generally listed in the *Bibliography*, or were otherwise gleaned from dusty government environmental impact statements, environmental assessments, photographs, rare technical reports, old maps, websites and decades of personal interaction with government officials (on and off the record), conservationists, ecologists, biologists, foresters and others. Each chapter was reviewed for accuracy by qualified experts in natural history and local geography before publication. Each is also grounded in the author's experience in over 40 years of scouting and visiting Oregon's forest wildlands and over 28 years advocating for their protection.

Tundra swans (*Cygnus columbianus*) on Davis Lake adjacent to the Davis Lake Lava Flow Unit of the proposed Upper Deschutes Wilderness. Although half the mountain is now a ski resort, Mount Bachelor's (in background) south and west faces are still of wilderness quality.

Bibliography

_____. 1999. *Oregonians want wolves.* Desert Ramblings (newsletter). Oregon Natural Desert Association (Bend, OR): 12 (2): 4. [*Wolf*]

Alaback, Paul B. 1989. Logging of Temperate Rainforests and the Green House Effect: Ecological Factors to Consider. USDA-Forest Service, Pacific Northwest Research Station. Juneau, AK. [*Carbon cycle*]

Arno, Stephen F. and Ramona P. Hammerly. 1997. NORTHWEST TREES: IDENTIFYING AND UNDERSTANDING THE REGION'S NATIVE TREES. The Mountaineers Books. Seattle, WA. [*Western larch*]

Ashworth, William. 1977. HELLS CANYON: THE DEEPEST GORGE ON EARTH. Hawthorn Books. New York, NY. [*Oregon wilderness protection*]

Associated Press. *State wildlife officials follow up on wolverine leads.* The Oregonian (July 17, 2001): B2. [*Wolverine*]

Bailey, Ric. 1987. H.R. 799, S. 1049, and the History of the Establishment of the Hells Canyon Wilderness Area Boundary. Hells Canyon Preservation Council. La Grande, OR. [*Oregon wilderness protection*]

Battaile, Connie H. 1998. THE OREGON BOOK: INFORMATION A TO Z. Saddle Mountain Press. Newport, OR: 504. [*Deforestation in Oregon*]

Behnke, Robert J. 2002. TROUT AND SALMON OF NORTH AMERICA. Free Press (Simon and Schuster). New York, NY. [*Bull trout, Pacific salmon*]

Belsky, A. Joy and Dana M. Blumenthal. 1997. *Effects of livestock grazing on stand dynamics and soils in upland forests of the Interior West.* Conservation Biology 11(2): 315-327. [*Forests and fire, livestock and forests*]

Bingham, Edwin and Tim Barnes. 1997. WOOD WORKS: THE LIFE AND WRITINGS OF CHARLES ERSKINE SCOTT WOOD. Oregon State University Press. Corvallis, OR. [*Charles Erskine Scott Wood*]

Bishop, Ellen. 2003. IN SEARCH OF ANCIENT OREGON: A GEOLOGICAL AND NATURAL HISTORY. Timber Press. Portland, OR. [*Oregon geology*]

Bourhill, Bob. 1994. HISTORY OF OREGON'S TIMBER HARVESTS AND/OR LUMBER PRODUCTION. Oregon Dept. of Forestry. Salem, OR. [*Deforestation in Oregon*]

Brown, Rick. 2001. Thinning, Fire and Forest Restoration: A Scenic-Based Approach for National Forests in the Interior West. Defenders of Wildlife. Portland, OR. (2nd printing). [*Forests and fire*]

Buchanan, David, Mary L. Hanson, Robert M. Hooton. 1997. Status of Oregon's Bull Trout, Distribution, Life History, Limiting Factors, Management Considerations, and Status. Tech. Rep. to Bonneville Power Administration, Contract No. 1994BI34342, Project No. 199505400 (BPA Report DOE/BP-34342-5). [*Bull trout*]

Bull, Evelyn L. 2003. "Pileated Woodpecker." Pages 372-374 in D. B. Marshall, M. G. Hunter, A. L. Contreras (eds.). BIRDS OF OREGON: A GENERAL REFERENCE. Oregon State University Press. Corvallis, OR. [Pileated woodpecker]

Bull, Evelyn L., Catherine G. Parks, Tool R. Jorgensen. 1997. TREES AND LOGS IMPORTANT TO WILDLIFE IN THE INTERIOR COLUMBIA RIVER BASIN. Gen. Tech. Rep. PNW-GTR-391. USDA-Forest Service, Pacific Northwest Research Station. Portland, OR. [Black bear]

Carroll, Carlos, Reed F. Noss, Nathan H. Schumacher, Paul C. Piquet. 2001. "Is the Restoration of Wolf, Wolverine, and Grizzly Bear to Oregon and California Biologically Feasible?" Pages 25-46 in D. Maher, R. Noss, J. Larkin (eds.). LARGE MAMMAL RESTORATION: ECOLOGICAL AND SOCIAL IMPLICATIONS. Island Press. Washington, DC. [Grizzly bear, wolf, wolverine]

Cede Holm, C. Jeff, David H. Johnson, Robert E. Bilbo, et al. 2000. Pacific Salmon and Wildlife — Ecological Contexts, Relationships, and Implications for Management. Special Edition Tech. Rep., prepared for D. H. Johnson and T. A. O'Neil (managing dirs.). WILDLIFE-HABITAT RELATIONSHIP IN OREGON AND WASHINGTON. Oregon State University Press. Corvallis, OR. [Pacific salmon]

Center for Biological Diversity. "Northern Goshawk" (factsheet). Available at www.biological-diversity.org/swcbd/species/goshawk/goshawk.html. [Northern goshawk]

Center for Biological Diversity. "Pacific Fisher" (factsheet). Available at www.biologicaldiversity.org/swcbd/species/fisher/fisher.html. [Fisher]

Costanza, Robert, Ralph d'Arge, Rudolph de Groot, et al. 1997. The value of the world's ecosystem services and natural capital. Nature 387: 253-260. [Wilderness economics]

Csuti, Blair, Thomas A. O'Neil, Margaret M. Shaughnessy, et al. 2001. ATLAS OF OREGON WILDLIFE: DISTRIBUTION, HABITAT AND NATURAL HISTORY. 2nd ed. Oregon State University Press. Corvallis, OR. [Elk]

Curtis, Robert O. and David D. Marshall. 1993. Douglas-fir rotations – time for reappraisal? Western Journal of Applied Forestry 8(3): 81-85. [Old-growth/mature/young forests]

DellaSala, Dominick A. and James R. Strittholt. 2000. Scientific Basis for Roadless Area Conservation — Review and Management Recommendations. Submitted to the USDA-Forest Service, Roadless Area Conservation Team. World Wildlife Fund. Ashland, OR; Conservation Biology Institute. Corvallis, OR. [Unroading the wild]

DellaSala, Dominick A., Stewart B. Reid, Terry J. Frest, James R. Strittholt, David M. Olson. 1999. A global perspective on the biodiversity of the Klamath-Siskiyou ecoregion. Natural Areas Journal 19: 300-319. [Klamath Mountains Ecoregion]

DellaSala, Dominick and Evan Frost. 2001. An ecologically based strategy for fire and fuels management in national forest roadless areas. Fire Management Today 61(2): 12-24. [Forests and fire]

Eder, Tamara. 2002. MAMMALS OF WASHINGTON AND OREGON. Lone Pine Publishing. Renton, WA. [Beaver, black bear, cougar, elk, fisher, grizzly bear, lynx, marten, Rocky Mountain bighorn sheep, wolf, wolverine]

Eifert, Larry. 2000. FIELD GUIDE TO OLD GROWTH FORESTS. Sasquatch Books. Seattle, WA. [Old-growth/mature/young forests]

Ercelawn, Ayesha. 1999. END OF THE ROAD: THE ADVERSE ECOLOGICAL IMPACTS OF ROADS AND LOGGING: A COMPILATION OF INDEPENDENTLY REVIEWED RESEARCH. Natural Resources Defense Council. New York, NY. [Roading Oregon's forests]

Ferris, Robert. M., Mark Shaffer, Nina Fascione, et al. 1999. Places for Wolves: A Blueprint for Restoration and Long-Term Recovery in the Lower 48 States. Defenders of Wildlife. Washington, DC. [Wolf]

Forest Ecosystem Management Assessment Team. 1993. Forest ecosystem management: an ecological, economic, and social assessment. USDA-Forest Service, Pacific Northwest Region. Portland, OR. [Mollusks]

Forsman, Eric D. 1998. "Northern Spotted Owl." Pages 672-673 in M. J. Mac, P. A. Opler, E. E. Puckett Haecker, P. D. Doran (eds.). STATUS AND TRENDS OF THE NATION'S BIOLOGICAL RESOURCES. Vol. 2. USDI-Geological Survey. Reston, VA. [Northern spotted owl]

Forsman, Eric D. 2003. "Northern Spotted Owl." Pages 319-320 in D. B. Marshall, M. G. Hunter, A. L. Contreras (eds.). BIRDS OF OREGON: A GENERAL REFERENCE. Oregon State University Press. Corvallis, OR. [Northern spotted owl]

Franklin, Jerry and Christen Theodore Dyrness. 1988. NATURAL VEGETATION OF OREGON AND WASHINGTON. Oregon State University Press. Corvallis, OR. [Oregon forests]

Frome, Michael. 1997. BATTLE FOR THE WILDERNESS (rev. ed.). University of Utah Press. Salt Lake City, UT. [The Wilderness Act, Oregon wilderness protection]

Gantenbein, Douglas. 2003. A SEASON OF FIRE: FOUR MONTHS ON THE FIRELINES OF AMERICA'S FORESTS. Tarcher/Penguin. New York, NY. [Forests and fire]

Gordon, David. 1992. FIELD GUIDE TO SASQUATCH. Sasquatch Books. Seattle, WA. [Bigfoot]

Gordon, David. 1994. FIELD GUIDE TO SLUGS. Sasquatch Books. Seattle, WA. [Mollusks]

Gorman, James. Faint hope for survival of a woodpecker fades. New York Times (June 10, 2002). [Pileated woodpecker]

Gorman, James. The outsider: in the shadow of extinction. New York Times (Feb. 8, 2002): E31. [Pileated woodpecker]

Hamburger, Robert. 1998. TWO ROOMS: THE LIFE OF CHARLES ERSKINE SCOTT WOOD. University of Nebraska Press. Lincoln, NE. [Charles Erskine Scott Wood]

Hart, John. 1975. HIKING THE BIGFOOT COUNTRY: THE WILDLANDS AND NORTHERN CALIFORNIA AND SOUTHERN OREGON. Sierra Club Books. San Francisco, CA. [Klamath Mountains Ecoregion]

Henjum, Mark G., James R. Karr, Daniel L. Bottom, et al. 1994. Interim Protection for Late Successional Forests, Fisheries and Watersheds: National Forests East of the Cascade Crest, Oregon and Washington. The Wildlife Society. Bethesda, MD. [Little Wilderness]

Hill, Richard. Agile Fishers' Future Shaky. The Oregonian (April 21, 2004): E12, E11.

Ingalsbee, Timothy. 1999. Learn from the burn: research natural areas for habitat and science. Wild Earth 9(2): 57-63. [Warner Creek fire]

Jensen, Edward C. and Charles R. Ross. 1995. TREES TO KNOW IN OREGON. Oregon State University Extension Service; Oregon Dept. of Forestry. Corvallis, OR. [*Western larch*]

Joslin, Les. 2000. THE WILDERNESS CONCEPT AND THE THREE SISTERS WILDERNESS. Wilderness Associates. Bend, OR. [*Oregon wilderness protection*]

Kendall, Katherine C. 1998. "Whitebark Pine." Pages 482-485 <u>in</u> M. J. Mac, P. A. Opler, E. E. Puckett Haecker, P. D. Doran (eds.). STATUS AND TRENDS OF THE NATION'S BIOLOGICAL RESOURCES. Vol. 2. USDI-Geological Survey. Reston, VA (sidebar in "Rocky Mountains" chapter). [*Whitebark pine*]

Kerr, Andy and Mark Salvo. 2000. *Livestock grazing in the national park and wilderness preservation systems.* Wild Earth 10(2): 45-52. [*The Wilderness Act*]

Kerr, Andy. 1980. *Hard choices in the political arena.* Earthwatch Oregon (Nov./Dec.): 14-16. [*Oregon wilderness protection*]

Kerr, Andy. 1995. *The browning of Bob Packwood.* Cascadia Times 1(6): 8-9. [*Oregon wilderness protection*]

Kerr, Andy. 2000. OREGON DESERT GUIDE: 70 HIKES. The Mountaineers. Seattle, WA. [*Elk*]

Kerr, Andy. *Naming wilderness after Hatfield is wrong.* Wallowa County Chieftain (Dec. 4, 1997). [*Senators Mark Hatfield and Bob Packwood*]

Komar, Paul. 1998. THE PACIFIC NORTHWEST COAST: LIVING WITH THE SHORES OF OREGON AND WASHINGTON. Duke University Press. Durham, NC. [*Oregon Dunes*]

LaLande, Jeff. 1989. *A wilderness journey with Judge John B. Waldo, Oregon's first preservationist.* Oregon Historical Quarterly 90(2): 117-166. [*Judge John B. Waldo*]

Larson, Jerry, Ron McLean, Stephen Cary. 1976. THE LIVING DUNES. Umpqua Publishing Company. Reedsport, OR. [*Oregon Dunes*]

Lichatowich, Jim. 1999. SALMON WITHOUT RIVERS: A HISTORY OF THE PACIFIC SALMON CRISIS. Island Press. Washington, DC. [*Pacific salmon*]

Loy, William, Stuart Allan, Aileen R. Buckley, James E. Meacham. 2001. ATLAS OF OREGON. 2nd ed. University of Oregon Press. Eugene, OR. [*Forest ecoregions, forest types*]

Loy, William, Stuart Allan, Aileen R. Buckley, James E. Meacham. 2001. ATLAS OF OREGON. 2nd ed. University of Oregon Press. Eugene, OR. [*Coast Range Ecoregion, Klamath Mountains Ecoregion, Cascades Ecoregion, East Cascades Slopes/Foothills Ecoregion, Blue Mountains Ecoregion*]

Mac, M. J., P. A. Opler, E. E. Puckett Haecker, P. D. Doran (eds.). STATUS AND TRENDS OF THE NATION'S BIOLOGICAL RESOURCES. Vol. 2. USDI-Geological Survey. Reston, VA. [*Grizzly bear, wolf*]

Marshall, David B. 2003. "Northern Goshawk." Pages 151-153 <u>in</u> D. B. Marshall, M. G. Hunter, A. L. Contreras (eds.). BIRDS OF OREGON: A GENERAL REFERENCE. Oregon State University Press. Corvallis, OR. [*Northern goshawk*]

Marshall, David B. 2003. "White-headed Woodpecker." Pages 364-367 <u>in</u> D. B. Marshall, M. G. Hunter, A. L. Contreras (eds.). BIRDS OF OREGON: A GENERAL REFERENCE. Oregon State University Press. Corvallis, OR. [*White-headed woodpecker*]

Marshall, David B., Mark W. Chilote, Hal Weeks. 1996. Species at risk: sensitive, threatened and endangered vertebrates of Oregon. 2nd ed. Oregon Dept. Fish and Wildlife. Portland, OR. [*Oregon fish and wildlife*]

Maser, Chris, Bruce R. Mate, Jerry F. Franklin, Christen Theodore Dyrness. 1981. NATURAL HISTORY OF OREGON COAST MAMMALS. General Technical Report PNW-133. USDA-Forest Service and USDI-Bureau of Land Management. Portland, OR. [*Black bear*]

Mathews, Daniel. 1988. CASCADE-OLYMPIC NATURAL HISTORY: A TRAILSIDE REFERENCE. 2nd ed. Raven Editions; Audubon Society of Portland. Portland, OR. [*Elk*]

Mathews, Daniel. 1999. CASCADE-OLYMPIC NATURAL HISTORY GUIDE: A TRAILSIDE REFERENCE. 2nd ed. Raven Editions. Portland, OR. [*Mollusks*]

Matthews, Mark. *Last chance for the whitebark pine.* High Country News (Dec. 4, 2000): 5. (available at www.hcn.org/servlets/hcn.Article?article_id=10133#). [*Whitebark pine*]

McNab, W. Henry and Peter. E. Avers. 1994. Ecological Subregions of the United States. WO-WSA-5. USDA-Forest Service. Washington, DC (available at www.fs.fed.us/land/pubs/ecoregions/toc.html). [*Coast Range Ecoregion, Klamath Mountains Ecoregion, Cascades Ecoregion, East Cascades Slopes/Foothills Ecoregion, Blue Mountains Ecoregion*]

Meehan, Brian T. *An Oregon century: the promise of Eden.* The Oregonian (Dec. 19, 1999): A14. [*Judge John B. Waldo*]

Merritt, Regna. 1999. *Rekindling the Greenfire: the wolf, wolverine and lynx make a comeback in Oregon.* Wild Oregon (newsletter). Oregon Natural Resources Council (Portland, OR) 26(2): 8-11. [*Fisher, lynx, marten, wolverine*]

Middle Rockies-Blue Mountains Planning Team. 2002. Middle Rockies-Blue Mountains Ecoregional Conservation Plan. The Nature Conservancy. Arlington, VA. [*Blue Mountains Ecoregion*]

Milstein, Michael. *Genetic tests show animal shot dead in Eastern Oregon was a wild wolf.* The Oregonian (Jan. 3, 2001): D1. [*Wolf*]

Milstein, Michael. *When wolves move in.* The Oregonian (Nov. 10, 2002): A11-A12. [*Wolf*]

Mortenson, Eric. *A judge in the wilderness.* Eugene Register-Guard (Aug. 9, 1987): B1. [*Judge John B. Waldo*]

Mortenson, Eric. *Writings of Judge Waldo.* Eugene Register-Guard (Aug. 9, 1987): B1-B2. [*Judge B. Waldo*]

Murray, Michael and Mary Rasmussen. 2000. Status of Whitebark Pine in Crater Lake National Park. Unpublished Final Report, Cooperative Cost-Share Agreement No. I19320000035. Copy on file at US Department of the Interior, Park Service, Crater Lake National Park, Resource Management Division. [*Whitebark pine*]

Nash, Roderick. 1982. WILDERNESS AND THE AMERICAN MIND. 3rd ed. Yale University Press. New Haven, CT. [*Oregon wilderness protection*]

National Assessment Synthesis Team. 2000. CLIMATE CHANGE IMPACTS ON THE UNITED STATES: THE POTENTIAL CONSEQUENCES OF CLIMATE VARIABILITY AND CHANGE. U.S. Global Change Research Program. Washington, DC. [*Carbon cycle*]

National Research Council. 2000. Environmental Issues in Pacific Northwest Forest Management. National Academy Press. Washington, DC. [*Old-growth/mature/young forests*]

Nehlsen, Willa, Jack E. Williams, James A. Lichatowich. 1992. *Pacific salmon at the crossroads: stocks at risk from California, Oregon, Idaho, and Washington.* Fisheries 16(2): 4-21. [*Pacific salmon*]

Nelson, S. Kim. 2003. "Marbled Murrelet." Pages 290-293 *in* D. B. Marshall, M. G. Hunter, A. L. Contreras (eds.). Birds of Oregon: A General Reference. Oregon State University Press. Corvallis, OR. [*Marbled murrelet*]

Newton, Michael and Elizabeth C. Cole. 1987. *A sustained-yield scheme for old-growth Douglas-fir.* Western Journal of Applied Forestry 2(1): 22-25. [*Old-growth/mature/young forests*]

Noss, Reed and Allen Cooperrider. 1994. Saving Nature's Legacy. Island Press. Covelo, CA. [*Across the Landscape and Over Time*]

Noss, Reed F. 1990. The ecological effects of roads, or the road to destruction. Available at www.wildlandscpr.org/resourcelibrary/reports/ecoleffectsroads.html (originally published as Diamondback. 1990. *The ecological effects of roads, or the road to destruction.* Special Paper. Earth First! Tucson, AZ.). [*Roading Oregon's forests*]

Olsen, Lance. 1992. Field Guide to the Grizzly Bear. Sasquatch Books. Seattle, WA. [*Grizzly bear*]

O'Neil, Thomas A. and David H. Johnson. 2000. "Oregon and Washington Wildlife Species and their Habitats." Pages 1-21 *in* D. H. Johnson and T. O'Neil (managing dirs.). Wildlife-Habitat Relationships in Oregon and Washington. Oregon State University Press. Corvallis, OR. [*Oregon fish and wildlife*]

Oregon Biodiversity Project. 1998. Oregon's Living Landscape: Strategies and Opportunities to Conserve Biodiversity. Defenders of Wildlife. Portland, OR. [*Coast Range Ecoregion, Klamath Mountains Ecoregion, Cascades Ecoregion, East Cascades Slopes/Foothills Ecoregion, Blue Mountains Ecoregion*]

Oregon Dept. of Fish and Wildlife. "Oregon Bighorn Sheep Auction Tag Nets $67,500" (press release). ODFW. Portland, OR (Feb. 23, 2001) (available at www.dfw.state.or.us/public/NewsArc/2001News/February/022301bnews.htm). [*Rocky Mountain bighorn sheep*]

Oregon Dept. of Fish and Wildlife. 1992. Oregon's Bighorn Sheep Management Plan 1992-1997. ODFW. Portland, OR. [*Rocky Mountain bighorn sheep*]

Oregon Dept. of Fish and Wildlife. 2000. Living with Wildlife: Black Bear. ODFW. Portland, OR. [*Black bear*]

Oregon Dept. of Fish and Wildlife. Oregon Big Game Statistics. Available at www.dfw.state.or.us/ODFWhtml/Wildlife/StatBooks/Table_of_Contents_00.htm (see "Elk" section). [*Elk*]

Oregon Dept. of Forestry. "25-Year Harvest History" (chart), available at www.odf.state.or.us/DIVISIONS/resource_policy/resource_planning/Annual_Reports/rpt25YearHistory.asp. [*Deforestation in Oregon*]

Oregon Dept. of Forestry. "Oregon's 2002 Timber Harvest Highest since 1997" (press release). ODF. Salem, OR (July 17 2003) (available at www.odf.state.or.us/divisions/resource_policy/public_affairs/news_releases/nr02180.htm). [*Deforestation in Oregon*]

Oregon Dept. of Forestry. 2000. A Study of Oregon's Forest Products Industry, 1998. Oregon Dept. of Forestry. Salem, OR. [*Wilderness economics*]

Oregon Wilderness Act, P.L. 98-328 (June 26 1984). [*Oregon wilderness protection*]

O'Toole, Randal. 2002. Reforming the Fire Service: An Analysis of Federal Fire Budgets and Incentives. Thoreau Institute. Bandon, OR. [*Forests and fire*]

Perry, David A., Reed F. Noss, Timothy D. Schowalter, Terrence J. Frest, Bruce McCune, David R. Montgomery, James R. Karr. 2001. Letter to Regional Interagency Executive Committee to implement Northwest Forest Plan (Sept. 4, 2001). [*Mollusks*]

Phinney, Wil. *Oregon wolf sightings include reports of "multiple animals".* Columbia Basin Bulletin (Jan. 24, 2003). [*Wolf*]

Pianin, Eric. *Scientists give up search for woodpecker.* Washington Post (Feb. 22, 2002). [*Pileated woodpecker*]

Power, Thomas Michael. 1996. Lost Landscapes and Failed Economics: The Search for A Value of Place. Island Press. Covelo, CA. [*Wilderness economics*]

Pyle, Robert. 1995. Where Bigfoot Walks: Crossing the Dark Divide. Houghton Mifflin. Boston, MA. [*Bigfoot*]

Quigley, Thomas M. and Sylvia Arbelbide (tech. eds.). 1997. An Assessment of Ecosystem Components in the Interior Columbia Basin and Portions of the Klamath and Great Basins. Vols. 1-4. Gen. Tech. Rep. PNW-GTR-405. USDA-Forest Service, Pacific Northwest Research Station. Portland, OR. [*Mollusks*]

Ross, Dennis. 1995. The Wilderness Movement and the National Forests. 2nd ed. Intaglio Press. College Station, TX. [*Oregon wilderness protection*]

Ruggiero, Leonard F., Keith B. Aubry, Steven W. Buskirk, et al. 2000. Ecology and Conservation of Lynx in the United States. University of Colorado Press. Boulder, CO. [*Lynx*]

Salvo, Mark. 1993. Senators Hatfield and Packwood and the Modern Environmental Movement. Honors thesis. University of Oregon Clark Honors College. Eugene, OR. [*Senators Mark Hatfield and Bob Packwood*]

Schommer, Tim and Melanie Woolever. 1998. A Process for Finding Management Solutions to the Incompatibility Between Domestic and Bighorn Sheep. Unpublished document in files of Wallowa-Whitman National Forest. Baker, OR. [*Rocky Mountain bighorn sheep*]

Schulke, Todd and Brian Nowicki. 2002. Effectively Treating the Wildland-Urban Interface to Protect Homes and Communities from the Threat of Forest Fire. Center for Biological Diversity. Tucson, AZ. [*Forests and fire*]

Scott, Douglas W. 2002. A Wilderness-Forever Future: A Short History of the National Wilderness Preservation System. Research Rep. 2001-1. Campaign for America's

Wilderness (updated June 2002; available at www.leaveitwild.org/reports/A_Wilderness-Forever_Future.pdf). [*Oregon wilderness protection*]

Scott, Douglas. 2001. A Wilderness-Forever Future: A Short History of the National Wilderness Preservation System. Pew Wilderness Center. Washington, DC. [*The Wilderness Act*]

Semeniuk, Robert. 2001. *Do Bears Fish in the Woods?* Ecologist 31(10): 32-35. [*Grizzly bear*]

Slauson, Keith, Bill Zielinski, Carlos Carrol. 2001. *Hidden in the shrubs: rediscovery of the Humboldt marten?* Mountains and Rivers. Siskiyou Field Institute (Cave Junction, OR) 1(2): 8-12. [*Marten*]

Smith, Jeff, P. Michael W. Collopy, et al. 1998. "Pacific Northwest." Pages 645-706 in M. J. Mac, P. A. Opler, E. E. Puckett Haecker, P. D. Doran (eds.). STATUS AND TRENDS OF THE NATION'S BIOLOGICAL RESOURCES. Vol. 2. USDI-Geological Survey. Reston, VA. [*Oregon fish and wildlife, mollusks*]

Soulé, Michael and John Terbough. 1999. CONTINENTAL CONSERVATION: SCIENTIFIC FOUNDATIONS OF REGIONAL RESERVE NETWORKS. Island Press, Covelo, CA. [*Across the Landscape and Over Time*]

Southwick and Associates. 2000. Historical Economic Performance of Oregon and Western Counties Associated with Roadless and Wilderness Areas. Fenandina Beach, FL. [*Wilderness economics*]

Steelquist, Robert. 1992. FIELD GUIDE TO THE PACIFIC SALMON. Sasquatch Books. Seattle, WA. [*Pacific salmon*]

Strittholt, James R., Nicholas Slosser and Kate Geise. 2002. Pacific Northwest Conservation Assessment. Conservation Biology Institute. Corvallis, OR (available at www.consbio.org/cbi/pacnw_assess/ecoregion-map.htm). [*Coast Range Ecoregion, Klamath Mountains Ecoregion, Cascades Ecoregion, East Cascades Slopes/Foothills Ecoregion, Blue Mountains Ecoregion*]

Tomback, Diana F., Stephen F. Arno, Robert E. Keane (eds.). 2001. WHITEBARK PINE COMMUNITIES: ECOLOGY AND RESTORATION. Island Press. Covelo, CA. [*Whitebark pine*]

Torgerson, Tim (ed.). 1999. OREGON BLUE BOOK 1999-2000. Office of the Secretary of State. Salem, OR: 5 (population); 185-188 (forestry). [*Deforestation in Oregon*]

Trail, Pepper. 2001. *Mollusks of mystery*. Mountains and Rivers. Siskiyou Field Institute (Cave Junction, OR) 1(2): 5-7. [*Mollusks*]

U.S. Fish and Wildlife Service. 2003. Bull Trout: *Salvelinus confluentus*. U.S. Fish and Wildlife Service. Available at library.fws.gov/Pubs/bulltrt03.pdf. (January 2003). [*Bull trout*]

U.S. House of Representatives, Committee of Conference. 1964. Establish a National Wilderness Preservation System. House Rep. 88-1829 to accompany S. 4. U.S. House of Representatives/Government Printing Office. Washington, DC. (Aug. 19, 1964). [*Oregon wilderness protection*]

U.S. House of Representatives, Committee of Conference. 1978. Conference Report on H.R. 3454. House Rep. 95-861. U.S. House of Representatives/Government Printing Office. Washington, DC. (Jan. 31, 1978). (Also published as Senate Report 95-626. U.S. Senate/Government Printing Office. Washington, DC. Jan. 31, 1978). [*Oregon wilderness protection*]

U.S. House of Representatives, Committee on Interior and Insular Affairs. 1983. Designating Certain National Forest System and Other Lands in the State of Oregon for Inclusion in the National Wilderness Preservation System, and for Other Purposes. House Rep. 98-13 to accompany H.R. 1149. U.S. House of Representatives/Government Printing Office. Washington, DC. (Mar. 2, 1983). [*Oregon wilderness protection*]

U.S. House of Representatives, Committee on Interior and Insular Affairs. 1982. Designating Certain National Forest System and Other Lands in the State of Oregon for Inclusion in the National Wilderness Preservation System, and for Other Purposes. House Rep. 97-581 to accompany H.R. 7340. U.S. House of Representatives/Government Printing Office. Washington, DC. (Dec. 9, 1982). [*Oregon wilderness protection*]

U.S. House of Representatives, Committee on Interior and Insular Affairs. 1964. National Wilderness Preservation System. House Rep. 88-1538 to accompany H.R. 9070. U.S. House of Representatives/Government Printing Office. Washington, DC. (July 2, 1964). [*Oregon wilderness protection*]

U.S. House of Representatives, Committee on Interior and Insular Affairs. 1972. Providing for the Addition of the Minam River Canyon and Other Areas to the Eagle Cap Wilderness, Wallowa and Whitman National Forests, Modifying the Boundaries of the Wallowa National Forest in the State of Oregon, and for Other Purposes. House Rep. 92-1525 to accompany H.R. 6446. U.S. House of Representatives/Government Printing Office. Washington, DC. (Oct. 4, 1972). [*Oregon wilderness protection*]

U.S. House of Representatives, Committee on Interior and Insular Affairs. 1975. Establishing the Hells Canyon National Recreation Area in the States of Oregon, Idaho and Washington, and for Other Purposes. House Rep. 94-607 to accompany H.R. 30. U.S. House of Representatives/Government Printing Office. Washington, DC. (Oct. 31, 1975). [*Oregon wilderness protection*]

U.S. House of Representatives, Committee on Interior and Insular Affairs. 1978. Creating the Indian Peaks Wilderness Area and the Arapaho National Recreation Area and to Authorize the Secretary of the Interior to Study the Feasibility of Revising the Boundaries of Rocky Mountain National Park. House Rep. 95-1460 to accompany H.R. 12026. U.S. House of Representatives/Government Printing Office. Washington, DC. (Aug. 9, 1978). [*Oregon wilderness protection*]

U.S. House of Representatives, Committee on Interior and Insular Affairs. 1979. Designating Certain National Forest System Lands in the National Wilderness Preservation System, and for Other Purposes . House Rep. 96-617. U.S. House of Representatives/Government Printing Office. Washington, DC. (Nov. 14, 1979). [*Wilderness grazing, "Colorado Grazing Language"*]

U.S. House of Representatives, Committee on Interior and Insular Affairs. 1984. Designating Certain National Forest Lands in the State of Arizona as Wilderness, and for Other Purposes. House Rep. 98-643, part I. U.S. House of Representatives/Government Printing Office. Washington, DC. (Mar. 30, 1984). [*Wilderness grazing, "Arizona Grazing Language"*]

U.S. House of Representatives, Committee on Resources. 2000. Steens Mountain Cooperative Management and Protection Act of 2000. House Rep. 106-929 to accompany H.R. 4828. U.S. House of Representatives. Washington, DC. (Oct. 3, 2000). [*Oregon wilderness protection*]

U.S. House Representatives, Committee on Interior and Insular Affairs. 1977. Designating Certain Endangered Public Lands for Preservation as Wilderness, Providing for the Study of Additional Endangered Public Lands for Such Designation, Furthering the Purposes of The Wilderness Act of 1984, and for Other Purposes. House Rep. 95-540 to accompany H.R. 3454. U.S. House of Representatives/Government Printing Office. Washington, DC. (July 27, 1977). [*Oregon wilderness protection*]

U.S. PIRG and Sierra Club. 1998. Wildlife Need Wild Places: The State of Disappearing Species and Their Habitat. U.S. PIRG and Sierra Club. Washington, DC ("Spotlight on Species: Grizzly Bear," available at www.pirg.org/reports/enviro/wildlife/grizzly.htm). [*Grizzly bear*]

U.S. Senate, Committee on Energy and Natural Resources. 1977. Endangered American Wilderness Act of 1977. Senate Rep. 95-490 to accompany H.R. 3454. U.S. Senate/Government Printing Office. Washington, DC. (Oct. 11, 1977). [*Oregon wilderness protection*]

U.S. Senate, Committee on Energy and Natural Resources. 1977. Oregon Omnibus Wilderness Act of 1977. Sen. Rep. 95-329 to accompany S. 658. U.S. Senate/Government Printing Office. Washington, DC. (July 6, 1977). [*Oregon wilderness protection*]

U.S. Senate, Committee on Energy and Natural Resources. 1979. The Oregon Wilderness Act of 1979 (S. 2031). Senate Report 96-421. U.S. Senate/Government Printing Office. Washington, DC. (Nov. 20, 1979). [*Oregon wilderness protection*]

U.S. Senate, Committee on Energy and Natural Resources. 1984. The Oregon Wilderness Act of 1984 (H.R. 1149). Senate Rep. 98-465. U.S. Senate/Government Printing Office. Washington, DC. (May 18, 1984). [*Oregon wilderness protection*]

U.S. Senate, Committee on Interior and Insular Affairs. 1963. Establishing a National Wilderness Preservation System for the Permanent Good of the Whole People, and for Other Purposes. Senate Rep. 88-109 to accompany S. 4. U.S. Senate/Government Printing Office. Washington, DC. (Apr. 3, 1963). [*Oregon wilderness protection*]

U.S. Senate, Committee on Interior and Insular Affairs. 1971. Designating the Minam River Canyon in Oregon as Wilderness. Senate Rep. 92-138 to accompany S. 493. U.S. Senate/Government Printing Office. Washington, DC. (June 2, 1971). [*Oregon wilderness protection*]

U.S. Senate, Committee on Interior and Insular Affairs. 1975. Establishing the Hells Canyon National Recreation Area in the States of Idaho, Oregon and Washington. Senate Rep. 94-153 to accompany S. 322. U.S. Senate/Government Printing Office. Washington, DC. (May 22, 1975). [*Oregon wilderness protection*]

University of Montana Wilderness Institute. Wilderness Information Network. Available at www.wilderness.net. [*The Wilderness Act*]

USDA-Forest Service. 1989. Fremont National Forest Land and Resource Management Plan Final Environmental Impact Statement. Appendix C. USDA-Forest Service, Pacific Northwest Region. Portland, OR. [*Fremont Rims Wilderness, Klamath Basin Wilderness*]

USDA-Forest Service. 1989. Ochoco National Forest Land and Resource Management Plan Final Environmental Impact Statement. Appendix C. USDA-Forest Service, Pacific Northwest Region. Portland, OR. [*Malheur Basin Wilderness, Ochoco Mountains Wilderness, South Fork John Day Wilderness*]

USDA-Forest Service. 1989. Rogue River National Forest Land and Resource Management Plan Final Environmental Impact Statement. Appendix C. USDA-Forest Service, Pacific Northwest Region. Portland, OR. [*Rogue-Umpqua Wilderness, Siskiyou Crest Wilderness, South Cascades Wilderness*]

USDA-Forest Service. 1989. Siskiyou National Forest Land and Resource Management Plan Final Environmental Impact Statement. Appendix C. USDA-Forest Service, Pacific Northwest Region. Portland, OR. [*Elk River Wilderness, Kalmiopsis Wilderness Additions, Siskiyou Crest Wilderness, Wild Rogue Wilderness Additions*]

USDA-Forest Service. 1990. Deschutes National Forest Land and Resource Management Plan Final Environmental Impact Statement. Appendix C. USDA-Forest Service, Pacific Northwest Region. Portland, OR. [*Newberry Volcano Wilderness, Metolius Wilderness, Three Sisters Wilderness Additions, Upper Deschutes Wilderness*]

USDA-Forest Service. 1990. Malheur National Forest Land and Resource Management Plan Final Environmental Impact Statement. Appendix C. USDA-Forest Service, Pacific Northwest Region. Portland, OR. [*Malheur Basin Wilderness, Malheur Canyons Wilderness, South Fork John Day Wilderness, Upper John Day Wilderness*]

USDA-Forest Service. 1990. Mount Hood National Forest Land and Resource Management Plan Final Environmental Impact Statement. Appendix C. USDA-Forest Service, Pacific Northwest Region. Portland, OR. [*Clackamas Wilderness, Columbia River Gorge Wilderness, Mount Hood Wilderness Additions, Santiam Wilderness*]

USDA-Forest Service. 1990. Siuslaw National Forest Land and Resource Management Plan Final Environmental Impact Statement. Appendix C. USDA-Forest Service, Pacific Northwest Region. Portland, OR. [*Coast Range Wilderness, Oregon Dunes Wilderness*]

USDA-Forest Service. 1990. Umatilla National Forest Land and Resource Management Plan Final Environmental Impact Statement. Appendix C. USDA-Forest Service, Pacific Northwest Region. Portland, OR. [*Blue Mountains Wilderness, Grande Ronde Wilderness, North Fork John Day-Elkhorns Wilderness*]

USDA-Forest Service. 1990. Umpqua National Forest Land and Resource Management Plan Final Environmental Impact Statement. Appendix C. USDA-Forest Service, Pacific Northwest Region. Portland, OR. [*North Umpqua Wilderness, Rogue-Umpqua Wilderness, Upper Willamette Wilderness*]

USDA-Forest Service. 1990. Wallowa-Whitman National Forest Land and Resource Management Plan Final Environmental Impact Statement. Appendix C. USDA-Forest Service, Pacific Northwest Region. Portland, OR. [*Blue Mountains Wilderness, Grande Ronde Wilderness, Hells Canyon Wilderness Additions, Malheur Canyons Wilderness, North Fork John Day-Elkhorns Wilderness, Upper John Day Wilderness*]

USDA-Forest Service. 1990. Willamette National Forest Land and Resource Management Plan Final Environmental Impact Statement. Appendix C. USDA-Forest Service, Pacific Northwest Region. Portland, OR. [*McKenzie Wilderness, Santiam Wilderness, Three Sisters Wilderness Additions, Upper Willamette Wilderness*]

USDA-Forest Service. 1990. Winema National Forest Land and Resource Management Plan Final Environmental Impact Statement. Appendix C. USDA-Forest Service, Pacific Northwest Region. Portland, OR. [*Klamath Basin Wilderness, South Cascades Wilderness, Upper Deschutes Wilderness*]

USDA-Forest Service. 2000. Forest Service Roadless Area Conservation Rule Final Environmental Impact Statement. Vol. 1, app. B. USDA-Forest Service. Washington, DC (available at www.roadless.fs.fed.us/documents/feis/documents/vol1/appendb.pdf). [*Wilderness economics*]

USDA-NASS. 1996. 1995 cattle and calf losses valued at $1.8 billion (press release). USDA-National Agricultural Statistics Service, Agricultural Statistics Board. (released May 17, 1996). [*Wolf*]

Verts, B. J. and Leslie N. Carraway. 1998. LAND MAMMALS OF OREGON. University of California Press. Berkeley, CA. [*Beaver, black bear, cougar, elk, fisher, grizzly bear, lynx, marten, Rocky Mountain bighorn sheep, wolverine, wolf*]

Watson, Jay and Ben Beach (eds.). 2000. THE WILDERNESS ACT HANDBOOK. 4th ed. The Wilderness Society. Washington, DC. [*The Wilderness Act*]

Weikel, Jennifer. 2003. "Brown Creeper." Pages 453-456 in D. B. Marshall, M. G. Hunter, A. L. Contreras (eds.). BIRDS OF OREGON: A GENERAL REFERENCE. Oregon State University Press. Corvallis, OR. [*Brown creeper*]

Western Native Trout Campaign. 2001. Imperiled Western Trout and the Importance of Roadless Areas. Center for Biological Diversity, Tucson, AZ; Pacific Rivers Council, Eugene, OR; Biodiversity Associates, Laramie WY. [*Bull trout*]

Western Native Trout Campaign. 2001. Imperiled Western Trout and the Importance of Roadless Areas. Center for Biological Diversity, Tucson, AZ; Pacific Rivers Council, Eugene, OR; Biodiversity Associates, Laramie WY. [*Roading Oregon's forests*]

Wood, Charles Erskine Scott. 1908. *Portland's feast of roses*. Pacific Monthly (Portland, OR) 19(6): 623-633. [*Charles Erskine Scott Wood*]

Wood, Wendell. 1999. *Why mollusks matter*. Desert Ramblings (newsletter). Oregon Natural Desert Association (Bend, OR) 12 (3): 8. [*Mollusks*]

Wuerthner, George. 1987. OREGON MOUNTAIN RANGES. American Geographic Publishing. Helena, MT. [*Coast Range Ecoregion, Klamath Mountains Ecoregion, Cascades Ecoregion, East Cascades Slopes/Foothills Ecoregion, Blue Mountains Ecoregion*]

Wuerthner, George. 1996. "The Potential for Wolf Recovery in Oregon." Pages 285-291 in Defenders of Wildlife Wolves of America Conference Proceedings; November 14-16, 1996; Albany, NY. Defenders of Wildlife. Washington, DC. [*Wolf*]

Young, Bob. Big Hoax: *The abominable truth can finally be told*. The Oregonian (Dec. 6, 2002): A1. [*Bigfoot*]

Appendix A
National Wilderness Preservation System in Oregon

Name	National Forest, BLM District, or National Wildlife Refuge	Ecoregion[i]	Acres[ii]	Year Established, Expanded[iii]
Badger Creek	Mount Hood NF	Cascades, East Cascades Slopes and Foothills	24,000	1984
Black Canyon	Ochoco NF	Blue Mountains	13,400	1984
Boulder Creek	Umpqua NF	Cascades	19,100	1984
Bridge Creek	Ochoco NF	Blue Mountains	5,400	1984
Bull-of-the-Woods[iv]	Mount Hood NF	Cascades	27,427	1984
Cummins Creek	Siuslaw NF	Coast Range	9,173	1984
Diamond Peak[v]	Deschutes, Willamette NFs	Cascades, East Cascades Slopes and Foothills	54,185	1964, 1984[vi]
Drift Creek	Siuslaw NF	Coast Range	5,798	1984
Eagle Cap[vii]	Wallowa-Whitman NF	Blue Mountains	349,987	1964, 1972, 1984[viii]
Gearhart Mountain[ix]	Fremont NF	East Cascades Slopes and Foothills	22,809	1964, 1984[x]
Grassy Knob	Siskiyou NF	Coast Range	17,200	1984
Hells Canyon[xi,xii]	Wallowa-Whitman NF, Vale District BLM[xiii]	Blue Mountains	131,133	1975, 1984[xiv]
Kalmiopsis[xv,xvi]	Siskiyou NF	Klamath Mountains	179,655	1964, 1978[xvii]
Mark O. Hatfield[xviii]	Mount Hood NF	Cascades	39,000	1984
Menagerie	Willamette NF	Cascades	4,800	1984
Middle Santiam	Willamette NF	Cascades	7,500	1984
Mill Creek	Ochoco NF	Blue Mountains	17,400	1984
Monument Rock	Malheur, Wallowa-Whitman NFs	Blue Mountains	19,650	1984
Mount Hood[xix]	Mount Hood NF	Cascades	47,160	1964, 1978[xx]
Mount Jefferson[xxi]	Deschutes, Mount Hood, Willamette NFs	Cascades, East Cascades Slopes and Foothills	107,008	1968, 1984[xxii]
Mount Thielsen	Deschutes, Umpqua, Winema NFs	Cascades, East Cascades Slopes and Foothills	54,272	1984
Mount Washington[xxiii]	Deschutes, Willamette NFs	Cascades, East Cascades Slopes and Foothills	52,738	1964, 1984[xxiv]
Mountain Lakes[xxv]	Winema NF	Cascades, East Cascades Slopes and Foothills	23,071	1964
North Fork John Day[xxvi]	Umatilla, Wallowa-Whitman NFs	Blue Mountains	121,352	1984
North Fork Umatilla	Umatilla NF	Blue Mountains	20,435	1984
Opal Creek[xxvii]	Willamette NF	Cascades	20,724	1996
Oregon Islands	Oregon Islands NWR	Offshore	575	1970, 1978, 1996[xxviii]
Red Buttes[xxix]	Rogue River, Siskiyou NFs	Klamath Mountains	3,750	1984
Rock Creek	Siuslaw NF	Coast Range	7,486	1984
Rogue-Umpqua Divide	Rogue River, Umpqua NFs	Cascades	33,200	1984
Salmon-Huckleberry	Mount Hood NF	Cascades	44,560	1984
Sky Lakes	Rogue River, Winema NFs	Cascades, East Cascades Slopes and Foothills	116,300	1984
Steens Mountain[xxx,xxxi]	Burns District BLM	Northern Basin and Range	174,744	2000

Name	National Forest, BLM District, or National Wildlife Refuge	Ecoregion[ii]	Acres[i]	Year Established, Expanded[iii]
Strawberry Mountain[xxxii]	Malheur NF	Blue Mountains	68,700	1964, 1984[xxxiii]
Table Rock	Salem District BLM	Cascades	5,500	1984
Three Arch Rocks	Three Arch Rocks NWR	Offshore	15	1970
Three Sisters[xxxiv]	Deschutes, Willamette NFs	Cascades, East Cascades Slopes and Foothills	286,708	1964, 1978, 1984[xxxv]
Waldo Lake[xxxvi]	Willamette NF	Cascades	39,200	1984
Wenaha-Tucannon[xxxvii]	Umatilla NF	Blue Mountains	66,417	1978
Wild Rogue	Siskiyou NF, Medford District BLM[xxxviii]	Klamath Mountains	35,818	1978

TOTAL PROTECTED WILDERNESS IN OREGON	**2,277,350 acres**
TOTAL OREGON LAND AND WATER AREA	**62,163,840 acres** [xxxix]
PERCENTAGE OF OREGON PROTECTED AS WILDERNESS	**3.7%**

Primary sources: Wilderness Information Network (www.wilderness.net); USDA-Forest Service. 1979. Oregon Map, Roadless and Undeveloped Area Evaluation II, Final Environmental (Impact) Statement. Washington, DC; Portland, OR.

[i]Oregon Level III Ecoregions: Blue Mountains, Cascades, Coast Range, Columbia Plateau, East Cascades Slopes and Foothills, Klamath Mountains, Northern Basin and Range, Snake River Plain and Willamette Valley.

[ii]This column represents the most accurate acreages available. "Approximate" figures in subsequent footnotes reflect estimates at time of designation as referenced in applicable statute.

[iii]The Wilderness Act, Sept. 3, 1964 (P.L. 88-577); Mount Jefferson Wilderness, Oregon (Act), Oct. 2, 1968 (P.L. 90-548); Public Lands — Wilderness Areas (Act), Oct. 23, 1970, (P.L. 91-504); Minam River Canyon Wilderness, Oregon (Act), Oct. 21, 1972 (P.L. 92-521); Hells Canyon National Recreation Area Act, Dec. 31, 1975 (P.L. 94-199); Endangered American Wilderness Area Act, Feb. 28, 1978 (P.L. 95-237) (incorporated "Oregon Omnibus Wilderness Act of 1978); Indian Peaks Wilderness Area, The Arapaho National Recreation Area and the Oregon Islands Wilderness Area Act, Oct. 11, 1978 (P.L. 95-450); Oregon Wilderness Act, June 26 1984 (P.L. 98-328); Oregon Resource Conservation Act, Sept. 30, 1996 (P.L. 104-208); Omnibus Parks and Public Lands Management Act, Nov. 12, 1996 (P.L. 104-333) [Both 1996 laws contain identical language protecting Opal Creek Wilderness. In a rare occurrence, conservationists' primary and backup legislative strategies both succeeded in Congress (involving attaching the Opal Creek language to two different bills), resulting in the area being "saved" twice.]; Steens Mountain Cooperative Management and Protection Act (P.L. 106-399), Oct. 30, 2000.

[iv]Originally designated with approximately 33,900 acres, 7,466 acres on the Willamette National Forest was transferred into the Opal Creek Wilderness upon its establishment in 1996. See footnote xxvii.

[v]Administratively established as Wild Area on Feb. 5, 1957.

[vi]Approximately 35,440 and 15,700 acres, respectively.

[vii]Administratively established as a Primitive Area in 1930; administratively designated as Wilderness on Oct. 7, 1940.

[viii]Approximately 216,250, 72,420 and 66,500 acres, respectively. The 1972 addition, while a net gain, also resulted in 7,220 acres previously designated as Wilderness being undesignated. The 1984 addition recovered 2,700 acres of the 7,220, thereby allowing Senator Hatfield to claim political credit for saving acres he had previously unsaved. The remaining 4,520 acres originally in the Eagle Cap Wilderness remain eligible for re-designation.

[ix]Administratively established as Wild Area on Nov. 11, 1943.

[x]Approximately 18,709 and 4,100 acres, respectively.

[xi]Includes three units: West Face, McGraw Creek and Seven Devil's (in Idaho). Also includes 83,811 acres in Idaho on the Nez Perce and Payette National Forests for a total of 214,944 acres.

[xii]In 1978, to facilitate construction of the Hells Canyon Rim Road, Congress — at the behest of Rep. Al Ullman and acquiescence of Senators Bob Packwood and Mark Hatfield — shrank the Wilderness between P.O. Saddle and Lookout Mountain. The original 1975 Wilderness boundary was congruous with the Hells Canyon Scenic Area (an administrative classification replaced by the Hells Canyon National Recreation Area Act of 1975), a line one-quarter mile west of the hydrologic divide between the Imnaha River and Snake River drainages. Approximately 1,120 acres were lost from the Wilderness when the boundary was moved. P.L. 95-625 (Nov. 10, 1978), 16 U.S.C. § 460gg.

[xiii]Wilderness consists of 130,095 acres on the Wallowa-Whitman National Forest and 1,038 acres on the Vale District of the Bureau of Land Management.

[xiv]Approximately 192,200 and 22,700 acres, respectively.

[xv]Administratively established as Wild Area on Sept. 10, 1946.

[xvi]In 1978, using a legislative "rider" to avoid public notice or hearing, Senator Hatfield moved the Wilderness boundary from northern side of Bald Mountain, which protected a trail, to the southern side, to allow construction of the Bald Mountain Road to allow de facto wilderness to the north to be logged. Approximately 102 acres were lost from the Wilderness. P.L. 95-586 (Nov. 3, 1978), 16 U.S.C. § 1132 nt.

[xvii]Approximately 78,850 and 92,000 acres, respectively.

[xviii]Originally, and more properly named, the Columbia Wilderness. Renamed in 1996. At least Hatfield is no longer in office.

[xix]Administratively established as a Wild Area on June 27, 1940.

[xx]Approximately 14,160 and 33,000 acres, respectively.

[xxi]Administratively established as a Primitive Area in 1930.

[xxii]Approximately 100,000 and 6,800 acres, respectively.

[xxiii]Administratively established as a Wild Area on Feb. 5, 1957.

[xxiv]Approximately 46,655 and 6,400 acres, respectively.

[xxv]Administratively established as a Primitive Area in 1930; administratively established as Wilderness on July 19, 1940.

[xxvi]Includes four units: Upper North Fork John Day River, Greenhorn Mountains, Middle North Fork John Day River and Tower Mountain.

xxviiContiguous with the Bull-of-the-Woods Wilderness. Separately designated for political benefit. The total acreage includes 7,466 acres previously in the Bull of the Woods Wilderness, allowing Senator Hatfield to receive political credit for "saving" the same acreage twice. See footnote iv.

xxviiiApproximately 21, 464 and 95 acres, respectively. Originally named Oregon Island Wilderness; changed in 1978.

xxixApproximately 16,500 acres adjoins the Red Buttes Wilderness on the Rogue River National Forest in California, increasing the total area protected to 20,250 acres.

xxxLivestock are expressly prohibited on 99,859 acres of the Wilderness, the first explicitly livestock-free Wilderness ever designated by Congress.

xxxiIncludes five units: Alvord Peak, High Steens, Home Creek, Little Blitzen and Upper Fish Creek.

xxxiiAdministratively established as a Wild Area on Feb. 9, 1942.

xxxiiiApproximately 33,004 and 35,300 acres, respectively.

xxxivAdministratively established as a Primitive Area in 1937; administratively established as Wilderness on Feb. 6, 1957.

xxxvApproximately 196,708, 45,400 and 38,100 acres, respectively.

xxxviContiguous with the Three Sisters Wilderness. Separately designated for political benefit.

xxxviiApproximately 111,048 acres adjoins the Wenaha-Tucannon Wilderness on the Umatilla National Forest in Washington, increasing the total area protected to 177,465 acres.

xxxviiiApproximately 25,658 acres on the Siskiyou National Forest and 10,160 acres on the Medford District of the Bureau of Land Management.

xxxixTorgerson, T. (ed.). 1999. OREGON BLUE BOOK. Salem, OR: 5.

Appendix B
Protected and Protectable Oregon Forest Wilderness

This table depicts the acreage in each of Oregon's Level IV Ecoregions (which comprise the state's five primarily forested Level III Ecoregions), the percentage of these ecoregions that are currently protected as Wilderness and the percentage that could (and should) be protected. Figures do not include non-forested protected Wilderness (Oregon Islands, Steens Mountain and Three Arch Rocks) or yet to be protected Oregon Desert Wilderness. As a result, figures are skewed somewhat for Level IV Ecoregions in the Blue Mountains Level III Ecoregion that are generally non-forested.

Additionally, the table does not include primarily forested wildlands in Level IV Ecoregions within Oregon's four primarily non-forested Level III Ecoregions (Columbia Plateau, Northern Basin and Range, Snake River Plain and Willamette Valley).

Total Wilderness percentages may not perfectly reflect the sum of their parts due to rounding. Also, data may vary from other published figures due to subtle differences in mapping and categorization.

Level III/IV Ecoregions	Total Area Acres	Protected Wilderness %	Protectable Wilderness %	Total Wilderness %
Coast Range				
Coastal Lowlands	405,183	0.0	6.1	6.1
Coastal Uplands	753,324	0.3	1.1	1.4
Mid-Coastal Sedimentary	2,392,590	0.2	4.4	4.6
Redwood Zone	20,031	0.0	37.5	37.5
Southern Oregon Coastal Mountains	443,475	3.9	14.9	18.8
Volcanics	1,307,732	1.3	3.0	4.3
Willapa Hills	481,064	0.0	0.0	0.0
Klamath Mountains				
Coastal Siskiyous	546,539	23.8	35.9	59.7
Inland Siskiyous	1,671,527	1.3	18.3	19.6
Klamath River Ridges	78,086	0.0	34.3	34.3
Oak Savanna Foothills	523,944	0.0	4.0	4.0
Rogue/Illinois Valleys	182,849	0.0	0.6	0.6
Serpentine Siskiyous	282,325	23.8	54.9	68.7
Umpqua Interior Foothills	589,309	0.0	0.0	0.04
Cascades				
Cascade Crest Montane Forest	1,221,581	33.7	26.9	60.6
Cascade Subalpine/Alpine	211,765	61.0	26.0	87.0
High Southern Cascades Montane Forest	586,226	26.3	45.7	72.0
Southern Cascades	905,572	11.5	1.5	13.0

Level III/IV Ecoregions	Total Area Acres	Protected Wilderness %	Protectable Wilderness %	Total Wilderness %
Cascades (continued)				
Western Cascades Lowlands and Valleys	2,498,504	2.2	9.8	12.0
Western Cascades Montane Highlands	1,746,174	12.5	26.2	38.7
East Cascades Slopes and Foothills				
Fremont Pine/Fir Forest	1,070,802	0.0	16.0	16.0
Grand Fir Mixed Forest	103,711	9.2	14.8	24.0
Klamath Juniper Woodland	502,455	0.0	9.6	9.6
Klamath/Goose Lake Basins	665,930	0.0	2.7	2.7
Oak/Conifer Foothills	295,610	0.6	4.0	4.6
Ponderosa Pine/Bitterbrush Woodland	689,027	1.0	5.9	6.9
Pumice Plateau	710,960	1.1	9.7	10.8
Pumice Plateau Basins	409,834	0.0	5.3	5.3
Southern Cascade Slope	330,330	0.03	1.2	1.2
Blue Mountains				
Blue Mountain Basins	693,911	0.0	0.05	0.05
Canyons and Dissected Highlands	700,045	10.9	23.2	34.1
Canyons and Dissected Uplands	698,733	15.7	42.0	57.7
Cold Basins	256,408	0.0	4.6	4.6
Continental Zone Foothills	2,377,136	0.0	5.3	5.3
Continental Zone Highlands	995,188	0.3	19.2	19.5
Deschutes River Valley	1,008,646	0.0	0.0	0.0
John Day/Clarno Highlands	1,583,783	1.5	13.7	15.2
John Day/Clarno Uplands	212,866	0.1	2.2	2.2
Maritime-Influenced Zone	890,128	1.5	15.9	17.4
Melange	786,132	6.4	17.5	23.9
Mesic Forest Zone	1,424,828	17.3	31.4	48.7
Subalpine-Alpine Zone	346,038	73.0	23.7	96.7
Wallowas/Seven Devils Mountains	337,057	10.7	10.6	21.3

Appendix C
National Wild and Scenic Rivers System in Oregon

Congress established the National Wild and Scenic Rivers System in 1968.[i] That legislation designated the Lower Rogue River segment as one of eight original Wild and Scenic Rivers.[ii] Congress added additional Oregon segments to the system in 1984,[iii] 1988,[iv] 1994,[v] 1996,[vi] and 2000,[vii] for a total of 49 segments and 1817.4 miles, approxi-

mately sixteen percent of the national system.[viii] These designations also protect approximately 574,960 acres of land that comprise the Wild and Scenic river corridors.[ix]

Stream Segment	Managing Agency	Established	Wild (mi.)	Scenic (mi.)	Recreational (mi.)	Total (mi.)	Upper Terminus[x]	Lower Terminus	Ecoregion
Big Marsh Creek	USFS	1988	0.0	0.0	15.0	15.0	NE1/4, S15, T26S, R6E	Confluence with Crescent Creek	Blue Mountains
Chetco	USFS	1988	25.5	8.0	11.0	44.5	Headwaters	Siskiyou National Forest boundary	Klamath Mountains
Clackamas	USFS	1988	0.0	20.0	27.0	47.0	Big Springs	Big Cliff Reservoir	Cascades
Crescent Creek	USFS	1988	0.0	0.0	10.0	10.0	SW1/4, S11, T24S, R6E	W line of S13, T24S, R7E	East Cascades Slopes and Foothills
Crooked*	BLM	1988	0.0	0.0	15.0	15.0	Crooked River National Grasslands boundary	Dry Creek	Columbia Plateau
Crooked, North Fork	BLM/USFS	1988	11.9	8.5	13.8	34.2	Source at Williams Prairie	One mile upstream from its confluence with Crooked River	Blue Mountains
Deschutes**	BLM/USFS	1988	0.0	30.0	143.4	173.4	(a) Wickiup Dam (b) Ogden Falls (c) Pelton Reregulating Dam	(a) Bend Urban Growth Boundary (SW corner, S13, T18S, R11E) (b) Upper end Reservoir Billy Chinook (c) Confluence with Columbia River.	Columbia Plateau East Cascades Slopes and Foothills
Donner und Blitzen	BLM	1988, 2000	87.5	0.0	0.0	87.5	Headwaters	Confluence with South Fork Blitzen and Little Blitzen, including tributaries: Little Blitzen River, South Fork Blitzen River, Big Indian Creek, Little Indian Creek, Fish Creek	Northern Basin and Range
Eagle Creek	USFS	1988	4.0	6.0	17.0	27.0	Headwaters below Eagle Lake	Wallowa-Whitman National Forest boundary at Skull Creek	Blue Mountains
Elk	USFS	1988	2.0	0.0	17.0	19.0	Falls on the North Fork; confluence of North and South Forks of the Elk River	Confluence with South Fork; confluence with Anvil Creek	Coast Range
Elkhorn Creek	BLM/USFS	1996	5.8	0.6	0.0	6.4	Willamette National Forest Southern boundary	Where the segment leaves BLM land	Cascades
Grande Ronde	BLM/USFS	1988	26.4	0.0	17.4	43.8	Confluence with Wallowa River	OR-WA border	Blue Mountains
Illinois	USFS	1984	28.7	17.9	3.8	50.4	Siskiyou National Forest boundary	Confluence with Rogue River	Klamath Mountains
Imnaha	USFS	1988	15.0	4.0	58.0	77.0	Headwaters of South Fork of the Imnaha River	Confluence with Snake River	Blue Mountains

Stream Segment	Managing Agency	Established	Wild (mi.)	Scenic (mi.)	Recreational (mi.)	Total (mi.)	Upper Terminus	Lower Terminus	Ecoregion
John Day*	BLM	1988	0.0	0.0	147.5	147.5	Service Creek	Tumwater Falls	Blue Mountains, Columbia Plateau
John Day (North Fork)	USFS	1988	27.8	10.5	15.8	54.1	Headwaters in North Fork John Day Wilderness Area	Confluence with Camas Creek	Blue Mountains
John Day (South Fork)	BLM	1988	0.0	0.0	47.0	47.0	Malheur National Forest boundary	Confluence with Smoky Creek	Blue Mountains
Joseph Creek	USFS	1988	8.6	0.0	0.0	8.6	Joseph Creek Ranch, 1.0 mile downstream from Cougar Creek	Wallowa-Whitman National Forest boundary	Blue Mountains
Kiger Creek*	BLM	2000	4.3	0.0	0.0	4.3	Headwaters	Where creek leaves Steens Mountain Wilderness Area	Northern Basin and Range
Klamath***	BLM	1994	0.0	11.0	0.0	11.0	J.C. Boyle Powerhouse	California border	East Cascades Slopes and Foothills
Little Deschutes	USFS	1988	0.0	0.0	12.0	12.0	Source in NW1/4 of S15, T26S, R6E	N line, S12, T26S, R7E	East Cascades Slopes and Foothills
Lostine	USFS	1988	5.0	0.0	11.0	16.0	Headwaters in Eagle Cap Wilderness Area	Wallowa-Whitman National Forest boundary	Blue Mountains
Malheur	USFS	1988	0.0	7.0	6.7 1	3.7	Bosonberg Creek	Malheur National Forest boundary	Blue Mountains
Malheur, North Fork	USFS	1988	0.0	25.5	0.0	25.5	Headwaters	Malheur National Forest boundary	Blue Mountains
McKenzie	USFS	1988	0.0	0.0	12.7	12.7	Clear Lake	Scott Creek, not including Carmen and Trail Bridge Reservoir Dams	Cascades
Metolius	USFS	1988	0.0	17.1	11.5	28.6	Deschutes National Forest boundary below Springs of the Metolius	Reservoir Billy Chinook	East Cascades Slopes and Foothills
Minam	USFS	1988	39.0	0.0	0.0	39.0	Headwaters at the South end of Minam Lake	Eagle Cap Wilderness Area boundary, 0.5 mile downstream from Cougar Creek	Blue Mountains
North Powder	USFS	1988	0.0	6.0	0.0	6.0	Headwaters in the Elkhorn Mountains	Wallowa-Whitman National Forest boundary	Blue Mountains
North Umpqua	BLM/USFS	1988	0.0	0.0	33.8	33.8	Soda Springs Powerhouse	Confluence with Rock Creek	Cascades
Owyhee*	BLM	1984	120.0	0.0	0.0	120.0	Three Forks downstream to China Gulch	Crooked Creek to Owyhee Reservoir; and "South Fork" from the Idaho border to Three Forks	Snake River Plain
Owyhee (North Fork)*	BLM	1998	9.6	0.0	0.0	9.6	Idaho border	Confluence with the Owyhee River	Snake River Plain
Powder*	BLM	1988	0.0	11.7	0.0	11.7	Thief Valley Dam	Highway 203 Bridge	Blue Mountains
Quartzville Creek	BLM	1988	0.0	0.0	12.0	12.0	Willamette National Forest boundary	Green Peter Reservoir	Cascades
Roaring	USFS	1988	13.5	0.0	0.2	13.7	Headwaters	Confluence with the Clackamas River	Cascades
Rogue (Lower)	BLM/USFS	1968	33.6	7.5	43.4	84.5	Confluence with the Applegate River	Lobster Creek Bridge	Klamath Mountains
Rogue (Upper)	USFS	1988	6.1	34.2	0.0	40.3	North boundary Crater Lake National Park	Rogue River National Forest boundary at Prospect	Cascades

Stream Segment	Managing Agency	Established	Wild (mi.)	Scenic (mi.)	Recreational (mi.)	Total (mi.)	Upper Terminus	Lower Terminus	Ecoregion
Salmon	BLM/USFS	1988	15.0	4.8	13.7	33.5	Headwaters	Confluence with Sandy River	Cascades
Sandy	BLM/USFS	1988	4.5	3.8	16.6	24.9	Headwaters	Mt. Hood National Forest boundary	Cascades
Smith (North Fork)	USFS	1988	8.5	4.5	0.0	13.0	Headwaters	California border	Coast Range
Snake****	USFS	1975	32.5	34.4	0.0	66.9	Hells Canyon Dam	An eastward extension of the north boundary of S1, T5N, R47E	Blue Mountains
Sprague (North Fork)	USFS	1988	0.0	15.0	0.0	15.0	Head of River Spring in the SW1/4 S15, T35S, R16E	NW1/4 S11, T35S, R15E	East Cascades Slopes and Foothills
Squaw Creek	USFS	1988	6.6	8.8	0.0	15.4	Source	800 feet upstream from McAllister Ditch intake	East Cascades Slopes and Foothills
Sycan	USFS	1988	0.0	50.4	8.6	59.0	NE1/4 of S5, T34S, R17E	Coyote Bucket at the Fremont National Forest boundary	East Cascades Slopes and Foothills
Wallowa***	BLM	1996	0.0	0.0	10.0	10.0	Confluence with Minam River	Confluence with Grande Ronde River	Blue Mountains
Wenaha	USFS	1988	18.7	2.7	0.2	21.6	Confluence of North and South Forks	Confluence with Grande Ronde River	Blue Mountains
West Little Owyhee	BLM	1988	57.6	0.0	0.0	57.6	Headwaters	Mouth	Snake River Plain
White	BLM/USFS	1988	0.0	24.3	22.5	46.8	White River Glacier	Confluence with Deschutes River	Cascades
Wildhorse Creek*	BLM	2000	9.6	0.0	0.0	9.6	Headwaters	0.36 stream miles into S34, T34S, R33E; and Little Wildhorse Creek from headwaters to its confluence with Wildhorse Creek	Northern Basin and Range
Willamette, North Fork of Middle Fork	USFS	1988	8.8	6.5	27	42.3	Source at Waldo Lake	Willamette National Forest boundary at Westfir	Cascades
TOTALS			**636.1**	**380.7**	**800.6**	**1817.4**			

* High desert, not forested, river.

** Upper portion forested, lower portion high desert.

*** State Scenic Waterway designated in 1988 and included in National Wild and Scenic Rivers System by the Secretary of the Interior at the request of the Governor of Oregon pursuant to Section 2(a) of Wild and Scenic Rivers Act (16 U.S.C. § 1273(a)).

**** Approximately one-half of protective corridor is in Idaho.

[i] Wild and Scenic Rivers Act, 16 U.S.C. §§ 1271 et seq.

[ii] 16 U.S.C. § 1274a(5).

[iii] 16 U.S.C. § 1274a(54)-(55).

[iv] Oregon Omnibus Wild and Scenic Rivers Act, 16 U.S.C. § 1274a(68)-(107).

[v] At the request of Governor Barbara Roberts, the Klamath River State Scenic Waterway was accepted into the National Wild and Scenic River System by the Secretary of Interior on Sept. 22, 1994.

[vi] At the request of Governor Barbara Roberts, the Wallowa River State Scenic Waterway was accepted into the National Wild and Scenic River System by the Secretary of Interior on July 23, 1996.

[vii] Steens Mountain Cooperative Management and Protection Act, 16 U.S.C. § 1274a—.

[viii] See National Park Service. 2002. River mileage classifications for components of the National Wild & Scenic Rivers System. Updated Feb. 1, 2002; printed Feb. 21, 2002. Available at www.nps.gov/rivers/wildriverstable.html.

[ix] Based on an average of a half-mile wide corridor of land, or 320 acres per linear mile of stream, except for Elkhorn Creek, which is 640 acres per linear mile, and deducting the Idaho portion of the Snake Wild and Scenic River (160 acres per linear mile).

[x] In the West Hills of Portland, Oregon, near the Sylvan interchange on US 26 (Sunset Highway), is the Willamette Stone State Park. Here a tiny monument marks the beginning of all land surveys in Oregon and Washington. The East-West baseline through the stone marks the ranges (R), while the North-South meridian defines the townships (T). A township is thirty-six square miles and divided into 36 one-square mile (640 acres) sections (S) and is specified by its "township" (T) and "range" (R). A section is further divided as necessary into halves, quarters, quarter-quarter sections, etc. So a legal description of SE 1/4, NW 1/4, T. 1 S., R. 3 E, S. 3, W.M describes the 40 acres in the southeast quarter of the northwest quarter of section 3 in Township 1 South, Range 3 East using the Willamette Meridian (or the first township south and three to the east of the Willamette Stone).

Appendix D
Other Congressional Conservation Designations in Oregon

In addition to Wilderness and Wild and Scenic Rivers, Congress has designated other conservation areas. Although units of the National Wildlife Refuge System also enjoy congressional protection,[i] since most Oregon refuges are wetlands and/or not generally forested, they are not further considered here.

Area	Agency	Est.	Federal Acreage*	Ecoregion
Bull Run Watershed Management Unit[ii]	USFS	1996	98,272	Cascades
Cascade Head Scenic-Research Area[iii]	USFS	1974	6,600	Coast Range
Cascade-Siskiyou National Monument[iv]**	BLM	2000	52,947	Klamath Mountains
Columbia Gorge River National Scenic Area[v]***	USFS	1986	43,058	Cascades
Crater Lake National Park[vi]	NPS	1902	183,244	Cascades
Hells Canyon National Recreation Area[vii]	USFS	1975	498,888	Blue Mountains
John Day Fossil Beds National Monument[viii]*/****	NPS	1974	14,000	Blue Mountains
Newberry National Volcanic Monument[ix]	USFS	1990	55,500	East Cascades Slopes and Foothills
Opal Creek Scenic-Recreation Area[x]	USFS	1996	13,048	Cascades
Oregon Caves National Monument[xii]*/**	NPS	1909	484	Klamath Mountains
Oregon Dunes National Recreation Area[xiii]	USFS	1972	31,000	Coast Range
Pacific Crest National Scenic Trail[xiv]	USFS/BLM	1968	NA[xv]	Cascades
Steens Mountain Cooperative Management and Protection Area[xvi]****	BLM	2000	496,135	Northern Basin and Range
Yaquina Head Outstanding Natural Area[xvii]	BLM	1980	100	Coast Range
TOTAL			**1,650,176**	

* Acreage from either statute or subsequent agency re-calculation.

**Most national monuments have been proclaimed by the President pursuant to the Antiquities Act of 1906 (16 U.S.C. § 431). Monuments can also be legislated. In Oregon, only the John Day Fossil Beds National Monument was Congressionally designated. Presidents have created the rest.

***Acreage only includes federal land in Oregon within the "Special Management Area." An additional 80,187 acres of non-federal land in Oregon are included in the "General Management Area," which usually provides inadequate protection from development. Total Oregon acreage in the CRGNSA is 123,245 acres. Total size of the NSA, including lands in Washington, is 292,500 acres.

**** Not located within the generally forested Oregon, but included for sake of completeness.

[i]16 U.S.C. §§ 668dd et seq.

[ii]16 U.S.C.A. § 482b nt. In 1892, the "Bull Run Forest Reserve" is established by presidential proclamation. In 1904, Congress prohibited human trespass and livestock grazing and strengthened penalties in 1909. In 1977, Congress shrunk the reserve to the Bull Run Watershed Management Unit and weakened protections to legalize previously illegal Forest Service logging. In 1996, Congress ended logging. In 2001, Congress added Little Sandy Watershed.

[iii]16 U.S.C. §§ 541 et seq.

[iv]Establishment of the Cascade-Siskiyou National Monument, Proclamation No. 7318, 16 U.S.C. § 431 nt. (65 Fed. Reg. 37249, June 9, 2000) (President Clinton).

[v]16 U.S.C. §§ 544 et seq.

[vi]16 U.S.C. §§ 121 et seq.

[vii]16 U.S.C. §§ 460gg et seq. (as amended).

[viii]16 U.S.C. § 431 nt. (Pub. L. 93-486, title I, sec. 101(a)(2), 88 Stat. 1461).

[ix]6 U.S.C. § 431 nt. (Pub. L. 101-522, 104 Stat. 2288).

[x]16 U.S.C. § 545b.

[xi]16 USC § 460oo.

[xii]Oregon Caves National Monument, Oregon, Proclamation No. 876, 16 U.S.C. § 431 nt. (36 Stat. 2497) (July 12, 1909) (President Taft).

[xiii]16 U.S.C. §§ 460z et seq. (as amended).

[xiv]16 U.S.C. §§ 1244 et seq. (While designation as a national scenic trail affords no formal protection to the trail corridor, it does tend to discourage (but has not always prevented) federal bureaucrats from logging along the route.)

[xv]The Oregon section of the trail is 369 miles (out of 2,350 total miles), from the California border to the Bridge of the Gods in the Columbia River Gorge. See Schafer, J. P. and A Selters. 2000. PACIFIC CREST TRAIL OREGON AND WASHINGTON. Vol. 2. Wilderness Press. Berkeley, CA.

[xvi]16 U.S.C. § 460nnn.

[xvii]43 U.S.C. § 1783.

Appendix E
Enjoying Oregon's Unprotected Forest Wilderness

Some might say, "Didn't you get lonesome?" Of course my answer would be, "No," for I have always loved nature's ways in the wilderness. There are so many things that are interesting to me. At night one can lie and gaze at the stars and Milky Way and listen to the breeze winding its way through the tree-tops, the night birds and all the rest. It's all interesting to study and think about. The wilderness is a friendly place if you can live up to its demands.

—George Wright (lifelong resident of Soda Mountain area)[1]

In spite of the name, it's a very nice hike in the proposed North Umpqua Wilderness.

Over two million acres of Oregon's forest wilderness is protected in the National Wilderness Preservation System. The Forest Service and private publishers have published detailed topographic maps for each area (except Grassy Knob and Table Rock).

All designated Wilderness areas in Oregon offer outstanding opportunities for solitude and primitive recreation. Parts of some areas, however — like Mount Hood, Mount Jefferson, Three Sisters, Diamond Peak and Sky Lakes — are recreationally overused, which reduces some wilderness experiences such as solitude.

But protected Wilderness is not the subject of this book.

Instead of visiting Oregon's already-protected Wilderness, choose to visit its unprotected wildlands. The former will likely always be there, the latter may not.

There are bookshelves full of excellent hiking guides that describe most hiking trails on Oregon's forested public lands. The thoroughness in their coverage tends to decrease as one moves east, with most eastern Oregon coverage devoted only to the major trails and hiking regions in Oregon's Blue Mountain Ecoregion. The eastern portion of Oregon's East Cascades Slopes and Foothills Ecoregion (a.k.a. the Fremont National Forest) gets little attention and only a few hiking guides give even cursory coverage of this area.

Most hiking guides are apolitical, so it will probably be up to the reader to deduce whether a particular hiking trail is part of a proposed Wilderness area described in this book (except that most hiking guides will inform you if a trail is in a designated Wilderness (and there are usually signs at the trailhead)). If a trail is in a roadless area of any significant size, it is probably located in one of the areas the Oregon Wild campaign proposes for Wilderness.

Nancy Peterson (the author is Mr. Nancy Peterson) has meticulously cross-refer-

enced each hike described in all currently available Oregon hiking guides with the areas proposed for Wilderness protection in this book, and vice-versa. If you are interested in exploring a particular trail, you can now identify which Wilderness proposal it is in. If you are interested in exploring a particular Wilderness proposal, you can now discover which trails and what hiking guides cover the area. Since guidebooks rotate in and out of print and are frequently revised, this valuable information is posted and constantly updated on the Oregon Wild Forest Coalition's web page at www.oregonwild.org/hikes.

If you are new to hiking, you should read up on the topic (see *Recommended Readings*, Appendix G). It's easy to have a safe and enjoyable time. Until grizzly bears return to the Oregon wilderness, perhaps the greatest inconvenience you will suffer from visiting Oregon's wild forests is a case of poison oak. As with most things, knowledge is power (www.andykerr.net/misc/poioakivy).

[1] Foley, Ann. 1994. On the Greensprings. Friends of the Greensprings. Ashland, OR: 46.

Appendix F
How You Can Help Save Oregon's Wilderness

Unfortunately, the sugar pine makes excellent lumber. It is too good to live, and is already passing rapidly away before the woodman's axe. Surely out of all of the abounding forest-wealth of Oregon a few specimens might be spared to the world, not as dead lumber, but as living trees. A park of moderate extent might be set apart and protected for public use forever, containing at least a few hundreds of these noble pines, spruces and firs. Happy will be the men who, having the power and the love and the benevolent forecast to do this, will do it. They will not be forgotten. The trees and their lovers will sing their praises, and generations yet unborn will rise up and call them blessed.

—John Muir[1]

Polite conservationists leave no mark save the scars on the land that could have been prevented had they stood their ground.

—David Brower[2]

Wilderness has value, but wilderness doesn't vote. Neither do fish, wildlife or plants.

If enough Oregonians give some of their time and money, Oregon's wilderness will be saved. Following are the three most important actions you can take to protect Oregon's remaining forest wilderness.

1. Contact your federal elected officials.

Only Congress can designate Wilderness areas. More importantly, if an entire state's congressional delegation (Representatives and Senators) wants an area protected as Wilderness, it will be protected. The Congress rarely denies a legislative request from a state's entire delegation. Please contact Oregon's congressional delegation at their addresses. It is best to keep your communications to one page and to the point. Be sure to say you want <u>all</u> five million acres in *Oregon Wild* protected as Wilderness.

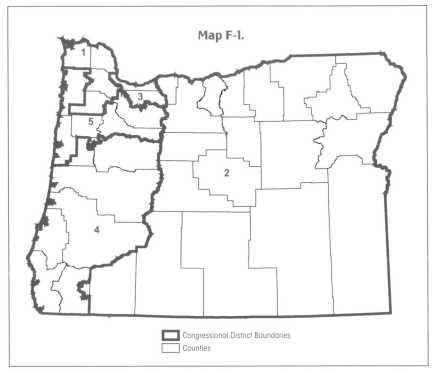

Map F-1.

Congressional District Boundaries
Counties

Oregon has five congressional districts. If it is not clear from this map, you can determine who represents you in the U.S. House of Representatives by calling your local library, county elections office, or by visiting to www.house.gov and entering your zip code.

Senator Ron Wyden (D)
503/326-7525 • 202/228-2717 (fax)
http://wyden.senate.gov/mail.htm
www.senate.gov/~wyden/

Senator Gordon Smith (R)
503/326-3386 • 202/228-3997 (fax)
oregon@gsmith.senate.gov
www.senate.gov/~gsmith/

mailing address:
United States Senate
Washington, DC 20510

---

[1] Buske, Frank (ed.). 1980. WILDERNESS ESSAYS. Peregrine Smith Books. Salt Lake City, UT: 250-251. (John Muir, "The Forests of Oregon and Their Inhabitants").

[2] Cole, Michelle. *Oregon conservationists mourned the death of David Brower on Monday, calling him an inspiration.* The Oregonian. (Nov. 7, 2000): A02.

Rep. David Wu (D, 1st)
503/326-2901 • 202/225-9497 (fax)
david.wu@mail.house.gov
www.house.gov/wu

Rep. Greg Walden (R, 2nd)
541/776-4646 • 202/225-5774 (fax)
greg.walden@mail.house.gov
www.house.gov/walden

Rep. Earl Blumenauer (D, 3rd)
503/231-2300 • 202/225-8941 (fax)
write.earl@mail.house.gov
www.house.gov/blumenauer

Rep. Peter DeFazio (D, 4th)
541/465-6732 • 202/225-0032 (fax)
peter.defazio@mail.house.gov
www.house.gov/defazio

Rep. Darlene Hooley (D, 5th)
503/588-9100 • 202/225-5699 (fax)
darlene@mail.house.gov
www.house.gov/hooley

mailing address:
United States House of Representatives
Washington, DC 20515

2. Support a conservation organization financially.

Eighty percent of democracy is showing up. Three-quarters of that is showing up with others. In numbers, there is strength. Consider joining the Oregon Natural Resources Council and/or one or more of the fine conservation and outdoor organizations that have endorsed *Oregon Wild* (see www.oregonwild.org).

MERLIN D. TUTTLE, *BAT CONSERVATION INTERNATIONAL*

The spotted bat (*Euderma maculatum*) is perhaps America's rarest mammal. In Oregon, one of the very few places it is found is the wildlands of South Fork John Day basin.

3. Volunteer with a conservation organization.

Volunteers, not professional staff, do most of the conservation work in Oregon. Volunteer with Oregon Natural Resource Council or another conservation organization working on *Oregon Wild*.

Appendix G
Recommended Readings

I have a low opinion of books; they are but piles of stones set up to show coming travelers where other minds have been, or at best signal smokes to call attention. Cadmus[1] and all the other inventors of letters receive a thousand-fold more credit than they deserve. No amount of word-making will ever make a single soul to know these mountains. As well seek to warm the naked and frostbitten by lectures on caloric and pictures of flame. One day's exposure to mountains is better than cartloads of books.

John Muir[2]

Oh John, lighten up! You wrote books and to good effect. You saved Yosemite more through your writing than your walking, though you much preferred the latter. Books can lead one to the wild and to a better understanding of it before, during and after a visit.

Ecology and Conservation Biology

To have fully functioning forest ecosystems, both across the landscape and over time, we need to conserve what is left and restore much of what has been lost. *Continental Conservation: Scientific Foundations of Regional Reserve Networks*, by Michael E. Soulé and John Terborgh, makes the case.

Oregon's Living Landscape: Strategies and Opportunities to Conserve Biodiversity, by the Oregon Biodiversity Project, provides lay people with an excellent overview of Oregon's biodiversity.

Natural Vegetation of Oregon and Washington, by Jerry Franklin and Christen Dryness, was first published in 1973 by the Forest Service. It is still quite useful and has been reprinted by Oregon State University Press. If you want to understand all those Oregon plant communities, this is your book.

Saving Nature's Legacy, by Reed Noss and Allen Cooperrider, explains why and how to maintain wildness.

A Sand County Almanac, by Aldo Leopold, is one of the books in the Old Testament of the Wilderness Bible.

Literature

Charles Erskine Scott Wood was a fascinating individual — and well ahead of his time. *Wood Works*, edited by Edwin Bingham and Tim Barnes, highlights Wood's varied writings. *Two Rooms: The Life of Charles Erskine Scott Wood*, by Robert Hamburger, brings this most original Oregonian to life.

Lasso the Wind: Away to the New West, by Timothy Egan, covers the American West, but several stories in the book could just as well have been set in Oregon. (One story involves the author of this book being hung in effigy.)

The only modern novel (thus far) on Oregon forests is *Forest Blood*, by Jeff Golden.

Listening for Coyote: A Walk Across Oregon's Wilderness, by William Sullivan, describes a 1,361-mile backpacking trek from westernmost Cape Blanco to easternmost Hells Canyon.

John Muir fans will appreciate *John Muir In His Own Words: A Book of Quotations*, compiled and edited by Peter Browning.

Natural History

Secrets of the Old Growth Forest, by David Kelly and Gary Braasch, was the first popular book about these endangered forests and helped set the stage for public debate, as did Elliot Norse' *Ancient Forests of the Pacific Northwest*.

Oregon Mountain Ranges, by George Wuerthner, is an excellent introduction to the geography and natural history of Oregon's forests. The *Field Guide to Old-Growth Forests*, by Larry Eifert, is a general introduction to westside ancient forest ecosystems.

A field guide to forests is always a handy reference. *Cascade-Olympic Natural History: A Trailside Reference* (2nd. ed.), by Daniel Mathews, is the most specific to the Cascade Range from the Columbia River to the Willamette-Umpqua Divide (between Eugene and Roseburg). *Western Forests*, by Stephen Whitney, is the next best field guide for Oregon forests. Mathew's *Rocky Mountain Natural History* covers Oregon's greater Wallowa Mountains region.

Several specific guides for trees have also been published. *Northwest Trees*, by Stephen Arno and Ramona Hammerly, is a nice little natural history of our sylvan siblings, but ignores forests south of the Willamette-Umpqua Divide on the west side and forests south of La Pine on the eastside. *Trees to Know in Oregon*, by Edward Jensen and Charles Ross, is a bit heavy on timber propaganda, but full of identification hints for the botanically challenged. The *National Audubon Society Field Guide to North American*

---

[1] Some guy of ancient Greek or Roman mythology, who either pleased and/or displeased the gods, who either suffered greatly and/or was greatly rewarded for it, then who either lived happily ever after and/or died tragically.

[2] Wolfe, Linnie Marsh. 1938. JOHN OF THE MOUNTAINS. University of Wisconsin Press. Madison, WI: 94-95 (originally published in John Muir, MOUNTAIN THOUGHTS in 1872).

Trees (Western Region), by Elbert Little, exhaustively covers the state. Less exhaustive, but lighter in the pack, is *National Audubon Society Pocket Guide to Familiar Trees of North America (West)*, edited by Jane Friedman.

One cannot have too many field guides. The *National Audubon Society Field Guide* series is well-done and has volumes on birds (western), butterflies, fossils, insects and spiders, mammals, mushrooms, night sky, reptiles and amphibians, rocks and minerals, wildflowers and weather, all of which occur in Oregon forests.

Birder's Guide to Oregon, by Joseph Evanich, Jr., is a general reference on well-known bird habitats. The new — and immediately classic — Oregon ornithological magnum opus is *Birds of Oregon*, co-edited by David B. Marshall, Matthew G. Hunter and Alan L. Contreras.

For identifying trees, shrubs, grasses, sedges and forbs in eastside forests, try *Common Plants of the Inland Pacific Northwest*, by Charles Johnson. This guide is a Forest Service (Pacific Northwest Region R6-NR-ECOL-TP-04-98) publication and is not distributed commercially. A second edition was published in 1998. Obtain a copy by contacting the Wallowa-Whitman National Forest office in Baker City where the author works.

For the lowdown on Sasquatch, *Where Bigfoot Walks: Crossing the Dark Divide*, by Robert Pyle, is the most authoritative and a rather nice piece of literature on the subject.

Land Mammals of Oregon, by B. J. Verts and Leslie Carraway, does not address Sasquatch, but does exhaustively cover every other non-sea mammal in the state. *Mammals of Washington and Oregon*, by Tamara Eder, is more general, but includes full-color images. *Mammals of the Pacific Northwest: From the Coast to the High Cascades*, by Chris Maser, is another fine source. Also useful is the second edition of the *Atlas of Oregon Wildlife*, by Blair Csuti, et al. It covers amphibians, reptiles and breeding birds, in addition to mammals.

Geology of Oregon, by Elizabeth L. Orr and William N. Orr, now in its fifth edition has long been the classic text to understanding the subject. Not anymore. Ellen Bishop's *In Search of Ancient Oregon: A Geological and Natural History* is infinitely more colorful and comprehensible.

Robert Pyle's *Butterflies of Cascadia*, the *Guide to Butterflies of Oregon and Washington*, by William Neil, et al., and *Macrolichens of the Pacific Northwest*, by Bruce McCune and Linda Geiser, may open whole new worlds to you.

Guide to Pacific Northwest Aquatic Invertebrates, by Rich Hafele and Steve Hinton (available from Oregon Trout, www.ortrout.org), can help you identify little bugs in the creek.

To get to know turtles, lizards and snakes, see *Reptiles of Washington and Oregon*, edited by Robert Storm and William Leonard, and *Reptiles of the Northwest*, by Alan St. John.

The Climate of Oregon: From Rain Forest to Desert, by George H. Taylor and Chris Hannon, is the most exhaustive word on the subject. (A companion volume, *Oregon Weather Book: A State of Extremes*, by George H. Taylor and Raymond R. Hatton, is also interesting, but unfortunately overlaps with much of Taylor and Hannon's other book.)

Oregon's forests host many diverse species, too many of which are now in trouble. *Rare, Threatened and Endangered Species of Oregon*, by the Oregon Natural Heritage Program (a project of The Nature Conservancy and the State of Oregon), gives you the skinny on the status of most organisms great and small. *Species at Risk: Sensitive, Threatened and Endangered Vertebrates of Oregon*, by the David B. Marshall and others (published by Oregon Department of Fish and Wildlife), presents further detail about these species' natural history.

The environmental impact statements and supporting documents that guide federal forest management often include important ecological information about Oregon's forests. The Interior Columbia River Basin Ecosystem Management Project for the eastside forests and the President's Northwest Forest Plan for the westside forests are available (just for the asking) from the appropriate Forest Service or Bureau of Land Management office.

Water: A Natural History, by Alice Outwater, especially chapter 3, makes the connection between water and forests crystal clear.

The Living Dunes, with photography by Jerry Larson, poetry by Ron McLean, text by Stephen Cary and edited by Lynne Word, is a beautiful picture book of the Oregon Dunes, one of the most unique ecosystems in Oregon. The *Pacific Northwest Coast: Living with the Shores of Oregon and Washington*, by Paul Komar, is a fine treatment of the Oregon Dunes. *Plants of the Oregon Coastal Dunes*, by Alfred M. Wiedemann, La Rea J. Dennis and Frank H. Smith, reminds us that the dunes are not just fascinating collection of sand, but of vegetation as well.

A Nature Notes Sampler, by Frank Lang, provides natural history tidbits about the Klamath Mountains of southern Oregon and northern California.

Shadow Cat: Encountering the American Mountain Lion, edited by Susan Ewing and Elizabeth Grossman, collects the experiences of a variety of writers and their interactions with North America's largest wild feline.

Salmon Without Rivers: A History of the Pacific Salmon Crisis, by Jim Lichatowich, is the single best read on what the Pacific salmon were, are and could be again.

Trout and Salmon of North America by Robert Behnke and illustrated by Joseph Tommelleri is beautifully written and illustrated. While continental in scope, one will learn much about fish in Oregon and the greater Northwest.

Nature Rambles in the Wallowas, by Elmo Stevenson, though first published in 1937, is still the best site-specific guide to this unique part of Oregon.

Forest Primeval, by Chris Maser, helps one understand the basic ecological functioning of a forest.

Outdoor Skills

If you do not know a thing about backpacking, consider the bible of backpacking, *The Complete Walker III*, by Colin Fletcher. Another favorite is *Backpacking: One Step at a Time*, by Harvey Manning.

Nature's Revenge: The Secrets of Poison Ivy, Poison Oak, Poison Sumac and Their Remedies, by Susan Hauser, debunks the pervasive myths about poison oak and presents the facts on how one contracts it, how to avoid it and how to treat it.

A slim but useful volume, *Wilderness Medical Society Practice Guidelines for Emergency Medical Care*, edited by William Forgey, helps you prepare for the time when things go wrong in the wild. *Wilderness Medicine: Beyond First Aid*, by the same author, is worth the read.

Proper defecation disposal is both a health and aesthetic matter. *How To Shit in the Woods: An Environmentally Sound Approach to a Lost Art*, by Kathleen Meyer, is the definitive work on the matter.

Wilderness

An incredible historical overview is *Wilderness and the American Mind*, by Roderick Nash. Nash explores our feelings toward wilderness from the roots of western civilization to the recent past.

Unmanaged Landscapes: Voices for Untamed Nature, edited by Bill Willers, is an anthology of essays from the likes of John Muir, Henry Thoreau and Rachel Carson, the intellectual giants who laid the groundwork for the modern Wilderness movement.

The Wilderness Movement and the National Forests, by Dennis Roth, is an excellent overview of the battle for wilderness on the National Forest System and includes two chapters specifically about Oregon. *Battle for Wilderness*, by Michael Frome, traces this struggle up to passage of The Wilderness Act of 1964.

For pretty pictures, the Time-Life American Wilderness series can still be found in used book outlets. *The Cascades* and *The Northwest Coast*, both by Richard Williams, cover Oregon forestlands. For more depth on the nation's remaining large wild areas, see *The Big Outside: A Descriptive Inventory of the Big Wilderness Areas of the United States*, by Dave Foreman and Howie Wolke. To read the legal and moral case for Wilderness, see

A Wilderness Bill of Rights: A Great Conservationist States His Case, by U.S. Supreme Court Associate Justice William O. Douglas (who spent a lot of time in the wilderness of northeast Oregon).

Hells Canyon: The Deepest Gorge on Earth, by William Ashworth, is a compelling narrative chronicling the epic battle to keep dams out of this magnificent canyon.

Oregon Desert Guide: 70 Hikes, by Andy Kerr, examines magnificent Oregon wilderness not known for having trees. (Okay, it's shameless plug, but some desert wilderness *does* have trees).

The Wilderness Concept and the Three Sisters Wilderness, by Les Joslin, is written from the perspective of a Wilderness manager and describes both the human and natural history of this premier Wilderness.

Return of the Wild: The Future of Our Natural Lands, edited by Ted Kerasote, is the first of a continuing series published by the Campaign for America's Wilderness to address history, environmental issues, current information and present the contemporary debate about Wilderness.

The Enduring Wilderness: Protecting Our natural heritage Through the Wilderness Act, by Oregon native Doug Scott, is a history of protecting land as Wilderness for the past four decades. It also looks to the future and the politics of wilderness preservation.

Political and Social History

The continuous struggle for the Oregon wilderness was accelerated and recast during the Northwest Forest Wars (ca. 1980±10 to ca. 2004±10). Several books have been written about the national effort to conserve the ancient old-growth forests of the Pacific Northwest. They include: *The Final Forest: They Battle for the Last Great Trees of the Pacific Northwest*, by Pulitzer prize winning author William Dietrich; *Showdown at Opal Creek: The Battle for America's Last Wilderness*, by David Seideman; *Coyotes and Town Dogs: Earth First! and the Environmental Movement*, by Susan Zakin; *Tree Huggers: Victory, Defeat and Renewal in the Northwest Ancient Forest Campaign*, by Kathie Durbin. All tell important, but different, parts of the story. A more scholarly treatise is *The Wisdom of the Spotted Owl: Policy Lessons for a New Century*, by Steven Lewis Yaffee. *A Common Fate: Endangered Salmon and the People of the Pacific Northwest*, by Joseph Cone, dwells mostly on dam problems, but also addresses critical forest habitat as it relates to salmon conservation.

"The Wisdom of the Owl at Dusk": Cultural Conflict and Moral Disagreement Over the Oregon Forests, by Sam Porter, is an unpublished PhD. dissertation from Emory University, which considers the forest wars through a lens not often used for such conflicts.

It really is a war, as David Helvarg points out in *The War Against the Greens: The*

"Wise Use" Movement, the New Right and Anti-Environmental Violence.

The lazy part of the media portrayed the story as "owls versus jobs" but Thomas Michael Power's *Lost Landscapes and Failed Economics: The Search for a Value of Place,* makes clear that there's more money in leaving trees standing than in cutting them down. It's mainly a matter of who gets the money.

Most journalists have ignored the eastside forests, but *Forest Dreams, Forest Nightmares: The Paradox of Old Growth in the Inland West,* by Nancy Langston, is an excellent account of the political and natural history of the federal forests of the Blue Mountains.

The history of eastside forests is written by fire and *Fire in America: A Cultural History of Wildland and Rural Fire,* by Stephen Pyne, is an exhaustive treatise that shows that Smokey Bear is an upstart. Oregon native Douglas Gantenbein has written a modern critique of forest firefighting follies in his *A Season of Fire: Four Months on the Firelines of America's Forests.*

Oregon Geographic Names, by Lewis L. McArthur, is the definitive reference of place names and includes many interesting tidbits of cultural and natural history.

Crater Lake National Park: A History, by Rick Harmon, tells the dramatic story one of the nation's oldest and Oregon's only national park.

Hiking and Boating

There are many hiking guides to Oregon's forests. Most describe trails in western and central Oregon. A complete listing of available guides with hikes cross-referenced to each proposed Wilderness area in this book is available at www.onrc.org/hikes. A few of these guides are particularly noted here because they have a political aspect or detail the natural history of their chosen area.

Oregon's Ancient Forests: A Walking Guide, by Wendell Wood, is an inspiration for this book. While out of print, it is still useful for locating many of Oregon's special forests.

Hiking Oregon's Geology, by Ellen Morris Bishop and John Eliot Allen, proves that you can walk and learn geology at the same time.

Exploring Oregon's Wild Areas, by William Sullivan, was the first Oregon hiking guide to expressly feature unprotected wilderness.

Hiking the Bigfoot Country, by John Hart, is a classic guide to the Klamath Mountains.

One can also float some of Oregon's unprotected forest wilderness. *Soggy Sneakers: A Guide to Oregon Rivers,* by the Willamette Kayak and Canoe Club; *Oregon River Tours* by John Garren; *Oregon's Quiet Waters: A Guide to Lakes for Canoeists and Other Paddlers* by Cheryl McLean and Clint Brown; and *Paddling Oregon,* by Robb Keller, describe routes

in several protected and unprotected Wildernesses.

As you drive to and from your wilderness explorations, take time to visit the signed wildlife viewing areas along the way. *Oregon Wildlife Viewing Guide,* by James Yuskavitch, details them all.

Hunting and Fishing

The *Flyfisher's Guide to Oregon,* by John Huber, and the *Wingshooter's Guide to Oregon,* by John Shewey, are helpful in flyfishing and game bird hunting Oregon's wild forests. Most exhaustive is *Fishing in Oregon* by Madelynne Diness Sheehan. Roadless and undeveloped areas provide excellent habitat and usually have lower hunting and fishing pressure than more developed areas.

Travel and Exploration

Oregon's National Forests, with photography by Robert Reynolds and text by Joan Campf, is a coffee table book that shows exactly *one* logging picture. While atypical of recent national forest history, the photography is nonetheless striking and reminds us that not all of the national forests have been logged.

Oregon Rivers, with photographs by Larry Olson and text by John Daniel, features every Wild and Scenic River or State Scenic Waterway in Oregon, save for those designated since the book was published.

The *Oregon Atlas & Gazetteer* (DeLorme Maps) and *Oregon Road and Recreation Atlas* (Benchmark Maps) have somewhat different approaches to providing the same topographic, cultural and recreation information. Carry both for all your Oregon explorations.

Activism

Keeping It Wild: A Citizens Guide to Wilderness Management, published by The Wilderness Society and the Forest Service, advocates keeping Wilderness wild and is also a useful overview of Wilderness management issues.

The *Wilderness Act Handbook,* also published by The Wilderness Society, includes the full text of the Act and also commentary on what each section means.

Selected Websites

Bureau of Land Management, Oregon State Office	www.or.blm.gov	Gateway to websites for each BLM district in Oregon.
Campaign for America's Wilderness	www.leaveitwild.org	Information about the Wilderness Act and wildlands that are and could be protected in the National Wilderness Preservation System.
National Oceanic and Atmospheric Administration	www.nwr.noaa.gov/1salmon/salmesa/index.htm	Presenting Pacific salmon stocks and their status (although their legal and biological status may change as the Bush Administration is capitulating to anti-salmon interests).
National Park Service Wild and Scenic Rivers Inventory	www.nps.gov/rivers/wildriverslist.html#or	Listing and information on each unit of the National Wild and Scenic Rivers System.
Northwest Trails Archive and Restoration Project	www.efn.org/~ntarp	The Forest Service and BLM often abandon old trails in areas they plan for later logging. NTARP documents and restores old trails.
Oregon Natural Heritage Program	www.natureserve.org/nhp/us/or	The scientific classification of nature in Oregon.
Oregon Natural Resources Council	www.onrc.org	A driving force for Oregon Wilderness since 1974.
Oregon State University, Trees of the Pacific Northwest	www.oregonstate.edu/trees/	On-line identification of Oregon's trees.
Oregon Wild	www.oregonwild.org	The latest details on the 5 million acre Wilderness proposal.
The Wilderness Society	www.wilderness.org	A national organization specializing in Wilderness protection.
U.S. Forest Service, Pacific Northwest Region	www.fs.fed.us/r6	Gateway to websites for each national forest.
Western Fire Ecology Center	www.fire-ecology.org	A project of American Lands.
Wilderness Information Network	www.wilderness.net	Information about the Wilderness Act, Wilderness management and wildlands already protected in the National Wilderness Preservation System.
Wilderness Watch	www.wildernesswatch.org	Monitoring and protecting Wilderness after it is protected.
Wildlands Center to Prevent Roads	www.wildlandscpr.org	Why we have too many roads and what to do about it.
World Wildlife Fund	www.worldwildlife.org/forests	Click on "roadless areas" for the document, "Scientific Basis for Roadless Area Conservation."

About the Author

I have flouted the wild;
I have followed its lure, fearless, familiar, alone; ...
Yet the wild must win, and the day will come,
When I shall be overthrown.

—Robert Service[1]

Andy Kerr worked for the Oregon Natural Resources Council from when he dropped out of Oregon State University in 1976, until 1996, when he burned out (on the job, not the cause). At ONRC he was first a field organizer, then served as conservation director and then executive director. He now serves as a Senior Counselor to ONRC. He'd rather not think about it, but the author has spent more than three years in Washington, DC — never more than a week at a time — laboring and lobbying on behalf of the wild.

Time magazine labeled Kerr a "White Collar Terrorist," referring to his effectiveness in working within the system and striking fear in the hearts of those who exploit Oregon's natural environment. In the course of his work he has been hung in effigy (at least twice) and received death threats (lost count). The Oregonian's Northwest Magazine characterized him as the timber industry's "most hated man in Oregon." The Lake County Examiner called Kerr "Oregon's version of the Anti-Christ." He participated, by personal invitation of President Clinton, in the Northwest Forest Conference held in Portland in 1993 for which Willamette Week gave Kerr a "No Surrender Award."

He is the czar of the Larch Company (a for-profit conservation organization whose membership are species who cannot speak and the generations of humans yet born, and where all profits are donated to environmental protection) and a freelance agitator for the wild through writing, consulting, lobbying and public speaking.

Presently, Kerr is also directing the National Public Lands Grazing Campaign (www.publiclandsranching.org; www.permitbuyout.net). He is also a founding board member of the North American Industrial Hemp Council (www.naihc.org).

His first book was *Oregon Desert Guide: 70 Hikes* (The Mountaineers Books). Others are in progress.

A sixth generation native Oregonian from the recovered mill town of Creswell in the upper Willamette Valley, he now lives in Ashland, a recovered mill town in the upper Rogue Valley with one wife, two dogs, one cat, one horse and no vacancies.

Andy Kerr's website is www.andykerr.net.

About the Cartographer

Erik Fernandez became involved with the Oregon Natural Resources Council after graduating from the University of Portland in 1997. As part of the Oregon Wild campaign he explores Oregon's roadless backcountry both virtually, via GIS (Geographic Information Systems) mapping projects, as well as actual hiking adventures. As ONRC's GIS Coordinator, Erik is the expert in mapping Oregon's wild areas. While continuing to explore the remote corners of Oregon, Erik has traveled extensively throughout the world, including New Zealand, Chile and Brazil.

About the Photographers

See how willingly Nature poses herself upon photographer's plates. No earthly chemicals are so sensitive as those of the human soul. All that is required is exposure, and purity of material. "The pure heart shall see God!"

—John Muir[2]

Sandy Lonsdale has been a volunteer conservation activist for nearly 20 years, defending Oregon's wild places and contributing to their protection by bringing the issues to the people and encouraging public participation in land management decisions. An Oregonian since 1972, Sandy knows the land like few others and has worked as a professional writer, photographer and speaker in Bend since 1989, contributing to many publications and conservation efforts. He also works to promote renewable energy alternatives. He contributed the photographs in *Oregon Desert Guide*.

George Wuerthner is an ecologist, photographer and writer with dozens of books to his credit (www.wuerthnerphotography.com). Among his books are *Oregon Mountain Ranges* and *Oregon's Best Wildflower Hikes*. His most recent book is *Welfare Ranching: The*

[1] Service, Robert. 1954. *The Heart of the Sourdough*, *in* COLLECTED POEMS OF ROBERT SERVICE. Dodd, Mead and Company. New York, NY: 7 (originally published in Robert Service, The Spell of the Yukon and Other Verses in 1907).

[2] Wolfe, Linnie Marsh. 1938. JOHN OF THE MOUNTAINS. University of Wisconsin Press. Madison, WI: 94-95 (originally published in John Muir, Mountain Thoughts in 1872).

Subsidized Destruction of the American West, co-authored with Mollie Matteson. He has over 220,000 images in stock and has sold photographs and articles to innumerable publications. He serves on the board of directors and/or is an advisor to a number of conservation organizations, including RESTORE: The North Woods and Alliance for Wild Rockies.

Elizabeth Feryl has documented forest ecology and practices for over a decade. Her photographs have been used by, against, and to persuade the federal government (by agencies, in court and in Congress, respectively) to protect forest wildlands. She produced the Ancient Forest Alliance book, *If you Think Our Forests Look Like This....* Her work appears in *Clearcut: The Tragedy of Industrial Forestry*, *Tree Huggers*, *Anatomy of a Conflict* and other publications. She has contributed photographs to over 50 conservation organizations. Elizabeth is also an artist, gardener and educator.

Gary Braasch of Nehalem covers natural history and conservation issues for magazines worldwide and is one of the most published assignment nature photographers. He is currently researching and photographing areas of high biodiversity in North and South America and documenting the effects of climate change worldwide. He has photographed the forests and wildlands of Oregon for 25 years and published the first national book on ancient temperate forests in 1988, *Secrets of the Old Growth Forests*.

David Stone has been a passionate environmental advocate since he arrived in Oregon in 1980. He co-founded the Waldo Wilderness Council and served as the Conservation Chair for Lane County Audubon from 1995 to 2003. He currently teaches Nature Photography at Lane Community College in Eugene and leads photo expeditions throughout the West on his mission to explore, reveal and celebrate the natural world. His photo credits include National Geographic, Oregon Outside and National Audubon Society guidebooks to the Southwest and the Pacific Northwest.

Ellen Morris Bishop is a photographer, writer and Ph.D. geologist who has worked to conserve rivers, watersheds and wild lands in eastern Oregon for two decades. Her books include *In Search of Ancient Oregon: A Geologic and Natural History* and *Hiking Oregon's Geology*. Her photographs have documented environmental issues in the Klamath Basin, Hells Canyon and the Cascades. Her next books are about the Pacific Northwest's geologic and ecological history and the Pacific Northwest's most endangered rivers. Her images are available through her website, www.ecosystemimages.com.

Larry N. Olson taught himself photography while earning a degree in biology at Lewis and Clark College. An avid backpacker, kayaker and backcountry skier, he has dedicated his career to photographing wild places. His exhibit format book Oregon Rivers features fifty-six rivers protected by the Wild and Scenic Rivers Act. His images of natural landscapes are exhibited in galleries throughout the West and have been published by the Audubon Society, The Nature Conservancy, the Sierra Club and The Wilderness Society. His studio and home is in Portland, Oregon.

Colophon

Book design by BryanPotter Design of Portland. Printing managed by Environmental Paper and Print of Portland (www.environmentalprint.com). Printing done by Millcross Litho of Portland. The book's protective wrapping reduces possible damage incurred in shipping and is projected to prevent the loss of at least 10% of copies shipped to bookstores.

NEW LEAF PAPER

ENVIRONMENTAL BENEFITS STATEMENT

This book published by ONRC is printed on New Leaf Reincarnation Matte, made with 100% recycled fiber, 50% post-consumer waste, processed chlorine free. By using this environmentally friendly paper, ONRC saved the following resources:

trees	water	energy	solid waste	greenhouse gases
125 fully grown	27,213 gallons	57 million BTUs	5,953 pounds	10,060 pounds

Calculated based on research done by Environmental Defense and other members of the Paper Task Force.

© New Leaf Paper   Visit us in cyberspace at www.newleafpaper.com or call 1-888-989-5323

A few references are made in this book to geographic features that have "Squaw" as part of their name. Of Algonquin origin, the word is a derogatory term for an anatomical feature unique to female mammals. It is also a racial slur. In 2001, the Oregon Legislature enacted a law prohibiting public bodies from using the word and also urged the Oregon and National Boards of Geographic Names to rename all inappropriately named landmarks in the state that include the term. The U.S. Geological Survey's Geographic Names Information System lists 146 such places in Oregon. In this book, where possible, reference is made instead to nearby landmarks.

Index